International Organizations and the Analysis of Economic Policy, 1919–1950

This book expands our understanding of the distinctive policy analysis produced between 1919 and 1950 by economists and other social scientists for four major international organizations: the League of Nations, the International Labor Organization, the Bank for International Settlements, and the United Nations. These practitioners included some of the twentieth century's eminent economists, including Cassel, Haberler, Kalecki, Meade, Morgenstern, Nurkse, Ohlin, Tinbergen, and Viner. Irving Fisher and John Maynard Keynes also influenced the work of these organizations. Topics covered include: the relationship between economics and policy analysis in international organizations; business cycle research; the role and conduct of monetary policy; public investment; trade policy; social and labor economics; international finance; the coordination problem in international macroeconomic policy; full employment economics; and the rich-country-poor-country debate. Normative agendas underlying international political economy are made explicit, and lessons are distilled for today's debates on international economic integration.

Anthony M. Endres is Associate Professor in the Department of Economics, School of Business and Economics, at the University of Auckland. He has also served as Lecturer in Economics at the University of Waikato and the University of Wollongong. Professor Endres has been a Visiting Fellow at the Research School of Social Sciences (Australian National University) and held visiting professorships at Kyotosangyo University, the University of Kyoto, and the University of Toronto. He is the author of *Neoclassical Microeconomic Theory: The Founding Austrian Version* (1997) and has published widely in the history of economic thought on questions on mercantilism, classical economics, institutional economics, and neoclassical economics. Professor Endres's research has appeared in the *European Economic Review*, *Journal of Institutional and Theoretical Economics*, *Journal of Monetary Economics*, *History of Political Economy*, and the *Journal of European Economic History*, among others.

Grant A. Fleming is Senior Lecturer in the School of Finance and Applied Statistics, Faculty of Economics and Commerce, at the Australian National University. He has also served as Lecturer in Economics at the University of Auckland and as Visiting Professor at Duke University. Dr. Fleming has published in a wide range of fields including the history of economic thought, economic and business history, international finance, and corporate finance. More than forty of his academic articles have appeared in journals such as *Business History Review*, *Cambridge Journal of Economics*, *Economic History Review*, *Financial History Review*, *International Labour Review*, and the *Journal of Monetary Economics*.

Historical Perspectives on Modern Economics

General Editor: Craufurd D. Goodwin, Duke University

This series contains original works that challenge and enlighten historians of economics. For the profession as a whole it promotes better understanding of the origin and content of modern economics.

Other books in the series:

William J. Barber, *From New Era to New Deal: Herbert Hoover, the Economists, and American Economic Policy, 1921–1933*

William J. Barber, *Designs within Disorder: Franklin D. Roosevelt, the Economists, and the Shaping of American Economic Policy, 1933–1945*

M. June Flanders, *International Monetary Economics, 1870–1950*

J. Daniel Hammond, *Theory and Measurement: Causality Issues in Milton Friedman's Monetary Economics*

Lars Jonung (ed.), *The Stockholm School of Economics Revisited*

Kyun Kim, *Equilibrium Business Cycle Theory in Historical Perspective*

Gerald M. Koot, *English Historical Economics, 1870–1926: The Rise of Economic History and Mercantilism*

David Laidler, *Fabricating the Keynesian Revolution: Studies of the Inter-War Literature on Money, the Cycle, and Unemployment*

Odd Langholm, *The Legacy of Scholasticism in Economic Thought: Antecedents of Choice and Power*

Philip Mirowski, *More Heat Than Light: Economics as Social Physics, Physics as Nature's Economics*

Philip Mirowski (ed.), *Natural Images in Economic Thought: "Markets Read in Tooth and Claw"*

Mary S. Morgan, *The History of Econometric Ideas*

Takashi Negishi, *Economic Theories in a Non-Walrasian Tradition*

Heath Pearson, *Origins of Law and Economics: The Economists' New Science of Law, 1830–1930*

Malcolm Rutherford, *Institutions in Economics: The Old and the New Institutionalism*

Esther-Mirjam Sent, *The Evolving Rationality of Rational Expectations: An Assessment of Thomas Sargent's Achievements*

Yoichi Shionoya, *Schumpeter and the Idea of Social Science*

Juan Gabriel Valdés, *Pinochet's Economists: The Chicago School of Economics in Chile*

Karen I. Vaughn, *Austrian Economics in America: The Migration of a Tradition*

E. Roy Weintraub, *Stabilizing Dynamics: Constructing Economic Knowledge*

International Organizations and the
Analysis of Economic Policy, 1919–1950

ANTHONY M. ENDRES

University of Auckland,
New Zealand

GRANT A. FLEMING

Australian National University

CAMBRIDGE
UNIVERSITY PRESS

PUBLISHED BY THE PRESS SYNDICATE OF THE UNIVERSITY OF CAMBRIDGE
The Pitt Building, Trumpington Street, Cambridge, United Kingdom

CAMBRIDGE UNIVERSITY PRESS
The Edinburgh Building, Cambridge CB2 2RU, UK
40 West 20th Street, New York, NY 10011-4211, USA
477 Williamstown Road, Port Melbourne, VIC 3207, Australia
Ruiz de Alarcón 13, 28014 Madrid, Spain
Dock House, The Waterfront, Cape Town 8001, South Africa

http://www.cambridge.org

First published 2002

Printed in the United Kingdom at the University Press, Cambridge

Typeface Times New Roman 10/12 pt.   *System* QuarkXPress [BTS]

A catalog record for this book is available from the British Library.

Library of Congress Cataloging in Publication Data

Endres, A.M.
    International organizations and the analysis of economic policy, 1919–1949 /
Anthony M. Endres, Grant A. Fleming.
        p.   cm.
    Includes bibliographical references and index.
    ISBN 0-521-79267-3
    1. Economic policy – International cooperation – History – 20th century.
    2. Commercial policy – International cooperation – History – 20th century.
    3. International economic relations – History – 20th century.   4. Economists –
History – 20th century.   5. Economic history – 20th century.   6. League of
Nations – History.   7. United Nations – History.   8. Bank for International
Settlements – History.   9. General Agreement on Tariffs and Trade (Organization) –
History.   10. International Labour Organisation – History.   11. Financial institutions,
International – History – 20th century.   12. Monetary policy – International
cooperation – History – 20th century.   13. Labor laws and legislation, International –
History – 20th century.   I. Fleming, Grant A.   II. Title.

    HD87   .E53   2002
    338.9′009′041–dc21   2001035702

ISBN   0 521 79267 3   hardback

Contents

Contents   ix

Figures and Tables

Abbreviations

BIS	Bank for International Settlements
CCI	Course and Control of Inflation
GATT	General Agreement on Tariffs and Trade
IBRD	International Bank for Reconstruction and Development
ICE	International Currency Experience
IFI	International Financial Institution
ILR	International Labour Review
ILO	International Labour Organization
IMF	International Monetary Fund
ITO	International Trade Organization
LON	League of Nations
LONJ	League of Nations Journal
UN	United Nations
UNEEC	United Nations Economic and Employment Commission
WEC	World Economic Conference
WES	World Economic Survey

Preface

This book is the culmination of eight years' research. It began with correspondence between the authors and Janie Gummer, the daughter of E.J. Riches, in 1993. Janie informed us that Riches, international civil servant and former ILO Deputy Director, was close to death and that some of his personal papers may be of interest to historically minded economists at the University of Auckland. These papers alerted us to the work of economists at the International Labor Organization. We were especially stimulated by conversations with A.W. (Bob) Coats when he visited the Antipodes in the mid-1990s; his unflagging enthusiasm for extending work on the intellectual history of economics to include the work completed by special cadres of economists and social scientists in both government and international agencies had a lasting influence, as the following pages attest.

The path to the final manuscript has been made easier by the wealth of comments from countless academic colleagues. We acknowledge the benefits of comments and conversations with conference participants at the History of Economic Thought Society of Australia conference (Freemantle), the European History of Economic Thought conference (Marseille), and two Economic Society of Australia Annual conferences (Canberra and Melbourne). More vigorous exchanges in seminars at the Australian National University, Duke University, King's College Cambridge University, University of Auckland, University of New South Wales, and University of Western Australia have sharpened our arguments and challenged our framework.

Research funding from the Australian Research Council Small Grant scheme (S6204012) helped us travel to key archival sources in Geneva where we received enthusiastic support from archival staff. They were not generally accustomed to having economists explore their records and that indicates just how much modern practitioners in the discipline have forgotten the value of these rich data sets. We are obliged in particular to Mr. A. Zoganas at the International Labor Organization and Ms. Blukacz-Louisfert and her staff at the League of Nations Archives in the United Nations Library (Geneva) for their energy, flexibility, and the ancillary archive resources placed so generously at our disposal. We also thank publishers for permission to use material that has previously appeared in book chapters (Edward Elgar and Ashgate) and in the *Cambridge Journal of Economics* (Oxford University Press), the *European Journal for the History of Economic Thought* (Routledge), the *International Labour Review* (International Labour Organization), and the *Journal of Monetary Economics* (Elsevier North Holland).

1 Economics and Policy in International Organizations: Introduction

PROLOGUE: A PERSPECTIVE ON THE LITERATURE

In the early twentieth century, John A. Hobson's *Toward International Government* (1915) reflected hopefully on the prospects for realizing the ideal of a "world community" or of "a society of nations" through the creation of an international organization. That organization would subordinate national advantage to the idea of international cooperation – an idea that Hobson did not fully articulate. Hobson could not have foreseen the evolution of international organizations committed to economic and social cooperation among nations over the twentieth century and the increasingly active role in international affairs that such organizations were to play from the creation of the League of Nations (LON) in 1919 onward.[1]

There are now available a plethora of institutional and organizational histories expatiating on the functions and influences of international organizations in the twentieth century.[2] Some recent studies have proceeded beyond recounting the history of administrative structures and functions to analyzing the nature, scope, and history of international economic cooperation – treating cooperation in connection with a flow of episodes, events, economic crises, and policy responses.[3] An abundant literature written by economists has focussed attention on:

---

[1] We mostly employ the term *international organization* in this book and regard it as synonymous with *international agency*, *transnational institution*, and *supranational institution*. All these terms are taken to refer to the institutional structures of intergovernmental or nongovernmental organizations. This broad usage is consistent with literature in the now specialized field of international organization. See Taylor (1990) and Willetts (1990).

[2] See, for example, Groom and Taylor (1990); Hill (1946); Luard (1966); Northedge (1986); and Walters (1952).

[3] Several studies in the field of international monetary cooperation stand out. See Horsefield (1969) and James (1996).

1. the macroeconomic stabilization, financial reconstruction, and enforcement programs of the LON and Bank for International Settlements (BIS) prior to 1939 (Pauly 1996; Santaella 1993; Schloss 1958);
2. the structure, function, and performance of international economic and financial institutions such as the International Monetary Fund (IMF) and World Bank (Black 1987; Gavin and Rodrik 1995; Krueger 1998; and MacBean and Snowden 1981); and
3. the economic rationale for the existence, development, and performance of supranational economic organizations (Frey 1997 and Vaubel and Willetts 1991 on public choice; Kindleberger 1986 on international public goods; and Simmons 1993 on dynamic contracting).

Furthermore, in the 1990s the Brookings Institution instigated a series of studies on the subject of "Integrating National Economies" (Bryant 1995; Kahler 1995). These studies have taken investigation of international economic organizations to a new and more sophisticated level; they consider the myriad of alternative possible forms of cooperation achieved through international organizations, locating each organization in a broad international movement aiming ultimately to coordinate national policies and minimize spillover effects on member nation states.[4] Again, the orientation in all this burgeoning research is structure, function, and performance at the operational level – it is institutional and organizational in character and not ideational or avowedly a study of doctrinal issues.

By comparison with the literature referred to so far, the purpose of this book is not to explain what organizational forms and structures were established or assess their performance. We intend to survey what was contributed in an intellectual sense to economic and social research by the social scientists – especially the economists – who worked in, or attached as consultants to, some of the principal international economic organizations from 1919 to circa 1950. This book aims to expand our understanding of the distinctive research and economic policy advice proffered by economists in international organizations. These organizations include the mostly Geneva-based LON Economic and Financial Section, various branches of the International Labour Organization

---

[4] The problem of managing and coordinating economic policies using international organizations has also been considered in the light of fundamental uncertainty facing international economic policy makers. See Ghosh and Masson (1994). Various definitions, forms, and methods of economic policy coordination have also been the subject of intensive study by economists. See, for example, Frenkel and Goldstein (1996a).

(ILO), the Bank for International Settlements (BIS), and various divisions of the United Nations (UN). As these organizations operated according to a certain set of guiding principles, their economic secretariats, analysts, and advisers were charged with the tasks of putting those principles into practice – of steering the specific organizations in a constructive direction. Apart from a long list of lesser known economists who were engaged in the work of these organizations as full-time employees or consultants (and whose work will be accorded wide coverage in the following chapters), some of the twentieth century's most eminent economists made significant contributions to the work of international organizations in the 1919–50 period, including: Gustav Cassel; Gottfried Haberler; Michal Kalecki; James Meade; Oskar Morgenstern; Ragnar Nurkse; Bertil Ohlin; Jan Tinbergen, and Jacob Viner. In addition, Irving Fisher and John Maynard Keynes commented on the work of several international organizations in the period under review.

Intellectual histories of economic research completed within and for international organizations have been rare and so far piecemeal. To be sure, the career and appointments processes, functions, and powers of economic secretariats have been investigated.[5] The first partly historiographical study of significance appeared in 1986 – *Economists in International Agencies: An Exploratory Study* (Coats 1986). That work's primary objective was to assess the role and status of economists as a "professional cadre" in "policy formulation, decisionmaking, and implementation" in various international agencies post-1945 (Ibid., 2). Further, some of the contributed chapters in Coats (1986) outlined the recruitment policies for economists; the place of economists within the agency and how economists' work infiltrated the policy-making process. Altogether, the intellectual history content in the Coats (1986) volume is largely a by-product.[6] Only the chapter by Sidney Dell (1986: 37ff.) considered the "influential ideas" on the problem of economic development offered by economists working for the UN secretariat from about 1947 onward. The evolution of ideas at the World Bank on the economic development process from the late 1940s is also treated carefully in Mason and Asher (1973: 457–90), although this is a comparatively brief intellectual history in a volume running over 900 pages concentrating on the origins, policies, operations, and impact of the group of institutions constituting the World Bank.

---

[5] On the secretariats see Bailey (1964), Hill (1946), McLean (1980), Menzies (1983), and Meron (1977).

[6] The same comment applies to Earlene Craver's (1986) study of Rockefeller Foundation grants to research work in international organizations over the interwar period.

Two important contributions of standing in the literature provide the background for this book. An obvious prototype is Neil De Marchi's work (in collaboration with Peter Dohlman) (1991) which produced a programmatic, path-breaking analysis of the work of LON economists in the 1930s. Here the very framing and content of economic research conducted by LON economists is adumbrated. We will have occasion at various points in the following chapters to comment on and extend the insights provided by De Marchi.[7] In addition, another model for our study resides in Jacques Polak's (1995) intellectual history of exchange rate research at the International Monetary Fund (IMF) post-1945.[8] Polak's work examines the development of research on, and policy attitudes toward, exchange rate matters by economists employed by an international organization. He was interested in the content of that research, associated policy advice, and the interaction between economics and policy, while admitting that linkages between economic research at the IMF and actual policy outcomes in nation states "is in no sense simple or direct" (Polak 1995: 735). Likewise, we are interested in the substantive ideational content of research and policy advice of economists in international organizations though on a much wider range of subjects. We also agree that the actual impact of ideas on policy cannot easily be estimated.

ECONOMICS AND POLICY IN INTERNATIONAL ORGANIZATIONS: HISTORIOGRAPHICAL ISSUES

That the following chapters focus on economic thought and policy, or economic thought as it relates to matters of practice at the national and international levels, raises some critical historiographical issues. Economists in international organizations from 1919 to 1950 acted as experts in the provision and interpretation of information and in the development of ideas; they were occasionally able to complete fundamental or "pure" economic research which had only remote bearing on immediate policy concerns; they planned operational programs in several fields and they participated in forums for the worldwide exchange of ideas and information on particular policy problems. We prefer to distinguish between all the above activities and economists' participation in decision making, policy making, and policy implementation as such. The economists whose work we wish to survey only participated *indirectly* in decision making and policy-making activities. In addition, on many economic

---

[7] Pauly (1996) has also assessed the analytic content of some early work at the LON on monetary problems. Again, Pauly's study will be mentioned at various points in this book.

[8] See also Polak (1997) for a treatment more along the lines of an institutional and personal history.

and social issues, international organizations had an educative, consulting, and advisory role rather than specific policy-making functions. Nevertheless, the work of their economists was frequently adapted to policy issues and critical episodes in economic policy confronting member nations. Our interest is in how the adaptation process altered the scope, content, and character of economic research in international organizations.

It would be a serious misapprehension to regard the work of economic researchers engaged by international organizations as being obviously "positive" in the traditional sense of dispassionate provision of analysis without manifest "normative" implications. It is not possible, generally, to disentangle positive and normative levels of discourse in the work we will consider. So much of that work was directed variously by the conventions, principles, and conference resolutions of the governing bodies of the respective organizations. The research considered in the following chapters acted both as an input into assessing what was feasible in relation to a particular policy response and it analyzed the effects of specific courses of action, often by observing and reporting on a range of country experiences and generalizing from these experiences. For example, we may acknowledge Pauly's (1996: 25) distinction between "operational" and "analytical" dimensions in the contribution of LON economists in the 1920s and 1930s. In the former dimension, LON economists were mere surveillance and reporting officers; they reported on LON- and BIS-sponsored financial reconstruction programs in Europe. In the latter dimension, LON economists conducted putatively pure economic analysis on international finance and business cycles. In general, however, we demonstrate in the following chapters that it is not easy to separate operational and analytical dimensions for the majority of research projects undertaken by economists in the international organizations considered, even where the research outputs were strongly analytical and published in scholarly journals or books.

The economics and policy analysis we survey in this book was didactic in style and sometimes hortatory; it contributed actively to reconciling differences in national policy initiatives or points of view on particular problems facing national policy makers; in some cases it critically appraises these initiatives (or lack of them as the case demanded). LON research in the 1920s in particular, contributed to the development of policy consensuses on a range of economic problems (Pauly 1996: 30–33).[9] ILO research over the entire period 1919–50 was openly

---

[9] Whether consensuses were generally contrived to create an impression of "liberal orthodoxy" on economic policy matters as Pauly claims (p. 17) is debatable. We shall discuss this point more fully below.

committed to advocacy, especially, as we shall demonstrate, from the late 1920s.[10] LON research was often transformed into "conventions" conceived as "models" recommended to member governments on a range of policy problems; and those governments were advised to "use these models . . . as far as they fit with . . . local conditions" in the process of bilateral negotiations over opportunities for policy harmonization (Loveday 1938b: 790). While economists and other social scientists engaged in work for international organizations in the period under review were deeply involved in policy discussion, they did not always explicitly admit to such involvement. Some tended to stress the "objective," "scientific," and mere "intelligence gathering" aspects of their work.[11] The "economic work of the League of Nations" up to 1927 was officially described as the output of "disinterested and technical experts" and wholly "scientific in character" (LON 1927b: 3, 40). Moreover, LON economists attempted to

> study the various problems selected . . . as profoundly and as widely as conditions permitted, and to interpret and express the results of the enquiries with scientific accuracy. But the final digestion of the facts collected has been left to the financial press and popular economic writers (Ibid., 40).

As one participant observed of the ILO's research output:

> this work would . . . go on no further than the simple collection and coordination of material. The solution of the various problems must lie either with the different Governments, in which case it would be purely national, or with the economic organization of the League of Nations, which can convene diplomatic conferences for the adoption of international arrangements (Oudegeest 1929: 2).

Later, Lewis Lorwin, economic adviser to the ILO, wrote an article on the "ILO and World Economic Policy" (1936) which expressly underscored the value-laden content of research at the ILO. That economists in international organizations were setting research agendas; frequently reflecting on the relationship between their research and policy problems; and developing independent conceptions of the main features of

---

[10] Of course we shall not be the first to make this point. See the official ILO history, Alcock (1971: 99–117). Our contribution will be to subject the relevant economic research to more thorough exposition and scrutiny from the perspective of the discipline of economics.

[11] See, for example, Thomas (1921b: 29–31). J.B. Condliffe (1938: 803), sometime LON secretariat member and later to act as an ILO consultant, viewed LON researchers as "international civil servants . . . [working in] a clearing house between civil services of various countries."

those problems, meant that they were in one way or another reflecting constantly on the role of the state, including supranational organizations, in economic life at the national and international levels respectively. Such reflection ipso facto infused their work with value judgements.[12] In assessing this work, we will notice parallels with the limited work on economic thought in national governments, except we shall be considering the work of economists in what may be regarded as international intergovernmental agencies.[13]

According to Donald Winch (1969: 19), to pose the existence of a relationship between economic thought and economic policy "entails both an over-optimistic conception of the technocratic status of economics, and a naïve view of the processes of political decisionmaking." This remark is made in the context of reviewing the interconnections between economics and policy for the most part where the debate on national economic policies in the Anglo-American situation held center stage. Winch's view deserves to be emphasized from the outset in our study. First, strict unequivocal disciplinary segregation between economics/ economists and other social sciences/scientists cannot be made for the period, or for the international organizations, under review. Economists as a professional group played a leading part in research secretariats, and they were assisted by statisticians, sociologists, and political scientists, all of whom from time to time contributed to economic thought and policy discussion. Second, it would indeed be naively ambitious to posit and then demonstrate a strong relationship between economic thought and decision-making outcomes (for example, the conference resolutions, declarations, and recommendations of international organizations). We may infer from specific policy pronouncements some connection to antecedent research by the secretariat and economic advisors in the organizations. This study will not attempt generally to estimate the impact of economic ideas and economic research on practice, that is, on international policy outcomes. Rather, the historiographical objectives in this book are delimited by the following questions:

1. What was distinctive, innovative, and significant in a doctrinal history sense, about research on economic and social policy issues in the international organizations over the 1919–50 period?
2. What policy questions stimulated the research undertaken and what policy positions flowed from research findings?

---

[12] See, for example, some of the work presented by economists working in, or for, international organizations at the Sixth International Studies Conference convened by the LON (International Institute of Intellectual Cooperation 1934; see also LON 1927b).

[13] Broad historical work on economists in national governments has a longer pedigree. See for example Coats (1981).

3. What intellectual influences acted on that research?
4. How did shifts in the prevailing orthodoxy on particular problems, especially the contemporary orthodoxy in the economics
   discipline, affect research in these organizations? Did that
   research reflect changes in academic economics, anticipate, or
   lead it?
5. What limitations may be identified in the economics as practiced
   by researchers in these organizations?

We intend to complement Winch's (1969) pioneering study of "economics and policy," adding an international dimension that was clearly
missing in his work on the interwar period. Winch adopted a strong
"Anglo-American focus" (p. 13). Accordingly, he concentrated on Anglo-
American economic thought which possessed distinguishing characteristics from French, German, and Scandinavian thought. To anticipate one
of our themes in the following chapters – economic thought and policy
in international organizations has a strong internationalist orientation
that sometimes and on some critical policy issues, differed significantly
from the prevailing, contemporary Anglo-American stream of economic
thought. Reasons for these differences will be canvassed in the following chapters. Suffice it to note at this point that the cosmopolitan group
of economists working at the LON, ILO, BIS, and UN between 1919 and
1950, together with the multifaceted, rich flow of information used in
their international-comparative work, accounted for the distinctiveness
of their research outputs.[14]

Much has been written in recent years on the "internationalization"
of the economics discipline (Coats 1997). On Winch's (1969: 14) reading,
economics "as a professional pursuit has become a more truly international discipline since the last war" that is, since 1945. In a formal academic sense, this view may be accurate. However, the explicit priority for
effecting substantial economic research at the ILO (and LON) before
1940 required recruitment of individuals with "economic training" from
a wide range of institutions and from as many member states as possible (Thomas 1921b: 24). Following a meeting of representatives of
national economic councils and economic research institutes held by the
LON in 1931, a recommendation was made to employ more "qualified"
economists in the LON secretariat (McClure 1933: 319). It was keenly
understood that any biases deriving from the nationality of economics
could be overcome by recruiting a cosmopolitan group (in terms of

---

[14] According to Henry Clay (1939: 575) the "usefulness" of the LON "as a centre of comparative economic studies" had *not* been negatively affected by the "political misfor-
tunes" besetting that organization by 1939.

nationality) and perhaps therefore a doctrinally diverse group as well.[15] In this special manner, the work of those with "economic training" in international organizations from the 1920s contributed to the internationalization of economics as a truly professional pursuit, well before Winch identified such a trend in the late 1940s. Doubtless we shall attempt to trace the national origins and international transmission of economic ideas on particular economic policy issues as the research unfolded in each organization.

THE IDEATIONAL CONTEXT OF RESEARCH IN INTERNATIONAL ORGANIZATIONS FROM 1919

Following creation of the LON, the Financial, Economics, and Statistics Section of the LON and the secretariat of the ILO (then a semiautonomous agency of the LON) undertook a wide range of economic research projects. In the opinion of one observer reflecting on the work undertaken during the 1920s, the LON "considered practically all the major world problems of economics."[16] Initially, the economic context and impetus for economic research at the LON was European financial reconstruction, but it quickly broadened to joint LON/ILO research on unemployment and international business cycles. The complete research effort from the early 1920s was cast in the background preamble to the founding LON constitution: "to promote international cooperation and to achieve international peace and security" (LON 1927b: 3). The Economic and Financial Organization (Branch) of the LON secretariat and its research economists used this broad background objective as a guide to justify all their projects, including economic surveillance and operational activities (Hill 1946). Furthermore, the 1920 Brussels Financial Conference was "unanimous . . . in believing that national action is not by itself sufficient. International co-operation . . . must continue and develop" (LON 1920: 11). In principle the term *cooperation* covered the entire spectrum of interaction among member states designed to create the preconditions for concerted action in response to cross-border economic and social spillovers. An early director of LON economic research

---

[15] For some broad remarks on the "experience" and "international character" of the LON Economic and Financial Section's secretariat see LON (1930b: 15–16).

[16] E.C. Wendelin, "Subject Index to the Economic and Financial Documents of the League of Nations" (1932), quoted in McClure (1933: xxiii). International conferences convoked and organized by the LON, or sponsored by the LON, initially provided the background and rationale for some of the research. The following three conferences in the 1920s were of some importance: 1. International Financial Conference, Brussels 1920; 2. International Economic Conference, Genoa 1922; and 3. World Economic Conference, Geneva 1927. On the relevance of these conferences to economic research at the LON see LON (1927b) and McClure (1933: 209–44).

remarked that international organizations promised "pacific communal co-operation of all nations irrespective of differences in their economic systems"; they had the potential to "devise and apply a set of principles which will restrict the uncontrollable action of individual States in imposing economic policies which react injuriously upon the interests of other countries" (Salter 1928: 6).[17] In practice, cooperation in the early 1920s amounted to intensive consultation over monetary arrangements and financial reconstruction in Europe through the LON; it involved confidential interchange of information between central banks and assessments of monetary conditions, rates of discount, stability of exchange rates, gold movements, and so on. These matters and the creation of politically autonomous central banks preoccupied LON economists. Eventually, information sharing and cooperation between various national authorities extended to the full range of monetary, fiscal, trade, labor, and social policy problems facing member states.

The *idea* of economic and social cooperation for those engaged by international organizations in the period under review was a symbol for a desire to manage deeper underlying economic processes at the international level. The economists perceived increasing interdependence and economic interaction between nation states that was not adequately supported by transnational, coordinated policy making. And the economic interdependencies could at least be analyzed, if not fully managed, by appropriate institutional arrangements such as multilateral organizations. Researchers for these organizations sought to develop insights into the possibilities for policy harmonization among nations on a range of economic problems; they analyzed differences between nations in the treatment of these problems. Recognition of economic interdependencies and on investigating demonstrable net gains from creating a truly international policy regime for managing cross-border policy spillovers soon advanced well beyond monetary matters. However, *cooperation* rather than planned *economic integration* (to use a modern, late twentieth-century term) was the goal; it was a voluntary form of "cooperation which brought peoples and governments together fructuously while not denying their diversity, their individuality and, above all, their sovereignty" (Groom 1988: 20).[18]

International economic and social cooperation provided an exceedingly broad background against which all international agency research

---

[17] Per Jacobsson (1928: 53) perceived even greater potential in the Geneva World Economic Conference of 1927: It "boldly drew up new lines on which to move toward a more rational economic organization on the basis of whole-hearted international collaboration." LON economics was seen as a crucial element in creating a "rational" basis for collaboration.

[18] See also Goodrich (1947: 19–20).

was conducted between 1919 and 1950; it was construed in different ways at the practical, policy-making level during that period. Throughout 1919–50, member governments made ongoing day-to-day decisions in a largely decentralized manner in respect of policy instruments used to deal with a wide range of macroeconomic and microeconomic problems. The international policy regime environment – the broad operational rules or framework for policy implementation – was agreed to episodically through participation in the resolutions of an international organization such as the LON and ILO; that regime, of course, varied as events demanded over the period 1919–50. For example, the international monetary regime or "rules of the game" agreed to at Genoa in 1922 differed from both the regime agreed to in the 1936 Tripartite Agreement between the United States, Britain, and France to stabilize exchange rates and the Bretton Woods regime established in the mid-1940s. The intellectual content of economists' contributions to international agency research and policy advice must always be considered against the changing background regimes (if any). We acknowledge that co-operation over economic and social problems as understood in the 1920s up to at least the early 1930s amounted to an extremely weak form by the standards set at Bretton Woods and by various UN development agencies in the 1940s. National autonomy was considered paramount prior to 1939; low-level cooperation obtained in which nations mutually recognized common interests, regularly consulted with each other, and shared data through international organizations. International prescriptive rules were rare prior to 1939, except in the case of international labor standards – although these were notoriously difficult to enforce.

Notwithstanding the foregoing contextual matters, it is vital that we focus squarely on the intellectual history, leaving international policy outcomes and questions of policy "influence" aside. As the Deputy Director of the ILO wrote in 1924:

> International action comes at the end and not at the beginning. There is no such thing as an international solution . . . which you can evolve theoretically and apply universally. Anything that is done internationally has got to be built up on the experience, the experiments of different countries, taking what is best out of each of them and generalising that into a principle which can be applied all over . . . In order to arrive at any international result there are three stages through which you have to pass – first study; then, discussion; and lastly, action (Butler 1924: 213–24).

It is precisely the "study" component as carried out by staff in the relevant international organizations that we distinguish and isolate for assessment in this book. Butler proceeded to explain the advantages of research in international organizations such as the ILO and LON: It can assist in establishing "uniform methods" for international-comparative studies; in securing data sets for international comparison; in "co-ordinating the work done in various national fields" on economics and social phenomena; and lastly, in "sifting the empirical results arrived at in one country by testing them over a wider area" (Ibid., 222). According to the reminiscences of one participant economist at the LON (who later acted as a consultant to the ILO), secretariat members had "no power but the power of persuasion"; they were involved in a serious tutelage role – "a continuous process of mutual education" (Condliffe 1951: 633). As their international comparative research developed, they were able to give expert assistance and training on what may or may not have been feasible policies for particular nations.[19]

The broad political economy context in which research was conducted in international organizations over the 1919–50 period cannot be set out in a simple thumbnail sketch. In the first place, we need to confront questions of definition. For Schumpeter (1954: 38) political economy involves expositions "of a comprehensive set of economic policies that the author advocates on the strength of certain unifying (normative) principles." We may apprehend an *international* "political economy" (in Schumpeterian terms) that each researcher engaged by international organizations declares allegiance to, or that may be distilled from their research contributions. Secondly, there is the existing literature to consider. The literature has so far offered some misleading conclusions in this matter. Northedge (1986: 170) presents a LON secretariat "persisting on often outmoded theoretical prescriptions while governments strove to cope with the economic and financial storms on the basis of crude calculations of national interest." Ostensibly, LON economists were interested in creating an institutional framework from the 1920s that preserved liberal, free market capitalism. Key operational criteria in this framework were adherence to the pre-1914 gold standard or some semblance of it, individual responsibility on social policy matters, fiscal conservatism, nondiscriminatory international trade, and unregulated labor markets. Thus, even in the face of mass unemployment and economic depression in the 1930s, the

> League's work on financial and economic co-operation suffered from a backward-looking complex: its language was that of revival, recovery, return to the free system . . . League experts needed to inform themselves why states had abandoned that system, rather than chide them with having done so (Ibid., 174).

---

[19] Harberger (1984: 110) provides a similar rationale for the tutelage function of IMF and World Bank staff in the 1970s and 1980s.

Now this passage is certainly an accurate characterisation of *some* LON economic research, but by no means the bulk of it over any significant period of years (as we shall demonstrate in the following chapters). Movement toward economic nationalism based on short-term considerations of national survival, was invariably viewed sympathetically in the research we consider; it was understood as either a reaction to the pernicious effects of international interdependence such as business cycle transmission or as a misunderstanding of the long-term net benefits derived from increasing economic interdependencies among nations. Consider, for example, the views of a leading figure in early LON economic research:

> Economic nationalism has grown up by unconscious individual pressure from this industry or that, or from emerging devices adapted to meet one successive difficulty after another (Salter 1934: 17).

Likewise, Alexander Loveday (1938a), Director of the LON Economic, Financial, and Transit Department in the 1930s, sympathized with nationalist "experiments in self-protection" as strategies designed to counter "economic insecurity" in a world where it was thought that the transmission of cyclical economic depressions could not be controlled.

The first director of the LON Economic and Financial Section held to a liberal, market-based political economy established within the framework of a secure, peaceful world, post-1919. In reflecting on the course of events up to 1931, international organizations such as the LON could assist in the creation of

> a monetary system, of a system of credit, of world commercial policy, of industrial organization and of world government ... Enterprise can still be both free and competitive, with planned direction guiding it so as to prevent its disastrous dislocation ... Man can then, freed alike from enfeebling impoverishment and harassing anxieties and insecurities, use the resources he has to give himself both a basis of secure material comfort and adequate leisure ... And then the real work of civilisation can at last begin (Salter 1932: 345–46).

There is nothing in this passage suggesting adherence to the dictates of laissez faire.[20] The content of economic research surveyed in this book usually adheres to the conviction that a mélange of national policies, in conjunction with "international State machinery" which coordinates

---

[20] In the same year, 1932, Salter attended the Amsterdam World Social-Economic Congress and maintained in an address that "we have learnt at last that unqualified *laissez-faire laissez-aller* involves intolerable waste and intolerable injustice" (quoted in Johnston 1932: 77). In this, Salter was expressing the prevailing ethos (or ideology) of international agency researchers from 1919 up to that date.

policies among different countries, may conceivably be created to confront problems common to all. There was no single, presumed, designated combination of national and international policies that would be applicable universally (Johnston 1932: 76–78).[21]

In Craig Murphy's *International Organizations and Industrial Change* (1994) and also Pauly (1996) there is the commonplace, frequent refrain attributing "failure" and "disappointment" to the international organizations in existence from 1919 to 1939 and not merely in the practical sense of organization failure. The content of economic and social research completed under the auspices of the ILO, LON, and BIS up to 1939 is also tarnished. Pauly (1996: 25–26) identifies "analytical oversight" in LON research through the 1920s until the mid-1930s and he associates the problem with a resurgent "liberal-orthodox" political economy underlying secretariat work. League officials and economists held to a political economy that was putatively laissez faire in spirit; it was based on a "dominant set of ideas [holding that] unemployment and illiquidity . . . would heal themselves. All that was needed was time and fortitude." Even as late as 1933, LON economists were still preparing conference briefing papers expressing "blind faith in market solutions" (Ibid., 20, 22). In the following chapters we will find this position difficult to sustain for the bulk of LON, including ILO, research *as it developed* over the interwar period and beyond. In addition, Pauly identifies a fundamental discontinuity in LON analysis in the mid-1930s when its orientation turned sharply to focus on "the deficiency of markets" and on the imperative of fostering "convergence in national economic policies deemed necessary for the effective operation of sound markets" (Ibid., 27). Again, when the full gamut of LON and ILO research is considered on the following pages, we find few obvious discontinuities of this kind.

Murphy (1994: 157–58) draws a distinction between the LON's "liberal fundamentalists" who were supposedly wedded for the entire interwar period to the interests of a "businessmen's peace movement" and the new age "Keynesians" who occupied the research and advisory ramparts of the UN from the late 1940s. This potted characterization of intellectual developments in international organizations is also unhelpful. An intellectual history must involve careful exegesis and documentation of the content of research and policy analysis in the relevant organizations and such an exercise must be distinguished from a history of the organization

---

[21] See also Lorwin (1936) where it is maintained that up to the mid-1930s there had occasionally evolved a "world economic policy" on several problems; the precise scope and content of policy depended on the circumstances of time and place. Alexander Loveday advanced a similar proposition in the mid-1940s. See LON Archives C1623, "Note on the Future of International Organisation Dec 1944 with Annex note by Loveday 1945."

as well as its practical achievements or failures. An intellectual history cannot, without qualification, pronounce on the success or failure of ideas but may comment on the applicability of economic ideas in respect of problems requiring practical resolution by policy makers.

The proposition that economic thought in international organizations over the 1919–50 period retained a rationalist faith in the methods of economic analysis which applied to international statecraft, *is* unexceptionable. All the researchers surveyed in this book desired that the results of their work might lead to a collaborative international policy regime on a range of problems. Indeed, the closer we advance to the 1940s, the greater the range of problems on which consensuses were being formed at the international level than might have been imagined in the early 1920s. Nevertheless, our researchers were not Utopian system builders or international regime builders, even if they tended to downplay (especially from the late 1930s) any counterproductive consequences of international economic and social cooperation. They generally appreciated practical political constraints at the national level. Moreover, many individual researchers remained open-minded to, and aware of, developments in formal, academic economics and they sometimes modified their work to take these into account. Indeed, as we proceed, some quite remarkable intellectual developments will be documented in treatment of specific policy-relevant problems including business cycles and monetary and fiscal policy responses to them; the economics of social policy and labor market regulation; trade policy; open economy macroeconomics, exchange rates, and international capital markets; the "full employment movement" and the economics of reconstruction and development.

The following chapters are divided along thematic lines corresponding to the foregoing policy problems. The material is not always organized along strictly chronological lines. Within each chapter there is serial development of each research theme. We consider the emergence and development of research on each theme often in conjunction with particular events, episodes, or pressing policy realities facing decision makers in the international organization. Each chapter, in other words, corresponds to a phase of economic thought on a policy problem. The research program on each theme is outlined, its achievements assessed against the background of contemporary economic thought on the subject, and its policy implications drawn out. We use published and unpublished material on each of the chosen themes and include work from all international organizations and all branch secretariats where it bears on each theme. Some of the material cited derives from publications and unpublished documents in the name of individual researchers rather than an international organization. In these instances, we presume that the ideas contained therein are a reflection of a line of thinking and a style of analysis that originated in, or contributed to discussion within, an international organization to which the individual was attached (as employee, adviser, consultant). What matters, given the historiographical objectives of our study, is that the ideas were an outgrowth of a distinctive brand of international-comparative research stimulated by the existence of an international organization.

2 Business Cycles: Conceptions, Causes, and Implications

INTELLECTUAL SETTING IN THE 1920s

Macroeconomic thought in the 1920s and 1930s produced various strands of economic analysis originating from European and American economists, though the appellation *macroeconomics* was not used at the time. The conventional wisdom was that economists could analyze chains of causation between major economic aggregates; fluctuations in these aggregates were used as representations of crises and business cycles. Economic policy responses drawn from economic analysis would turn on the means of stabilizing economies to prevent or at least mitigate what were then variously understood as crises, business fluctuations, or trade cycles. In this chapter, we review developments in theoretical work and associated applications on the subject completed in international organizations. The following two chapters will survey recommendations offered on macroeconomic stabilization policy by the ILO and LON designed to deal with crises and cycles.

Recent research on the development of macroeconomic ideas in the 1920s up to the mid-1930s has been less concerned with the pervasive influence of J.M. Keynes – who was doubtless, as we shall see, active in the debates on crises and cycles prior to the appearance of his *General Theory of Employment Interest and Money* in 1936 – and more so with other macroeconomic perspectives which emerged and evolved contemporaneously with Keynes's ideas (Dimand 1993, 1995; Jonung 1979; Laidler 1991, 1999). There were also other sources of research on business cycles in particular. Many national economic advisory councils, official economic commissions and business cycle research institutes were established in Europe during the 1920s and 1930s.[1] Some later

---

[1] For a full list of these organizations see Ohlin (1931a: 9–11). Up to 1931, official economic organizations and research institutes had been established in Austria, Belgium,

prominent academic economists came to serve as principals in these organizations.[2]

The intellectual setting after the First World War nurtured an attitude in the European economics profession in which "[s]tabilisation was a key word in every discussion of the economics of Europe ... A rapid return to the prosperous conditions that made the fifty years before World War I a kind of (European) golden age was the obvious target" (Barkai 1993: 3). Contemporary European thought on macroeconomic stabilization sought to establish the key variables requiring stabilization in the face of recurring economic fluctuations. In this context the extensive economic research of economists at the ILO and LON deserves consideration. What was distinctive about their contributions? We shall respond to this question first by using as benchmarks the ideas already available in the contemporary, formal economics literature, especially in the fields of business cycles and monetary economics. Work in these fields developed over the period under review; it also advanced along different, sometimes competing, sometimes complementary lines among different groups or schools of thought. Therefore, we will need to be aware of crucial timing differences and special characteristics that align economic thought in relevant international organizations with one or another school of thought, where appropriate. It is expected that insights generated from the work of international organizations sometimes led, or alternatively lagged (and hence implicitly or explicitly borrowed from), developments in the formal literature in economics. What also matters for our account is that establishing distinctiveness in economic thought requires some nuances, some ideational differentiations, with respect to the questions given priority by the mostly Geneva-based researchers, and to novel elements in their answers on the problem of crises and cycles.

THE ILO-LEAGUE RESEARCH PROGRAM ON CRISES AND CYCLES TO 1931

The Fourth International Labour Conference of the League of Nations resolved that,

Czechoslovakia, Denmark, Finland, France, Germany, Hungary, Italy, Netherlands, Poland, Portugal, Spain, Sweden, and the Soviet Union. See also Morgan (1990: 64–68) for a brief survey of some work completed at European business-cycle research institutes in the 1920s.

[2] Notable economists included: Hayek and Morgenstern (Austria); Wagemann (Germany); Gini (Italy); Pedersen (Denmark); Lipinski (Poland); Henderson (United Kingdom); and Verrijn Stuart (Netherlands). These, among others, were called to a LON conference on "economic depressions" held at Geneva in 1931. They recommended further work on the problem going beyond existing research which had concentrated on North America and Europe, to full a study "on a world basis." See McClure's (1933: 319) report on the conference taken verbatim from the League of Nations Journal (*LONJ*) December 1931.

with a view to combating unemployment crises, the International Labour Office shall be instructed to make, in collaboration with the Economic and Financial Section of the League of Nations, a special study of the problem of the crises, of unemployment, their recurrences and the fluctuations of economic activity, to collate and compare, in particular, the results of the investigations made in various countries, and to make known the measures taken with a view to sustaining economic activity, and thus stabilising the labour market (ILO 1924b: introductory note).

Pursuant to this instruction, a long-term research program was established. The main purpose was to reveal opportunities for policy makers as to the means "for preventing periodic crises of unemployment" (ILO 1924a: 6). The ILO researchers were quick to realize that the conditions of labour per se (wages, living standards, working conditions, wage-setting practices), while of immediate concern to many ILO Conference participants, could not be analyzed in isolation from the imposing macro-economic trends associated with monetary forces and the macrodynamics of the business cycle in industrialized economies. In fact, monetary aspects of the business cycle, including the so-called monetary causes of unemployment, were to become the centerpiece of the research program.

Working in a similar vein to that of North American researchers, Wesley Clair Mitchell (1913, 1923) and Warren Persons (1916), the ILO-LON economists first endeavoured to provide statistical representations of cyclical movements in major economic aggregates. The objective was to marshal quantitative evidence determining the relative strength of different causal factors in business cycles as a preliminary to finding means by which governments may respond to them. A descriptively realistic account of crises and cycles was preferred over idealized, formal theorizing; a motive for lowering the level of abstraction and formulation was to derive operational rules for economic policy. No concern was held at the ILO-LON, *à la* Mitchell (1913: 20), for canvassing all the available pure theories of crises and cycles and then testing or applying them to assess their explanatory power. More immediate policy implications were sought even if fundamental causes could not immediately be isolated or understood. Indeed, some frustration was expressed over the contemporary state of cycle theory: "no theory has yet been advanced which commands wide acceptance," yet policy makers were pleading for solutions (ILO 1924b: 13). Briefing documents for delegates attending the 1927 World Economic Conference reflected on LON cycle research up to that date with similar sentiments:

Since 1924 the [ILO-LON] enquiry . . . has proved beyond doubt that excessive fluctuations in trade activity are highly prejudicial to the stability of employment, and that it would be very desirable, if possible, to diminish the intensity of such fluctuations (LON 1927a: 36).

We find acceptance of a loose monetary approach to crises and cycles advanced from the outset of the research program. A prominent theme is the interaction of changes in money and credit with changes in economic activity considered in aggregate terms – particularly actively associated with, and measured by, the general level of prices, total output, and total employment. The ILO-LON program subscribed to the view that a simple classical, quantity theory of money best explains broad contours of crises and cycles and conveniently links monetary phenomena with other key, measurable economic variables. Thus, "[m]odern industry and commerce are based on a money economy and the movement of the general level of prices . . . is an important factor affecting fluctuations." Furthermore, variations in the general price level were readily observable representations of underlying economic changes. Now there "is a close connection between changes in the general level of prices and variations in the volume of currency" (ILO 1924b: 13). Changes in the volume of money and credit and the level of prices that have a cyclical character, were to be distinguished from autonomous monetary impulses especially on the supply side such as increases in the production of gold. Under the gold standard regime in vogue before 1914, higher gold output tended to increase banks' gold reserves and the volume of currency. With the gold standard in retreat in the 1920s, the link between the volume of currency and banks' gold reserves was breaking down. More than before 1914, "changes in the volume of currency have had a marked effect on fluctuations in economic activity" independently of gold supply influences (Ibid., 14). Therefore, a simple monetary theory of the business cycle was initially adumbrated in which prominence is accorded to the link between the money supply and prices (implicitly in a closed-economy context). The report of the ILO economist J.R. Bellerby for the International Association on Unemployment in 1923 was discussed approvingly in an unsigned article (ILO 1924c). Here there is recurrent emphasis on the money supply-price level nexus. It is submitted that "banks, by . . . the issue of 'money' of all kinds, can influence the movement of the price level [and] are handling a most powerful and sensitive instrument for industrial welfare" (Ibid., 79). The proposition that monetary factors cause price-level variations was considered unexceptionable (for example, Fuss 1927: 603).

It was considered supererogatory in ILO-LON research during the 1920s to search for an original propagating mechanism (specific monetary shocks) for a crisis or cycle. From a practical standpoint, limitations in available data did not allow a resolution of fundamental causes in this sense. However, that is not to gainsay policy-relevant, sometimes temporary, real effects of monetary disturbances – effects which arise because it takes time for decision makers in a decentralized economy to adjust to changes in real magnitudes (relative prices) and nominal magnitudes (absolute, money prices):

> whether due to the cumulative effects of individual action or . . . to currency policy [of commercial banks] reactions [are caused] which involve readjustments in the process of production. Further, one of the immediate effects of a movement in the general level of prices [consequent upon such currency changes] is a change in distribution, and readjustments caused by this change are often accompanied by friction and disorganisation. Production, exchange, distribution and consumption endeavour to accommodate themselves to the new level of prices. The lessons due to instability of the nominal measure of real values are well known and appear far to outweigh any chance of gain of an exceptional character which sometimes arise (ILO 1924b: 14–15).

The central idea here makes monetary disturbances, in particular periodic expansions and contractions of credit, the observable, controllable cause of economic dislocation which expresses itself in employment and investment fluctuations, among other things. By contrast, the speed of adjustment of decision makers' perceptions is not directly observable or controllable. As formulated in the 1920s, the ILO-LON "theory" of the business cycle concentrates on a straightforward notion that variations in the quantity of money (or "currency") is largely responsible for price-level variations and subsequent economic disorganization.[3] This rather banal conclusion (for the times) is distilled from the writings of Irving Fisher (1923), Ralph Hawtrey (1919, 1923), and J.M. Keynes (1923).

Writing in 1928 Fisher paid obeisance to the work of the ILO economists in particular; they clearly specified crucial links between "unstable money – unstable employment" (Fisher 1928: 92). More accurately the ILO-LON economists' work considered as a whole included an intermediate link here, namely, unstable money – unstable price level –

---

[3] Not that every credit expansion, for example, that leaves price levels stable is necessarily legitimate. We shall point out later how the ILO-LON program was keenly aware of credit expansions which, while keeping price levels stable, were doing so unwarrantedly in situations where positive productivity changes demanded price level reductions. The ILO-LON theorizing on monetary aspects of cycles, such as it was, allowed for deeper causes originating in overinvestment (following such unwarranted monetary expansions). They had knowledge of Austrian ideas on the cycle, for example, Hayek (1933); Hayek attended the Geneva meeting on "economic depressions" (see footnote 2 above). On Austrian approaches to both the business-cycle and monetary theory in the interwar years see Laidler (1999: Chapter 2).

unstable employment, though that was implicit in Fisher's nexus.[4] We might remark summarily that the initial ILO-LON research program on cycles was a loosely articulated amalgam of Fisher's, Hawtrey's, and Keynes's ideas *for the 1920s*, with Fisher playing a leading role. Central to Fisher (1923) is the idea that money illusion is pervasive, that is, decisions in the economy are based on misperceptions about the changing relationship between real and nominal magnitudes. His well-known proposition is captured in the title of his early work: "Business Cycle Largely a 'Dance of the Dollar'" (1923). For Fisher, fluctuations in the purchasing power of money had real consequences (Dimand 1993). The ILO-LON research program was substantially equivalent to Fisher's; it accepted, like Fisher, the "old" quantity theory of money at least as a point of departure, though it cannot be maintained that the ILO-LON program was as analytically sophisticated as Fisher's work in the 1920s. In addition, Bellerby's (1923a, 1923b) work at the ILO contained clear recognition of the Cambridge (U.K.) cash-balances version of the quantity theory of money, so well embedded in Hawtrey (1919) and Keynes (1923), and this recognition produced some important conclusions when considering monetary policy responses to cycles.[5]

In various country profiles presented in ILO-LON work, it is evident that as early as 1924 a monetary theory of the business cycle was generally accepted by Geneva economists. At least, "a most powerful determinant of activity and enterprise is controlled through the monetary machine" (ILO 1924c: 79). It was not, therefore, mere coincidence that Hawtrey's *Monetary Reconstruction* (1923) was also cited frequently in this 1924 article. Hawtrey had proclaimed tirelessly that the "trade cycle is a purely monetary phenomenon" (1923: 141). The cycle propagating effects of nonmonetary factors were minimized. For example, the flows of tradeable goods were stated to have "had very much less bearing on unemployment in most countries than fluctuations in home prices." The gold standard, or some variations on the standard, had tended to "internalise price fluctuations" and those countries which attempted to adopt independent currency policies (and so abandoned the gold standard) had merely postponed but not avoided the eventual transmission of price fluctuations and hence the business cycle (ILO

---

[4] The contrast with Keynes (1923) (a book cited frequently in ILO-LON reports), was only slight on this point: for Keynes in the 1920s the business cycle was foremost *represented by* price level fluctuations, and *constituted by* systematic effects of price level changes on other variables – employment, investment, consumption, and the like.
[5] Bellerby's contributions to the debate on monetary policy are of some significance and will be discussed in Chapter 3. A comprehensive exposition of monetary ideas developed in the Cambridge economics tradition for the period under review is now available in Laidler (1999: Chapter 5).

1924a: 143–44). Trade fluctuations were the result, for the most part, of price fluctuations.

ILO-LON applied research in the 1920s owed much directly to Fisher's work.[6] Short-run price level fluctuations of sufficient magnitude during a business cycle were thought to have been associated with employment and output instability and research was undertaken to measure this association (ILO 1925f: 224). Extensive empirical evidence was gathered in support of this general association, and considerable support was offered in Fisher (1926), some of which was supplied by the ILO.[7] In their copious empirical studies and country profiles the ILO-LON researchers drew heavily on Fisher's paper. Fisher calculated the correlation between unemployment and a linear distributed lag of movements in a price index. Using data from the United States 1915–25, Fisher demonstrated a short-run positive relationship between price level changes and total employment. His influential data are shown in the (adapted) Figure 2.1.

P' denotes a moving weighted average of the past price changes. Fisher interpreted the statistical correlation between the two series as evidence of a relation between price changes and (subsequent) employment. The lag distribution concept inherent in Figure 2.1 was Fisher's invention and it influenced work at the ILO. His analysis indicated a unidirectional casual sequence running from price changes to unemployment; the source of causation is located in inertia, fixed contracts, and general institutional arrangements in markets that prevent costs adjusting as fast as prices when output prices change. When costs lag prices, output price changes impact on profits and hence on other variables – investment and employment. ILO researchers seized on this work because it confirmed the results of their empirical cross-country studies up to 1926.

Surprisingly, institutional impediments on the cost side were largely ignored; instead the Fisher relationship was used as a shorthand by the ILO economic research director – Belgian trained economist Henri Fuss

---

[6] Fisher (1926), published in the *ILR*, was highly regarded. It sparked continuing work along the same lines at the ILO. See the commentary entitled "Statistical Evidence Showing the Relation of Prices to Unemployment," ILO Archives, 1929, L5/1000/4/2, pp. 14–29. Here Fisher's (1926) work on this subject is extended and updated, drawing on considerably more cross-country data. See also the ILO report: "Unemployment: Some International Aspects" (1929) for similar work.

[7] During 1924, Fisher corresponded with the ILO Director thus: "I have been making a lengthy study of the relation of the purchasing power of money to the so-called business cycle including unemployment and I find a strikingly high degree of correlation," ILO Archives, Z1061/74/5. He met leading ILO economist, J.R. Bellerby twice to discuss these results in Chicago in December 1924 and again during 1926.

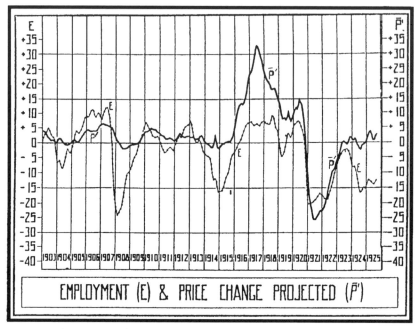

EMPLOYMENT (E) & PRICE CHANGE PROJECTED (P')

Figure 2.1 Irving Fisher's Results: Comovements between Lagged Price Changes ($\bar{P}'$) and Employment (E) (*Source*: Adapted from Fisher [1926: 791]; Used by permission.)

– as one that may in principle be exploited by economic policy. That policy should aim "to ensure that the instrument of payment shall increase at a rate corresponding exactly to the expansion of production" (Fuss 1927: 605). The ILO-LON had a prima facie case for a policy of price stabilization to mitigate business cycles. That policy would carry employment stability in its train (this policy stance included several important qualifications as we shall point out in Chapter 3). Achieving price stability was all the more critical in the United States and Great Britain if they were to become leading reserve currency centers. Stable price levels would connote both stable exchange rates and a stable monetary standard for smaller countries on the gold-exchange standard. Here the ILO economists were quick to recognize the importance of Keynes's *A Tract on Monetary Reform* (1923) – a book which, as ILO commentaries noted, emphasized the need for internal price level stability in the United States and Great Britain (ILO 1924a: 153; also Fuss 1927: 606).

In a survey of unemployment across Europe, the United States, and British Empire in the period 1920–23, the ILO (1924a: 6) concluded that "there is a close relationship between price fluctuations and the financial and credit policy of the different countries from which the existence of a general relation between such a policy and unemployment may be deduced." While ILO-LON research in the first half of the 1920s found in favor of a clear-cut relationship between money and prices, it did not readily accept that price changes and employment are so straightforwardly connected. Collating evidence from many League member countries, high levels of employment or reductions in unemployment appeared to be associated with stable or mildly rising price levels (ILO 1925f: 223). A 1924 report submitted that "a certain upward movement in prices is an invariable and inevitable accompaniment of the process of recovery" (1924c: 84); by implication some price inflation is tolerable on employment grounds. There were, in short, certain limits in which it was believed a rise in prices could be accepted as a tradeoff for reductions in unemployment but these limits were not quantified. A pastiche of quotations and research results from the work of prominent economists – Gide, Cassel, and Keynes – were used to support the case for tolerating a gently rising price level; Fisher and Taussig, among others, figure as pronouncing against significant price level *fluctuations* which, if they occurred, were not merely representative indicators of the general path of the business cycle; price level fluctuations had economic consequences in that, given the slowness of decision makers to adjust to changes in the relation between real and nominal values, investment plans and decisions to employ labor were disrupted. It was concluded that "a violent rise in prices" would result in a catastrophic increase in unemployment. In between the extremes, moderate inflation may also be acceptable provided that it was immediately followed by a monetary policy response which sought to stabilize the price level, but not necessarily reduce it to its old level. Evidence in this case was adduced to demonstrate that, following stabilization, "the rapid improvement in the labour market which had accompanied the [moderate price-level] rise has continued or the high level of activity reached has been maintained" (ILO 1924a: 135, 139–41).

A serious complication arose in the interpretation of the relationship between price and employment data, which was recognized as follows: "a rise in prices does not always mean that trade is active, and a decline does not always point to depression" (ILO 1924c: 84). To be sure, there was confidence only that a *rapid* fall in prices had been "always" accompanied by "a marked increase in unemployment" (ILO 1924b: 135). Wesley Mitchell's work on business cycles was expressly used as a source for these insights. In particular, important productivity improvements leading to downward secular price level movements were well known to Geneva economists. Such secular movements were an obvious motivation for the remark that price level declines do not always connote depression (also Bellerby 1923b: 326). To repeat our earlier observation, however, the desultory treatment of nonmonetary factors in the business cycle was the hallmark of ILO-League research in the 1920s. And this is scarcely surprising given the dominant streams of economic thought in the period; reliance upon the work of Hawtrey, Fisher, and Keynes was in no small measure responsible for this orientation.[8]

Extensive statistical investigations by the ILO, under the rubric of "economic barometers" deserve our attention because they analyzed the relationship between aggregate price and employment fluctuations during the business cycle.[9] The principal investigation was made by the ILO (1924b) and it was a synthetic contribution drawing on lessons from Persons (1916, 1919) and subsequent Harvard-sourced studies on business barometers; the work of the London and Cambridge Economic Service (under the direction of economist-statistician Arthur Bowley) which produced the "British Index Chart," and the work of the Swedish Board of Trade (under the direction of Johan Åkerman). Some (now) elementary statistical techniques developed by these national organizations were freely adapted to ILO research in the 1920s, for example, the method of isolating secular trends using moving averages and curve fitting and the method of two variable correlation. It was also noted in the ILO report how the chart produced by the London and Cambridge group included the value of exports from the United Kingdom in the index of leading cyclical indicators – unlike the Harvard barometer where such an indicator did not figure so highly, presumably because of

---

[8] In late 1925 the Swedish economist Johan Åkerman wrote a memorandum to the ILO-LON commenting on "the organization of research on economic cycles." Discerning that the favored research orientation was skewed toward monetary factors and price level movements, he averred: "the large unsolved problems concerning the cause of economic cycles are, however, no longer of a purely monetary nature." Further, "what asks for investigation [are] . . . the role played by the stocks of raw materials, semi-finished goods and finished products – such are the problems that remain unsolved." He maintained that the tasks of international organizations was to coordinate statistical work undertaken in various countries and provide "an analysis of the different countries' positions in the [various] phases of the cycle," ILO Archives U6/1/2/3, 10/10/1925.

[9] See Morgan (1990: 56–63) for an appreciation of the "business barometer" movement in statistical research during the 1920s. The movement was motivated by the forecasting potential of statistical analysis for private business decisions. The ILO researchers drew different conclusions: Economic barometers could "be used for the purpose of guiding some authority in an endeavour to render economic life more stable in the interests of the community as a whole" (ILO 1924b: 18).

the relatively closed nature of the American economy. The lesson for an international organization studying different phases of the economic cycle was salutary: It must account for variability in "the structure of economic life" across countries. Accordingly, criteria for compositing series of data in an index of the business cycle must be specially selected for each country (ILO 1924b: 18–20).

Uncertainty was expressed about the price level–total employment relationship because seasonal, accidental, and secular trends could be responsible for changes in the price level and these all occur simultaneously in the aggregate data. Data sets need variously to be "de-trended" so that investigation of the causes and solutions to short term "cyclical movements" could be isolated (ILO 1924b: 17). In 1924, statistical methods available for isolating cyclical phenomena were only just beginning to be refined and the ILO survey on "economic barometers" found no general agreement as to the most applicable and reliable methods (Ibid., 29–38).

Altogether, the result of ILO-League research on the business cycle turned on the issue of price stability. Price stability was generally regarded as the harbinger of employment stability. This was a macroeconomic perspective in which "stability" had an elastic meaning; it allowed for slightly rising (or falling) aggregate price levels. Furthermore, the "controlling" monetary factors are potentially destabilizing of the price level, the labor market, and industry in general (Bellerby 1923b). Research completed at the end of the 1920s embodied a theme representative of work in the ILO-LON over the entire preceding decade: Usually, it concluded, "the monetary factor really does influence the labour market and, what is more, . . . it predominates over other factors capable of acting in the opposite direction" (ILO 1929: 8). This recognition derived from much empirical research. There were obvious intellectual linkages in all this research to Keynes in the 1920s who made a similar argument without giving it a strong empirical basis (unlike Fisher).[10] Bellerby (1923a, 1923b, 1924, 1925) elaborated on the ILO research at great length; he insisted that, however expressed, national and international monetary stability, stable price levels (or "stability in the purchasing power" of money as Fisher expressed it), all meant that employment would thereby be stabilized across countries.

A critical outcome for international economic policy analysis may be remarked upon at this juncture. Explanations of unemployment, fluctuations in total employment and production which turned on institutional structures in product and labor markets and their operation in

---

[10] Thus on Laidler's (1999: 161–62) authority, for "Keynes in 1925, unemployment was primarily a monetary problem, not one centred on the labour market."

particular national settings, were necessary but not sufficient considerations for understanding causes and for offering policy responses. Nationally focused explanations were severely inadequate given recognition of the international nature of business cycles. ILO-LON research on cycles across countries found another enduring explanation – locating causes of macroeconomic change including total unemployment in the determination of money and credit policies. It is scarcely surprising, therefore, that institutional arrangements for monetary policy formulation and implementation (at the national and international level) were a prime subject for discussion and research in international organizations during the 1920s (see Chapter 3).

The first comprehensive discussion by an international organization of the international transmission of business cycles (originating in monetary disturbances) was offered by the LON Gold Delegation (1930a).[11] Again, the assumed source of an impending downturn in the cycle characterized first by price level deflation, was an unstable flow of money (and specifically bank credit) based on gold. Monetary disturbances developed cumulatively through the 1920s; they were not random, instead originating in the growing "inadequacy of the supply of new gold available for money." The Delegation observed a tendency toward an international gold shortage which was "likely at no very distant date to exercise its influence in depressing prices" (Ibid., 5). Insufficient gold production, and the maldistribution of gold among countries, exacerbated by existing legal and customary gold reserve requirements for commercial and/or central banks, were expected to have an on going deflationary effect. In the Delegation's view, policy makers had little room to maneuvre. On the reading of ILO researchers, if there was no central bank collaborative action on an international basis, the gold shortage would be tantamount to "a restriction of credit"; it would lead to unemployment and a precipitate fall in price levels which, following results of the ILO research in the 1920s, was portentous of rising unemployment.[12] The ILO work on the putative "gold shortage" makes

---

[11] LON Archives, Official Doc. c.375.m.161 1930 II, League of Nations, Gold Delegation of the Financial Committee, Interim (First) Report. Another Interim (Second) Report was issued in 1931 and the Final Report in June 1932. See LON (1931, 1932a). Irving Fisher (1935: 289) credits Gustav Cassel, a leading Swedish economist represented on the LON Delegation, as being responsible for the formation of the delegation in late 1928. Note also a similar treatment of the issues contained in these reports by ILO economists – see ILO (1931g).

[12] See A.A. Evans (a Cambridge, U.K. trained economist) who was engaged at the ILO: "The Effects of a Possible Inadequacy of Means of Payment on Unemployment: Memorandum of the International Labour Office," ILO Archives L5/1000/4/2, Geneva, 17/10/1930.

extensive use of Hawtrey (1930); it relates the unstable flow of bank credit to a reduction in consumers' expenditure and a highly elastic response to investment in inventories by merchants ("producers and dealers") in goods markets. Expectations also contribute to the deflationary spiral in that the "monetary circumstances in which a restoration of credit takes place are so intimately associated with a fall in the commodity price level that the merchant expects a fall and acts in the same way as if the fall had actually taken place."[13] Now these comments were written at the beginning of the economic depression of the 1930s. The international transmission process is also made patent:

> In practice the effects of inadequacy of the means of payment in one country tend very rapidly to spread to other countries; this tendency manifests itself both in the reduction of purchasing power of a country leading to reduction in the volume of imports, and in the fall in the commodity price level which occurs in all countries. Thus, in periods of falling prices unemployment will rise in practically all countries owing, firstly, to the effect of inadequacy in the means of payment on unemployment in each country and, secondly, to the effect of the inadequacy of means of payment in the countries which are their usual customers (Ibid., 11–12).[14]

This conclusion is drawn following analysis of data on the relationship between money and short-term price level fluctuations, and unemployment from twenty-three countries. The variable requiring immediate policy action is identified squarely as a monetary one. Monetary policy changes are urged "to prevent future occurrence of periods of ... fall[ing] prices" (Ibid., 37), though it is not made clear how an internationally organized, collaborative monetary policy would operate. By contrast, the LON Gold Delegation and the newly created BIS accepted deflation as the outcome of the operation of an anonymous gold standard mechanism. BIS pronouncements held strongly to this orthodox line.[15] Price level reductions were entirely natural or normal economic

---

[13] Evans, ILO Archives L5/1000/4/2, 1930, p. 7.

[14] The ILO emphasis on unemployment effects is not surprising given that organization's founding objectives. See Evans (1995: 2–6) for personal memoirs on the 1930 report on the gold shortage.

[15] See the BIS *Annual Report* for 1930/31 (BIS 1931) and 1931/32 (BIS 1932). The resolution of the BIS governing board on 11 July 1932 is typical: "The Board of the Bank for International Settlements, recognising the necessity of the re-establishment between nations of a monetary system with a common basis, in order to facilitate international settlements under more stable and secure conditions, is unanimously of opinion that the gold standard remains the best available monetary mechanism and the one best suited to make possible the free flow of world trade and of international financing; it is desirable, therefore, to prepare all the necessary measures for the re-establishment of the

adjustments inherent in the cycle such that complete, universal price level stabilization was neither desirable nor possible. The Gold Delegation's conception of the business cycle in its final report owes much to an orthodox, classical line on cycles as essentially equilibrating phenomena in the long run:

> *We view the business cycle as a more or less rhythmical oscillation* of a very complex price structure and business activity *around a hypothetical norm of stable relationships.* The normal position of the equilibrium is never reached and never can be realised except upon the assumption of a static society (LON 1932a: 134, emphasis added).

REFLECTIONS ON THE INTERNATIONAL BUSINESS CYCLE: FURTHER ANALYTICAL WORK IN THE 1930s

The LON Gold Delegation's reports marked the end of an era inasmuch as they constituted the last substantial piece of advisory work giving pre-eminence to monetary aspects of the cycle, especially the money supply (read: gold supply)–price level nexus and the consequent normal, "rhythmical" price level dynamics of the business cycle. The Delegation's reports were quickly overcome by events, not least the worldwide, indefinite abandonment of the gold standard, including the looser gold-exchange standard arrangements that were constructed in the 1920s.

Bertil Ohlin's LON-sponsored research report on "The Course and Phases of the World Economic depression" (Ohlin 1931a) represented a fundamental break from the orientation of ILO-LON business cycle studies in the 1920s. Ohlin's work also ushered in a series of well-known LON-based contributions in the 1930s (Haberler 1937; Tinbergen 1938, 1939). Ohlin remained faithful to the title of his report; it was mostly a recent economic history of the course and phases of the Depression up to late 1931 and it bore no obvious economic theoretic trademarks of a distinctive Stockholm School line of macroeconomic argument.[16] The work has a strong applied, empirical content and it gives few hints as to what was to come in the extensive Swedish work on the business cycle and in Ohlin's subsequent contributions in particular.[17] In the former,

---

functioning of the gold standard" (quoted in Martin and Riches 1933: 27). BIS officials remained wedded to the gold standard and the system of complete multilateral currency convertibility that the gold standard embodied, though Per Jacobsson's reflections on his early experience at the BIS suggest that a minority, including himself, were expressing dissent in late 1931 (Jacobsson 1958: 21–24).

[16] The distinctive Stockholm School "macrodynamics" was then only in fledgling form in the Swedish economic literature (Laidler 1999: 51–75).

[17] Ohlin (1931a) is not mentioned in Haberler (1937), the latter purporting to be a comprehensive survey of business cycle theory up to that date. We cannot agree with Craver (1986: 213) that Ohlin (1931a) served as an "influential" book on "macroeconomic theory"; its influence resided elsewhere.

reference to critical psychological, expectational, and confidence-related phenomena are not weaved into Ohlin's work for the LON; in respect of the latter, Ohlin (1933b) turns tentatively toward analyzing the determinants of *output* variations in their own right as distinct from assessing monetary and price-level disturbances – but this orientation is absent in his LON report. What is notable about Ohlin's report is the acute sensitivity to international interdependencies and the open economy spillover effects of crises – arguably a hallmark of Swedish research on cycles at about the same time.[18]

On appointment by the LON in late 1930, Ohlin set out to study "facts and special characteristics of the present depression." He had a year to report and called on the assistance of economists and statisticians employed by the Geneva-based ILO and International Institute of Agriculture as well as the LON economics secretariat. Drafts of the report were presented (before final publication in September 1931) to conferences of representatives of economic and advisory councils and economic research institutes held in Geneva in March and July 1931.[19] The outcome was a truly international study, sensitive to some of the wide variations in the pattern of the depression across countries. Nonetheless, the report illustrated the "length, depth and universality of the depression" (McClure 1933: 320–21). It underscored key macroeconomic interdependencies between countries that prevailed in the face of policies and natural impediments to trade and payments. These interdependencies are discussed at length (Ohlin 1931a: 216–23). Four principal factors are isolated as being responsible for the international transmission of what Ohlin described as a "financial crisis" (p. 221):

1. reduction in the demand for, and international trade in, commodities (raw materials, for example);
2. output inelasticities in agriculture, such that production of wheat and food-related products in particular did not decline in line with price falls – so that trade balances of primary producers deteriorated;
3. sudden changes in international capital movements detrimental to countries (especially primary producers) that had accumulated large international short-term capital obligations (partly

[18] See, for example, Johan Åkerman ([1931]: translated 1932, Chapter IX: "International Interdependence" (pp. 144–64). Here, as later in Swedish economic thought, reasons for considering "international" as opposed to interregional issues within nations turn on restrictions to exchange and currency flows, and to the flows of goods, labor, and capital between nations (Ohlin 1933a).

[19] For a full list of attendees, see Ohlin (1931a: 10–11).

because of the permissive use of gold exchange standards established in the 1920s);[20]
4. increasing resort to restrictive trade policies and currency adjustments as the cycle turned down.

These four factors are now commonplace considerations in any standard account of the economic history of the early 1930s. In 1931 their significance was only just beginning to become understood. Ohlin relied on a general distinction between industrialized, manufacturing-based economies and primary product-dependent economies. Leading industrialized economies seemed eventually to suffer more-or-less equally the same macroeconomic consequences of the crisis. Size in an economic sense or relatively low dependence on trade did not bring effective insulation; nations less dependent on trade were usually net creditors in the world economy with large international investments and obvious negative feedback effects occurred when these investments produced poor returns. Altogether, the

> effect of these developments on the leading nations and other manufacturing countries was ... [just as] serious. Their exports of manufactures to the impoverished countries dependent on primary products declined heavily and employment in the export industries fell off. To some extent this fall in their export trade was due to the increased duties and other impediments to the import of foodstuffs which they had themselves imposed (p. 220).

Furthermore, a "striking characteristic of this interaction of international economic relations" was that it "tended to reduce the value of investment in lending and borrowing countries alike." The depression was foremost a financial phenomenon – it would be, in Ohlin's estimation, "a serious mistake to treat the present depression as ... principally an unemployment crisis" (p. 233).[21] Tribute is paid to the conventional classical price-flexibility argument in economic theory. Countries might avoid some of the worst consequences and international spillover effects of the economic crisis and enjoy speedier recovery by promoting price and wage flexibility. This part of Ohlin's analysis is hedged about by

---

[20] Countries with accumulating obligations faced deflationary consequences as the supply of long-term international capital decreased; short-term capital also became "increasingly difficult" to source (p. 219). We will have occasion to review more specialised LON studies of the sources and consequences of fluctuations in international capital movements in Chapter 7.

[21] This statement could not be further from the general Stockholm School line that developed a few years later which was "willing to ask questions about macrodynamic processes in which output and employment variations were of the essence, processes which might begin with unemployed resources" (Laidler 1999: 75).

qualifications for particular cases and countries though his first impulse is to recommend relative price and wage flexibility coupled with freer capital and labor mobility within and between nations and implementation of freer trading arrangements worldwide (pp. 262–73). Greater flexibility in all these respects would normally result in crisis amelioration, faster adjustment, and recovery.

In tracing the international variations over the course of the cyclical downturn from 1929 to mid-1931, Ohlin depicts sources and tendencies in Figure 2.2. Countries falling under the first three headings are labelled "foyers de crise."[22] Groups 1, 2, and 3 acted as originators and transmitters of depression to Groups 4 and 5.

The extent of the depression's effects on living standards, and the speed of recovery, were very different matters; they depended on the "flexibility and adaptability of the economic systems of the various countries" (p. 238). Nevertheless, Ohlin detected problems in simply presuming that circumstances in the cyclical downturn were "normal" on this occasion. The standard prescription to increase economic "flexibility," if applied universally, that is in a concerted manner internationally, may not be sufficient to afford a rapid recovery. Observing the first round of output price and input price deflation up to mid-1931, he suggested that a fallacy of composition might be underwriting arguments that proposed ongoing *downward* wage and cost flexibility alone to effect a genuine international recovery:

> [A] reduction of certain costs and prices, if undertaken by one country alone and not by others, would increase the competitive power of the export industries of that country and thus have a greater effect on the volume of sales and employment than if the same policy were simultaneously adopted in all countries (p. 268).

This portentous passage anticipated the competitive rounds of currency devaluation to follow in the early 1930s. Ohlin was mindful of complications introduced by the open economy cases: Only some countries had the luxury of a low degree of openness and so could be insulated to some extent in the short run from the spillover effects of changes in competitiveness consequent upon price-level declines and currency devaluations.

When Ohlin turns attention to cases in which significant unemployed and underemployed resources are presented after the first round of deflation up to 1931, he judges that it is "uncertain" to what extent the price and cost flexibility solution would lead to "an increased volume of

---

[22] South Africa, Portugal, Turkey, and Central American countries could not be classified as they may just have well been placed in one category as in another in respect of the factors mentioned in the foregoing paragraph.

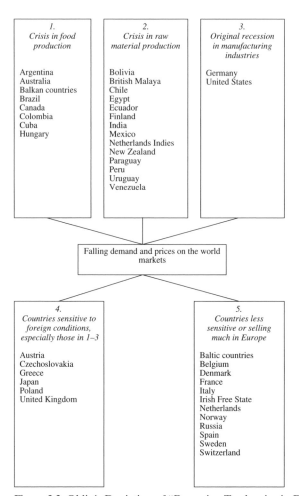

Figure 2.2 Ohlin's Depiction of "Recession Tendencies in Different Countries" (*Source*: Ohlin [1931a: 240, chart 32].)

production and employment" (p. 268). The focus on downward wage flexibility, in particular, might not be satisfactory afterall. Wage stickiness could support purchasing power and place a brake on the downward spiral in production.[23] There are features of an argument here that resem-

---

[23] Thus, it seemed to him "uncertain whether during the present depression general reductions of prices and wage rates would have enabled output to be maintained at a higher level." And, while the benefits of downward flexibility in all input prices are acknowledged, this event "might be offset by a strengthening of the tendency of purchasing power to decline" (p. 270).

ble debates that would come to the fore in the pending academic economics literature initiated by Ohlin and some other Swedish economists, as well as Keynes and his followers. In 1931, however, the analytical tools were not available to the LON (and to Ohlin); they could not provide a satisfactory explanation of the determinants of aggregate output and employment in the short-run situation of a depression. They had to be satisfied with a comprehensive, detailed account of past events not integrated by an overarching theory of economic crises or cycles.

Two other aspects of Ohlin's report deserve comment before we proceed further. First, it does not expressly set out policy priorities or explicit policy prescriptions for each country. Second, it did not conclude emphatically (as the Gold Delegation of the LON had done) that international monetary factors were fundamentally responsible for cyclical downturns of the kind then being experienced and that such downturns were "normal." To be sure, the crisis was constituted by disarray in international financial markets. Measures taken to make major monetary reforms, on their own, were not likely to be successful and were certainly not implied by his report. Indeed, Ohlin maintains that "[s]ensitive analysis . . . of the whole problem of business cycles is still at an early stage," therefore rendering premature any definite policy conclusions.[24]

The dearth of policy reflection, let alone specific recommendations, was continued in Gottfried Haberler's work completed for the LON in Geneva (Haberler 1932, 1937, 1943a, 1943b). Haberler's *Prosperity and Depression: A Theoretical Analysis of Cyclical Movements* (1937) was the culmination of five years' research. A critical change in perspective (and by implication in policy orientation) is evident in Haberler's first Geneva-based publication. While in Geneva he delivered a lecture to the Harris Foundation in 1932 on the theme of "money and the business cycle." His analysis was quite different from the standard ILO-LON approach to this subject in the 1920s. Like Ohlin in 1931, Haberler was critical of "traditional monetary explanations" (1932: 74) of the cycle that proposed strictly monetary policy reactions acting on price levels as sufficient to dampen, if not negate, cycles. He associates this traditional, general line of thinking with Cassel, Fisher, and Hawtrey (he excepts Keynes) and does not go so far as to identify the ILO-LON synthesis of these writers' work in the 1920s as part of the same tradition. Monetary and price level phenomena are acknowledged as both important impulse factors and observable factors of any business cycle.

---

[24] Therefore what are we to make of all the academic work and work in international organizations on the subject prior to 1931? At about the same time, ILO economists were less patient. See Martin's (1931a,b) reviews of the Macmillan Committee's (U.K.) Report (1931) for the ILO. The ILO economists' views on policy responses in 1931 and beyond will be discussed in Chapters 3 and 4.

However, the "rational regulation of credit" to stabilize price levels will not suffice because

1. the price level is frequently a misleading guide to monetary policy and that its stability is no sufficient safeguard against crises and depressions, because
2. a credit expansion has a much deeper and more fundamental influence on the whole economy, especially on the structure of production, than that expressed in the mere change of the price level (Haberler 1932: 53).

Factors on the supply side of the economy – inventions, human skills, and technical improvements – can affect price levels by lowering costs of production independently of monetary influences. Haberler stresses the importance of deflation caused by general cost reductions consequent upon supply-side improvements, as opposed to deflation caused by monetary forces such as a shortage of gold. The LON Gold Delegation (1930a) had explained the 1929–30 cyclical downturn – observed through falling price levels – as a consequence exclusively of the latter. *Per contra*, for Haberler, a "scarcity of gold could result only in a relative deflation, which could never have such disastrous results as the present depression" (Haberler 1932: 55). To elaborate on this position he adopts what would now be described as an "Austrian" (or specifically a "Hayekian") vision of the vertical structure of production in advanced industrialized economies.[25]

Haberler proposed an explanation for the Depression in the 1929–32 period that stresses monetary overinvestment more than monetary disequilibrium (*à la* Fisher, Hawtrey, and the ILO-LON in the 1920s) as the preeminent cause. The originating factor in the overinvestment theory is an unstable supply of bank credit; long-run natural rates of interest and temporary money market interest rates subsequently diverge and that divergence distorts the time profile of capital investment. For example:

> a credit expansion by the banks which lowers the rate of interest below that rate which would prevail, if only those sums, which are deliberately saved by the public from their current income, come on the capital market . . . will induce the business leaders to indulge in an excessive lengthening of the process of production, in other words, in overinvestments. As the finishing of a productive process takes a considerable period of time, it turns out only too late that these newly initiated processes are too long. A reaction is inevitably produced . . . which raises the rate of interest again to its natural level or even higher. Then

---

[25] In fact Haberler cites Hayek and the English economist Dennis Robertson as offering similar analysis to his own (p. 66).

these new investments are no longer profitable, and it becomes impossible to finish the new roundabout ways of production. They have to be abandoned . . . This process of adjustment of the vertical structure of production, which necessarily implies the loss of large amounts of fixed capital which is invested in those longer processes and cannot be shifted, takes place during, and constitutes the essence of, the period of depression (Haberler 1932: 60–61).

In short, there were identifiable instabilities in the real sector made up of durable fixed capital goods. The "business leaders" are clearly victims of imperfect foresight in not correctly assessing the relative prices between present goods and future goods, thus creating an overinvestment boom. The smooth, continuous flow of investments in both shorter and longer ("roundabout") production processes is disrupted and such disruption constitutes the business cycle; proportions of "money streams" devoted to producing consumers' goods as opposed to producers' goods will be altered. Vertical maladjustments in the real structure of production did not suggest an obvious set of monetary policy responses of the kind favored by the ILO-LON in the 1920s. The dislocation which purportedly occurs in the structure of fixed or physical capital, as distinguished from purely financial capital and working capital, "can in no case be cured in a very short time" by monetary and price level changes (p. 70). The LON was therefore entertaining a new, "monetary overinvestment" explanation of the 1930s depression which had largely Austrian origins. The shift in thinking, directly connected to the change in personnel working on the LON business-cycle research program, is quite marked. Haberler insisted that the causes of the cycle were "complicated" – so much so that he could not venture upon offering specific policy responses. In 1932, a sentiment of powerlessness was widely held in international organizations – the depression seemed intractable from the standpoint of internationalists bent on finding solutions in a collaborative, truly international package of policy responses.

In the Preface to the original 1937 edition of *Prosperity and Depression*, the Director of the Financial Section of the Economic Intelligence Service of the LON, Alexander Loveday, remarked: "our knowledge of the causes of depression has not yet reached a stage at which measures can be designed to avert them" (Haberler 1937: v). A modern reader might be surprised that the first edition of Haberler's work on cycles did not contain a section directly addressing economic policy responses to the cycle.[26] His work was intended to act both as a review of economic

---

[26] In a retrospective on *Prosperity and Depression* Officer (1982: 151) commented that "today's reader . . . is struck by [the] . . . minimal attention . . . devoted to policy measures to counteract the cycle." In fact, the main policy conclusion was mostly implicit

theory and as a preliminary to statistical testing, later carried out by Jan Tinbergen (1938, 1939). Haberler's *Prosperity and Depression* was contributed on the cusp of some important developments in pure economics – the formulation of complete mathematical models of business cycles in aggregative form (Frisch 1933; Samuelson 1939a) and Keynes's celebrated reformulation of macroeconomic theory which would have a strong bearing (in due course) on the potential range of policy measures available to avoid depressions (Keynes 1936).

Tinbergen arrived in Geneva in 1936 and some years later he produced *Statistical Testing of Business Cycle Theories* (1938) and *Business Cycles in the United States of America 1919–1932* (1939).[27] The core scientific contribution of these LON-sponsored publications was the construction of aggregate econometric models coupled with tentative estimation of coefficients in these multiequation models for the United States. A peer review of Tinbergen's early results in September 1937 was rather optimistic (with hindsight).[28] The ILO's econometrician Hans Staehle, was understandably concerned to derive policy implications from Tinbergen's research; his report anticipated favorable outcomes, that is, policy recommendations in due course. There is, argued Staehle

> the increasing recognition that mere qualitative statements would never enable any successful economic policy to be undertaken, since the effect of such policy may be quite different according to the weight which must be attributed to the various tendencies it calls forth. The task is essentially a quantitative one (Ibid., 11).

In executing the task Tinbergen's prime initial focus was on econometric methodology and his underlying economic-theoretic orientation is masked by this preoccupation. Essentially he was to analyze cycles caused by nonmonetary factors, especially in the second instalment (Tinbergen 1939) – an orientation far removed from work in international organizations on the subject of cycles in the 1920s and early 1930s, but not essentially at odds with Haberler's early articulation of the Austrian overinvestment theory.

and negative especially in the first edition, insofar as it raised doubts about the potency of traditional monetary responses.

[27] De Marchi (1991: 153–54) outlines the sequence of institutional developments associated with the LON research program in business cycles from 1933. See Morgan (1990: Chapter 4) for a complete assessment of Tinbergen's econometric work.

[28] Staehle (1937) – "Report on Meeting of Business Cycle Experts held at League of Nations' Secretariat, September 8–11 1937." The meeting was attended by Tinbergen, O. Anderson, A.L. Bowley, G. Haberler, R. Harrod, L. Pasvolsky, D. Robertson, and H. Staehle. ILO Archives 02/8/2.

Tinbergen acknowledged the importance of his work for economic policy, that is for business cycle control: "the purpose of business-cycle policy is to prevent the development of cumulative processes" (1938: 39). In one model he constructed, a hypothetical compensatory public works policy is introduced as an "outside" influence changing relevant model coefficients and dampening cumulative processes making for a depression in total output (Ibid., 34–35). Whether the amplitude of a cycle is permanently dampened by active public works policy is uncertain – everything depends in Tinbergen's multiequation, macroeconometric modelling on the source of a shock or shocks to an economy that propagated the cyclical movement in the first place. The conclusions for those pressing for immediate policy relevance are uninspiring. His policy responses are the result of mental experiments and may conceivably prevent in practice the development of a real-case cyclical movement, but it all depends. Tinbergen's achievement still merits praise because, as Staehle at the ILO maintained, business-cycle modeling should illustrate the potential for using quantitative measures of relations between aggregate economic variables to inform policy making. Tinbergen illustrates how policies can influence economic structure (that is, policies affect coefficients of established macroeconomic relationships by simulation or the policy effects may be monitored *ex post*) and how policies may change the average levels of macroeconomic variables (again by simulation or monitoring). Policy applications, therefore, could be made more precise. It is not until at least the late 1940s, in tandem with improvements in national income accounts, that econometric modeling along the lines of Tinbergen's work for the LON is broadened to simulate the likely effects of a wider range of economic policy initiatives.[29]

Keynes's (1939a) well-known review of Tinbergen's work treated only the first, methodological volume (for example, Tinbergen 1938). Two aspects of Keynes's critique are relevant for our exposition: discontent over the lack of realistic policy conclusions and scepticism over Tinbergen's attitude to nonmeasurable phenomena. Thus Keynes (1939a: 561):

> [I]f [as Tinbergen insists] it is necessary that *all* the significant factors should be measurable, this is very important. For it withdraws from the operation of the method all those economic problems where political, social and psychological factors, including such things as government policy, the progress of invention and the state of expectations may be significant.

Keynes suspected that many of these nonmeasurable factors might be of interest to international organizations such as the LON whose task it was

---

[29] See Zarnowitz (1992: 172–75).

to offer member nations and their policy makers means of responding to business cycles. The context of such responses mattered given the peculiarities of the political, social, and business institutions. Furthermore, statistical conventions varied among nations; data needed to operationlize key variables in his *General Theory* (1936) *viz.* savings and investment, were seriously deficient so that international comparisons were well-nigh impossible.[30] Yet Tinbergen had pressed on seemingly oblivious to these problems and to the concurrent work of the LON Committee of Statistical Experts (whose membership included economists Morgenstern, Clay, and Lindahl). The Committee deplored the fact that there existed "no common agreement . . . as to the meaning of such basic terms as 'savings', 'capital', or 'investments'; their definition depends on the theoretical conceptions of different students and on the practical purposes of the study in which such terms are introduced" (LON 1938a: 7). Keynes was also bemused with the orientation of LON economic research taking Tinbergen's work as representative: that "as far as 1939 is concerned the principal activity and *raison d'etre* of the League of Nations" should have been to closet away their best economists to work on "computors" (sic) and engage all their energies "in arithmetic" (1939a: 561). Certainly in Keynes's mind there were larger issues in international political economy deserving the LON economists' attention and the international policy implications of Tinbergen's work were difficult to discern.

Notwithstanding Keynes's critique on the foregoing aspects, Tinbergen's pioneering statistical effort made some advances in the analysis of business cycles proper – apart from advances in the application and refinement of econometric techniques (on the latter see Morgan 1990). He concentrated on a specific nonmonetary variable and developed a model of investment activity. Indivisibilities in current investment expenditure and leads and lags in that expenditure were translated into "cycles." For the purposes of Tinbergen's operational analysis business cycles were conceptualized as endogenously generated movements in key economic variables especially investment in relatively closed economies (De Marchi 1991: 164–65). Fluctuations in investment expen-

---

[30] On statistical issues Keynes made some telling points. There were glaring deficiencies in data sets of profits and investment available in some highly developed economies yet these data were used uncritically by Tinbergen (Keynes 1939a: 562–63). A LON (1938a) Committee of Statistical Experts had just reported on these problems and Keynes (1939b) reviewed their work in connection with data on capital formation, savings, and investment. It was therefore exceedingly unwise to use with confidence any of Tinbergen's results – say, those for the United States and generalize them for other countries. These statistical issues have retained their relevance in the late twentieth century despite vast improvements in econometric technique. See Patinkin (1976: 1094–96).

diture are explained by profit variations, so that if profits fluctuated cyclically, then investment would tend to do so perhaps with a lag. Now Keynes was not impressed with Tinbergen's treatment of investment expenditure. Tinbergen apparently excluded profit expectations; expectations were becoming a crucial theoretical consideration in macroeconomic theory by the late 1930s, not least in Keynes (1936). For Tinbergen expectations, while not directly measurable, are not on that ground strictly excluded in his modeling work. He takes expectations as a simple, *stable* function of past experience: "[t]he simplest type of expectations at moment t on the value [of] some variable x will have at moment $t + 1$ is that it is assumed equal to the last-known value of that variable say $x(t-1)$" (Tinbergen 1940: 147). Keynes (1940: 155) remained unsatisfied with this simplification; he harbored a more theoretically sophisticated appreciation of the role of expectations in the cycle in which "expectations of change" matter. Tinbergen's modeling used an innocuous class of expectations based on the notion "that the future will resemble the recent past" and that seemed too convenient.

While in Tinbergen's work international aspects of the cycle were mentioned perfunctorily, Jacques Polak (who assumed the mantle of senior LON researcher on business cycles following Tinbergen's departure) explicitly modeled the international propagation mechanism (Polak 1937–39). Since the price of domestic currency in terms of foreign currency in the long run reflects domestic economic fundamentals relative to foreign fundamentals, currency exchange rates and their variation can transmit fluctuations in those fundamentals (usually with a lag). Immediate fluctuations in international trade and payments are quickly transmitted regardless of currency exchange rates. In addition, international capital movements were also a symptom of, and often induced by, the business cycle and they also acted as an independent source of transmittal. Haberler's survey had foreshadowed salient theoretical features of economic research (up to 1943) on "international aspects of business cycles."[31] Polak's and Haberler's recognition of open economy complications – both international economic interdependencies and international cycle transmission conduits – led to greater awareness in international organizations of (1.) the effects in principle of short-term international capital movements; (2.) the differential impact of business cycles in different countries that depended on the commodity

---

[31] See Haberler (1943a: 406–51). Notable inclusions in Haberler's review are the ideas of Oskar Morgenstern (later to be associated with the LON Delegation on Economic Depressions – see the next section), and Ragnar Nurkse's (1935) work on international capital movements. Nurkse was later associated with important open economy macroeconomic research for the LON (see Chapter 7).

composition of trade with other countries and different currency regimes, and (3.) the importance of events in large industrialized countries that acted as cycle originators, especially the United States. In fact Polak (1937–39: 93–96) modeled the United States as a cycle propagator and depicted smaller open economies as recipients of exogenous shocks from the United States' business cycle. It would nonetheless take until the 1940s explicitly to link all this work with the idea that leading industrial countries in a business-cycle sense ought somehow to coordinate their macroeconomic policies in order to counter endogenously generated economic fluctuations and thereby reduce the spillover effects on other countries. That nearly a decade of research on cycles at the LON yielded paltry policy conclusions and only implicit allusions to the benefits of international macroeconomic policy coordination, lends weight to Keynes's solicitude over the direction of the LON research program.[32]

TOWARD A KEYNESIAN REORIENTATION FOR BUSINESS-CYCLE ANALYSIS AND POLICY IN THE 1940s

The 1940s ushered in new research interests at the ILO-LON, though business cycles were still on the agenda under a new guise. There emerged deep theoretical points of separation between the business-cycle research program in the 1930s and the new war-related work in the 1940s. The first hint of a change in economic thought on cycles appeared in the early months of 1940. The "Economic Intelligence Service" of the LON reoriented its work primarily to consider macroeconomic issues likely to be of importance when the time came for postwar economic reconstruction. That work acquired what we would now recognize as a broad Keynesian outlook; it was preoccupied with the short-run determinants of aggregate output, price levels, and employment. The objective was to stabilize these variables in the face of an expected international shock, in this case, the cessation of a world war which had the potential to cause major macroeconomic fluctuations.[33]

---

[32] De Marchi (1991: 167) viewed Tinbergen's and Polak's work as serving "the emerging consensus in favour of coordinated policies to promote stability in a dynamic and changing world." That consensus was indeed fostered by work in international organizations but LON business-cycle work up to 1940 made only a minor contribution in this respect.

[33] A preliminary plan for research was developed in early 1940 by the Director of the Economic, Financial, and Transit Department of the LON "in consultation with high officials and economists of various countries" (LON 1945b: 21). In May 1940 a Princeton, New Jersey, Mission of the Economic, Financial, and Transit Department was established (with assistance of the Rockefeller Foundation). Economic and statistical staff at Geneva were considerably reduced. Some ILO economics staff were removed to a Montreal mission. All collaborated on the business-cycle research led by the LON staff in Princeton during the 1940s. See LON Archives C1739 and C1755–1757.

The post-World War One (1918–22) experiences of the United States and the United Kingdom were used as case studies. A central purpose was to predict the short-run cyclical effects of the transition from war to peace, and more importantly, to draw out lessons for government policy from the transition (LON 1942a). As Alec Cairncross (1944: 253) remarked, these case studies did not constitute "an academic study of the trade cycle, but a dossier on Government policy." In the United States case, an economic "crisis" is identified from the middle of 1920; it was attributed to postwar efficiencies in production and transportation due to input price reductions. From the vantage point of early 1942, the LON economists inquired whether "by appropriate measures of economic policy" this crisis could have been avoided or mitigated (Ibid., 30). Policy failures were adduced as causal factors in amplifying the immediate postwar cyclical upturn in 1919 that subsequently made price level (and money wage) declines in 1920 more precipitous: The United States government "through deficit financing" (p. 34) coupled with weak monetary control by the Federal Reserve accentuated the late 1919–early 1920 cyclical peak. Similarly at the outset of the downturn in the second and third quarters of 1920, policy inertia allowed the downward movement to accelerate into a "crisis." While postwar relative price and wage changes were expected by government and market participants, "a protracted process of deflation" as occurred in 1920 was generally not expected and of an entirely different order; deflations of that kind should be averted by macroeconomic policy responses. First, "wage rates on average should be kept stable" by a wages policy (p. 36). It is implied that direct government intervention in money wage-setting practices is desirable and effective on these occasions. Second, timely monetary policy action to lower interest rates should be on the government's agenda. Gold reserves were certainly adequate in the United States to permit such a policy response (unlike the United Kingdom where reserves were not sufficient to sustain the postwar higher price level). If private investment demand is not responsive "with sufficient rapidity or strength, Governments may have to embark on a program of temporary deficit spending . . . by an extension of public works, the payment of war bonuses or the release of savings" (Ibid., 36). Here we have, at least on first reading, a recommendation to avoid protracted cyclical downturns using a crude Keynesian approach. On the LON economists' assessment of the historical record, such an approach would have been credible and effective if implemented in the United States during 1920.[34] Against this

---

[34] Earlier, the Fiscal Committee of the League of Nations (1939a) produced a report which recounted the 1930s debate on the advisability of unbalanced budgets during depressions. Its conclusions were equivocating: deficit financing all depended on national

interpretation is the remaining strong belief at the LON in the power of a carefully crafted monetary policy at critical business-cycle turning points – an emphasis that makes economic thought at the LON in the 1940s less rabidly Keynesian than a first reading might suppose. During wartime, the Federal Reserve "felt compelled to adjust their policies to the requirements of the Treasury" and operated an accommodating, easy monetary policy. It is speculated that the Federal Reserve lost its ability to correctly and adroitly time its policy responses, so much so that the "restrictionist banking policy [which] started at the end of 1919 continued after the 1920 turning point till well into 1920" thus tending "to aggravate the depression" in subsequent years (LON 1942a: 38).[35]

In the second case study, the United Kingdom economy is subject to a similar analysis but the conclusions are significantly different. Comprehensive data are used to construct broad economic trends (1918–22). Again, like the United States experience, "errors and hesitations in the formation of policy" are underscored (Ibid., 39). Monetary policy was too easy, in retrospect, though any other policy stance "was not considered politically practicable" given the short-run desire to expand employment for a demobilizing army (Ibid., 77). Fiscal policy in the period was considered inappropriate. Keynesian-type fiscal actions would not have enjoyed credibility and may well have had "limited effectiveness" given "the then state of public opinion [dictating that] deficit financing as an instrument of cyclical policy could not have been employed." No "deliberate anti-depression policy" is discerned (Ibid., 40). Notwithstanding the disapproving tone of the LON report, it is remarkably sensitive to the policy-making context in 1918–22 in the United Kingdom case. The (modern, late-twentieth-century) policy credibility issue comes to the fore, that is, fiscal policies of a Keynesian type will not have potency if public opinion, broadly understood, did not believe in them.

Expecting parallel economic trends post-Second World War, namely a short postwar boom followed by depression, a macroeconomic policy mix which stabilizes aggregate expenditure is recommended. The mix

circumstances, including political sensitivities and the state of confidence and opinions held by the public.

[35] The LON's reading of the effects of Federal Reserve action in 1919 and 1920 accords closely with an authoritative study of the early years of the Federal Reserve system. Thus Friedman and Schwartz (1963: 239) aver sympathetically: "from 1919 to 1921 ... [t]here was no strictly comparable American experience on which to base policy or judge the effects of actions designed to stimulate or retard monetary expansion. In particular, there was no evidence on the length of lag between action and effect. There was a natural, if regrettable, tendency to wait too long before stepping on the brake, as it were, then to step on the brake too hard. ..."

should include a prices and incomes policy to control cost inflation and stabilize wages. The British action in 1918–19 in resetting minimum wage rates were badly synchronized with the dynamics of market prices and wages in the postwar cycle:

> [m]inimum but not maximum rates were enforced even when the risk became an inflationary rise, and [subsequently] these minima were removed when the danger was a fall in wages and other prices (Ibid., 76).

The lesson was that centralized wages policies must be formed as part of an overall macroeconomic policy package and not in isolation. The British case also illustrated how microeconomic reforms were crucial to reduce inflation originating in inevitable postwar supply side inelasticities – the housing industry, in particular would have benefited from a relaxation of rent controls (Ibid., 77–79).

In both case studies of experience in two leading industrial countries post-1918, the LON report did not recommend retention of stringent rationing or ongoing price controls; there was also doubt expressed about the usefulness of rent controls. Both price and rent controls were used extensively post-1945 in the United Kingdom, and many other countries. In keeping with the spirit of research on wages policy and the business cycle in the 1930s, some key results of which were published in the *International Labour Review* (ILR), LON research on the subject in the 1940s considered centralized wages policies essential ingredients in the macroeconomic policy mix designed to mitigate an expected economic postwar boom and crash.[36] For example, if according to this view a wages policy became part of general macroeconomic policy, a general rise in money wages in line with labor productivity could be mandated during an economic expansion. That way profits would be restrained as would the potential for an overinvestment boom and following recession. By contrast, research in international organizations in the 1920s opted for the familiar line that labor markets clear in the long run, subject to wise policy interventions at the microlevel to remove market imperfections and promote smoother, quicker adjustment of labor supply to labor demand.[37] By the 1940s it became more widely accepted, following the implications of Keynesian macroeconomics and the lead taken at the ILO, that a macropolicy on wages could assist in stabilizing and

---

[36] See the papers published in the *ILR* in the 1930s, especially E.R. Walker, "Wages Policy and the Business Cycle" (1938) which expounded the rationale for an activist, centralized wages policy. See also Mitnitzky (1935) and Lederer (1939) which consider wage dynamics in the cycle and macropolicy responses.

[37] On the microeconomic policy reforms needed in labour markets, see Chapter 6.

regulating the path of the general wage level and thence the general business cycle.

A special Delegation on Economic Depressions (hereafter, Delegation) was appointed in 1938 to compile advice on what was termed *contracyclical* economic policies; its reports made special reference to the determination of aggregate output and the volume of employment in the short run (LON 1943, 1945a).[38] By comparison with the 1920s, the dynamic path of price levels (wage levels excepted) over the cycle were relegated to a position of secondary interest. A postwar depression was expected, with a likely relapse toward "policies of intense economic nationalism" as occurred in some parts of the world in the 1930s (LON 1943: 7). The Delegation's reports devote much space to antidepression measures administered and coordinated on an *international* basis, doubtless informed by positive, more formal work on the international aspects of business cycles being conducted by Oskar Morgenstern (1943) – a leading member of the Delegation. Specifically, the Delegation aimed to promote the philosophy that "we should think in terms of consumers' needs first" and deny "the belief that the difference in standards of living of different peoples is a menace to social order and international understanding." It was in favor of sharing the world's "mechanical, human and scientific means for satisfying [consumers'] needs" and that must not be read as advancing a "nationalistic doctrine" (Ibid., 11–12).

The Delegation's reports eschew highly theoretical deliberations and make very limited citations to academic literature in economic theory. They document as "preparatory" work on business-cycles research completed in Geneva by Haberler and Tinbergen. Emphasis is placed on controlling fluctuations in economic activity rather then dispassionately theorizing about causes (*à la* Haberler) or statistically testing hypotheses (*à la* Tinbergen).[39] A purported "very remarkable development in . . . economic and social doctrine" eventuated (LON 1945b: 33). The Delegation prosecuted a change in the "fundamental assumptions of economic thought" (LON 1943: 10). Management, through government intervention, of macroeconomic stabilization was certainly a central idea in the Delegation's reports. The idea was not new, though it was expressed with great timidity and accompanied by frequent qualifica-

---

[38] Two leading economists from academia were appointed to the Delegation to work on "The Transition from War to Peace Economy" (LON 1943) and "Economic Stability in the Post-War World" (LON 1945a): Bertil Ohlin (who was involved in the early work on the former but not involved in drafting), and Oskar Morgenstern (formerly Director of the Austrian Institute for Business Cycle Research). Gottfried Haberler attended meetings at which early drafts were discussed.

[39] In addition the LON (1942a) report on the U.K.–U.S.A. experience is considered mere "background" work (LON 1945b: 30).

tions in the work of international organizations prior to 1943.[40] Unlike most other studies (Polak's excepted), the Delegation's work was distinctive in stressing the essentially international character of business cycles and the need, therefore, for internationally coordinated, collective action to respond to cycles. Depression was an especially immediate bogey:

> Depressions may have many causes. They vary in nature, and may require the adoption of different policies on different occasions. There is no single simple remedy ... Moreover, they are international phenomena ... and we have to consider the influences of policies adopted in one country upon economic activity in another (LON 1945a: 291).

Furthermore, "independent action by each country for the achievement of full employment and economic stability would inevitably be self-defeating [;] ... national policies should be coordinated on the basis of an agreed international plan" (LON 1943: 7). Policy coordination would take the form of international action coalescing around a common set of broad policy objectives. The LON's economists recognized an incipient new policy consensus paraphrased in the following capsule summary statements (from LON 1943: 113):

1. employment of nations' resources should be maintained at a high level;
2. frictional unemployment is tolerable, any other form of unemployment requires immediate policy responses;
3. all nations should be able to share in world markets, so progressive removal of trade policy restrictions is recommended;
4. "courageous international measures of reconstruction and development" coupled with (3) above, should be supported so that all nations may accelerate their growth rates.

These statements may now seem like platitudes; they give no clear guidance for "contracyclical" policy. The Delegation's 1945 report was perhaps more comprehensive and more nationally focused in advising that a nation should "maintain its national income at a level corresponding to the fullest possible employment of its resources" subject to containing inflation and balance of payments problems (LON 1945a: 307).[41] In this the Delegation was expressing some "idealism and *élan de vie*"; its policy prescriptions presupposed a "stably expanding world, not

---

[40] For example, LON (1939a) did not embrace the idea of deficit financing to counter cyclical downturns.

[41] D.H. Robertson (1945: 401) rightly characterizes the 1945 LON report as "the economic swan-song ... of the League of Nations," though we consider LON (1946) as an important accompaniment. See Chapter 7 for an exposition of LON (1946).

a stagnant one" (Robertson 1945: 404). There are no ready-made blue-prints for managing business cycles in the Delegation's work, although in separate chapters some potent closed economy macroeconomic policy responses are broached. The chapter separation between closed and open economy issues is an expository convenience and closed economy matters should not be divorced from consideration such as international currency and monetary arrangements, the effects of international capital movements, and trade policy reforms.[42]

A standard, elementary aggregate relationship is posited: "the level of employment depends on the amount of expenditure" (LON 1945a: 291). The most powerful variable on the side of expenditure, expressly fol-lowing the lead given by Tinbergen, is investment.[43] It is proposed that investment constitutes "that part of demand which is particularly unstable" (Ibid., 46). Fluctuations in investment expenditure, including foreign-sourced direct investment, spread depression internationally. The prices of raw materials are believed especially sensitive to invest-ment fluctuations. There is characteristic Keynesian concern for the demand and supply of output as a whole. Thus it is observed that there is often "insufficient . . . spent to buy the whole output that can be pro-duced" so that unemployment appears. Moreover, expressed in the lan-guage of Keynesian economics, "changes in investment plans do not always synchronise with decisions to save. When savings outrun invest-ment, they go to waste and unemployment is caused." Declining invest-ment expenditures result in unemployment and unemployment "can only be overcome if that demand is made good." We are led perforce to the components of "Aggregate demand . . . (1.) private consumption; (2.) private investment; (3.) public expenditure on current goods and ser-vices; (4.) public investment expenditure; and (5.) net foreign invest-ment" (Ibid., 291–92). The object of national macroeconomic policy is to maintain aggregate demand. The 1943 report of the Delegation, referred to a new "economics of production" (LON 1943: 10), boldly setting the scene for the 1945 report which nominated properly managed govern-ment investment expenditure as a variable susceptible to diligent man-agement with the purpose of smoothing out the business cycle, though government investment impulses need not compensate for the whole of any decline (or alternatively, rises) in private expenditure.[44] There is

---

[42] Open economy issues are treated contemporaneously in two other LON studies – Viner (1943) and Nurkse (LON 1944). See Chapters 5 and 8 respectively.

[43] See LON (1945a: Chapter V) treating the "strategic role of investment" (pp. 50–75).

[44] The Delegation carefully outlines a key aspect of the Keynesian story turning crucially on the power of public expenditure and associated fiscal policy instruments *viz* the "mul-tiplier" effects of different types of expenditure. Haberler's treatment of the multiplier effects in *Prosperity and Depression* is cited and not Keynes's or Kahn's contributions (LON 1945a: 176–78).

strong preference for the deliberate use of public finance both on the revenue and expenditure sides. In addition, the clear implication is that public investment may stimulate private investment either directly or indirectly by first boosting private consumption (LON 1945a: 163–200).

Fiscal and monetary policies must be finely designed in such a manner as to maintain confidence and support private investment (Ibid., 299–300). Nonetheless, there is a noteworthy underreliance on monetary measures in genuinely identifiable depression conditions compared with the tenor of similar analyses written by international organizations in the late 1920s and early 1930s. Monetary policy would have a cameo role only, at least during depression conditions in industrialized economies (unlike less-developed economies where fiscal policy implementation may be problematic, therefore placing a greater burden on monetary actions). Monetary policy must be formulated to keep interest rates low, though not indefinitely. Interest rates must be allowed to rise in time of boom otherwise, in the Delegation's view, resort must be had to less desirable policy instruments such as price controls, direct controls on both investment and resource allocation more generally. The severity of a business cycle (together with the degree of price level inflation in an upswing) can be dampened by relying less on wartime planning techniques and controls, and more on creating an economic environment conducive to greater relative wage and price (including interest rate) flexibility. As far as fiscal policy is concerned, it should be allowed that a government's tax and expenditure policies need tailoring to circumstances; different types of public expenditure and tax policies were required in raw materials or primary product-dependent economies as opposed to industrialized, manufacturing-dependent economies.[45]

Gottfried Haberler advised on drafting the two Delegation reports, not long after completing the final 1943 edition of *Prosperity and Depression* which was updated to include, *inter alia*, reflection on Keynes's *General Theory of Employment* (1936). The Delegation's 1945 report reveals Haberler's influence especially, though not exclusively, in its disdain for direct controls over prices, wages, and investment, and in Haberler's admiration for Keynes's style of macroeconomic analysis. Haberler quoted Keynes approvingly in this connection:

> The object of our analysis is . . . to provide ourselves with an organised and orderly method of thinking out particular problems; and, after we

---

[45] Primary producing cases are considered in detail. Special policies available to them included export subsidies; government guaranteed price schemes; domestic government producer schemes and various production controls (Ibid., 250–75). The sympathy for direct controls in this context contrasts with the view of BIS economists who railed against "perpetuating . . . the methods of the war economy" in any country, irrespective of its economic structure. See BIS (1948: 163 passim).

have reached a provisional conclusion by isolating the complicating
factors one by one, we then have to go back on ourselves and allow, as
well as we can, for the probable interaction of the factors amongst
themselves. This is the nature of economic thinking (Haberler 1943a:
233 quoting Keynes 1936: 297).

As observed already, the Delegation's reports are neatly divided into an
analysis of domestic economic factors and policies first, followed by
studies of complications introduced by international economic interdependencies. No mention is made of Keynes's theoretical apparatus, yet
there is obviously considerable Keynesian conceptual content at least in
a vulgar, popularist form.[46] Haberler's *Prosperity and Depression* devotes
some space to a review of the multiplier concept, including the foreign
trade multiplier, and the efficacy of fiscal policies under varying conditions. And none of these topics were exclusively or uniquely Keynes's
creations. The 1943 edition of Haberler's work devotes a full, final
chapter to thorough examination of Keynesian policy formulations.
Critically important differences between Haberler and proponents of
Keynesian-type policies are clarified in that chapter and these differences carry over into the Delegation's report. Up to 1945, Haberler's
work bears some scepticism toward Keynes's contribution so far, specifically, as finding a resolution to business cycles is concerned. Thus,
Keynes "does not furnish a ready-made answer to the riddle of the business cycle"; Keynes offered many "bare contentions" and contributed a
closed-economy analysis far inferior to work which attempted, however
imperfectly, to grapple with international complications (Haberler 1943a:
233, 245).

   Richard Kahn (1937: 678) referred to Haberler's procrastination in
the first edition of *Prosperity and Depression* over matters of appropriate policy responses to depression. Haberler was accused of equivoca-
tion on the use of, and best method of financing, public works schemes
immediately after the breaking of an economic boom. Even in other
stages of the cycle Haberler (1937: 281) remarked less than favorably on
the "numerous and complicated problems of fiscal, administrative and
political nature connected with such schemes." These remarks raised
Kahn's ire; he evinced concern at Haberler's apparent disdain for expansionary policies, quoting Haberler's statement about reliance on an
"alarming expansion of central bank money" to finance all kinds of government expenditure in cyclical downturns. Furthermore, Kahn fulmi-
nated against Haberler's inadequate treatment of the role of the rate of
interest in the cyclical process; Haberler was presumably ignoring the

---

[46] The only avowed Keynesian text cited in the report's total of 437 pages is one reference
to Alvin Hansen's *Fiscal Policy and Business Cycles* (1941). See LON (1945a: 181n).

power of liquidity preference to disrupt the allocative power of the rate of interest to equate savings and investment.[47]

Haberler's (1943a) account of the Keynesian literature deserves our consideration since it contains explicit reservations on the application of what he referred to as "pump priming" public expenditure policies as putative remedies for cyclical movements (p. 228). Barring institutional rigidities (aggressive trade unions, resource supply inelasticities, and so forth) which could lead to cost-push inflation long before full employment is attained by "pump priming," Haberler argued that the course of a cyclical upswing as full employment is approached required more analysis than it was accorded in Keynes's *General Theory*. The contemporary Keynesian literature had also been neglectful of this phase of the cycle and the policies appropriate to it. That literature had generally presumed universal excess capacity and unemployed resources in all industry sectors; it "was essentially depression economics" possibly of questionable relevance at the time (Haberler 1943a: 503). Again, writing in the same year as the LON Delegation's 1945 report, Haberler (1945: 309) underscores the immediate policy problem: in fact the "employment objective . . . will hardly be an important factor after the war; at least it should not be one in a rational system of economic policy, because it is not likely that there will be general unemployment due to a general deficiency of effective demand."[48] Haberler was adamant that the long-run policy issues associated with management of economies at or near full employment were exceedingly complex; they present

> a much more difficult task than a spending policy *pure et simple*. The result of our analysis can be summarised by saying that it is comparatively easy to lift the economic system out of a deep depression, but that it is much more difficult to maintain the high level of employment and output which is reached at the end of the upswing (Haberler 1943a: 506).

---

[47] Resolution of the ensuing debate between Kahn and Haberler on the pages of the *Economic Journal* requires familiarity with some of the finer points of pure economic theory in the 1930s that need not detain us here. Haberler replied to Kahn by pointing out, first, that in both terminology and substance, he could not be counted as being in the company "of Keynes and his followers [including Kahn]" (Haberler 1938: 329). On matters of substance we agree with Laidler (1999: 297, 297 n. 18) that an aspect of Haberler's objection to Keynes (1936) involved Keynes's "exaggerated [position on] the capacity of liquidity preference to disrupt the coordination of savings and investment decisions by interest-rate movements, *except perhaps temporarily at times of crisis*" (emphasis added).

[48] The BIS (1945: 53) made precisely the same point, though it proceeded to recommend that "the principles of compensatory business-cycle policy . . . in the present situation" in the majority of countries demanded budget surpluses and "the postponement of all such government projects as are not urgently required."

Now for all its occasional expressions of "idealism" as charged by Robertson (1945: 404), the Delegation's 1945 report resounded with expressions of problems associated with maintaining high levels of output. Unemployment due to "chronic depression" may present a quite straightforward problem requiring expansionary Keynesian policies (LON 1945a: 224–29). Arguments in the report clearly maintain that a mere expansionary fiscal and monetary policy cannot for all times and places solve the problem of maintaining output and employment without interruption.

The path of the price level is an indicator of pending disruption; that path will have a different trajectory depending on national institutional conditions, as illustrated in several case studies in the Delegation's report. Inflation is discussed extensively in the 1945 report. Firstly, inflation can arise because fiscal and monetary policies are inappropriate in those situations where aggregate expenditure is stimulated but cannot reduce unemployment in particular industries or regions.[49] Second, inflationary influences may be observed from ill-timed, easy fiscal, and monetary policies during the cycle. Third, cost push inflation may derive from specific supply side pressures.[50] Macroeconomic demand management was therefore more problematic than merely adopting a pump priming policy (LON 1943: 50–66). Moreover, government deficit financing must "not restrict the supply of investible funds for the other uses"; and must be so managed as to avoid crowding out private expenditure and not be coupled with policies that are cost raising (Haberler 1943a: 504). Admittedly the above prescription is a general counsel of perfection though it is offered in an ideational context in which inflation took on an almost pathological aspect. "Contracyclical" management of the business cycle must, in this view, be geared to counteract "conditions likely to lead to inflation or accentuate inflation . . . Were the market left free, the risk of an inflation of the prices of raw materials, of local currency inflation and of subsequent general and local collapse would, we believe be greatly enhanced" (LON 1943: 79–80). All this runs contrary to a modern perception that the problem of latent inflation was minimized in the think-

---

[49] Haberler's influence is again evident on this point. During 1945 he gave evidence to the U.S. Senate Hearings before the Subcommittee on Banking and Currency dissenting from the general tenor of the "Full Employment Bill" on the grounds that "[i]ncreasing total effective demand . . . could not deal with unemployment specific to particular industries or regions without endangering price stability" (as paraphrased by Barber 1996: 163).

[50] See LON (1945a: 184–85; 201–04; 213–15, and 304–05); also LON (1943: 91–95, 117) and LON Archives "Princeton Mission Files," C1738, R. Nurkse Correspondence. See also Ragnar Nurkse's contemporary study for the LON (1946) on the subject of inflation and first use of the term *inflationary gap* in the BIS *Annual Report* for 1948–49 (BIS 1949: 68–69).

ing of economists working in international organizations in the 1940s because they were so enamored with popular, simplified Keynesian policies (Pauly 1996: 29). The prevailing antiinflation attitude at the LON (and also the BIS and ILO) can be attributed as much to impending supply side bottlenecks created by wartime controls and the likelihood that price controls and rationing would be removed, as to expected mismanagement of fiscal and monetary policies at specific stages of the business cycle. A more sceptical perspective on Keynesian and "contracyclical" macroeconomic management had infiltrated the economic work of international organizations from an early date.[51]

Contracyclical policies could not be expected to work without paying heed to another dimension – organized, concerted international fiscal and monetary initiatives based on agreement and continuous consultation between policy makers across national boundaries. Previously it may have been thought that international agreement might only need to be formed around international monetary arrangements and trade policy. Now, according to the LON experts, international organizations would play a leading research, facilitation, and tutelage role; they would convene international meetings and conferences to assist national policy makers with contracyclical policies. A key presumption was that international cooperation or consensus formation would be forthcoming in a spontaneous manner among nations. In respect to policies designed to smooth out cycles and "secure a stable but expanding [world] economy," formulating an internationally compatible package of policies was imperative, though no specific policies are outlined or regarded as a priority (LON 1945a: 316). Instead the *direction* of international policy reforms are indicated as follows:

1. the adoption of more liberal and dynamic commercial and economic policies;
2. the creation of an international monetary mechanism;
3. the creation of an international institution which will stimulate and encourage international movement of capital for production purposes and . . . impart a contracyclical character to this movement;

---

[51] ILO economists were concerned about wage inflation arising from labor shortages in any postwar recovery (ILO 1945: 594–95); the BIS always took a conservative line on inflation in its *Annual Report* in the late 1930s and through the 1940s (drafted mostly by Per Jacobsson, BIS economic adviser from inception in 1930 and later IMF Managing Director). Already in 1942, Jacobsson was predicting a postwar inflationary boom (BIS 1942: 22). Jacobsson frequently expressed strong dissent from policies which relied on unsophisticated, Keynesian solutions to cyclical fluctuations. See E.E. Jacobsson (1979: 111, 159–60, 209–22, 405–40).

4. the creation of a buffer stock agency;
5. the international coordination of national policies for the maintenance of a high and stable level of employment (Ibid., 316).

The Delegation's 1945 report endorsed the role of emerging international organizations as informal (rather than controlling or enforcing) intermediaries for promoting cooperation and coordination over policies to thwart the international transmission of business cycles. It supported the institutions to be formed as a result of the Bretton Woods Conference, the new United Nations agencies, the ILO, and "an international organization which might help governments to devise commercial policies conducive to stability" (then unnamed, most probably the proposed International Trade Organization [ITO]). Overall, the Delegation conceived of a bipolar arrangement of all these organizations postwar, but it remained open to the idea that mutually compatible regimes designed to deal with business cycles could be organized regionally or on a multipolar basis (Ibid.).

The Delegation believed its work had demonstrated how the spread of depression in the world economy is likely to result in competitive devaluations and various protectionist, beggar-thy-neighbor measures. Application of the old mantra of isolationism and economic insulation potentially offered damaging results for all. If national policy programs did not run in concert with other nations, "one country will tend to spread depression in order to avoid it at home, and . . . the world will be divided into a number of autarkic pugnacious units" (Ibid., 315).

SUMMARY AND CONCLUSIONS

When, in the first three years of the 1930s, the LON Gold Delegation (along with the BIS) exhibited strong attachment to the gold standard together with an associated belief in the natural rhythm of business cycles – where cycles had positive net benefits – they were indeed advocating a most orthodox position compared to what international organizations offered before and after the entire 1919–50 period. Yet even recourse to such orthodox conceptions included allowance for monetary authorities to develop more predictable, stable policies which would combat excessive price level fluctuations then considered the hallmarks of, if not the precursors for, significant economic depression. The Gold Delegation represented a line of thought that held the market economy to be inherently stable and the business cycle was considered a natural self-adjusting process; stability could be disturbed by erratic, misguided monetary policies that did not heed the imperatives of the gold standard regime.

In the 1920s we find arguments from Geneva-based ILO-LON economists which are seldom as orthodox as those of the Gold Delegation;

they are constructed in the belief that there is no reliable automatic process in the market economy ensuring full resource utilization. Accordingly, the cycle should be combated with an active macroeconomic stabilization policy. Monetary causes were underscored and dominated over institutional, labor market, and nonmonetary phenomena. International spillover effects were recognized and international monetary policy coordination recommended. Adjustment to business cycles was not seen as a problem for stabilizing nations without serious implications for others. More deliberate international action is frequently proposed, concentrating exclusively on monetary responses. The Geneva economists believed, along with most other professional economists prior to the 1930s, that "stabilisation was synonymous with monetary policy" (Jonung 1979: 483). Active countercyclical fiscal policy did not come within their purview in the 1920s. All this gives their doctrine a modern flavor, especially the idea that the monetary regime should concentrate on price stability – an idea achieving prominence again in the 1990s.

What then was distinctive about the view from Geneva in the 1920s? By the standards of contemporary British, American, and Scandinavian economics, the program was essentially a synthesis of conventional theory (as it developed in the 1920s). Some structure to the applied research at the ILO was given by Fisher's empirical work relating price level changes to changes in employment. This work supported the price level stabilization theme in ILO-LON business-cycle policy analysis. Furthermore, the ILO-LON research program on business cycles in the 1920s was an authoritative source on the use of "barometers" of economic activity to profile cyclical patterns.

Ohlin's work for the LON signaled doubts about the continued application of orthodox ideas promoting market-led wage and price flexibility coupled with freer trade and factor mobility as the most effective route to recovery from a severe business-cycle downturn of the kind experienced over 1929–32. Haberler arrived in Geneva (from Austria) in 1932 with the idea that the cycle functions to bring about necessary structural economic adjustments though the effects are basically negative and unfavorable to output in the short term. The economic boom constitutes the infertile soil upon which depressions are raised; monetary forces are the conduit for change through business "overinvestment." By the completion of his survey of business-cycle theory in 1937 Haberler had begun to adopt a more eclectic position. Nevertheless, the LON economists were still apt to lament at this time that their understanding of cycles was so incomplete that they could not feel confident pronouncing on measures to mitigate them.

A major shift in thought and research practice in the 1930s came with Tinbergen's exercise in quantitative modeling. Tinbergen emphasized nonmonetary forces as fundamental causes and as operational variables that economic policy might manipulate. Again, deliberate government responses to cycles are countenanced; policy can be effective in modifying the cycle, especially its more predictable, cumulative elements. When the Delegation on Economic Depressions completed its reports in the 1940s the shift from direct interest in business cycles per se, to the determinants of levels of aggregate output and employment in the short run was complete – with the time frame being restricted to expected events in immediate postwar years. The bases of Keynesian "contracyclical" policy are established. This change in the late 1940s both in terminology and doctrine marked an intellectual discontinuity in the economic work of international organizations, paralleling contemporary developments in formal macroeconomic analysis.

The shift in doctrine was not unqualified. Serious doubts were expressed over the adequacy of Keynesian prescriptions, as then understood, because they did not appear to offer a genuine, complete package of policies to respond to cycles. The Haberler-Morgenstern (Austrian) influence on the Delegation's reports in the 1940s seems manifest in some sections. There are doubts about the egregious simplification of monetary policy into a mere handmaiden of expansionary fiscal policy, and more extensively, there are many words devoted to the costs of inflation arising on the path toward providing high levels of output and employment over a short time period. In this view, macrodemand management may be *mis*managed: Compensatory expansionary monetary and fiscal policies useful for overcoming a significant depression are in practice easily conflated by policy makers and politicians with a procyclical (and thence ultimately destabilizing) inflationary monetary and fiscal policy package responsible for a cyclical upswing and subsequent economic boom.

The LON Delegation on Economic Depressions agrees that Keynesian policies may well have a stabilizing effect if the short-run determinants of output and employment are both well-understood and quantifiable, but there is an added proviso: To be effective, those policies must be coordinated on an international basis. On this score the recommendation is identical with international organizations in the 1920s and 1930s. Now, however, there is greater realism about the possibility of success. That possibility can be enhanced if business-cycle policies do not promise too much and if dangers and difficulties are envisaged. The Delegation therefore warns against ignoring complications in the application of Keynesian policies, especially those relating to inflation.

The work of international organizations on business cycles in the 1940s, as represented by the Delegation's reports, while advancing some grand policy goals around which a postwar international consensus might be formed, is in fact quite modest and in places skeptical about the possibilities of formulating a rational business-cycle policy. We shall explore this observation in more detail in the following two chapters where attention turns to proposals on economic policy designed by international organizations to respond to specific aspects of economic crises and cycles.

3   The Role and Conduct of Monetary Policy in the 1920s and 1930s

DOCTRINAL SUPPORT FOR INTERNATIONAL ECONOMIC CONFERENCES IN THE EARLY 1920s

In the monetary field a great deal of preparatory work was completed at the LON in the early 1920s to establish a framework of ideas concerning postwar monetary reconstruction. In addition, economists in international organizations attempted to articulate some principles that might act as focal points for general international monetary cooperation. The ultimate purpose of cooperation was to counteract the international transmission of business cycles. Two conferences were convoked by the LON: The Brussels Financial Conference in 1920 gave initial impetus to the preparatory work on monetary issues; a clear, formal expression of principles was arrived at in 1922 at the Genoa International Economic Conference.[1]

The Genoa conference provides a leading example of the rationale for international organizations such as the LON in the 1920s as noted in our first chapter. Such organizations can develop principles on which economic policies are formed and executed in the interest of international peace and progress. Given that international monetary arrangements were in disarray in the early 1920s following the breakdown of the pre-1914 gold standard, monetary policy and exchange rate issues came to the fore. The conference emphasized exchange rate stabilization through currency reform, making all currencies exchangeable against gold. Rather than gold acting as a means of settlement or as an international monetary reserve, currencies firmly on the gold standard (the U.S. dollar and eventually sterling) were to act as reserve currencies.[2] In this,

---

[1] On the Brussels Conference see LON (1920). Much more was written on, and for, the Genoa Conference; see, for example, LON (1922) and Hawtrey (1922).

[2] The purported shortage of gold as an international exchange medium was the reason for this Genoa conference recommendation. The Financial and Economic Council of the

monetary conditions in the United States and Great Britain were pivotal; they would, in the Genoa scenario, impact on money supplies in other gold-exchange standard countries. The object of exchange rate stabilization in the above sense was intended to assist international economic adjustment to external imbalances. According to Nurkse (LON 1944: 215–16) the Genoa conference resolutions were

> anti-deflationary . . . and therefore in that sense [were] 'inflationary.' Without [them], the shortage of international currency might have led to a general deflation which would have 'corrected' the situation through a reduction in the value of international transactions and an increase in output of new gold. With [them], the gold shortage was made good by exchange reserves.

The League of Nations would play a central role because it was charged with organizing stabilization loans to bolster exchange reserves in countries facing high inflation (and hence exchange rate problems); those countries would be required in turn to commit to the new proposed gold exchange standard and to an ordinance denying their central banks from monetizing budget deficits and sterilizing gold flows (Eichengreen 1985: 139–40). Central banks would coordinate their actions internationally but this could only be assured if they were free from direct political interference. In that happy situation, currencies would be stabilized as would the domestic currency price of gold, and the League would organize loans to effect monetary and, *pari passu*, economic adjustment (Jacobsson 1979: 47–57).

The prevailing doctrine at the LON (and among central bankers for that matter) was that a return by each nation to a fixed exchange rate – a fixed gold parity – should occur as quickly as possible. This belief, coupled with greater autonomy conferred on central banks to conduct monetary policy with the ultimate aim of achieving fixed gold parities resulted

> in a country-by-country approach to stabilization with little attention paid to the vital question of the viability of exchange ratios. The question of the value of the gold parity was viewed as a sovereign national choice and the chief concern of the central bankers was whether stabilization could be maintained at the chosen rate (Meyer 1970: 5–6).

While the conventional gold-standard view of the international adjustment process to international payments imbalances was still quietly accepted (along with its deflationary bias), the new found emphasis on

---

League assisted many European countries to make amendments to their central bank legislation enabling them to hold interest-bearing reserves in gold-convertible balances and foreign bills (LON 1944: 204–05).

central bank autonomy meant that the process was likely to be slower, more deliberate, and painstaking than under a pure gold-standard regime. Adjustment was to be no longer automatic; central banks could adopt their own, proximate monetary policy objectives that may depend on unique national economic circumstances (Clarke 1967: 43).

While what was proposed at Genoa was *not* an international system based on laissez faire, it was tantamount to restoring "Anglo-American hegemony over the international financial system" (Silverman 1982: 58). Certainly the Genoa ideal of adopting a gold exchange standard was predicated on a managed monetary system, loosely linked to gold and strongly dependent on a coordinated international network of central banks. Nations without central banks were urged to create one. The ideal could hardly be realized without allowing central banks some independence over influencing their domestic economic conditions. Central bank interdependence on an international scale provided opportunities for cooperation and coordination, but the speed of adjustment along the path of economic restructuring in any one country had to remain, at least in part, a matter of discretion. Central banks would be informed by local institutional conditions to take discretionary actions. It is precisely at this point that the ILO research program on monetary aspects of the business cycle found its raison d'être. Here was an opportunity to offer a more liberal approach to domestic economic management which traded off international obligations against the need to maintain a modicum of internal balance, in particular with respect to the level of employment. Like Keynes in the early 1920s, the ILO researchers inveighed against necessary return to old gold parities between the currencies of leading industrial nations, for example, the reinstatement of the old parity between sterling and gold. Keynes's position in fact inadvertently summarizes the prevailing ILO view:

> [W]hen stability of the internal price level and stability of the external exchanges are incompatible, the former is generally preferable; and that on occasions when the dilemma is acute, the preservation of the former at the expense of the latter is, fortunately perhaps the line of least resistance (Keynes 1923: 132).

The ILO research rejected the "old" gold standard because it had consequences quite antithetical to ILO principles; it necessitated monetary stabilization through severe deflationary measures and higher unemployment in many countries. The director of the ILO reported in 1923 that in

> the course of investigations ... the International Labour Office has been enabled to realize clearly the close relation between rates of exchange and the condition of the labour market in each country. The

stabilization of the rate of exchange and the improvement in the monetary situation have undoubtedly resulted in renewed or increased unemployment.[3]

Stabilization at the expense of unemployment would not do. How then were central banks to behave without completely sacrificing the goal of stable employment and without relinquishing policy variations attuned to differing economic structures and institutional conditions? This question would be answered in the Geneva research program. The program adopted a general view that policy coordination between central banks involving "permanent co-operation between nations for controlling credit" and close "collaboration between central banks" in the larger countries (such as Great Britain and the United States) would need to be allowed time to develop; coordination was an "ideal" which would not occur immediately. The first ILO commentary on the Genoa conference accepts the possibility of achieving the ideal but international action required formulation of practical guidelines for managing money and credit at the national level – guidelines broadly consistent with the recommendation for a managed international financial system (ILO 1924c: 93–94). A notable omission in this ILO commentary was any explicit tribute to the Genoa nostrum proposing maintenance of fixed gold parities effected by continuous cooperation among central banks. International central bank cooperation meant something quite different to ILO economists; it could be molded to achieve a broad set of economic policy goals – not just exchange rate stability. Certainly, while accepting the gold exchange standard, the ILO researchers were on the side of those who did not favor reconstructing the old, pre-1914 gold standard on a durable basis. Not only was this position quite prescient; in a more positive sense it led to the development of a thoroughgoing set of monetary policy rules for central banks committed to operating in a loosely cooperative world monetary system and to modifying the course of the business cycle ultimately to achieve employment and output stability. In this view, the old gold standard, together with the monetary policy actions it dictated, merely accommodated the business cycle.

A DISTINCTIVE ILO PERSPECTIVE ON THE APPROPRIATE MONETARY POLICY FRAMEWORK

The scope, nature, and content of the proposed monetary policy framework emanating from ILO research in the 1920s deserves thorough examination. Most of the substantive analysis was completed by James R. Bellerby, a Cambridge (United Kingdom)-trained

---

[3] *LONJ* (1923: 963).

economist.[4] He contributed to the formal academic literature on monetary economics in the 1920s and that literature was replete with proposals for stabilizing price levels. The Geneva economists tended to ignore subtle differences between many prominent economists on the precise meaning of this policy objective.[5] Two points are certain however: They perceived that major causes of unemployment were significant changes in the price level brought about by inappropriate monetary policies, and they did not favor stabilizing price levels in any country at a level significantly lower than that which was obtained in the early 1920s. The unpleasant consequences of severe deflation were to be avoided. Confidence was urged in "the existing level of prices" (ILO 1924c: 91, quoting Keynes's *Tract*).

If price level stability was the main target of monetary policy what was the nature of the goal structure underlying this objective and how was it rationalized? Doubtless, "if price level movements could to *some extent* be controlled and stabilised . . . the risk of unemployment would thereby be much reduced" (ILO 1924a: 144, emphasis added). Again in 1927 the economic research director at the ILO claimed that "[a] monetary policy aiming at stabilizing . . . the *general* level of prices – in other words, at maintaining a constant relation between the ever-growing volume of production and the instruments of payment need for exchange of goods – would eliminate an important economic cause of unemployment" (Fuss 1927: 614, emphasis in original). Here the price level was perceived as a target variable. A managed national monetary system was preferable. Money and credit would systematically be controlled with the assistance of a target variable – the price level. The ultimate long-term goal was employment stability. This point was also made repeatedly in

---

[4] Bellerby was trained in the Cambridge monetary tradition of the late 1910s and early 1920s; he was later made a fellow of Gonville and Caius College for a short period. In 1924, Keynes noted that Bellerby was involved in "the almost revolutionary improvement in our understanding of the mechanism of money and credit and of the analysis of the trade cycle" (Keynes 1924a: 419, 419n). Bellerby spent some time in Cambridge, U.K. during the early 1920s and was probably influenced by Keynes's ideas at that time. In H.M. Robertson's (1983: 408) recollection, Bellerby "was close to Keynes."

[5] The views of Cassel, Gide, Fisher, Hawtrey, Keynes, Pigou, Stuart, and Wicksell are all canvassed in ILO (1924a: 144–154). See also ILO (1924c: 85–94) where the opinions of Bullock, Donham, Seligman, and Sprague are mentioned. A broadly representative view, closely mirrored in ILO-League publications, is Keynes's *Tract*. Keynes (1923: 149) stressed that the proper objective of a managed monetary system was internal price level stability. Similarly, throughout the 1920s Irving "Fisher regarded price-level stabilisation as not merely helpful, but sufficient for the stabilisation of business activity in general" (Laidler 1999: 185). The ILO cited Keynes and Fisher more frequently than other economists on this matter.

Keynes's speech to a conference on unemployment organized by the ILO (Keynes 1924b: 185–86, 190, 192).

National differences relating to exchange rate setting did not gainsay the prime task of monetary authorities to remove uncertainty about price levels. In the United States with an exchange rate pegged to gold and large gold reserves, the Federal Reserve interposed between perceived short-term gold flows and their impact on domestic conditions. From the ILO perspective, depending crucially on the state of relevant indicators (discussed below), gold flows may be sterilized. In other countries, such as Britain (before the return to gold in 1925 and with slender gold reserves), policy makers should stabilize exchange rates near currently prevailing levels. Thereafter, some type of managed, adjustable exchange rate was envisaged; gold must be used to stabilize the exchange rate only in an emergency. The competitive struggle for gold was discouraged. Mechanisms were suggested to minimize the need for gold: maintaining reserves in the form of foreign balances, gold exchange standards, or an international clearing system. The ILO urged international coordination of demands for gold by collaboration between central banks. Wide fluctuations in internal prices should therefore be avoided by an international system superimposed on monetary management at the national level.

The U.S. Federal Reserve was presented as an exemplar because it closely followed the ILO conception of a monetary policy strategy which attempted "conscious direction" of economic activity to attain price stability using a "scientific system of credit regulation" (Bellerby 1926: 59). The accompanying recommendations were also more specific. The adoption of a preventative countercyclical monetary policy was advocated which ultimately stabilized output and employment at high levels. Any policy aiming for price stability would need to demonstrate that it was able, in due course, to maintain industry "at a higher *average* level of activity than has ever been previously achieved" (ILO 1924c: 85, emphasis in original).[6] Stabilization of the price level was emphatically not an end in itself, although the time horizons could differ over which price stability and employment stability may be achieved. The employment goal may be a long-term one, whereas the intermediate target variable – the price level – was best conceived as a short-term policy desideratum. Mitigating large short-term variations in the price level was expected to have long-term benefits for achieving the employment goal. The concern to make price stability the servant of employment stability

---

[6] This sentiment is expressed in ILO (1924a: 143) in terms of "a higher permanent level of employment" and Bellerby (1925: 14): "the chief purpose of credit policy should be to maintain industry at its highest possible permanent level of activity."

was consistent with the ILO charter which elevated to the status of a guiding principle the value of social justice, meaning, in practice, the maintenance of high levels of employment and living standards for the entire workforce (Thomas 1921a).

Now an active monetary policy would ideally be formulated subject to: (1.) the specification of a desired path for relevant indicator variables which are purveyors of economic information to policymakers; (2.) an understanding of the relationship of this path to price stability, and (3.) an understanding of the relationship between price stability and employment stability. An additional overarching requirement was that monetary policy be able to take "anticipatory" action to stave off sharp movements in the price level (ILO 1924a: 151). By implication, real variables such as employment would also be stabilized, but, according to ILO research, the precise links between the money supply (as indicated by changes in the monetary base), prices and employment were avowedly obscure given the limited state of knowledge and available data. Perhaps this modest outlook explains why they reported on the two most useful policy instruments without commenting on their relative effectiveness. This was unlike Keynes (1923: 145) who regarded the discount rate instrument as an intolerably slow means of transmitting the impact of changes in bank reserves to prices. He favored open market operations.[7]

Mapping the desired path of indicator variables was part of any rational monetary policy. If the data sources used by policy makers were narrowly based or poorly designed, achievable employment levels could be lower than otherwise as a result of inconsistent policy reactions in the short term. Consistent indices of output and employment were absolutely necessary in addition to price indices. The ILO (1924b) report on "Economic Barometers" was an especially important landmark in the statistical study of business cycles in the 1920s. It advanced beyond synthesizing all relevant work up to 1924 to the point of suggesting what indices could legitimately be interpreted as indicator variables in a monetary policy framework targeting price stability. If the "laws relating to the sequence of economic fluctuations" could be estimated statistically, the time path of relevant indicator variables could then be observed "for

---

[7] Keynes's reasoning in the 1920s was more sophisticated than anything available in ILO publications. For Keynes (1924c: 208), changes in the volume of real cash balances (and hence the velocity of circulation) was *the* significant indicator variable: "We no longer believe that prices can be kept as steady as they might be simply by securing a constant volume of money, and we hold, rather, that we can only keep prices steady by varying the quantity of money to balance changes in k [where k = real purchasing power required by the public]." Hence his preference for open market operations. That the habits of the public were not directly controllable by monetary authorities possibly dissuaded Geneva economists from mentioning this important theoretical insight.

the purpose of guiding some authority in an endeavour to render economic life more stable" (Ibid., 8, 18).[8]

It was in the United States during the 1920s where the ILO researchers found the most advanced use of economic barometers informing a discretionary monetary policy. Price level stabilization was an accepted norm in the United States in this period – a norm easier to satisfy in that large, relatively closed economy than in a small open economy (Fisher 1935: 409). Research during the 1910s and early 1920s resulted in the production of time series representations of cyclical activity adjusted for "unwanted fluctuations," and stimulated the establishment of a number of university business-cycle institutes and commercial forecasting agencies (Morgan 1990: 58). The task of developing and using economic barometers to inform monetary policy was pioneered by economists at the Federal Reserve. This was a period in the Fed's history when "a conscious attempt . . . to use central bank powers to promote internal economic stability" had led the Fed to "face explicitly the need to develop criteria and standards of monetary policy" (Friedman and Schwartz 1963: 240). The Tenth Annual Report of the Federal Reserve in 1923 embodied these attempts by setting out statements on the importance of open market operations and rediscounting for general credit policy. The work of Carl Snyder, General Statistician of the Federal Reserve Bank of New York, on statistical barometers and a contingent monetary policy rule appeared contemporaneously with some rules formulated in Geneva which we shall explore below. Snyder (1923a: 278–79) argued that "accurate and reliable" indices designed by Mitchell, Persons, and Irving Fisher could be drawn upon to "establish an index figure wherewith automatically to control the amount of currency to be issued, and therefore . . . the total of bank credit." With this economic information the Fed "should be required by law" to undertake open market operations or rediscounting in order to "keep the amount of currency and credit in balance with the price level, and maintain the latter at as nearly a constant figure as is practically possible"(Ibid., 284).[9]

Federal Reserve research made an immediate impact on Geneva economists, who felt that Snyder had enunciated "the most complete system for the control of industry through the regulation of credit" (ILO 1924a: 151). To this work they added insights from British and European

[8] In other words: "One of the possible future uses of economic barometers is indicated here, namely, that of providing the central authority with the information necessary for the guidance of its credit policy" (ILO 1924a: 151 n. 5).

[9] Snyder's (1923a: 284) comment that legislation would ensure "that this control . . . be automatic and free from the possibility of intervention by any kind of influence, political, financial, or otherwise" has a modern flavor. See also Snyder (1923b, 1924) and Garvy (1978).

research. The suggestion by E.C. Snow (1923: 342) that a "general prosperity index" be constructed from sectoral data to guide credit policy was endorsed so long as such a barometer indicated "the regularity of sequence, if any, between the movements in different industries." Monetary authorities would then have the requisite information to base predictions "not only on periodicity but especially on an established sequence of movements" (ILO 1924b: 19 n. 2). Bellerby's (1926: 54–58) case study of Federal Reserve experience demonstrated that data on the volume of production, employment, retail and wholesale trade, and stocks were used to guide credit policy. A general price index was in his estimation an utterly "indispensable" part of policy makers' data set; it was in fact weighted highly in the monetary policy-making process, going by Bellerby's evidence gained from the testimony of leading decision makers in the process.[10] However, the precise weighting of other data in that decision process remained opaque. Furthermore, Bellerby's insight into the operation of monetary policy in the United States revealed that data on the rate of turnover of bank deposits and the volume of transactions of all kinds were used by the Federal Reserve Bank of New York as anticipatory barometers (of future price level variations), whereas the price index was regarded as a "laggard barometer." The process of data gathering and interpretation was not perfect in Bellerby's opinion. Given the desire to target price level stabilization in the United States then the development of more specialized, detailed data sources giving leading indications of future price changes was imperative.

THE ILO MONETARY POLICY RULES

Bellerby's research at the ILO led him to formulate some rudimentary monetary policy reaction mechanisms. Two contingent monetary policy rules are offered. The first rule is similar in form to Snyder's suggestion that the monetary base be linked to deviations of the price level from its target path. Monetary authorities should choose a "price level . . . as a 'normal' around which it is felt desirable to stabilise prices. After that level has been reached, the endeavour would be made to keep prices from moving more than, say, 3 percent. above or 3 percent. below the level" (Bellerby 1923b: 329). An algebraic representation of the above statement illustrates its insightfulness. Let m_t = the monetary base in time t so that:

$$m_t = m_{t-1} + \mu_1 (p^*_{t-1} - p_{t-1}) \tag{1}$$

with μ_1 = the responsiveness of the monetary base to a change in the price level, p^*_{t-1} = the target price level and p_{t-1} = the actual price level.

---

[10] The list of statisticians and economists interviewed by Bellerby is impressive (see Bellerby 1926: ix–x).

This rule allows policy makers to operate with an elastic price standard so that monetary policy need not react automatically to price variations within the chosen range.[11] It was taken for granted that employment stabilization would automatically follow in due course. It was also presumed that such a rule would be infeasible in the face of factor supply shocks (migration, capital movements) or productivity shocks (climate changes, inventions). We shall return to this point shortly.

The second rule advanced beyond those developed in the United States and related to deviations in output, stating that "[i]t is at [the] point where unemployment has fallen to an average of about 2.5 to 3 percent, and where industry has reached a high level of efficiency without as yet causing a rapid rise in prices, that any measure for the . . . restraint of currency [should be introduced]" (Bellerby 1923b: 310). Here,

$$m_t = m_{t-1} + \mu_2(x^*_{t-1} - x_{t-1})$$ (2)

where x^*_{t-1} = the target path for nominal gross national product (GNP) and x_{t-1} = nominal GNP. Provided inflation is not accelerating (that is, inflation is not "attaining any degree of rapidity"; Bellerby 1923a: 90) the magnitude μ_2 is chosen so as to ensure employment levels remain at 2.5–3 percent.[12] In an era before national income accounting Bellerby suggested that an employment index and well-chosen "sample" production indices be used to provide information on economic activity and, in conjunction with price indices, the target path of GNP.[13] Two points should be noted about this second rule. First, it assumes that there is a natural (or average) rate of unemployment and the role of monetary policy is to stabilize fluctuations in unemployment around this rate.[14] Second, rule (2) acknowledges the possibility of supply-side phenomena affecting prices and employment. Now, in principle, stabilizing the price level (that is, rule (1)) subject to the condition that general productivity changes should be allowed for, would have satisfied the Geneva economists. For their publications explicitly hedged the price target by

[11] That monetary policy could be conducted with an elastic standard is recognized in more sophisticated work in the 1980s; for example, Hall (1984).

[12] The full pertinent text reads: "the employment index, rough as it may be, if taken in conjunction with the movement of the price level itself, would form an admirable criterion for the guidance of discount policy. A tendency on the part of the employment index to turn down . . . coupled with an upward turn of the price index number, would be the strongest possible evidence that the time had come to regulate credit strictly . . . In other words, after this point had been reached, the movement of the price level would be the principal guide, the object of credit policy to prevent the rate of movement from attaining any degree of rapidity" (Bellerby 1923a: 90).

[13] The reader may note similarities between rule (2) and some modern versions of nominal GNP targeting; for example, McCallum (1987).

[14] This general insight formed the basis for monetarist rules in the 1980s (Taylor 1981: 146).

stressing the importance of employment as the ultimate goal (see, for example, Bellerby 1925). Otherwise a secular price level decline due to productivity advances could stimulate an easing of monetary policy leading to an overinvestment boom of the kind feared (and predicted) by Austrian economists (for example, Hayek 1932). A more useful rule such as (2) would incorporate productivity considerations; thus, "[t]he criteria on which to base a [monetary policy] judgment should not be made dependent so much on the rate of fall of prices, as on the extent to which it is depressing trade" (Bellerby 1923b: 326). The norm of price level stability has since been set against the productivity norm as an alternative monetary policy target (Dowd 1995; Selgin 1995a,b). In the late twentieth century it is accepted that these norms are distinctly different, because, among other things, a productivity norm necessitates making nominal spending or nominal GNP *the* monetary policy target variable; it does not value price level stability per se. The view from Geneva exuded confidence that monetary stabilization following one of the proposed rules was feasible given the availability of data, the right instruments, and their timely use.

For all the ingenuity with which the research reported above sought to identify statistical barometers for the guidance of the proposed active monetary management, the problem of additivity or weighting in the decision process could neither be ignored nor buried by a plethora of data, or by tendering simple policy rules. An early, coherent expression of this problem arises when Bellerby (1925: 27) contemplates the possibility of formulating a discretionary monetary policy strategy:

> [i]mmediately a decline of prices threatened or forecast depression – and particularly if subsidiary indices of employment and production gave a similar indication – credit would be eased . . . This method of combining different indices in support of the price index may, therefore, reasonably be designated the 'composite' system.

The problem of relative weight in the interpretation of indices in the "composite" meant that wise "discretion" had to be exercised (Ibid., 29). That the Geneva-based economists could on the one hand believe that wider use of statistics of various kinds could make a managed monetary system more "scientific" and therefore more credible, and on the other hand admit of discretionary judgement, is hardly surprising.[15] The contemporary enthusiasm for barometers of the business cycle was founded on a desire to improve the basis of decision making. Keynes (1923: 148

---

[15] The view that monetary policy making could be rendered more "scientific" by using statistical barometers is oft-repeated in ILO (1924a: 6; 1924c: 94) and Bellerby (1923b: 326; 1924: 181).

passim) had early on favored discretionary monetary policies. Like the ILO economists, he advised central banks to use data on employment, output, interest rates, and other indicator variables to supplement price data. Just as in ILO publications in the 1920s there is no suggestion in Keynes's *Tract* that interpreting these data should be rigidly circumscribed – it all depended on a country's history, institutions, and policy makers' experience in designing and using data (Meltzer 1988: 217–18). Developing a measure of reputation and credibility was not a one-time event for a monetary authority. For ILO economists the accumulation of more sophisticated data sources and use of more technical forecasting techniques would produce policy credibility. Premature and unwise experimentation were to be avoided. Problems of timing and insufficient understanding of policy impact lags were resolvable matters of implementation once the monetary authority was furnished with relevant quantitative information.

No country-specific recommendations on monetary policy were made available. There is no discussion of practical problems accompanying any attempt to synchronize national and world price level stability, yet the attempt is signaled in the plea for an "international policy of price stabilisation" (Bellerby 1923b: 327; ILO 1924a: 152–54). Ostensibly, the interdependence of economies implied that no country (unless it was completely closed to international trade) could operate an independent monetary policy for very long. Given this interdependence, especially between major world economies, it was critical that monetary authorities in those economies collaborate in following the new procedure which set the target of price level stability. In the absence of a new international body (perhaps linked to the LON) which might set and somehow enforce the rules for controlling credit and achieving price stability, sufficient cooperation between monetary authorities in all major world economies would stabilize price levels for all countries by default. The ILO-League role would then be one of data collecting and information gathering.

POSTSCRIPT: THE ILO CONTRIBUTION TO MONETARY POLICY ANALYSIS IN THE 1920s

There is an extensive modern literature on determining the best monetary policy rule for central banks.[16] That literature has given scarcely any attention to the historical development of ideas on monetary policy rules, and yet many issues addressed in the late 1980s and 1990s were featured in earlier work. The discussion of rules versus discretion is a case in point.

---

[16] See, for example, Fair and Howrey (1996) and the literature cited therein.

Alan Blinder (1987: 404) summarizes the commonly held, yet misinformed, view that our retrospective needs to begin with J.M. Keynes and *The General Theory*: "[b]efore Keynes, the rules-versus-discretion debate hardly existed because few economists saw any rationale for what we now call demand management, nor had any idea how to accomplish it." In fact, Geneva-based economists in the 1920s had worked through issues concerning price and employment stability, at least within a fixed exchange rate framework. The ideational context should not be mistaken: Demand management in the 1920s was synonymous with conducting a monetary policy aimed at bringing about price stability; it had no place for the "Keynesian" notion of an optimal fiscal-monetary policy mix.

Now while the Geneva Conference had recommended international collaboration among central banks, the ILO interpreted this recommendation differently both from orthodox economists at the League and central bankers. Not only did the ILO research program in the 1920s offer some practical suggestions over which collaboration could be brought into effect and which would assist in dampening the impact of business cycles, it actively advocated a unique interpretation of the Genoa recommendations and belied any notion that researchers in international organizations must function as mere arbiters. As befitted the cosmopolitan collection of economists in Geneva during the 1920s, their research bore the stamp of a truly international range of intellectual influences, with Cassel, Hawtrey, Keynes, Fisher, and other luminaries receiving frequent citation. A synthesis of ideas was produced, culminating in a basic framework for a monetary policy strategy that embodied a moderate, qualified form of policy activism. The proposed strategy anticipated some of the main recommendations of the (British) Macmillan Committee (1931) on Finance and Industry. In their work, the Geneva economists were able expressly to introduce aggregate employment into the price stabilization discussion – so much so that employment stabilization (at a high level) was articulated as an ultimate monetary policy goal.

The central features of the ILO framework for the conduct of monetary policy may be identified as follows:

1. establish politically independent central banks;
2. give central banks a clearly defined target of price stabilization subject to the proviso that the price level could be regarded as an elastic or moving target. That is, price level variations would be permissible within a small range, partly to allow for seasonal productivity and wider secular considerations;

3. the credibility of monetary policy and reputation of policy makers would develop over time; policy makers would be required to make consistent use of a variety of statistical indicator variables in order accurately to time the use of policy instruments and monitor their effects;

4. if the reaction function of policy makers was oriented toward price level stabilization, general expectations of monetary policy will be confirmed and decisions in the economy at the microlevel would create employment stabilization.

This framework was constructed on the belief that there is no reliable automatic process in the market economy ensuring full resource utilization. The Geneva economists were convinced of the need for a monetary stabilization policy to counter the business cycle. Active, expansive countercyclical fiscal policy did not come within their purview in the 1920s. All this gives their doctrine a modern flavor, especially the idea that the monetary regime should concentrate on price stability which has achieved prominence in the 1990s.

By the standards of contemporary British, American, and Scandinavian economics, the ILO program was essentially a synthesis of conventional theory (as it developed in the 1920s), but it was more insistent about the need to design practical goals, rules, and methods for the conduct of monetary policy. There was one nuance of some distinction in the price level stabilization focus: They reasoned in terms of a price stability target which they idealized and from which they drew the conclusion that there was no conflict between price stability and high, stable levels of employment in the long term. A monetary policy attuned to price stability was a necessary condition for high employment. The program was also an early authoritative source on the construction and use of macroeconomic statistics in the monetary policy process. They thought in terms of quantified barometers of economic activity and appreciated the actual and potential use of barometers in the conduct of monetary policy. Perennial issues in the twentieth century debate on monetary policy – quantitative rules, the role of discretion, the nature of the price stability target, and use of relevant indicators – were well understood.

INTERNATIONAL MONETARY ORGANIZATION AND POLICY: IDEAS EMERGING AT THE LON AND BIS IN THE 1930s

Under the direction of the LON Economic Consultative Committee, LON monetary research in the 1920s was conventional and conservative; it dealt with monetary problems in two "phases." First, to promote currency stability, its work focused on means to achieve prewar gold parities. Secondly, its research considered ways of conducting monetary policy to avoid "undue fluctuations in the purchasing power of gold" (that is, obtain price stability). Both phases rested on articles of faith in respect of predicted economic outcomes: Success in the first phase would "increase international trade" and achievement of the second would automatically lead to high domestic output and employment.[17] In short, it was thought that no long-run clash existed between external stability and domestic prosperity. This creed endured in the early 1930s; it was essentially a logical extension of the Genoa conference resolutions whereas the direction of ILO research (as we shall see in the material that follows), at least from the standpoint of the LON economists, must have been considered an adulteration of those resolutions.

The agenda for the "monetary and credit policy" session of the 1933 World Economic Conference, drafted by the LON economics secretariat, aimed "to consider how the conditions for a successful restoration of a free gold standard could be fulfilled."[18] The newly created BIS, which immediately became a center for economic and monetary research and consultation primarily focused on Europe, chimed in with a similar message. The BIS initially favored reestablishment of the pre-1914 gold standard. In the BIS view, there was a clear alternative between an international gold standard and nationalistic, inflationary credit expansions. Deliberate, conscious, managed credit policies could have no credibility; they would entail damage to private sector confidence and economic stability. The political autonomy of central banks was only meaningful if the impersonal gold standard rules were slavishly followed by domestic monetary policy makers. Otherwise, in the BIS perspective, *quis custodiet custodem*? The gold standard was the only international monetary regime that could produce a system of complete multilateral currency convert-

---

[17] See the Report of the Economic Consultative Committee 1928 in *LONJ*, July 1929, pp. 1032–33. The relevant section of the report reads: "The Consultative Committee, while recognising the great benefit to international commerce that has already resulted from the stabilisation in terms of gold of the currencies of most countries of the world, recalls the fears entertained by the Genoa Conference of the dangers that might arise from undue fluctuations in the purchasing power of gold. In view of the detrimental effects upon industry, agriculture and the conditions of employment that would result from such fluctuations, the Committee appreciates the great interest which the central banks take in this problem and recommends it to the attention of the Financial and Economic Organization of the League."

[18] See "Annotation to the Agenda I. Monetary and Credit Policy" submitted by the Preparatory Committee of Experts. LON Archives: Doc C.48.M.18 1933 II. spec. 1. The Agenda is reprinted in World Economic Conference (1933). See especially Part II, pp. 29–47.

ibility and in which all contemporary market participants could have confidence. It was believed, erroneously or otherwise, that contemporary market perceptions of various national government attempts to extricate themselves from the gold standard rules and their deflationary bias, would inevitably undermine confidence in any national currency (Beyen 1949: 88–90). The LON and BIS researchers reacted with studied nonchalance to the onset of the economic depression of the 1930s. Yet the domestic policy implications of the depression seemed obvious in retrospect. A benign monetary policy would not necessarily eliminate the source of the extraordinary cyclical fluctuation then in evidence. There was only one fairly insignificant concession, at least as it was conventionally interpreted at the LON and BIS: Central bank cooperation was required to deliver a truly concerted international monetary policy response to the depression and to facilitate a revival of international trade (in conjunction with other policy initiatives such as trade policy liberalization).[19] And any shortage of gold as a means of international payment would require the necessary extension of international credits, again effected by central bank collaboration.[20]

The final LON Gold Delegation's (1932a: 50) report repeated the usual shibboleths common in the work of international organizations in the early 1930s:

> Those responsible for monetary policy in each country must take account both of domestic and international considerations and these may not be easily reconcilable. It is for this reason that we attach particular importance to the development of methods of continuous consultation and co-operative effort to maintain the international equilibrium without sacrificing national interests.

There are no carefully nuanced recommendations here or in the remainder of the Delegation's report. What was the most efficacious monetary technique or the appropriate method of cooperation which would minimize the clash between "domestic and international considerations"? Altogether, the speed with which central banks could consult, cooperate, and willingly act in concert (and consistently with a resurrected gold standard) seemed to be egregiously overrated.

The BIS economic commentaries during this period and toward the mid-1930s appeared more concerned with setting out first principles. When the BIS considered the purposes of international central bank cooperation over monetary policy it arrived at some important

---

[19] On trade policy issues see Chapter 5.
[20] These were standard lines of argument evident in BIS reports in the early 1930s. See Dulles (1932: 452).

conclusions, advancing on the platitudes offered by the LON Gold Delegation. The main purposes of central bank cooperation were:

1. To evolve a common body of monetary doctrine and assure the widest possible measure of common agreement on monetary theory, problems and practice, including agreement upon what the international standard is to be and how to maintain it . . .
2. To comprehend by interchange of information and counsel the difficulties which confront one's neighbor as well as oneself, and thus to perceive the true motives and necessities for the lines of conduct respectively followed . . .
3. To learn how to avoid doing harm to one another, especially when one central bank is operating in the market of a neighbor . . .
4. To gather and exchange data and information of a monetary and economic character, domestic and foreign, thus helping to form a basis of judgment in guiding credit policy and deciding the proper course of conduct (BIS 1935: 41–48).

In respect of the first purpose of cooperation it was perhaps extraordinarily naive to hope for a consensus on monetary doctrine across countries. Otherwise these "purposes of cooperation" seemed eminently modest in formulation; they reveal a preeminent concern to minimize negative international spillover effects of central bank actions. There is no suggestion that cooperation along the lines suggested could occur quickly or be instantly effective – only that cooperation was desirable. The BIS envisaged, well before Bretton Woods, that central bank cooperation through a formal institution such as the BIS could help broadly to maintain "more stable business conditions," protect currency stability, and achieve balance of payments equilibrium (Ibid.) All these objectives may be thwarted or rendered more difficult to sustain if the actions of central banks were significantly incompatible.[21] The suggestion in the mid-1930s of a degree of monetary cooperation effected through one central *international* institution (the BIS) was a new departure. The argument in the 1935 BIS *Annual Report* turned on the viability of loose cooperation rather than rigorous, binding cooperation based on a formal blueprint or international agreement. Presumably flurries of concentrated cooperative activity would be episodic and based on special economic events. In 1935 the BIS was still primarily a European-centered institution. Later it was observed that the "spirit of cooperation" especially among European central banks working through the BIS in fact

---

[21] On the limits (which emerged in practice) of central bank cooperation in the interwar years see Mouré (1992). On the role of the BIS in this connection from 1930, see Schloss (1958: 58–62).

"evolved spontaneously and not as a result of any formal regulation and it has grown stronger with the years and has become powerful enough to survive even under the most extraordinary circumstances" (Auboin 1955: 37). In Chapter 7 we shall have occasion to reinforce this point on the advantages of spontaneous cooperation when we consider ideas developed at the LON in the 1940s on international monetary organization leading up to Bretton Woods.

THE ILO's DEPARTURE FROM MONETARY POLICY ORTHODOXY IN THE 1930s

Just as in the 1920s, ILO publications in the 1930s offered alternative lines of thought on monetary policy to more orthodox, conventional views presented by the LON and BIS. For the ILO researchers, a properly focused, well-timed, and consciously designed monetary policy did not destabilize the private sector. Without "active measures" and the international monetary cooperation upon which such activism must be founded, national governments might have recourse to potentially damaging policy instruments – higher tariffs and taxation and reductions in the general level of money wages (Martin 1931a: 370, 372).[22] Martin turned selectively to sections of the Macmillan Committee's (1931) report which he identified as marking "a revolution in economic thought." Quoting the Report's finding that "entrepreneurs as a whole are failing to receive back proceeds the equivalent of what they had paid out as costs of production" (p. 374), Martin perceived a rejection of the orthodox economic doctrine that a general overproduction is impossible (Say's Law). Ignoring the time horizon intended in arguments accepting Say's Law, Martin believed that the depression in economic activily in the early 1930s demonstrated that this Law was invalid and certainly not universally applicable. He interpreted Say's Law as maintaining that there would be an invariable sufficiency of purchasing power available to buy goods. Now that an *in*sufficiency had in fact been demonstrated, active monetary policies were required to boost "effective demand" to a level necessary to provide high output and employment (Martin 1931a: 374). Furthermore, international monetary action was essential, and its precise basis is adumbrated in a second article (Martin 1931b).

Contrary to the Macmillan Committee (1931), the "automatic" gold standard is emphatically rejected. Domestic monetary policies should rest on a "more scientific system" which enabled "buying to keep pace

---

[22] The publications of P.W. Martin, an ILO economist, especially his interpretations of the Macmillan Committee (1931) were consistent both with the 1919 ILO founding Charter (ranking employment and social justice goals highly) and the ILO monetary policy framework developed in the 1920s. The following section draws heavily on his work.

with the volume of goods offered for sale" (Martin 1931b: 688; Martin and Riches 1933: 28–30). The ILO economists favored regular use of open market operations and discount rate instruments of monetary policy in light of the movement in a broad range of statistical indicators of economic activity (Martin 1931b: 691–93, 695). A central objective must be to stabilize the "world price level" and in the circumstances prevailing in 1931, to in fact allow price levels to *rise* at least to the level of 1928 to effect a concomitant rise in output prices. International central bank agreement to proceed along these lines was essential – nations could not act in isolation for fear that isolated action may compromise their external position and currency exchange rate in particular. ILO economists urged sterilization of gold movements where they occurred if domestic economic conditions were temporarily unstable or seriously imbalanced. Again central bank collaboration could determine the criteria for assessing "instability" and "imbalance."

Notwithstanding the proclivity toward monetary activism, there is a nagging theme in ILO publications in the early 1930s that monetary policy will not be successful on its own. Other policy instruments including public investment programs and wages policy would be required.[23] This position is broadly consistent with Keynes's view in the *Treatise on Money* published in October 1930, though Keynes's work is not cited in Martin's articles. In Keynes's *Treatise*, especially Chapter 37, there are extensive reflections on the greater effectiveness of fiscal relative to monetary policy in open economies (Dimsdale 1988: 322–23). In a later article the ILO economists argue that "cheap and plentiful credit unquestionably helps to make a revival possible; but there is no assurance that it will revive and sustain the volume of buying when this latter is insufficient to keep industry reasonably fully employed" (Martin and Riches 1933: 38). In a 1933 article on the "Social Consequences of a Return to Gold" the ILO economists hardened their position against a return to anything resembling a genuine international gold standard. Indeed, they not only rejected the "automatic" pre-1914 gold standard; they blurred the distinction between different types of "managed" gold standard along with all the domestic monetary policy actions associated with these types. By expatiating on the possibilities of making monetary policy reaction functions more flexible and adaptable to national economic structures and circumstances, the LON Gold Delegation (1932a) had inadvertently assisted the more liberal ILO economists. A paragraph from the Delegation's report is seized upon as arguing for a more liberal monetary policy framework which did not sacrifice internal economic

---

[23] Public investment and wages policy are discussed in Chapters 4 and 6 respectively.

balance or immediate exchange rate stability. Here the ILO researchers were writing with some skill and acuity in taking advantage of existing confusion and lack of consensus in the formal literature on monetary policy.[24] In this they did not underestimate difficulties in the way of achieving internal balance with the assistance of monetary policy. Thus, according to the LON Gold Delegation quoted approvingly by Martin and Riches, monetary policy should be conducted carefully, sometimes according to data that are country and event specific:

> With reference to the other indices which should be taken as a guide to monetary policy, varying opinions, in our present state of knowledge, are likely to be held. They are all those indices which reflect business activity – the market rates of discount, the value of building permits, the debits to individual deposit accounts, the production of various primary products, the international movements of capital etc. The significance of these will vary from country to country and from epoch to epoch. No set rules for their interpretation can be laid down (LON Gold Delegation quoted in Martin and Riches 1933: 35 n. 1).

This passage is interpreted as urging national governments to "give more play to judgement and discretion in monetary and banking policy" (Ibid., 36). There is nothing new here in terms of the substance of this recommendation compared with the ideas of their ILO predecessors in the 1920s. However, Martin and Riches advanced beyond earlier conceptions of the role of monetary policy by insisting that policy must be geared to "maintaining purchasing power" recognizing that such an objective could conflict, from time to time, with price stability. Their arguments nevertheless exuded considerable modesty about what monetary policy in isolation could accomplish.

ILO research papers implicitly proceeded as if they were treating monetary policy issues in one closed (world) economy rather than addressing problems facing individual open economies. It is scarcely surprising therefore that they did not elevate exchange rate stability above employment and output stability. They tended to abstract from small open economy dilemmas where speculative, short-term international

---

[24] The nonexistent consensus is referred to in contemporary monetary policy debate. For example: "There is as yet no general agreement as to whether internal management can be accomplished most satisfactorily by monetary measures of control, or whether it is primarily a non-monetary problem requiring conscious and deliberate adjustments of prices to each other, interest rate adjustments, physical output adjustments, and the like. And if the control should primarily be monetary, what should be the criteria? Is it primarily a matter of stabilizing prices, or of stabilizing and adjusting the component parts of the national income, or of stabilizing production, or of stabilizing employment?" (Williams 1934: 305).

capital flows in connection with uncertainty over the probable movement of exchange rates became inevitable and intractable.[25]

In setting proximate targets for monetary policy the ILO economists in the early 1930s rejected the simple price stability objective, warning more openly than their predecessors in the 1920s that a monetary system designed primarily to secure price stability in the first instance, may carry profit inflation in its train (Martin and Riches 1933: 41–42, 47). The costs of price level inflation are contrasted with social conflict likely to arise from the distributional consequences of widespread profit inflation. To be sure, the problem was recognized by the ILO in the 1920s, but it was more forcefully stated in the 1930s: "it is clear . . . that if approximate stability of the general price level is to be maintained [by monetary policy] at a time when productivity is increasing, some measure must be devised to prevent the development of profit inflation and consequent investment booms and exchange fluctuations" (Ibid., 41–42). For the first time Keynes's *Treatise* (1930: 125) is cited in support of an ILO objective *viz.* to ensure that increases in productivity were rapidly reflected in higher wages. That the practical, macrolabor market policy instruments such as centralized wage fixing institutions were not established in some countries sometimes made implementation difficult. One implication was that monetary policy had limited effectiveness in achieving the broad range of objectives that the ILO economists had in mind; wages policy also needed centralized direction. Certainly the ILO concurred with the LON and BIS that monetary policy responsibilities conferred on central banks ought to be isolated from the reach of day-to-day politics. Nevertheless, for the ILO, central banks were inseparable parts of governmental institutional machinery and monetary policy is ultimately a matter for governments not technicians or elites. By the mid-1930s, thinking at the ILO could no longer entertain the view that monetary policy be narrowly confined to achieving stability in a price index, however formulated.

Martin and Riches were in no doubt that the ILO must play a leading role advising on world economic reconstruction following the depression of the 1930s. Their focus on monetary issues was defensible since "monetary mismanagement can at any moment make a living wage and an adequate return to enterprise unattainable, [and] social justice, even in its most attenuated form, is out of the question" (Martin and Riches 1933: 50). They concede that differences in approach and emphasis in monetary economics "to be found in different schools of economics" coupled with "widely different national outlooks on economic and mon-

---

[25] LON research on these open economy issues was demonstrably stronger and more convincing, at least by the 1940s. See Haberler (1943a: 431), LON (1944: 131), and Chapter 7.

etary questions" make a world consensus on the role of monetary policy "exceedingly difficult" to imagine (Ibid., 49).

Economists in international organizations in the early 1930s were faced with finding practical solutions to an extraordinary economic event. Their monetary policy solutions were not well presented in the sense that they did not offer highly formal analytical frameworks; they could not match, for example, Keynes's *Treatise* (1930) where a formal theory of monetary policy relates central bank actions to price level fluctuations, interest rate changes, and changes in investment. This is not to say, however, that the ideas of these economists in international organizations were not evolving with the impact of circumstances and new ideas gradually filtering through their policy deliberations. Unlike academic economists who were attached to formal deductive theorizing, economists in international organizations favored less formal, inductive analysis of monetary problems.

In an article on a theme that preoccupied ILO economists in the 1920s and 1930s Bertil Ohlin's "Employment Stabilization and Price Stabilization" (1937) would have seemed understandable to them at an earlier date, though it would have been incomprehensible to those at the LON and BIS in earlier years. Contrary to pre-Keynesians at the League, Ohlin argued that "*a simple program for the stabilization of the price level ... is not acceptable.* The stabilization of employment at the desired level assumes a policy which is primarily directed to preventing maladjustments in the sphere of investment activity" (Ohlin 1937: 328, emphasis added). That this argument could confidently be submitted less than a decade after the ILO view on monetary stabilization policy in the 1920s had fully matured is testimony to the impact of events and "Keynesian" ideas in the 1930s. The epoch-making change in economic thought on macrostabilization policy in particular was imminent in Ohlin's work for the LON (Ohlin 1931a: 224–26) on "The Course and Phases of the World Depression"; he implicitly doubted the now older League monetary policy proposals because, by 1931, the standard monetary instruments became ineffective in conditions of rapidly falling prices, crises of confidence, interest-insensitive investment demand and insufficient international monetary cooperation. Similarly Keynes (1936) doubted the ability of monetary policy to stabilize employment and investment mainly because movements in long-term interest rates were unlikely to be able to offset sharp fluctuations in the marginal efficiency of capital. (We shall examine a key policy implication of all this, namely, public investment programs, in the next chapter). Without accounting for all theoretical complexities, ILO research was moving in the same direction. There was retarded, reluctant acceptance of the limited effectiveness of monetary policy at the LON and BIS by the 1940s. Work at the LON and BIS in the 1930s was strongly influenced by the Austrian economist Gottfried Haberler and Swedish economist Per Jacobsson respectively. Neither Haberler nor Jacobsson wanted to downplay the closely aligned price and exchange rate stability objectives of monetary policy. Research agendas at the ILO changed earlier and more radically to the extent that the topic of monetary policy attuned to the price stability norm was relegated to obscurity in the ranking of research priorities by the mid-1930s.

4   Public Investment Programs in the Interwar Period: Pre-Keynesian, Proto-Keynesian, and Keynesian Perspectives

INTRODUCTION

From its inception in 1919, the ILO conducted extensive international research on economic and social conditions. The purpose of this chapter is to document the history of the rich vein of economic thought and policy advice on public investment programs that was proffered in ILO publications through the 1920s and 1930s, and supplemented by the work of economists at the LON. Many ILO member countries attempted to use countercyclical public works policies to maintain employment during the interwar years. These policies were monitored and compared by the ILO in the light of developments in the economic analysis of public expenditure over the period. Indeed, in perspicacious research reports, ILO economists anticipated some important developments in economic thought later to be recognized as essentially "Keynesian." They were quick to seize on the latest work in economics which helped them formulate policy responses to international unemployment, with public works enjoying prominence.

Our account of the ILO perspective as it developed over the period under review is given impetus by a neglected remark in J.M. Keynes's *General Theory* which was made with direct reference to the achievements of ILO researchers. A feature of Keynes's policy recommendations arising from the theoretical apparatus of the *General Theory* was the operation of an active public sector investment program:

> [A] national investment programme directed to an optimum level of domestic employment . . . is twice blessed in the sense that it helps ourselves and our neighbours at the same time. And it is the simultaneous pursuit of these policies by all countries together which is capable of restoring economic health and strength internationally, whether we measure it by the level of domestic employment or by the volume of international trade (Keynes 1936: 349).

In an accompanying footnote Keynes praised ILO researchers under the leadership first of Albert Thomas and later Harold Butler, because of their "consistent appreciation of this truth," that is, of the need for active public investment programs involving concerted international initiatives (349 n. 1). In the following discussion we will trace the development of ILO research on this matter and consider the accuracy of Keynes's tribute. First we provide a survey of standard pre-Keynesian propositions issuing from the ILO on the role of public works in the 1920s. We then illustrate the impact of ideas on the economics of underconsumption on the ILO position in the late 1920s. The eclipse of pre-Keynesian notions evident in ILO publications from the late 1920s is documented. We then present the intellectual background to the remarkably prescient ILO plan for world economic reconstruction through public investment programs first given official ILO sanction in 1932. We conclude that ILO researchers provided some precursory foundations of Keynesianism, at least with respect to the role of public investment in the Depression policy response and recovery phase.

A PRE-KEYNESIAN PUBLIC WORKS STRATEGY FOR THE 1920s

The Anglo-American financial conservatism following the First World War bore on deliberations at the first session of the Washington ILO Conference in 1919. An innocuous conference recommendation suggested that ILO member governments "coordinate the execution of all work undertaken under public authority, with a view to reserving such work as far as practical for periods of unemployment and for districts most affected by it" (ILO 1919 quoted in 1931b: 70). There is no question here that public authorities might need to create entirely *new* capital works for combating cyclical unemployment or geographically concentrated unemployment. The proposition that a certain amount of given, planned public expenditure be postponed to periods of economic stagnation was thoroughly discussed in policy debate in Britain before 1914 and this did not escape the ILO's attention. One early advocate of the policy, British economist and statistician A.L. Bowley, suggested the idea to the 1909 Poor Law Commission. He maintained that such "a scheme need involve no [additional] expenditure save of thought and forethought; it was in the nature of prevention rather than of cure."[1] Just as with the 1919 ILO Conference recommendations, the intent was to keep some planned work in reserve. From the standpoint of 1919, rises in unemployment were expected to be modest and intermittent rather than

---

[1] Quoted from Part II of the *Minority Report of the Poor Law Commission*, 1909 (ed. Sidney and Beatrice Webb), in ILO (1931a: 5), bracketed insert added.

historically large and endemic; public works were then an incidental tool to be used as the case allowed, to smooth out periodic employment fluctuations. In short, there was no urgency or doctrinal change in the 1919 recommendation.

Research on rising unemployment in ILO member countries in the first half of the 1920s does not formulate policy proposals in favor of public works (Fuss 1926; ILO 1924a, 1924d, 1925f). Favorable acknowledgment is given to governments that had carefully organized relief work for the unemployed and contributed to reducing frictional unemployment by establishing systems of state labor exchanges (ILO 1923). Going by research priorities at the ILO, adoption of unemployment insurance was considered to be a more preferable means of ameliorating an unemployment problem.[2] Otherwise, ILO research concentrated entirely on macroeconomic remedies: targeting price level stabilization through active, countercyclical monetary policies (Fuss 1927; ILO 1924c). While much scope was envisaged in the 1920s for discretionary monetary management, this was not matched by a similar attitude to fiscal management and recurrent public expenditure variation on such things as public works. That monetary policy responses to unemployment were to form the centerpiece of ILO reports in the first half of the 1920s is scarcely surprising given general scepticism in the economics literature over the potency of fiscal policy in general and public works in particular.

The ILO researchers, consistently with the prevailing *Zeitgeist* and with experiences of unemployment in the first half of the 1920s, did not recognize that governments had responsibility for long-term productive work for the unemployed in the 1920s (Garraty 1978: 151–60). However, concessions were made for public works that had some utility in altering the time distribution rather than the long-run level of unemployment. The earliest statement of this principle appeared in an ILO research report on "remedies for unemployment":

> public works ... may become an important factor in stabilising the employment of labour if they are systematically distributed in date, in order to neutralise as far as possible, the effects on the labour market of fluctuations in individual orders [for the products of labour] (ILO 1922a: 116).

Having a public works policy meant making public expenditure plans so that national responses to rising unemployment could be made using fiscal surpluses generated in the past. The policy stance was articulated in a closed-economy context. Support for this stance in the formal

---

[2] A full appraisal of unemployment insurance schemes is contained in ILO (1925a). See Chapter 6.

economics literature came from leading pre-Keynesian British economists in the first quarter of the twentieth century – Beveridge, Bowley,
Pigou, and Robertson. These economists demonstrated that public *relief*
works, as opposed to genuine, enduring capital investment programs,
could reduce unemployment but only if financed from budget reserves
(Hancock 1960, 1962). Public expenditure could legitimately be made on
public works as a countercyclical measure. Moreover, in a society where
taxpayers left considerable amounts of income in "storage" or idle,
higher taxes could be used to fund relief works. As Bridel (1987: 1072)
affirms, the result is a balanced budget multiplier effect; the pre-
Keynesians understood that public works, "even without any budget
deficit, can lessen unemployment."[3] The ILO shared this pre-Keynesian
outlook which was quite progressive for the 1920s.

The ILO advanced beyond the classical line on public works usually
associated with Ricardo and, in the contemporary literature, with R.G.
Hawtrey and the British "Treasury view."[4] In this literature emphasis is
laid on *annually* balancing the government budget. Hawtrey gave a standard critique of the pre-Keynesian position on public works. Hawtrey
applauded expansive monetary policies as a remedy for unemployment
in economic downturns since they would lower interest rates and
stimulate private investment expenditure. Easier money need not be
accompanied by public works which, if activated, would be badly
managed, wasteful, and crowd out employment-creating private outlays.
Altogether, "public works are merely a piece of ritual, convenient to
people who want to be able to say that they are doing something, but
otherwise irrelevant" (Hawtrey 1925: 44). This classical line asserted the
existence of a fixed wages or capital fund so that employment on public
works would be substituted for employment in private industry. At no
time did ILO researchers entertain this view. An expansive monetary
policy may not succeed in regularizing employment quickly enough. The
ILO's primary object was the immediate employment effect of public
works rather than with the long-term "self-correcting" nature of a cyclical depression assisted by a flexible monetary policy. Nevertheless, there
was always the connotation of temporary "relief" in ILO discussion of
public works pre-1926.

---

[3] Formal analysis of the balanced budget multiplier effect – that, for example, a given
increase in government expenditure financed by an equal increase in tax revenue will
raise national income by the same amount as that given increase – is not available in the
economics literature until 1945 (Blaug 1991: 187 n. 22). However, the ILO economists
seemed to grasp the essence of the idea even though their discourse did not include a
definitive statement that "the balanced budget multiplier is equal to one."

[4] For a detailed, comprehensive assessment of the British Treasury view for the entire interwar period see Peden (1984).

A surge in the international experience of unemployment later in the 1920s prompted more attention to public works at the ILO Conference. For the first time we find a resolution requesting investigation of the link between public finance and public works. The Conference recommended

> the organization of public works so as to counteract the fluctuations of private business . . . In particular [it] requests the International Labour Office . . . to seek the advice of the Joint Committee on the *financial obstacles* to . . . putting into operation . . . public works (Eighth Session of the ILO Conference 1926 quoted in ILO 1931a: 1, emphasis added).

This was an important advance on the 1919 Washington proposal on public works. A Joint Committee of researchers at the ILO and LON set to work to report on the public finance implications of an active public works policy. In addition ILO economist J.R. Bellerby was sent to the United States to provide further case study material for future ILO conferences. His incisive report entitled *Stabilisation of Employment in the United States* (Bellerby 1926), had far-reaching implications. After surveying the experiences of authorities in the United States with public works, Bellerby observed that "it seems doubtful whether any country can justly be said to have succeeded up to the present in giving full effect to the [Washington] proposal" (p. 68) on public works. This opinion seemed to have been widely held at the ILO. Impetus was given in the 1921 President's Conference on Unemployment to carefully timed use of official financial reserves on public works so as "to abolish acute unemployment" (especially in the construction industry).[5] Despite the political goodwill, Bellerby could not rate very highly the actual delivery of public works in the United States up to 1925.

In the United States there were some vital indications that the original Washington proposal was made at too high a level of generality. First, public works required advance planning. Planning would broach technical, logistical, administrative, and financial matters, and the problem of timing. Secondly, public works as conceived in 1926 had a very limited scope; they could not legitimately replace private industrial or service activities but were meant to be supplementary to them. That is, "the establishment of state-controlled establishments as competitors to private industry in times of slump could not improve and might aggravate the general situation of business itself. Public competition would force all weaker competing units out of the market" (Bellerby 1926: 68). Infrastructural services (public utilities, road construction), afforestation, health, and community services were all considered eminently suitable, yet limited, spheres of employment creation for public authorities.

---

[5] Barber (1985: 19). Barber gives a full exposition of the 1921 *President's Report*.

Bellerby's research introduced a critical principle that infrastructural works required a long-term planning horizon as against the shorter horizon of the market and private industry; the long horizon for public works meant that they could not easily be set aside or delayed and then activated at a moment's notice when an economic crisis supervened. There were also practical lessons in Bellerby's work: Advanced planning of public works required data on the state of the labor market preferably by industry and region – data not readily available. And the *structure* of unemployment in a major economic downturn usually meant that countercyclical public works, very limited as they were in the United States at the time, would not usually require the identical labor profile that was typical of those represented amongst the unemployed. Thus Bellerby's research concludes that "[m]iners, metal workers and engineers, who frequently suffer most in a period of depression, would be affected only in a minor way by public works" (p. 70). Public works were most useful in dealing with general mass unemployment in a depression rather than with unemployment affecting a single industry or unemployment due to specific noncyclical causes.

As for administrative difficulties with public works, these were considerable in the system of government observed by Bellerby. A multiplicity of federal, state, and municipal authorities had become involved in making provision for public works; provision was made in a discoordinated fashion with the authorities timing their activities imperfectly *vis-à-vis* general fluctuations in the level of unemployment (pp. 75–77). Financing was a matter of public authorities being able "to secure the funds . . . by other means than heavy taxation during depression. The desirable course would be . . . to collect the whole of the funds during the period of prosperity so that taxation could be eased during depression" (p. 73). The latter scenario was recognized as "somewhat Utopian"; Bellerby's observations on the experience in the United States was that the second-best option – *viz.* raising taxation for use on public works – could still yield some gains in employment. Raising loans, that is, deficit financing, while not beyond the purview of the authorities up to 1926, was given passing consideration by Bellerby. The "principles of sound finance" dictated that only "permanent revenue-producing works such as harbours, transport facilities, electrical plant" should be financed by loans, but avowedly as a last resort (p. 75).

The Report of the Director of the ILO reinforced what was a pre-Keynesian consensus among ILO researchers: Fully financed balanced budgets that made periodic allowance for public works would be worthwhile because "the total amount of capital available is the only factor which determines the possibilities of employment at a given moment but the use made of capital must also be taken into consideration" (ILO

1927: 136–37). In circumstances of rising rates of unemployment, the use made of capital in private hands was patently below capacity. During the 1920s, ILO researchers observed member governments responding by planning and implementing public works on a more regular basis. They were informed initially by practice rather than pure economic analysis. A fundamental presupposition was that while the business cycle was inevitable, sharp fluctuations in the level of unemployment were not. In this pre-Keynesian vision, public works came to be conceived as an *economic* policy instrument affording the organization and maintenance of employment rather than just a social policy response distributing relief work.

CHALLENGES TO PRE-KEYNESIAN DOCTRINE ON PUBLIC WORKS

Proceeding with caution, the ILO canvassed a wide range of arguments in the public works debate in the 1920s and early 1930s. By the end of the 1920s its researchers revealed a penchant for linking underconsumptionist explanations of economic depression to the provision of public works. A significant shift in perspective occurred in the early 1930s in favor of loan-financed public investment programs. Such a position seemed to run counter to the sacred principles of orthodox, "Treasury view" public finance. The work of ILO economist P.W. Martin was published in the *International Labour Review* and, while his contributions were independent, they nevertheless illustrated that an auspicious change was in the air among ILO researchers.[6]

Martin (1926a, 1926b) followed American economists Foster and Catchings (1925) who maintained that countercyclical expenditure on public works was not only desirable if reserve surplus funds were available, but imperative irrespective of the state of government reserves. In the United States, "Foster and Catchings did much to raise public consciousness on the necessity of aggressive fiscal intervention to counteract deficiencies in private spending" (Barber 1985: 54–55). Likewise, Martin popularized fiscal intervention for an international audience. For Martin, the international economy contained an inherent bias toward underconsumption. Employment stability targeted indirectly through the instruments of monetary policy would not be achieved if, periodically, the demand side of the world economy was slow to respond to monetary policy. A noninflationary fiscal policy was required to support an

---

[6] Born in London, Percival William Martin was later educated at Columbia University where he came into contact with underconsumptionist doctrine in courses taught by Wesley Mitchell and others. He was a member of the ILO staff from 1920–34. See the unclassified papers labeled "Martin Archive Group" in the LON Archives.

expansive monetary policy in periods of rising unemployment. Reasoning in terms of a closed economy, presumably equivalent to the world economy as a whole, Martin (1926b: 51–52) argued that "buying power can be reinforced so as to provide markets for all that industry can produce."[7] Furthermore "an adequate market for goods would mean an adequate market for labour to make these goods and the consequent diminution of ... mass unemployment." There were many varieties of "underconsumptionist" doctrine available in the interwar period. Martin produced his own version of that doctrine, which unlike most other versions did not emphasize the problem of overinvestment.[8] Nevertheless, like other contributors to the doctrine such as Foster and Catchings he stressed the independence of decisions to save and invest and traced the causes of unemployment to the failure of decisions to invest to offset decisions to save. In addition, he adopted the position that production in a monetary economy does not automatically sustain consumption at high levels sufficient to prevent declines in the price level and in actual and expected profits, and cumulative falls in output and employment. Here Martin finds a place for loan-financed public works: A policy, in other words, of deficit-financed public investment reinforces purchasing power when, given a low level of inflation, unemployment was historically high and rising. A general rise in unemployment was due to a general overproduction relative to consumers' ability to pay (1926b: 45). The rationale is purely macroeconomic. This underconsumptionist case is attenuated because it does not propose policies to address specific microeconomic causes of unemployment such as structural or technological unemployment.[9] Martin was silent on how public works might be organized to provide employment opportunities by region or industry where unemployment was increasing.

The macroeconomic theme containing a vision for making public investment central to governmental demand management is contained in Martin's published work in the 1930s. The economic crisis of 1929–32 added to his conviction that

---

[7] That Martin was taking a global view is only made explicit much later in Martin (1931b: 690) where his point of departure is "the world view as a whole."

[8] On Martin's brand of "underconsumptionist" doctrine see King (1990). For a survey of theories of underconsumption, which emphasizes the point that, compared with Keynesian theories, underconsumptionists remind us "that there is a limit to the extent to which employment can be increased by increases in investment alone," see Schneider (1987: 744).

[9] The underconsumptionist perspective also ignored general supply-side causes. The importance of underconsumption as a factor explaining fluctuations in unemployment and the countervailing role of a public works program is later reinforced by Ansiaux (1932) in a more formal academic article in the *ILR*. Again, supply-side issues are ignored.

large sums are held relatively idle, both by business undertakings and by private individuals, in the form of stagnant bank deposits or actual hoards. A government loan for the purpose of financing public works tends to galvanise these idle funds into activity; and thereby to reinforce the volume of buying . . . If the public works programme is accompanied by measures tending to increase the quantity of currency and credit in circulation, the influence on business activity is likely to be still more pronounced. In such a case public works will be financed, directly or indirectly, in part or whole, by what is . . . new money (Martin 1932: 201–02).

In this passage Martin alluded to the need for an accommodating monetary regime which in the extreme would allow governments to "print money . . . to meet its liabilities" (1926b: 45). The liabilities incurred from public works would have prominence here. If public works are organized in combination with an appropriate monetary policy their successful integration would "present a direct means of increasing effective demand."[10]

Dissent in ILO publications from Martin's line of thought was quickly registered by Swedish economist Gustav Cassel (1932). In pre-Keynesian mode, Cassel insisted on immediately balancing government budgets; the use of public works was an emergency measure – a response of very last resort – presumably in conditions of severe civil strife. The crowding out of private expenditure by public expenditure was advanced not as a hypothesis but as an article of faith. More compelling are Cassel's reflections on sequencing issues associated with economic reconstruction following the world economic depression. Easier monetary policies must be implemented first and could be relied upon to effect high levels of employment without public works (Cassel 1932: 647). Balanced budgets would promote investor confidence; there is no suggestion that private investment demand, for instance, would be interest inelastic. Even without public works, Cassel was mindful of unfavorable international balance of payments consequences of easier monetary policies, especially if smaller economies experienced rates of inflation higher (consequent upon easier money) than their larger trading partners. International cooperation on monetary policy was therefore a pre-eminent consideration; public works policy had a subordinate role as a method of unemployment relief. In responding to this point of view the editor of the *ILR* commented bluntly: "It is undeniable that such a

---

[10] See also the important paper published by Martin and an ILO research colleague, E.J. Riches (1933: 39), where it is asserted that government maintenance of "effective demand" should be instituted as a "*permanent* policy" (emphasis added). No mention is made in this article to the functions of public works in such a policy.

change in the order of remedies would constitute a fundamental change in the programme which the [ILO] Office has formulated" (editorial note in Cassel 1932: 643).

In fact, by 1931 pre-Keynesian ideas on public works of the kind advanced by Cassel had been fully eclipsed in ILO research. Adoption of ideas on underconsumption made a significant difference in this connection (ILO 1931a: 27, 29–30, 100 n. 1).[11] But underconsumptionism was not the only influential doctrine. In the United Kingdom Keynes had long been familiar with a short-run, disequilibrium interpretation of the quantity theory of money in which a continual increase in the supply of money is transmitted, at least in part, to output and employment and did not simply lead to price level inflation. According to Blaug (1991: 182) the "standard pre-Keynesian framework for demonstrating the efficiency of loan-financed public works" was rationalized on this basis: It was "already present in Keynes's and Henderson's 1929 tract 'Can Lloyd George Do It?' " Furthermore, Keynes's *Treatise on Money* gave the ILO economists some intellectual authority in their quest to encourage governments to use budget deficits when financing public works. By 1930, Keynes was becoming less sanguine about the use of monetary policy *exclusively* to stabilize employment. He mentioned public works in this context, as an investment either fully funded by governments or as an industrial subsidy. His argument is premised on open international capital markets:

> [I]t is not sufficient for the *central authority* to stand ready to lend – for the money may flow into the wrong hands – it *must also stand ready to borrow*. In other words, *the Government must itself promote a programme of domestic investment*. It may be a choice between employing labour to create capital wealth, which will yield less than the market rate of interest, or not employing it at all. If this is the position, the national interest, both immediate and prospective, will be promoted by choosing the first alternative. But if foreign borrowers are ready and eager, it will be impossible in a competitive open market to bring the rate down to the level appropriate to domestic investment. Thus the desired result can only be obtained through some method by which, in effect, the Government subsidises approved types of domestic invest-

---

[11] Underconsumption is used to justify deficit-financed public works and high wages policies. Thus, citing J.A. Hobson, the ILO (1931c: 218) considered that the immediate implications of general underconsumption was "a state of disequilibrium between the productive forces of society and its purchasing power, the former being far in excess of the latter." Critical *desiderata* for ILO researchers were the effects of the aggregate level of money wages and "high" wages policies on unemployment when unemployment is caused by insufficient purchasing power (pp. 219–22). ILO Director H.B. Butler (1931a: 314) also broaches these issues.

ment or itself directs domestic schemes of capital development (Keynes 1930, vol. II: 337, emphasis added).

For Keynes, government-created capital assets were economically justifiable over an extended time horizon. Public investment programs and subsidies to private employers were warranted even though they may not yield a return greater than or equal to the current market rate of interest. Speculative foreign capital flows may distort the picture; what Keynes called the "prospective" or long term social *and* economic return of lowering the level of domestic unemployment in "the national interest" was a more important referent than the current market rate of interest.

Now for the ILO, the brief remarks on public investment in the *Treatise*, together with Keynes's pronouncements on the matter in the popular press were regarded as unexceptionable.[12] The Report of the Director of the ILO made much of Keynes's endorsement of the virtues of active public investment programs although no mention is made of Keynes's other option – subsidies directly to spur expansion of employment. Keynes left open the option for governments – they could undertake the investment themselves or give assistance in terms of preferential interest rates to public authorities (both countenanced by the ILO) or offer preferential interest rates to the private sector (not explicitly recognized by the ILO). Keynes's public investment schemes were to "act not merely as a palliative, but as a positive remedy" (ILO 1931b: 72).[13] In 1931 an ILO research report on public works demonstrates close knowledge of Keynes's extensive but less formal journalistic contributions urging an expansion of public investment in Britain; the report contrasts Keynes's view with the contrary classical arguments of Hawtrey, the British Treasury, and the standard pre-Keynesian line as represented by Henry Clay's *The Post-War Unemployment Problem* (1929) (ILO 1931a: 27–30). Keynes is grouped with P.W. Martin of the ILO on the side of the new view in favor of deficit-financed public works. "There can be no doubt" the report concludes, "as Mr J.M. Keynes says, that an active public works policy involves an increase in

---

[12] Laidler (1999: 273 n. 29) comments that in the *Treatise* "Keynes had been only a reluctant advocate of counter-cyclical public works expenditure." And Lee (1989: 138) correctly points out that Keynes only mentions public works "obliquely" in the *Treatise* and that Keynes's ideas on this matter are not given "a solid basis in theory" until his *General Theory* appeared in 1936. Perhaps so. But contemporary practitioners, policy advisors and policy makers attributed considerable authority to his views pre-1936, not the least ILO economists.

[13] Throughout 1929 and 1930 Keynes referred to public works as his "favourite remedy" (Clarke 1988: 115).

credit facilities" (p. 179). In the perspective of the ILO, by contrast with pre-Keynesian proposals, Keynes envisaged public investment as an integral part of a policy of reflation at certain stages of the business cycle. Keynes's position pre-*General Theory*, was also interpreted by the ILO as one in which the state of private-sector expectations was stabilized or even stimulated by public-sector investment programs; the *volume* of investment would change but there is no interpretation that the state would function to plan the overall structure and composition of investment or that it should effect the complete socialization of investment.[14] Thus:

> Extensive schemes for works of public interest, by helping in some measure to raise prices and increasing the demand for materials, stimulate economic activity generally and produce a psychological reaction that is far from negligible in economic fluctuations (ILO 1931b: 72).

Complementing these reflationary actions was a grand ILO plan to assist in "organising the labour market" as a whole, permanently to prevent a sharp acceleration in the rate of unemployment (p. 74). Economic fluctuations (or the business cycle) were no longer inevitable. The events of 1929–31 illustrated that the cycle produced mass unemployment for a long period of time. Reliance on the automatic self-correcting forces of the market economy would be tantamount to accepting a significant element of market failure evidenced by labor market *dis*organization. Measures to prevent such disorganization were required. Therefore "public authorities should take advantage of the opportunity and carry out works of public interest on profitable terms" (pp. 71–72). Consistently with Keynes, there is no hint here that "profitable" meant a profit rate above the ruling market rate of interest.

Financing issues were regarded as straightforward especially in larger industrialized economies with the capacity to borrow on the international capital market (ILO 1931a: 94–96, 103). Smaller countries will have difficulty financing public investment if the government accounts are in a parlous state, as they tend to be in depression conditions. Therefore the importance of international cooperation in intergovernmental lending in particular has to be underscored – as it was in ILO (1931a)

---

[14] The debate that developed in the late twentieth century over Keynes's purported view in the *General Theory* that the State should take responsibility for planning the overall level and structure of investment is summarized in Laidler (1999: 267 n. 22). The researchers in international organizations surveyed in this book never held this view on investment expenditure independently and did not interpret Keynes's writings at any stage as seriously suggesting comprehensive socialization.

and more stridently so in ILO (1935).[15] As one leading commentator on financing claimed, the ILO had an intellectual and moral role, rather than a practical, organizational role in ensuring that public works finance was made widely available:

> [I]nternational cooperation is desirable; so it is fortunate that the *International Labour Office* has established a special committee at Geneva to study the question, and that this committee . . . [has produced a] report about "Unemployment and Public Works" . . . in 1931. It is very desirable that this Institution should have an influence on the policies of the various Governments. In all countries there are some parties and classes that are more interested in public works than others, and, as this policy is best for the whole world, it is most desirable that these parties should get *moral support from an international institution*; indeed it should become a question of honour for all countries to take part in this activity (Warming 1932: 224, emphasis in original).[16]

Evidence gathered on administrative difficulties with public investment from the 1920s to 1930 made the ILO objective of using public works to organize labor markets look rather ambitious. Administrative systems could thwart an enlightened program even if deficit finance is accepted.[17] What was intellectually justifiable was not always administratively possible or politically acceptable. Variations in "proto-Keynesian"-type responses to mass unemployment in the early 1930s across ILO member countries have since been attributed at least in part to state structures (Weir and Skocpol 1985). ILO researchers were well aware of the multiplicity of authorities responsible for public works in various countries. Using the example of Germany, they recommended a stronger, centralized system of control which would coordinate the activities of local authorities and public utility undertakings. Further, to avoid undue influence "by electoral considerations" at all levels, the centralized system should be operated by a "permanent and non-political body" such as a Public Works Committee (ILO 1931a:

[15] See also James Meade (1932: 13–16) which also afforded much importance to international cooperation in respect of lending for public works. Correspondence between Meade and the ILO on the subject of international cooperation over public works is contained in the ILO Archives U15/1/25/5/2 6th July 1937; 9th July 1937.

[16] Warming implored the BIS to become actively involved in organizing finance "on fair terms." However, BIS *Annual Reports* in the 1930s were decidedly cool on the idea. The closest those *Reports* came to acknowledging such a role was in 1937. We will have occasion to present the BIS position presently below.

[17] This seemed to be a common experience in Britain during the early 1930s. See Booth (1993).

181–82).[18] As well, long-established systems of State labor exchanges in many European countries were readily available to recruit labor for public works. Finally, drawing on an exhaustive survey of international practices, the ILO recommended that authorities schedule public works according to "a reliable index of the intensity of unemployment" (ILO 1931a: 84). Up to 1931, Germany and the United States were presented as exemplars in this connection, always activating public works when aggregate unemployment reached a certain level. Public works were activated to prevent a further deterioration in unemployment; they would reduce the *scale* of unemployment rather than eliminate it (pp. 85–86). While the level of unemployment was a useful "warning index," other "economic barometers" should also be consulted (p. 88). General indices of the state of industrial production disaggregated geographically and by industry would materially assist authorities in applying public works, but ILO member countries had not, by 1931, reached this high level of readiness in the fight against rising unemployment.

THE 1932 ILO RESOLUTION REGARDING PUBLIC WORKS: TOWARD GLOBAL ECONOMIC RECONSTRUCTION

The 1931 ILO survey of the theory and practice of public works distinguished three types of unemployment: 1. unemployment of a "more or less permanent" character, 2. cyclical unemployment, and 3. seasonal unemployment. Category (2) was identified as being relevant to public works activity, provided work could be varied upward in cyclical downturns and vice versa. However, these three categories of unemployment became less relevant to circumstances in 1931–33. The economic crisis of the 1930s presented a special case of mass unemployment which was severe and prolonged. In these conditions, "[s]ooner or later a point is reached at which there are no more public works on the programmes of the authorities concerned" (ILO 1931a: 4–5, 25–26). Some important points in favor of public works were made in this 1931 ILO investigation. First, employment was preferable to relief work of any kind. Secondly, public works have positive downstream effects on the demand for goods, services, and labor in other private industries, but these were difficult to estimate quantitatively. Thirdly, public works expenditure raises the purchasing power of the community as a whole.

An essential feature of policy recommendations on public works in the 1920s as outlined in the 1931 ILO survey was the planning and coordination of work at the *national* level on a relatively *small* scale. As gen-

---

[18] Copious evidence was also presented from the United States where a central Employment Stabilization Board had been established to regulate public investment schemes (Butler 1931b: 72–73).

eralizations, these recommendations were realistic given the amplitude of economic cycles in the 1920s; public works would serve as a response to short-lived economic downturns. The survey was submitted to the April 1932 ILO Conference. The Conference adopted a resolution marking a major shift in thinking on public investment:

> Government delegates . . . should as soon as possible be given instructions to draw up a list of *big international works* for economic equipment and for national works on a *large scale* calculated to encourage the general development of the economic situation of the countries concerned, to make the necessary financial arrangements therefore and to have them put in hand without delay (ILO 1932: 221, emphasis added).[19]

The necessity for "planning on a world basis" had been presaged in a report on the 1931 World Social Economic Congress by an ILO official (Johnston 1932: 58). In the same year the deputy director of the ILO considered the time ripe for "international solutions to the world's difficulties" (Butler 1931a: 323). So by 1932 the ILO advocated international planning of public works in a manner that moved decisively beyond ILO studies and Conference resolutions in the 1920s – resolutions focusing on smaller, nationally based countercyclical public works schemes conceived as genuine investments.

The analytical groundwork for the historic 1932 resolution on an internationally based, large-scale public works policy, was completed by ILO economists Martin and Riches. Other ILO investigatory work concentrated on the direct social consequences of the economic crisis, for instance, on employment problems in particular countries or for particular social groups, and on methods of ameliorating these consequences at the local level.[20] Martin and Riches formulated a macroeconomic perspective linking international monetary policy coordination with large-scale public investment schemes. They envisaged a sequence of schemes beginning with developments in the larger industrialized and creditor nations. As part of the agenda for world economic reconstruction they presupposed that price level stability achieved through an appropriate monetary policy on its own would not suffice to maintain a high level of employment. Expansionary monetary policies must be aimed at financing public works "directly or indirectly [via downstream activities] . . . by what is to all intents and purposes new money" (Martin 1932: 202). Since capital and raw materials supplies were available, and cheap capital was

---

[19] See ILO (1932: 220–21) for the full text of the resolution adopted by the Sixteenth Session of the ILO Conference. The Conference passed the resolution on public works 80 votes to 1 (Alcock 1971: 104).

[20] For example, Fuss (1935), Fuss and Tait (1933), ILO (1933a), and Thibert (1933a,b).

not readily invested by private industry, then the only feasible alternative was for large-scale, government-directed public works. Public works would mobilize otherwise idle bank balances. In the 1931 ILO study of public works it was recognized that expansionary monetary policies at that time would release "a superabundance of money seeking investment" as the rate of interest declined. That private investment expenditure was interest inelastic in some economies was not stressed in this 1931 study at all. Intense aversion to unbalanced budgets in many countries was also ignored. Nevertheless, evidence reported in Martin (1932) and Martin and Riches (1933) indicated low confidence among private investors and thus a reduced likelihood of cheaper credit being quickly or fully utilized. In the event public works expenditure would not be acting as a deterrent to private investment expenditure, employment would not simply be diverted from so-called more productive private employment to public sector employment, and inflation was not inevitable. For as Keynes explained in 1929 (quoted *in extenso* in ILO 1931a: 27):

> In so far as the greater volume of employment and business means that wage earners carry in their pockets increased purchasing power in bank notes and that business men keep at their banks an increased purchasing power in bank deposits, there can be an increased volume of credit of an entirely innocent and non-inflationary description.

Martin was definitely thinking along these lines when addressing the 1932 ILO resolution on public works. Official sanction was given to this perspective in the Report of the ILO Director to the 1933 Conference wherein public investment expenditure was hailed as "a method of compensating the loss of purchasing power caused by unemployment" (ILO 1933b: 21).

In the context of the 1932 Conference resolution, the question arises whether public investment could be implemented internationally. Provided central banks in surplus countries pursued expansionary monetary policies and provided public authorities carefully planned public works schemes, then activity in one country would have demonstration effects for others and lead to a revival of employment internationally (Woytinsky 1932). Moreover, the revival would be enduring if public works ceased to be regarded as temporary measures; ongoing public works schemes may be required for a long time to maintain a level of purchasing power consistent with high employment. Martin (1932: 202) promised that the ILO would assist authorities in ILO member countries with planning, given that the Office had collected much detailed information on suitable schemes. In 1931 it seemed reasonable to conclude that "public works would *not* be put in hand for *long* [periods] of time" (ILO 1931a: 32, emphasis added). Now, in 1933, inspired by the

ILO Conference resolution, the position of ILO researchers was that carefully planned public works not only helped revive economic activity, they also had a long-term place in economic development by maintaining investment and purchasing power at high levels. Again, in the determination of the ILO Director, "public enterprise is an indispensable method of stimulating industrial activity" (ILO 1933b: 23).

By 1933, ILO economists had become concerned about the speed of adjustment of private sector investment intentions following introduction of easier monetary policy (for example, Martin and Riches 1933: 50). In some countries loan finance would be needed to activate public investment. While the 1933 Conference resolved that public investment should give "an assured economic yield" (ILO 1935: 2), that yield was not operationally defined. The question of yield drops completely from view in the lengthy resolutions adopted by the International Public Works Committee at the 1937 Conference (ILO 1938: 754–57). Any focus on the rather static concept of "yield," that is a rate of return on each public investment in isolation, would need precise quantitative expression and must incorporate the current market rate of interest and an arbitrary discount rate. Instead, ILO research emphasized the long-term self-financing aspects of public investment. First, the cost of social transfer payments and *ad hoc* relief works would decline. Secondly, increased tax revenue could be expected as national income and employment expanded *pari passu* (Martin and Riches 1933: 39–40). Thirdly, as early as 1931 a new analytical dimension was introduced: the employment and expenditure multipliers. Keynes's and Henderson's *Can Lloyd George Do It?* (1929) is paraphrased approvingly in respect of the former, and research in the United States is used to suggest that the latter must be greater than unity (ILO 1931a: 14–19). And Martin (1932: 202) asserted a "two-fold increase in the volume of buying" as a result of every additional unit of public investment expenditure.[21] The ILO researchers grasped very early on the basic mechanism of the multiplier process by showing a lucid understanding of primary and secondary effects of exogenous expenditure impulses originating from additional public investment. Lastly, while it was admitted that public investment, so justified, might lead to a significant increase in foreign imports of raw materials in some countries, this concern was allayed given the objective of

---

[21] R.F. Kahn's (1931) celebrated article which gave formal quantitative expression to the multiplier notion was later used in ILO publications to give explicit endorsement to deficit-financed public works (ILO 1935: 73). Unfortunately statistical estimates of employment multipliers in different countries are not made in ILO research, although see Mitnitzky (1934) in the *ILR* who does attempt to quantify the effects of public works on employment.

expanding public works *internationally*; in the event, all nations should benefit from an increase in international trade stimulated thereby (ILO 1931a: 25–28; Martin 1933: 243).

The ILO researchers, along with J.M. Keynes, had not merely made a leap of faith in the early 1930s in advocating expansionary public investment schemes, for there were sound logical reasons for such schemes. While most ILO publications referred in great detail to experiences with public expenditure in a wide range of countries, most of the cited intellectual background up to 1933 is Anglo-American with frequent citations to Keynes, Mitchell, Hawtrey, Clay, Foster, Catchings, and the National Bureau of Economic Research in that order.[22] In Sweden, Myrdal, Lindahl, and Ohlin had also published extensively between 1932 and 1934 on countercyclical application of public sector deficit finance, but they did not receive explicit recognition in ILO work until 1935 (ILO 1935: 74 passim).[23] In 1936 an economic advisor to the ILO, L.L. Lorwin (1936: 462–63) reflected on the achievements of the ILO in the 1930s and understood public investment as one of the "large measures" promoted for economic recovery, equal in priority with monetary policy reform and the expansion of international trade. The meaning of public investment was now transformed: It applied to any government activity designed for industrial development including housing, education, and health care – these are all considered on the same plane as means of counteracting employment instability. The ILO survey entitled "Public Works Policy" in 1935 showed that it did not need the formal conceptual framework of Keynes's *General Theory of Employment Interest and Money* (1936) for governments vigorously to promote public works. In 1935 however, the intellectual linkages now went beyond Keynes and were more cosmopolitan. There is reference to European theoretical contributions *and* European practice: German, Swedish, Russian, and French literature on public works is brought to the fore.[24] Bertil Ohlin contributed an article to the *ILR* which, perhaps unintentionally, endorsed the pragmatic, internationalist position adopted at the ILO:

> [I]n financially strong countries it is sound and practicable to resort to large scale borrowing during periods of depression . . . It is time to learn

---

[22] The NBER was involved in an extensive study of public works in the United States. See Gayer (1935) which cites ILO research frequently.

[23] That ILO researchers were up-to-date with Swedish developments is indicated by their desire to publish an English translation of the Myrdal-authored appendix to the 1933 Swedish Social Democrat government budget. Myrdal declined (Jonung 1991: 28).

[24] The works of Myrdal, Ohlin, Woytinsky, and Milhaud figure prominently in ILO references. Extensive discussion of public investment schemes in Europe up to 1935 may be found in ILO (1935), ILO (1938: 737–43), and Ohlin (1935: 679–86) for details on schemes in Sweden.

> the lesson of recent experience that intelligent and sound public finance
> does not require the budget to be balanced each year but only over a
> number of years (Ohlin 1935: 685).

Toward the middle of the 1930s a more tolerant attitude toward fiscal
imbalances due to public works had become the norm in Eastern Europe
(Aldcroft 1993: 178). A reader of the 1935 ILO survey would nonetheless observe a disparate, modest set of uncoordinated works schemes in
various European countries, rather than an internationally integrated
approach as recommended by ILO economists. Many cases were presented of schemes which were in fact procyclical in the late 1920s and
early 1930s – schemes which exacerbated depression conditions because
they were progressively reduced in scale and concentrated on merely
giving the unemployed basic relief rather than genuine asset-creating
work (ILO 1935: 6 passim).

In a rare allusion to loan-financed investment expenditure, Per
Jacobsson at the BIS weighed in with a negative (or, more charitably
understood, noncommittal) view on the subject in the 1936/37 BIS
Annual Report:

> There has been much controversy as to the part that the public spend-
> ing of borrowed funds can play in overcoming a depression. In fact,
> the budgets of most countries have shown large deficits and the policy
> of defraying expenditure from proceeds of loans has thus been almost
> universal. In some countries where this occurred, recovery set in
> early while in others it was delayed. The conclusion would seem to be
> that only if general conditions making for an equilibrium between
> costs and prices are in process of being established will government
> spending assist recovery; if these conditions are lacking the result of
> such spending may on balance be directly injurious, for continuous bor-
> rowing to meet excess expenditure may undermine confidence (BIS
> 1937: 10).

Jacobsson was surely right to add the sort of warning one would expect
from an international central banker. A country's particular financial
circumstances and general public attitude to deficit financing would be
crucial in determining the efficacy of public works programs. Furthermore, in his set of "general conditions" the consistency of policies being
pursued in parallel with deficit finance was all-important and conceivably differed between countries. The fragility of private sector
expectations and confidence were uppermost in Jacobsson's mind.[25] At
the LON, Haberler also took a similar, fairly guarded position on

---

[25] The practical international difficulties in organizing finance for public investment in
some countries were also probably lurking in the background as well, given that the BIS
might be given an expanded, possibly onerous task as chief organizer and monitoring
agency. The BIS *Annual Reports* did not broach the matter.

financing public works; his argument also turned on the dangers in damaging confidence:

> It is by no means easy (though it is not impossible) to find methods of raising the necessary funds, apart from an alarming expansion of central-bank money, without giving rise at the same time or later to a decrease in the flow of money at some other point of the economic system.
>
> This much may be said at this point – that, if a net increase in demand for goods is effected by such measures, and if disturbing psychological repercussions on business enterprise are avoided, such a policy may very well initiate a process of general expansion (Haberler 1937: 281).

Unlike the ILO, expansion of central bank credit to finance public investment is here regarded as (potentially at least) "alarming"; other "methods" of financing and their effects are not elaborated, much to the chagrin of a major academic reviewer of LON research (Kahn 1937: 679; 1938: 335). Richard Kahn's earlier correspondence in 1933 with researchers at the ILO clarified the differences in theory and practice between financing public works out of taxation and financing by loans; he also corrected some misunderstandings at the ILO on the difference between employment and income multipliers.[26] Later he evidently had no communication with the LON economists on these subjects relating to public works yet he was an international authority on theoretical aspects of the subject during the 1930s.

In 1938 the *ILR* reported favorably on ILO initiatives under the heading "Public Works as a Factor in Economic Stabilisation" (ILO 1938). This article was based on Resolutions adopted by the 1937 ILO Conference. It took for granted what a few years earlier would have been heretical, *viz.* the "objective of national planning of public works is to maintain purchasing power" (p. 731); that the issue of public works "embraces public expenditure in general" (p. 732); that public expenditure should promote developments in capital (human and physical) and be accompanied, where necessary, by an accommodating monetary policy and, initially, by unbalanced budgets (p. 734). There was a new emphasis on public investment outlays as a core element of fiscal policy. ILO studies of leading industrialized nations' attempts to coordinate "public investment planning" (as it came to be known) helped disseminate information and experiences in different institutional contexts (for example, Higgins 1944). Doubtless, the intellectual impetus for the shift in per-

---

[26] See ILO Archives U15/1/25/5/3 22nd August 1933; 13th September 1933; 26th September 1933.

spective was due to the *General Theory* which, according to Lerner (1936: 436) was keenly discussed in Geneva immediately after publication.[27] One policy implication of Keynes's contribution, quickly appreciated in Geneva, was underscored in Lerner's well-known review: "the amount of employment can be governed by policy directed towards affecting the amount of investment." When for psychological or institutional reasons lowering the rate of interest did not prove effective, "investment by the authorities" must be implemented. Public investment was necessary, in fact, increasingly so "as the wealth and capital equipment of the community [tends to] increase. For this means that on the one hand people wish to save more out of the larger income corresponding to full employment while on the other hand the accumulation of capital lowers the marginal efficiency schedule of capital." Public investment "whose efficiency is less than the rate of interest" would then be necessary to ensure equilibrium with full employment (Lerner 1936: 452).

An activist monetary policy was required – one which was not invariant to the fiscal policy stance (ILO 1935: 116; 1938: 736–37). The ILO Conference in 1937 favored international agreements enabling public investments in different countries to be developed on "parallel lines, so that an expansion of credit and an increase in the volume of public works may be as far as possible simultaneous in all countries." Furthermore, an International Public Works Committee was created to collect data, analyze, and share information between member countries; it would have the far-reaching responsibility of promoting international public works, of planning and then assisting in implementing schemes where works in some debtor countries would be financed by stronger creditor countries (ILO 1938: 744–45, 751).[28] This framework could be used to justify a wide range of schemes depending on national circumstances. Hence the following guiding principle directed the Committee:

> A public works policy should not be thought of merely as a means of combatting unemployment and aim solely at providing employment. It should contribute to an ordered development of national economic activity and should consequently be adapted to the needs of each country (ILO 1935: 158).

Here was a responsibility portentous of the link, to be so well developed in the 1950s, between foreign investment and foreign aid flows and public

---

[27] The editorial introduction to Lerner's review of Keynes (1936) in the *ILR* states that the *General Theory* "has an important bearing on many of the questions which are at present in the forefront of the interests of the International Labour Organisation" (in Lerner 1936: 435).

[28] The full text of the ILO Conference resolutions in respect of the International Public Works Committee is reprinted in ILO (1938: 754–59).

works in recipient (debtor) countries. Later, this was to become a principal responsibility of the World Bank.[29]

CONCLUSION

We are now in a position to reflect on Keynes's footnote endorsement of ILO research in the *General Theory* (1936). As quoted in the introduction to this chapter, Keynes praised the ILO for appreciating a "fundamental truth" that national investment programs could play a significant role in maintaining "optimum levels of employment." To be sure, by 1932 the ILO economists viewed public investment as part of general government outlays. And the discourse which had once exclusively used public "works" had merged imperceptibly with a new language expressing "works" interchangeably with "investment." The equivalence of public "works" and "investment" would not have been widely accepted in the 1920s. Increasingly in the 1930s, the Geneva researchers recommended deliberate deficit-financed outlays for long-term social and industrial development and to bolster aggregate demand rather than for temporary unemployment relief. It was a long road, however, to this proto-Keynesian policy stance.

Initially the ILO adopted a pre-Keynesian view that public works were to be financed from extant contingency reserves. Unemployment crises were a temporary lapse from high employment and high employment could ultimately be achieved by flexible monetary policies. Short-term unemployment could be ameliorated by ad hoc public works schemes. A new emphasis on deficient purchasing power emerged in ILO research from the late 1920s, with underconsumptionist ideas providing arguments for more vigorous, discretionary public expenditure programs to maintain aggregate demand in recessions. A fundamental shift in perspective toward "Keynesianism" at the ILO had to wait until the economic crisis of the late 1920s and early 1930s. Loan-financed public investment was openly and frequently endorsed. The ILO researchers made themselves familiar with international practice in respect of public works in this period; they drew on extensive data sources including case material from ILO member countries.

Predominantly informed by practice therefore, and bolstered by theoretical contributions from Keynes, other British and American

---

[29] The idea of a World Bank did not escape ILO researchers. Keynes had lectured to Geneva researchers (including the ILO) on the structure and role of an international bank as part of a lecture series on international economic policy in 1929 (Fleming 2000). In ILO (1935: 118) it is suggested that "an international financing institution" be created to act as a conduit for international lending on public works presumably because it was thought that the BIS could not easily take responsibility for that function.

economists and later by Swedish economists, they developed a frame-work justifying a wide variety of public investment schemes. While ILO economists did not provide a single, uniform, robust theoretical case for the scope and function of public investment over the interwar period, this is *not* to say that they did not have logical cases for sets of policy conclusions on the matter. To be sure "in the [economics] literature of the 1920s as a whole, where the case for public works was . . . something of a commonplace . . . it lacked a coherent theoretical base" (Laidler 1999: 329 n. 17). Economists working in international organizations worked close to real country experiences with public investment and pressing policy issues; they did not have the luxury of waiting for wide-spread endorsement of a high-level theoretical base for their changing positions on the matter. It would be uncharitable to conclude that they appeared to draw on what theoretical literature was available in an ad hoc fashion to bolster their outlook without acknowledging that much of the material they consulted earnestly on the subject was less formal and often highly descriptive by comparison with some contemporary academic economics.

The ILO agenda on public works fully matured by 1935. It accepted that private investment expenditure could be unresponsive to interest rate reductions as evidenced by experience between 1929 and 1933. The notion that public investment may not yield a rate of return sufficient to match the current market rate of interest was left to languish in the background; policy makers were driven actively to respond to the unemployment crisis by taking a long-term horizon for public investment which involved concern for less easily quantifiable social returns. Moreover, even taking a purely economic perspective, the full consequences of public investment expenditures were best understood in terms of their *total* multiplier effects on employment and national income. The ILO formulation for public investment post-1936 strengthened the connections between Keynesian macroeconomic management, public expenditure, and the pursuit of high and stable employment. Social spending, broadly conceived, was to be integrated with the idea of discretionary, macroeconomic demand management (we shall consider broader aspects of social expenditure from the late 1930s in Chapter 6). In any case, by the mid-1940s it became conventional to regard public investment as a vital tool of fiscal policy.

In conclusion, the Geneva researchers were progressive and innovative in their promotion of public investment in the interwar years. The ideal of world economic reconstruction through international collaboration over public works reached a high point in programmatic ILO publications in the mid-to-late 1930s. The ILO researchers' access to data and the fact that they kept in close association with practical affairs enabled them to reach policy conclusions which Keynes also appreciated and acknowledged. By contrast, Keynes's (1936) choice of an academic audience required him to encapsulate similar policy conclusions in a coherent macroeconomic theory. The ILO economists worked at a lower level of abstraction and only used Keynes's contributions pre-1936 as *ex post facto* rationalizations for policy conclusions reached from an intensive study of the practice and real-case potential of public investment. Nonetheless, these reports deserve recognition as supportive of those who were moving in a "Keynesian" direction before 1936. Would that Keynes had given the contribution of researchers at the ILO a more fitting tribute than a footnote reference in the *General Theory*.

5   Trade Policy Research: Geneva Doctrine and the Scandinavian Connection

INTRODUCTION

The rise of trade policy interventions in the interwar years has been well documented (for example, Kindleberger 1989). By contrast, the intellectual history of trade policy doctrine for this period has been accorded scarcely any attention. Recent contributions have emphasized the authority and momentum given to trade policy interventions by J.M. Keynes's putative apostasy on free trade dating from the early 1930s. Thus Jagdish Bhagwati (1994: 234–35) maintains that "Keynes's renunciation of the doctrine of free trade remained a potent source of disbelief in the doctrine . . . [and his] apostasy turned the 1930s into the most deadly episode among the challenges to the doctrine of free trade." And Douglas Irwin (1996: 206) concludes that "Keynes succeeded for many years in placing the free trade doctrine in doubt and putting its advocates on the defensive."

In this chapter we present evidence suggesting that there is much more to the intellectual history of trade policy discussion from the late 1920s to the mid-1940s than is available in Keynes's fragmentary remarks on the subject. There was a potent source of belief in *freer* trade at least, emanating from significant research undertaken under the auspices of international organizations in Geneva during the period under review. Specifically, there is evidence linking much of this research with Ohlin's pivotal publications in international economics in the interwar years. Unlike Keynes, Geneva economists remained consistent advocates of freer trade. A vast array of research reports on trade policy matters were forthcoming from Geneva-based international organizations in the interwar period.

The purpose here is to assess the content and intellectual significance of the Geneva research program on trade policy mostly with respect to real trade flows (the international monetary dimension demands separate treatment in Chapter 7). We consider that program in terms of its logical coherence and development; these are separate questions from whether or not it exerted an influence on economic policy in any country or on international economic policy. Indeed, if the course of world trade policy up to the mid-1940s is anything to gauge "influence" by, then the Geneva emphasis on freer trade failed. Dearth of immediate policy influence notwithstanding, we submit that a distinctive stream of economic thought originating in Swedish economics is discernible in Geneva research and is worthy of consideration in its own right. The Geneva advocation of freer trade was largely independent of, and was unmoved by, Keynes's apparently authoritative, often shifting position on the subject. As early as 1930, Keynes became primarily concerned with what was best for Great Britain (Cammarosano 1987: 150).[1] By contrast, the foreign trade thinking of Geneva researchers was largely determined by wider international considerations.

THE WORLD ECONOMIC CONFERENCE AND OHLIN'S LEAGUE OF NATIONS REPORT

The phrase "policy of Geneva" was first used in a Romanian publication which railed against the League of Nations' dependence "upon the classic doctrine of free trade" (Manoilesco 1931: 205). Manoilesco made extensive reference to discussion papers and reports of the 1927 World Economic Conference (WEC) in the course of submitting a case for a program of general tariff protection to avoid mass unemployment and employment at low wages. If correct, his claim of a Geneva free trade bias ran counter to the League's original Convenant, Article 23, which made provision *only* "to secure and maintain freedom of communications and of transit and equitable treatment for the commerce of all members of the League."[2] This provision did not amount to recommending removal of all extant trade restrictions; if anything it merely idealized the notion of equity in trading opportunities between nations.

The League of Nations convoked the 1927 WEC in Geneva; it surveyed the whole field of trade restrictions and was practically unanimous regarding the necessity for a pause and then gradual reduction in the range and extent of trade controls. The official WEC report declared uncategorically that "the time has come to put an end to the increase in tariffs and to move in the opposite direction" (LON 1927a: 32). Confer-

---

[1] Eichengreen (1984: 364) refers to "Keynes's repeated shifts on the need for protection." We note Keynes's conviction by the 1940s that to "restore the balance of international commerce by restriction and discrimination" was a "false approach" after all (Keynes 1979: 223).

[2] Quoted in Heilperin (1946: 147).

ence memoranda and subsequent discussion were well aware of contemporary realities; they were adamant for instance, that "stability" of tariff systems was paramount although it was recognized how rapidly changing exchange rates gave impetus to change tariff regimes (Rappard 1930: 143). An undeniable implication of the "stable tariffs" argument was that the volume and value of trade can expand without altering existing tariffs in an upward direction.

To reorganize *ab ovo* international protectionism and by implication world production was not on the WEC agenda. Containing and reducing existing levels of protection was, however, the essence of the conference final reports. In addition, the conference attempted to clarify the meaning and practice of dumping (conceived pejoratively), assisted by important technical input from LON adviser Jacob Viner (1926). The conference also urged greater international uniformity and modernization of tariff nomenclature (LON 1927a: Part vi).

Altogether, the WEC discussions, resolutions, and reports culminated in a manifesto in favor of moving, through a process of nonbinding international cooperation, toward *freer* trade. That is what the WEC final report meant by "liberty of trading" (Ibid., 22).[3] The direction rather than the timing and extent of the movement toward free trade seemed paramount. Three lines of action were envisaged in that movement: unilateral tariff reductions, bilateral treaties, and multilateral conventions. An Economic Consultative Committee was established at the LON in Geneva to monitor these actions. An underlying current of censure and moral approbation, as the case demanded, pervades its annual reports. In its early reports it expresses general satisfaction, after some quite detailed international surveys, that upward movement in tariffs had been arrested (LON 1928, 1929). An implicit presumption in these post-WEC League discussions was that tariffs confer a reduction in living standards in all countries – and not that some may lose and others gain by a tariff change. The notion of optimal tariffs designed for one country was either not at this stage understood in Geneva or more likely it was disregarded as impractical.

A tendency to support free trade is noticeable in all LON research reports, including the work of researchers at the International Labour Organization. A report originating from the ILO Research Division averred confidently that "[e]conomic *rapprochement* and the reduction

---

[3] The eminent Italian economist, Carrado Gini, captured the spirit of the WEC. He remarked portentously in conference discussion that the "complete execution of the free trade solution . . . would not be opportune unless a 'Super State' could guarantee the continuity of such a policy, even in times of economic crisis" (quoted in Manoilesco 1931: 223 n. 1).

of tariff barriers as foreshadowed by the World Economic Conference of 1927 will facilitate the permanent improvement of real wage standards" (Richardson 1928: 201). Furthermore, the League's annual *World Economic Survey* (*WES*) produced by LON economists J.B. Condliffe and later James Meade, did not desist from dealing with problems of international trade policy that involved value judgements in favor of liberal, freer trade policy.[4] Bertil Ohlin prepared a study which was the forerunner to the *WES* (Ohlin 1931a). He collaborated with the Economic Intelligence Service of the League and ILO economists in surveying the course of the economic depression up to mid-1931. Another principal set of intellectual inputs for this survey were submissions by eighteen economic research institutes and advisory councils from League member countries.[5] Ohlin held the requisite outlook for Geneva: He had already aligned himself with the "policy of Geneva" in his earlier "Plea for Freer Trade" (Ohlin 1928).

The Ohlin (1931a) report made three main points with respect to world trade policies. First, the rise of import duties evident from 1929 had increased "the general feeling of uncertainty" (p. 222), with deleterious effects on investment expenditure and employment. A study commissioned by the ILO supported this conclusion: Commercial policies can "beget uncertainty" when continual "changes in tariffs make it impossible to place long contracts." As well, upward shifts in protective duties tended to raise domestic production costs in some countries imposing those duties to the point of neutralizing the protective employment effect of the tariff. A subsequent assertion that "it does not seem to be in the least doubtful" that, following such upward shifts, the net outcome for all countries since 1927 was a contraction in (some vaguely defined) aggregate world output and employment could not be corroborated (Ansiaux 1931: 148, 151, 155, 170–71). The assertion contained a normative comparison of well-being between losing and gaining nations.

The second finding of the Ohlin report derived from careful empirical work that illustrated that "Belgium, Holland and Scandinavian countries whose domestic markets are the least sheltered against the varying forces of international competition" had, by mid-1931, been the least

---

[4] Roy Harrod (1937: 707) noted that the author of the *WES* embarked upon "occasional essays in interpretation," exposing the "fallacies and excesses" in international economic policy. From 1947 the *WES* became the reponsibility of the United Nations. The retitled *World Economic Reports* were written by staff at the Economic and Stability Section, under the direction of Kalecki until 1954.

[5] Ohlin worked on the report in Geneva from January–August 1931. A list of institutes and councils is contained in Ohlin (1931a: 9–11). Notable individuals consulted included: Hayek and Morgenstern (Austria); Ernst Wagemann (Germany); Verrijn Stuart (Netherlands); and H.D. Henderson (United Kingdom).

affected by depression conditions (p. 235). This historically contingent evidence indicated that by not reacting to greater foreign protectionism nations may avoid damaging their domestic economies twice-over: Simply retaliating by raising tariffs or using other trade restrictions can reduce the efficiency of local production.

Thirdly, the Ohlin report demonstrated that terms of trade had moved in favor of nations producing tradeable manufactures as opposed to primary products (p. 233). At first glance, the terms of trade data in the report suggested support for the views of Graham (1923), Manoilesco (1931), and other contemporary economists whose work pointed to the need for permanent protection for nations wishing to sustain an import-competing, labor-intensive manufacturing sector. Protection, under certain conditions, could transfer labor (and other factors) from low-wage (for example, primary activities) to high-wage industries.[6] In the League's and Ohlin's view, the policy implications of terms of trade arguments for protection were not obvious. At least three grounds were presented in League research for demurring from the protectionist implications of data in Ohlin's report. The first ground derived from close study of real cases and country experiences and of data produced by the Economic Intelligence Service of the League; the second turned on monopolistic phenomena evident in different countries and the third concerned the relationships, if any, between trade restrictions and international transmission of the business cycle. We will discuss these matters *seriatim*.

In taking an ardent liberal, internationalist perspective on the economic conditions prevailing in the early 1930s, Ohlin's report observed a world which was heterogenous with countries in markedly different stages of development, with different degrees of dependence on tradeable goods and exhibiting asymmetries in economic responses to tariff changes. Therefore the differential effects of a downturn in the international business cycle could not easily be forecast, and the extensive use of trade restrictions to create a viable manufacturing sector in any country was no guarantee of immunity from depression:

> Some economists . . . argue that countries in which a balance between the different industries exists – for instance between agriculture and manufactures – are able to resist better than others the disturbing effects of a worldwide depression . . . It is difficult to see how one relationship between various industries should be more natural or ensure greater stability than another. Obviously, however, countries depending only on one or a small number of industries suffer to an exceptional

---

[6] Of course, the subsequent income-distribution consequences were later analyzed and formalized by Stopler and Samuelson (1941).

degree if their industry or industries happen to be severely depressed. Such has been the case of a great number of countries in Latin America and Africa. On the other hand, conditions have been favourable in certain countries with specialised industries which have been relatively little affected. The majority of European States have a varied economic life. Such countries have reached a degree of self-sufficiency as a result of which disturbances in the outside world, acting on their foreign trade, affect them relatively little. During the present depression, the prices of commodities entering into international trade have in general fallen considerably more than those of goods produced for the home market only. Hence countries for which foreign trade is of great importance, such as Great Britain and most extra-European countries with a specialised type of industry, felt the effects of the slump more quickly and more acutely than most others (Ohlin 1931a: 234).

In addition, the variety of international experiences was also brought into sharp focus when considering the internal mobility of factors after market imperfections supervened. In short, monopolistic phenomena blurred the terms of trade argument for protection. Factor mobility in particular was not always perfect within nation-states such that it did not respond quickly to market price signals or tariff-influenced price signals. The internal adjustability of prices and factors figured as a major consideration in Ohlin's report. He referred to the widespread "inelasticity of wages" (p. 231). Moreover, he argued that greater "flexibility in the price system" (p. 269) may encourage greater mobility of factors between industrial sectors, occupations, and regions. However, an overwhelming body of evidence submitted through the League suggested extensive wage and price inflexibility in member countries.[7] Imperfect competition was also a feature of labor markets; noncompeting groups were the norm.[8] Consequently, if a nation's trade pattern alters unfavorably it is not able to respond quickly by changing that pattern appropriately. Increasing labor transference by subsidizing the use of labor in specific activities was considered a better response from an international standpoint, compared with various forms of external trade protection. Always preferred in Geneva research (for example, at the ILO) were *direct* domestic policy responses to market failure over trade interventions.

The Ohlin report set in motion League research on the international transmission of the business cycle in the context of rising protectionism in the 1930s. Folke Hilgerdt, who joined the League Secretariat in 1933,

---

[7] Thus, the "present economic system is based on adjustment through changes in the prices mechanism. Into this mechanism elements of rigidity have been introduced, which affect and to some extent impede its working" (p. 273).

[8] The problem of factor market distortions is taken up in a more formal analysis in Ohlin (1931b).

cast doubt on the benefits of trade restrictions of any kind for countries specializing in the production of manufactures for domestic consumption and/or for export. Hilgerdt (1933: 289) granted that "the policy of economic isolation" pursued in some countries and by the United States from the late 1920s, had the objective of stabilizing domestic production and prices. Nevertheless, despite tradeable goods forming a low proportion of national output in the United States, that country was not completely closed from the influence of the international business cycle since it was highly dependent on foreign raw materials. Under these circumstances, it was a patent error to maintain that the observed rise in tariffs could prevent changes in price relations originating from an external source. According to Hilgerdt, tariffs could not immunize a country from being drawn into the international business cycle. If the purpose,

> as is generally the case, is the protection of manufacturing industries, then raw materials are generally duty-free or only liable to very low rates, while manufacturing goods have to pay rates which increase with the degree of manufacture. The United States tariff is probably one of the most refined in this direction (p. 289).

Here tariffs can stabilize the prices of manufactures, but they were not regarded as useful at the time to stabilize marked fluctuations in the prices of raw materials. Drawing on data from the United States, Hilgerdt demonstrates that capacity constraints tended to raise the price margin between manufactures and primary products creating a temporary industrial boom.[9] Even without retaliatory tariffs, the demand for manufactures in raw-materials-producing countries will decline. Now a "liberal trade policy" mitigates against an ensuing, significant economic depression. The foreign demand for manufactures "has a stabilising effect upon industrial activity" (p. 290).

Two case studies are adduced to support Hilgerdt's contentions. First, in Germany, "no economic isolation of the same kind as in the United States prevailed before the depression and where, accordingly, a large part of the manufacturing industry was working for export, the export industry was an important stabilising factor." Second, in the United Kingdom, high raw materials prices are accompanied by increased foreign demand for industrial products and vice versa. That foreign raw materials producing countries are the main consumers of British exports

---

[9] In a contemporaneous article Keynes (1933) reflected on the drive for "national self-sufficiency." He recognized that self-sufficiency and hence internal stability through trade interventions (and possibly currency devaluations), would enable a country to break away from external price level fluctuations. Temporary trade benefits would ensue, although, and this is the point of Hilgerdt's contribution, the transmission of inflation can weaken the case for self-sufficiency.

compounded the problem of economic depression in the 1930s. So up to 1933, while some "modern economists seem to have deprived this doctrine [of free trade] of the bulk of its theoretical significance" (p. 289), Hilgerdt's evaluation of data collected by the League concluded that at least *freer* trade had much practical significance. The increasing trade policy interventions from the late 1920s created only very short-term benefits, and then only for the relatively closed economies such as the United States and France. National measures taken in isolation were fraught with dangers, one of which Hilgerdt identified as domestic inflationary pressures that contributed to the amplitude of the business cycle in the early 1930s.

In these early studies, the overriding conception of the world economy and international trade policy was one which emphasized interdependence. Exchange rate stability is usually assumed, perhaps reflecting misplaced confidence in eventual return to a gold standard. The world economy was not held together by one predominant trading nation, but many countries diverse in their degrees of dependence on tradeable goods. These countries were bound by long-run equilibrating tendencies in their economic interconnections, that is, by tendencies effected through compensatory internal price adjustments. Trade restrictions of any kind masked, but did not ultimately thwart, such adjustments. A debatable normative conclusion, at least from the stance of any *individual* country, was also drawn: Every nation is at a maximum in the long run with freer trade.[10]

DISTURBANCES TO INTERNATIONAL EQUILIBRIUM: LEAGUE ASSESSMENTS IN THE 1930s

Against the background of the Hawley-Smoot Tariff of 1930 and the new British tariff regime of 1931–32, the League's *World Economic Survey* (*WES*) presented a simple, "contracting spiral of world trade" in diagrammatic form (LON 1933a: 8) (see Figure 5.1).

Owing to a considerable fall in prices over the period, the value of trade figures (measured in terms of gold) are somewhat misleading, although the Economic Intelligence Service of the League also collected data on trade volumes (which declined by 25 percent, 1929–34; Condliffe 1935b: 23). John B. Condliffe, the author of *WES*, attributed the contracting spiral primarily and directly to "a veritable rise of economic armaments" due to a breakdown in the fragile spirit of international

---

[10] This normative proposition was formally explored by Samuelson (1938). The welfare economics of free trade in the late 1930s demonstrated that trade restrictions can improve the terms of trade and welfare of the country imposing them. It is not a foregone conclusion that world welfare improves since the gain of one country has to be set against the losses of others. This issue was *not* faced squarely in early Geneva research.

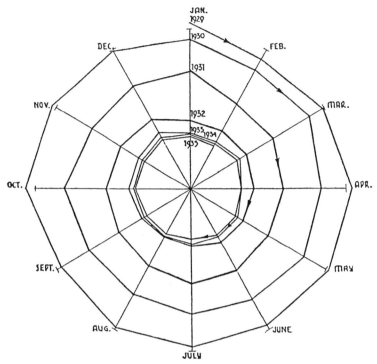

Figure 5.1 Contraction in the Value of World Trade Measured in Terms of Gold 1929–35 (*Source*: Condliffe [1935b: 24]. An earlier version appears in LON [1933a: 8].)

trade policy cooperation originally created at the 1927 WEC (Ibid., 25, 29). Quotas, prohibitions, higher tariff, and nontariff barriers and competitive devaluations compounded the problem. Diagrammatic analysis of the contracting spiral of world trade represented an early attempt to conceive of the world trading system in a dynamic sense by expressing trade as a recursive relationship; current trade flows depended on declining levels of earlier trade. While Condliffe's diagram was certainly rudimentary in nature (with no attempt to express trade relations in any quantifiable two dimensional space), it hinted at the more elaborate analysis of trade and economic development that was to be the hallmark of Swedish sequence analysis in the 1930s.[11]

---

[11] Erik Lundberg's (1930; 1937) research on the concept of economic equilibrium in particular adopted the sequence method in the study of macroeconomic fluctuations. Lundberg's "ultimate objective was to explore economic change on the general or total system level" through examining the possible transition paths of the economy with first-order

League research produced data showing relatively price-inelastic demand for agricultural commodities in importing countries. Now, if the elasticity of foreign demand is not great, this provides a rationale for any *one* country autonomously to introduce restrictions on trade and increase domestic employment. The latter would be bolstered if actual or potential retaliatory measures did not have much potency for the country in question (Condliffe 1933b: 654–55; Ohlin 1936: 103). Here immediate domestic employment effects may be the *singular* trade policy desideratum rather than the value or volume of trade. Notwithstanding this well-understood rationale in Geneva (and even the "optimum tariff" argument was vaguely recognized in relevant research reports from the early 1930s), it did not seem to League researchers that these arguments were applicable to a world which had embraced a generalized acceleration of trade restrictions. That these restrictions were accompanied by an ongoing reduction in the volume and value of trade reinforced their skepticism. The other argument which could have been made but was not, would have likened tariffs to monopoly restrictions in which case the loss imposed in some countries may be represented, under certain conditions, as being greater than the gain to the tariff implementing country. The maintenance of all the resource allocative inefficiencies implied thereby would have strengthened the League's preference for freer trade. However, not until the mid-1940s was this argument formally expressed in the literature on trade theory.[12]

Condliffe (1933b: 655) concluded gloomily that "a reduction of tariffs" from 1933 "will not alone suffice to restore world trade." The wholly provisional, bilateral character of international trade policy negotiations post-1932 was not a cause for celebration. The "new protectionism" or "new mercantilism" as it was later dubbed, made extensive use of discriminatory bilateral tariff treaties, monetary and quantitative restrictions (LON 1937a: 192; Condliffe 1941: 307). The *WES* surveyed the content of these developments, concluding that they were invariably "short-term compromises . . . designed to make possible the continuance of at least a minimum of foreign trade," especially in raw materials (LON 1933a: 206). The noticeable trend toward bilateralism had the policy

difference equations (Henriksson 1996: 349). This approach was later applauded by Baumol as forming the foundations of formal economic dynamics (Baumol 1991; see also Jonung 1991: 12).

[12] Samuelson, Scitovsky, and Lerner were the leading theorists on this matter. See Metzler (1949: 74–75). Broader efficiency considerations bearing on this argument are canvassed in Ohlin (1936: 63) and we find Ohlin's (1938: 506) review of Haberler (1936) anticipates results of the relevant positive trade analysis in the 1940s: "Surely if a free-trade country alone raises tariffs during a depression, it can bring about a large increase in employment, and part of it may be retained even if other countries retaliate."

objective of trade balance equalization; narrow arrangements were the norm so that combining certain import-export arrangements with "most favoured" third parties was usually ruled out. Presumptively, trade-diverting effects were thought to dominate trade-creating effects. There-fore, while the trend toward bilateralism led to some downward tariff adjustments, it could not quell the "present riot of nationalism." However "defensible such policies may have been in particular cases, they are in aggregate a flight from reality. The reality is that the peoples of the world are, and must be, interdependent" (LON 1936a: 192).[13]

The impulse exclusively to adopt bilateral policy reforms was demon-strably linked to the difficulty in procuring raw materials. The outcome was a set of complex, disparate, and unstable short-term relationships. Reciprocation was subject to political factors and power considerations. A new trend was discernible in trade relations: In order to avoid retal-iatory measures, each country imposed new restrictions on the products of countries in relation to which its bargaining power was strongest, that is, with which it had a positive trade balance (LON 1933b: 30). This was a contagious policy which had little to do with a more liberal approach to commercial policy or a "second best" option to freer trade. The League's report on raw materials trade concluded that bilateral agree-ments had not significantly facilitated access to markets for manufactures (LON 1937b: 28). The "new protectionism" was changing the structure of world trade. The Geneva researchers occupied a sheltered observa-tory so to speak – speculating on an intensifying international struggle resulting in the domination of underdeveloped countries by strong indus-trial nations which would ultimately endanger world peace. Moreover, the League observed trade policy regimes informed by the erroneous belief that there was a constant market which each country can reserve for itself.[14]

---

[13] In the view of one commentator – Herbert Feis, sometime consultant to the ILO – this Geneva doctrine of internationalism, as applied to trade policy, had severe limitations: "Those who formulated the doctrine . . . often pointed out the great variety of differ-ences between countries. But they insufficiently appreciated the importance of these dif-ferences, and the extent to which they lead to differences of policy as between countries. They under-estimated the possible advantages to *some* countries at *some* times of forming *special* and perhaps *exclusive* economic connections. The uniform policy set forward as a guide often could not provide the result that particular countries, with their individual difficulties and characteristics, at the moment wanted most. They turned to other possibilities, though often the advantage was temporary or illusory" (Feis 1940: 41, emphasis in original).

[14] Later Condliffe (1941: 288) used a more sweeping generalization to describe those trade policy developments in the 1930s which relied on bilateralism: They had "been used to complete the destruction of nineteenth-century trade and investment and with it the organization of world production by private enterprise." The LON (1942b: 71) chimed

The *WES* (LON 1937a: 183–84) denounced the bilateral "canalising" of world trade because it broke the "essential links in the chains of transactions; it cause[d] the unprecedented fluctuations in prices, the disorganization of production, default on financial obligations and piling up of stocks . . . [which] are still leading to fresh disturbances of international economic relations." Folke Hilgerdt, the LON specialist researcher in trade policy, wrote in 1935 that a

> bilateral system of trade leads, sooner or later, to the division of this [world] market into several, with different price levels and no free admittance. Already certain countries in Central Europe have been partly shut out from the world market and compelled to pay higher prices for their imports than those prevailing in that market. This system, if any, is full of confusion and complications (Hilgerdt 1935: 187).

Further, if the proponents of bilateralism thought that the policy would guarantee participating nations insulation from cyclical fluctuations transmitted from wider international sources, they were quite mistaken, at least on Hilgerdt's review of the evidence.[15] Previously League research conceived of the world economy as an organized series of closely interlocked and interdependent markets that adjusted comparatively smoothly. The Geneva ideal of competitive, multilateral trade based on equivalence of trading opportunities was an anachronism elsewhere.[16] In seeking intellectually defensible economic arguments for their disdain of bilateralism the League economists conjoined, rather casually, their more applied work on trade patterns and policies with general equilibrium analysis in the Walras-Cassel tradition (and Ohlin's innovatory work in that tradition in particular).

Condliffe's articles in *Svenska Handelsbanken (Index)* illuminated the idea that international trading relationships are underpinned by an "economic equilibrium" which "has proved a very powerful instrument of analysis if only because it emphasizes so strongly the multilateral and interdependent nature of all causation that must be reckoned with in all economic phenomena." The foundations of equilibrium are located in

in with the remark that each "bilateral agreement was *sui generis*, designed to meet the special trade requirements of, and to afford effective reciprocal advantage to, the signatories. Commercial agreements, in truth, became instruments of commercial warfare."

[15] See Hilgerdt (1935: 183–86).

[16] That the now "normal" function of the nation-state was to *plan* foreign trade was anathema in Geneva (see Condliffe 1941 and Heilperin 1946). And the direction of policy formulation had deviated from a clear focus on tariff instability which preoccupied post-1927 WEC discussions. Tariffs *per se* were playing a "much less important role than formerly" (LON 1937a: 185). More insidious controls were now in place internationally.

"the theory of pricing" (Condliffe 1933a: 226). Multimarket, country, and regional interdependence had taken the form of competitive "price bargaining" over tradeable goods and services, where the prices were conferred with integrity and stability by an internationally accepted gold standard. Condliffe paid obeisance to Ohlin and Haberler for extending the theory of pricing, as he called it, to international trade. Indeed, in his "Preface" to *Interregional and International Trade*, Ohlin (1933a: vii) acknowledged that he had constructed a theory of international trade "in harmony with the mutual-interdependence theory of pricing," citing, *inter alios*, Walras, Wicksell, and Cassel as precursors.

Condliffe contributed a loose concept of "international equilibrium" constructed at a lower level of abstraction from that found in the contemporary formal, high theory of Ohlin and Haberler. He wished to move fluidly between observation of actual trade relationships, patterns, and problems, and analytical developments in contemporary trade theory. Ohlin's work became a subject for critical scrutiny. Condliffe claimed that his general perspective encompassed "dynamic" economic forces in a real "network of international trade" (1933a: 229; LON 1932b: 273). He perceived a "series of intersecting equilibria set in space as well as time," thus advancing beyond the static, spatial notions which were the hallmark of Ohlin's contribution. We are treated to a glimpse – only a hint of recognition – that Ohlin's theoretical apparatus was difficult to apply to the evolution of international trade in the 1930s.[17] Condliffe's is still a nonmonetary, classical "theory" of international trade with price changes (rather than, say, Keynesian effective demand or income changes) acting as the centerpiece of international adjustment. The purported increasing inflexibility of national price structures during the early 1930s had not merely shattered any semblance of international equilibrium; it also undermined the possibility of smooth, low-adjustment cost transitions from one equilibrium to another as world trade and living standards increased *pari passu* (Condliffe 1933a: 233). The world economy was no longer an organized, "developing organic whole" precisely because price signals were not able to operate in a manner that automatically supported world trade.

Following Ohlin and Haberler (as we noted in Chapter 2 the latter joined League researchers in 1934 through 1936), the imposition of

---

[17] Ohlin (1938: 498 n. 1) later remarked in a characteristic, self-effacing manner: "a great defect of my own work . . . [is] that the "dynamic" parts – which occupy a large part of the book [Ohlin 1933] – are interwoven with the "static" parts in a confusing manner. By "dynamic" I mean anything that is relative to *time*, that is, deals with *successive* stages – while a "static" theory compares *alternative* positions, without considering the transition from one to the other" (his emphasis).

higher trade barriers is interpreted as being equivalent to creating more space barriers, pushing national markets apart and thereby adding more noise in the transmission of market prices. International competition working through price changes in fact brought spatially dispersed markets into a closely bound network that could adjust quickly to exogenous shocks (Condliffe 1933a: 236–37; LON 1936a: 184). In a subsequent article Condliffe (1935a: 3) did not explicitly recognize the Heckscher-Ohlin result on factor price equalization, but he broadened the idea in asserting that the international gold standard operating in an environment of "relatively free trade" produced "harmonisation, by international competition, of the different national price and cost structures." Trade restrictions disrupt these stable "natural" structures. However, to the extent that trade restrictions, especially tariffs, are not altered too frequently the price system could work within and through such barriers. By contrast, quotas and quantitative prohibitions place "insuperable obstacles" to the operation of market prices since they cut off price signals altogether.

In view of the foregoing considerations, by early 1935, Condliffe communicated what was a carefully reformulated Geneva position. Tariff changes and price changes effected by currency adjustments were adjudged to be more acceptable responses to balance of payments problems for any country. These instruments were tolerable, second-best, short-run adjuncts to a long-run policy agenda emphasizing freer trade. Careful sequencing of trade policy changes will usually be important. Thus a distinction is drawn between tolerable short-run trade interventions and long-run liberalization through negotiated, reciprocal tariff reductions.[18] No country, in this view, could afford to adopt a freer trade policy if other countries persisted with the opposite policy. The Agenda for the 1933 Lausanne WEC drawn up by LON economists after wide consultation with experts from member nations, singled out nontariff barriers, including exchange controls and special bilateral clearing agreements affecting international payments, as universally pernicious. Altogether

> they operate so as to divert trade into artificial channels, to give artificial advantages to producers in the countries employing them, and to involve discrimination in the discharge of accumulated and current debts as between creditors of different nationalities (WEC 1933: 58–59).

In promising to render a purely bilateral character to international economic relations without any demonstrable trade-creating benefits, the

---

[18] See WEC (1933: 63) and LON (1936b).

Conference Agenda roundly denounced such barriers; the anonymous LON drafters of the 1933 WEC Agenda were "unanimous in affirming the necessity that action for removal of the [nontariff] restrictions on international trade . . . should be taken as soon as possible" (p. 61). In the long-run scenario constructed in Geneva during the mid-1930s, all countries were exhorted to adopt a general principle turning on "gradual removal . . . of trade restrictions" – especially of quotas and exchange controls – a principle little changed from that adopted at the 1927 WEC.[19] It was also fully endorsed by ILO economists (Martin 1936: 640–41; 1937: 196). There is a crucial shift in perspective here; it contains an insight predating Samuelson's (1939b) positive, analytical contribution on the gains from international trade. Condliffe's argument, deriving for the most part from analysis of data flowing into the League's Economic and Financial Section, was similar to Samuelson's, for it reduces to the proposition that some degree of trade, however restricted by tariffs in particular, is necessarily better for all countries than no trade.[20] We turn in the next section to the Geneva proposition that multilateral trade is economically superior to other trading relationships in the long run.

FOLKE HILGERDT'S PIONEERING CALCULATIONS AND REVISIONS IN GENEVA TRADE POLICY DOCTRINE

When Hilgerdt (1942) operationalized Condliffe's "network of world trade" idea, Geneva researchers were no longer subjecting to censure the whole host of trade interventions introduced during the 1930s. Hilgerdt's data may have engendered some confidence in the system of multilateral trade (which he depicted in a flow diagram reproduced as Figure 5.2 as follows). His calculations for 1938 in Figure 5.2 present a system of economic interdependence which had not been extinguished by the expansion of trade barriers in the 1930s; only a "gradual disintegration" was observed compared to a similar model constructed for 1928, so the network was still intact (Hilgerdt 1942: 78, 91).[21]

---

[19] Condliffe (1935a: 16). This exhortation was entirely consistent with a 1936 tripartite agreement on commercial policy between France, the United Kingdom, and the United States which vowed to "attach the greatest importance to action being taken without delay to relax progressively the present system of quotas and exchange controls with a view to their abolition" (Martin 1937: 189). Again, tariffs were conspicuously excepted.

[20] Condliffe's view diverges from Samuelson's results which held for tariffs or quantitative controls.

[21] See also LON (1941: 80) which demonstrates how many European countries "managed to maintain their trade with some degree of success during this period of hampered international transactions." It was accepted at the League that *substantive* most favored nation clauses granting benefits to third parties in trade agreements, preferential agreements in other spheres and regional agreements, were all conducive to the maintenance

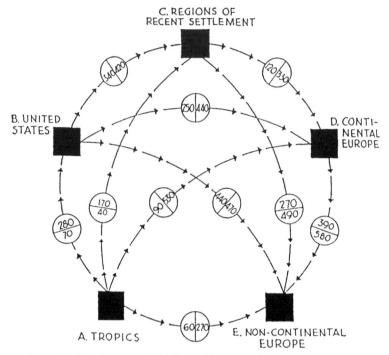

Figure 5.2 The System of Multilateral Trade, as Reflected by the Orientation of Balances of Merchandise Trade in 1938 (*Note*: The balances derived from [this figure] are given in millions of dollars. Both import and export balances are shown: the smaller of the two figures in each circle represents export balances of the group from which the arrows emerge, and the larger figure the import balance of the group to which the arrows point. The difference between the amounts in question is due largely to the inclusion in imports of transport costs between the frontiers of the exporting and importing countries. In certain cases, however, it appears due to the overvaluation of imports by countries applying exchange control (as conversion to dollars was made at official rates of exchange).) (*Source*: Hilgerdt (1942: 90).[22])

His influential, pioneering model demonstrates the immense quantitative significance of multilateral trade in 1938, and was described in League publicity as a depiction of a well-functioning "worldwide vascu-

---

of international trade that in practice advanced beyond narrow bilateralism. These agreements were legitimate second-best options (LON 1939c: 159; Condliffe 1941: 295–327; LON 1942b: 58, 70, 127).

[22] As early as 1935, Hilgerdt had experimented with diagrammatic representations of international trade and payments flows. See his "triangular" representations focussing on the trade balances of the United Kingdom in Hilgerdt (1935: 179).

lar system" (LON 1942b: 165). Hilgerdt's (1943) paper in the *American Economic Review* represented his calculations as providing evidence for arguments promoting multilateral trade – they were not to be regarded as mere historical artifacts. His data for 1938 show a latent degree of international integration. The full potential of multilateral trade may be actualized through postwar international organization and coordination on an extensive scale (p. 407). Just how that outcome might be effected remained opaque.

Disturbances to the network of world trade in the late 1920s and early 1930s were not directly attributable to modifications in commercial policy, but to deeper cyclical causes. Conversely, the improved state of international trade identified in the *WES* for 1937–38, "was the result rather of general economic recovery than of any great change in commercial policy" (LON 1939c: 137). That each country's trade interventions reduced the volume and value of trade in the aggregate from the early 1930s was viewed as an unwanted consequence of rational, temporary actions taken to meet the exigencies of international balance in the face of an exogenous economic disturbance. Trade policy responses were often destabilizing of the international "vascular" flow. The supervening impact of war made the matter worse and the "temporary" expedients tended to persist and be extended. Condliffe and Stevenson (1944: 64), reporting for the ILO, reviewed Hilgerdt's model, concluding that "economic systems are no longer meshed into a stable international equilibrium." War, not trade interventions as such, was also a prime cause of breakdown. And, notwithstanding the influence of economic forces, together with the advent of full-scale war in 1939, the motive of national aggrandizement and political power was not underestimated as a separate influence, in principle, explaining the rise of protectionism. Noneconomic forces were attributed considerable weight, though perhaps rather belatedly, by researchers in international organizations. For example a widely held view in Geneva though, at least in retrospect, was that:

> during the five or six years that led to the outbreak of war in 1939 ... [e]conomic considerations were increasingly subordinated to political ends. Commercial policy became increasingly a form of economic warfare (LON 1944: 209).

Influenced by the effect of trade policies on labor in particular, ILO economists also shared the shift in perspective in Geneva toward accepting the need for trade interventions in the short run. The ILO director averred in 1939 that economic "isolation is no solution to the problem presented by the unequal distribution of natural resources and the need for markets." The gradual "withdrawal of nations from the world system of trade" observed in the 1930s was tantamount to requiring workers to work longer, eat less and lower quality food, and tolerate poorer housing conditions (ILO 1939a: 32). The consequences notwithstanding, trade restrictions in the 1930s needed to be appreciated as policy responses used to maintain high levels of employment, "at least for a limited time" (ILO 1940a: 5–6, 69–70). Another influential researcher in Geneva characterized this view as a legitimate socioeconomic argument. Thus, William Rappard's 1938 Cobden Lecture rated this position as "[m]uch more important than either the purely economic or financial" case for trade interventions. The objective of governments is "to avoid the sudden dislocation of the social and economic structure . . . [;] to combat unemployment or to protect its balance of payments" (Rappard 1938: 56).[23]

The ILO regarded real wages, and not just the prevention of both mass unemployment and social instability, as a prime consideration. A special study investigated the matter at length (ILO 1940a). Its main theme – that the relationship between foreign trade, wages, and employment "rests on an *a priori* basis and is not therefore merely a historical accident" – caused some consternation among ILO officials.[24] One controversial result was that under certain conditions, factor prices, especially real labor incomes, were positively responsive to the degree of trade dependence. The data were presented (see Table 5.1):

These data were interpreted to mean that greater trade dependence in terms of the maintenance of the volume of exports and imports of manufactures implied higher real labor incomes than otherwise. Reference to the level of employment in this ILO analysis is conspicuously absent (and was probably a reason for the debate which ensued at the ILO over publication and interpretation of these data). In the countries listed in Table 5.1, changes in the level of protection from 1929 to 1932 were not taken into account. The conclusion drawn is that insofar as trade regulation inhibits trade in manufactures, it must reduce real wages in countries specializing in manufactures. Two critical variables were acknowledged: (1.) the proportion of output of separate countries dependent on exports and imports and (2.) the terms of trade faced by separate countries. Now Table 5.1 and the accompanying interpretation relied on the first variable to the exclusion of possible terms of trade effects. The relative importance of (1.) and (2.) in relation to real wages and employment were uppermost in the minds of those interested in the total effects of trade policy. Considering (2.),

> it is conceivable that a country which has restricted its foreign trade might nevertheless be able to maintain a higher level of real income for labour than other countries *in which the volume of international com-*

[23] Rappard was Director of the Geneva Graduate Institute of International Studies.
[24] ILO Archives EP/04 "Memorandum Concerning International Trade Study" (Robert M. Carr), 17/8/1939.

Table 5.1. Real Wages and Trade Dependence

1929–32 (1929 = 100)						
Quantum of Manufactured Imports, 1932		**Payrolls, 1932**		**Quantum of Manufactured Exports, 1932**		
Great Britain	65.2	Great Britain	96.7	Italy	75.8	
Italy	61.2	Italy	81.0	Great Britain	61.2	
United States	54.0	Germany	63.6	Germany	59.1	
Germany	46.4	United States	54.6	United States	38.4	
1932–36 (1932 = 100)						
Quantum of Manufactured Imports, 1936		**Payrolls, 1936**		**Quantum of Manufactured Exports, 1936**		
United States	160.0	United States	162.8	United States	160.4	
Great Britain	140.3	Great Britain	121.5	Great Britain	123.4	
Italy	74.3	Italy	102.8	Italy	88.5	

Source: ILO (1940a: 68).

> *merce remains unchanged.* For instance, the adverse effect of trade restrictions on the terms of trade of the latter might more than offset their advantages of specialisation arising from international commerce (ILO 1940a: 69, emphasis added).

Individual countries may, under the special conditions outlined in the foregoing passage, use protectionist policies "at least for a limited time" (Ibid.) to achieve both higher employment and real wages.[25] Grudging concessions to protectionism aside, the ILO report returned to the impact on allocative efficiency of trade interventions and, when considering uses of "the world's economic resources" rather than those of any one country, "a loss of efficiency" is implied by a general move toward extensive restrictions. Hence the imperative to focus on long-run international efficiency.

Researchers at the League appreciated the ILO point of view. There was much rigidity observed in economic structures, particularly in

---

[25] Not long after the ILO study, Stopler and Samuelson (1941) published their celebrated theorem stating that factor prices, including labor income, were positively responsive to changes in domestic prices caused by trade policy adjustments when those adjustments favored a labor-intensive, import-competing sector.

industrialized nations with highly specialized physical capital investment, and organized labor. The resistance of both capital and labor to cuts in nominal profits and wages respectively, induced attempts "to buttress existing industries by all appropriate means," notably by trade interventions (LON 1942b: 121–22). The Economic and Financial Section of the League went so far as to sympathize with exchange controls as "an essential prerequisite" for some countries aiming to defend their currencies against the background of a deteriorating trade balance (LON 1938b: 5). Emphatically *not* countenanced was the use of exchange controls or other trade interventions to maintain large export surpluses rather than to reduce unsustainable deficits. Exchange rate realignments were preferred as a means of preventing a cumulative decline in the volume of world trade and restoring capital movements between countries. Such realignments were an integral part of a long-run agenda for a freer world trading system. However, exchange rate changes should not in principle be used in a manner analogous to other trade restrictions simply to export unemployment – a distinction which in practice was often difficult to make. By contrast, in the plethora of reports from the ILO, the League, and the Geneva Graduate Institute of International Studies in the 1940s on trade-related issues, it is difficult to find one kind word for quantitative trade controls. The following message epitomizes the attitude widespread in international organizations in the mid-1940s:

> We may characterise [quantitative trade controls] as a 'noncomfortable' type of interference, a foreign substance, as it were, in the body of the free economy which necessarily leads to dangerous ulcerations and suppurations and threatens to weaken or undermine the individualist economy altogether. On the other hand, customs tariffs, even high ones, [are] ... 'comfortable' interferences which do not destroy the price mechanism on the functioning of which a private enterprise economy must depend (Haberler 1943b: 20).

The Haberler-led study for the League denounced quantitative controls regarding them as a resort to "the line of least resistance" when less damaging forms of intervention allowing the price mechanism to function could have been employed. If quotas were still preferred then, at the very least, import licenses should be auctioned to the highest bidder (Haberler 1943b: 37, 41).[26]

---

[26] This penchant to use the price mechanism wherever possible is the result, for the most part, of an *a priori*, "liberal" position on international political economy. Thomas Balogh (1944: 258, 260) correctly discerned that the Haberler study sometimes expressed "liberal" preconceptions that were "wholly unsupported by analysis."

FREER TRADE, INTERNATIONAL AGREEMENTS, AND MACROECONOMIC MANAGEMENT

In the realm of positive trade analysis, when Tibor Scitovsky (1942) reconsidered the theory of tariffs he unwittingly provided the intellectual rationale for a long-running Geneva theme insisting on the need for international cooperation in trade policy making.[27] Intractable political constraints were often deliberately set aside when League researchers prescribed more cooperation (LON 1939b). They knew well that economic and political factors were intimately connected and the mere desire for cooperation was insufficient to ensure successful collaboration. Scitovsky demonstrated two outcomes that tariff retaliation would have: bilateral barter arrangements or unstable short-term tariff bargaining games. Tariffs were a rational reaction by one country in order to profit (or at least to obtain a more favorable trading position) *vis-à-vis* the actions of others. The effect of *all* countries following a policy of retaliation could be to reduce the welfare of each of them – but this was not foreseen by any one player. Once the game had begun, this "rational" interest in higher tariffs not only (and unintentionally) described aspects of actual trade policy practice in the 1930s quite well; it was remarkably consistent with the Geneva researchers' interpretation of trade interventions in that period. Furthermore, Scitovsky characterized an "ideal" free trade world as a cartel which contained forces tending toward disintegration unless some international trade conventions were established and enforced.

Viner's (1943) study for the League seemed to have Scitovsky's results in mind. Viner accepted as given that some countries rigidly controlled their trade relations. To avoid complete disintegration and regression toward state-controlled bilateral arrangements he suggested a multilateral conference – not merely for a rapprochement between countries – but to formulate a binding "international convention." That convention would set a time schedule for reducing trade restrictions postwar, define illegitimate trade practices, and establish an international agency to monitor and arbitrate on changes to trade interventions. All this accorded well with the normative exhortations from Geneva throughout

---

[27] The best capsule summary of this theme is Condliffe (1941: 355–94). It is also a theme in James Meade's work before he joined the League in 1937 (see Meade 1933). The WES which Meade compiled from 1938 also reiterates the international cooperation theme in relation to trade policy (LON 1939c: 165). Although Keynes championed the ideal of international cooperation he specifically nominated monetary arrangements and public investment rather than trade policy (Keynes 1981: 151–53). See also Rappard (1925: 70–85) on League efforts to effect international cooperation in the early 1920s.

the 1930s in favor of freer trade through international cooperation. These were not empty, pious exhortations because they derived from extensive empirical work and case studies and turned on the consequences of trade interventions (although they sometimes lacked formal theoretical foundations). The policy desiderata were nevertheless quite transparent; microeconomic liberalization must be assisted by an international management mechanism for meaningful trade policy reform incorporating something like an international code of conduct. Later, of course, this was ultimately realized by the machinery of the GATT.[28]

Microeconomic liberalization coupled with macroeconomic management (including international management) were central to League reports in the 1940s. Were these ideas compatible? The problem of how to engender greater efficiency and order in international trade through liberalization had to be reconciled with "Keynesian-type" macroeconomic policies which were vital instruments available to policy makers desiring to increase employment in a world of persistent demand deficiency (LON 1945a: 160–68). Employment levels were no longer permitted to fluctuate markedly from a high level. Discriminatory trade and exchange restrictions could therefore be justified to reduce the propensity to import when the high employment objective conflicts with exchange rate stability and the maintenance of favorable terms of trade. Keynes's (1936: 338–39) important caveat was that the avowedly "treacherous instrument" of trade restrictions should *not* be part of an "immoderate policy" to secure and maintain a maximum favorable trade balance.

The full employment objective could conflict with measures to preserve and extend international collaboration on trade policy, especially when the volatile forces of international competition might be allowed full dominion. Freer trade would be resisted by vested interests, often even more stridently when macroeconomic conditions were not favorable to them. As James Meade wrote in the League's *WES* for 1937–38, "attempts to secure freedom of trade are intimately connected with the maintenance of buying power" (LON 1939c: 165). In accepting the basic Keynesian position – advocacy of monetary and fiscal policy activism in pursuit of full employment – League economists were set free to argue vigorously that commercial policy no longer be used as an instrument of national countercyclical policy. If trade restrictions are embedded

> in the international economic structure, they raise the question whether any nation can afford to permit an internal revival to stimulate an

---

[28] Haberler collaborated with League researchers to produce a report on quantitative trade restrictions which came close to anticipating postwar developments. The report recommended international supervision of trade intervention and the use of an international veto mechanism (Haberler 1943b: 45).

expansion of imports when there exists the possibility that . . . special discriminatory devices may be employed to prevent the subsequent closing of the gap [in trade balances] thus created . . . [E]very country would be compelled to adopt similar devices in order to prevent its internal revival from stimulating its import requirements . . . Stability would be purchased at the cost of poverty (LON 1945a: 109).[29]

ILO reports reflected on deeper issues in this connection. Full employment may well be achieved but living standards for those employed could be improved by adopting freer trade. Further, the long-run *maintenance* of full employment depended on the growth of world trade (Condliffe and Stevenson 1944: 75–76, 112; Martin 1937: 196). A more liberal commercial policy assured more "efficient employment" (LON 1945c: 30). Allocative efficiency, it was insisted, must not be forgotten if the growth of world trade was an objective. Instead of the terms of commercial agreements made by governments *primarily* determining trade relations, competition between buyers and sellers and associated market prices should be allowed greater sway by comparison with events in the 1930s. Moreover, commercial agreements that contemplated trade *and* payments arrangements bestowing more extensive powers on the rights of private individuals to trade on the basis of mutual benefit were eminently preferable. (By contrast intergovernmental – especially bilateral – agreements in the 1930s tended to restrict and regulate to the point where private international financial relations were superseded.) It was now thought (by the mid-1940s) that with careful macroeconomic management the stability-poverty tradeoff may be avoided. General adoption of Keynesian macroeconomic policies would provide the prerequisites for international cooperation on other matters including trade policy (LON 1945c: 64). Though, and this recognition was crucial for distinguishing the LON position from later UN obfuscation of the matter, Keynesian domestic policy instruments by no means guaranteed high levels of economic growth and development. The volume of world trade was critical in respect to the latter; less-developed nations, so dependent on commodity exports, relied on freer trade, in particular, access to the markets of larger industrialized nations, to promote growth.[30] Many small open economies in fact relied on freer trade to

---

[29] A similar line of argument is pursued in Nurkse's report for the LON in 1944: "[C]ommercial policy was influenced to a great extent . . . by attempts to use it in a general manner as a form of national anti-depression policy." The deleterious consequences are then outlined (LON 1944: 206–07).

[30] Compare remarks made by the U.N. Secretary-General in 1947 to the effect that other factors influencing "the underdevelopment of many areas of the world are much more serious and fundamental in their effect on the volume of world trade than the restrictive practices which are often merely the secondary phenomena of profound economic

secure full, efficient employment. In this connection, the League's (1945a: 242) report looking toward postwar stability remarked on the need to combine domestic Keynesian-type policies with trade policy reform. It noted

> the dependence of many agricultural and mining countries upon foreign trade; but certain highly industrialized countries are scarcely less dependent. When capital goods constitute a large proportion of their exports, these countries are particularly susceptible to fluctuations in economic activity abroad. When in addition their imports consist largely of indispensable foodstuffs, their balance of payments becomes particularly vulnerable. Neither these countries nor certain of the smaller industrialized states with highly specialized export industries can hope to maintain a high and stable level of employment by means of domestic compensatory polices alone.[31]

A clear sequencing preference emerged in Geneva research: Liberalization of trade policy encourages microeconomic adjustments only *after* domestic monetary and fiscal policies were used to manage aggregate demand and the exchange rate used to manage trade imbalances. *A fortiori*, exchange rate management would be more effective with freer trade. Exchange rate adjustments could also be implemented in an orderly fashion by establishing a managed world currency system but this was dependent on international collaboration. Ragnar Nurkse (LON 1944: 208) explained the preferred course of action at the League in respect of commercial policy:

> [A]nything tending permanently to restrict and distort the international division of labour must lower the efficiency of economic effort and the standard of material welfare in all the countries concerned. While some of the social priority considerations inherent in commercial policy may have to be accepted as a datum . . . liberalization [can be promoted] by lessening the need for . . . the general uses of commercial policy in relation to the balance of payments.

Trade policy reform is more easily implemented against the wishes of sectional interests when there is full domestic employment. While the desirable direction of reform was clear, the difficulties of the reform task were not underestimated. Bilateral arrangements and, more crucially,

---

instability" (Brown 1957: 107). Here the positive contributions of a freer trade regime are minimized.

[31] Cf. Keynes's view in the *General Theory* which placed greater weight on the power of domestic policies: "[I]f nations can learn to provide themselves with full employment by their domestic policy . . . [i]nternational trade would cease to be what it is, namely, a desperate expedient to maintain employment at home by forcing sales on foreign markets and restricting purchases" (1936: 382).

multilateral negotiations were required postwar (LON 1942b: 163; 1945c: 27–29). That the terms of reference for these negotiations may be dominated by institutional imperatives contrived by one or two nation-states did not disconcert Geneva researchers. Scitovsky's (1942) message may well have been heeded: Freer trade would have to be enforced by international agreement or imposed by dominant, large nations against each country's selfish, myopic requirements. Condliffe (1941: 394) advanced further; he concluded proceedings of the 1939 Bergen conference on international trade and world peace with remarkable foresight: "[I]t must be an American dominated system, based on Pax Americana."[32]

Researchers in international organizations increasingly recognized during the 1940s that mere commitment by governments to full employment policies did not mean all opportunities will be seized when employment was at high levels to put liberal commercial policies into effect. Indeed,

> [e]xperience has shown that commercial policies do not automatically become more liberal when conditions permit them to do so. Direct and determined action is essential to secure a reduction of trade barriers and the creation of greater equality of treatment [among trading partners] (LON 1945c: 62).

International structures through which a general liberal objective could be prosecuted were not made clear in the early 1940s, although the American ITO proposals led the debate from the mid-1940s.[33] There were also some tentatively worded memoranda produced at the LON in 1944–45 on the history and possible structure of future customs unions.[34]

---

[32] According to J.H. Williams (1947: 101), the leading American economist specializing in trade policy and international monetary economics in the 1940s, in "creating conditions favorable to the restoration of a multilateral trade system, the heaviest responsibility will be our own" [*viz.* that of the United States]. However, Thomas Balogh, writing from the perspective of the United Kingdom, feared that the contributions on trade policy analysis forthcoming from the LON in the 1940s (notably Haberler's and Viner's) would justify "a system of 'absolute morality' in international economic relations." Masquerading as a form of economic "liberalism," that approach "would enable the United States to have its cake and eat it, retain its export surplus . . . for purely internal economic reasons (to stimulate employment without domestic reform)" (Balogh 1944: 259).

[33] LON (1943: 107) first broached the problem of organization and structure (see also LON 1945c: 63). An international body with appropriate powers to deal with questions of commercial policy was not something readily formulated by national governments in the interwar years. James Meade is credited with a commercial union proposal in July 1932 that was mainly a charter of rules reflecting British interests (Zeiler 1999: 28). The ITO structure was the first full-fledged, government-promoted, genuinely international charter.

[34] See LON Archives C1738: "Economic Aspects of Customs Unions: Some Historical Illustrations" (May 1944) and "Outline for a Note on Minimum Attributes Necessary For a Successful Customs Union" (23/3/1945).

Certainly, by 1945 binding multilateral freer trade agreements with specific rights and obligations of contracting parties were widely endorsed. Ideas promoted through ILO-LON reports from 1927 were now coming to fruition.

The Americans had originally envisaged a system of international trade governance through the ITO structure with parallel functions to those of the IMF in international monetary relations. It was also thought desirable to coordinate the full employment policies of participating nations with an attempt to expand existing reciprocal trade agreements into a comprehensive multilateral trading scheme with rules and mutual obligations (United States Committee on International Economic Policy 1944). Notwithstanding numerous escape clauses and exceptions to national sovereignty the principles of the ITO charter underscored an urgent need not to allow upward revisions of the base level of protection in existence circa 1947. The fixed, adjustable exchange rate rule created by the IMF charter had to be matched by similar rules aimed to prevent free use of commercial policies to perpetuate international disequilibrium. Protectionist trade policies were especially not sanctioned to create large surpluses on current account of the balance of payments or used with an expressed or implicit purpose of sustaining an existing surplus (Nurkse 1947a).[35] Although the ITO proposal was not implemented, the international cooperation, freer trade philosophy was kept alive in the underlying principles of the GATT.[36] The preamble to the GATT recognized that the *direction* of reform must be toward liberalization under the presumption that higher living standards internationally would ensue (GATT 1952: 13).

GENEVA TRADE POLICY RESEARCH: CAPSULE SUMMARY

A cosmopolitan group of economists working on trade policy matters in Geneva – Condliffe, Haberler, Hilgerdt, Meade, Nurkse, Ohlin, and Viner – were responsible for producing a substantial, Scandinavian-influenced

---

[35] As we have already seen, consistent with the general trade policy line emanating from international organizations in the 1940s, Nurkse continued to press policy makers on the imperative not actively to use commercial policy in relation to the balance of payments. It is not obvious that Keynes's general remarks on the subject of commercial policy at the time were congruent with ILO-LON doctrine. For example, his 1945 speech to the House of Lords implies active use of commercial policy as the case demanded: "In working out the Commercial Policy ... [my] proposals are devised to favour maintenance of equilibrium by expressly permitting various protectionist devices when they are required to maintain equilibrium and by forbidding them when they are not so required" (Keynes 1945: 393).

[36] See Diebold (1952) on the failure of the ITO charter. On the ITO-GATT connections see Diebold (1996) and Reisman (1996).

research program. The sterile debate between impossible alternatives of completely free trade and autarky is avoided; instead the focus of attention is actual policy problems and changing trade patterns. It was a program informed by evolving, real case trade interventions and negotiations, and by an impressive (for the time) data base – both quantitative and institutional – collected by the League's Economic Intelligence Service.

If there was a major theme in Geneva research it was the unrelenting internationalist perspective. It was therefore always skeptical of single-country motivated optimal tariff arrangements and of the general applicability of cases for trade intervention aimed at securing balanced industrial development (with a labor-intensive, import-competing sector usually demanding protection). Ohlin's influence is manifest on Geneva researchers who understood the importance of factor market failure (factor price inflexibility and factor immobility) which was best dealt with by internal microeconomic policies rather than trade intervention. It would not do, according to the Geneva program, to cite the business-cycle experience of the early 1930s as a reason for resorting to permanent protection. The international business cycle was eventually transmitted with or without increased trade intervention. Hilgerdt's early empirical work suggested that freer trade in the 1930s would have reduced the depth of the 1930s depression since it would have dampened inflation pressures in the larger, relatively closed economies.

Contemporary advances in the pure theory of international trade had tangential implications for trade policy issues. Some of these implications were eventually heeded in Geneva, others disregarded. Whereas trade theory reasoning was formal and axiomatic, Geneva research was preoccupied with practical international economic relations and concrete trade policy problems constrained by institutions and history. While not using formal models, some important theoretical constructs were presented: For example, Condliffe forged links between Ohlin's general equilibrium approach to internal trade by contemplating a dynamic "network of world trade" – a multilateral network integrated by market prices rather than quantitative, administrative controls. He insisted on this network's essential stability and on its resource allocative benefits provided it was not too frequently disrupted by shifts in trade interventions, or by discriminatory bilateralism. Hilgerdt operationalized the network for 1938; used it to demonstrate considerable trade integration despite the rise of protectionism in the 1930s and to indicate the potential for greater multilateral trade if only trade were liberalized.

The Geneva perspective advocated freer trade; it represented a case for genuine multilateralism. Early on the prescription that each country was at a maximum in the long run with freer trade (an argument under certain conditions later questioned by Samuelson) gave way to a distinction between warranted, short-run depression or employment policy expedients and international agreements and conventions designed to realize freer trade in the long run. Scitovsky's reassessment of the theory of tariffs ran parallel with research in Geneva. Rather than rely on homilies (and there were many of these in the conference resolutions of international organizations) about the need for more international cooperation, this research emphasized the importance of binding international agreements to expand multilateral trade and avoid aggressive bilateralism.

Keynes's ideas on trade policy in the interwar period, unlike the implicit freer trade message in Ohlin's work, did not hold sway in Geneva; at any rate they were not cited. Yet the influence of the elementary "Keynesian" idea that aggregate demand could actively be managed by monetary and fiscal policy was acknowledged. This idea was then enlisted when promoting microeconomic liberalization through freer trade. By the 1940s the Geneva researchers superannuated the notion of general trade interventions (for whatever nominated national objective). No longer were these interventions considered a necessary instrument for pursuing short-run internal balance. However, specific interventions for economic purposes were favored, such as exchange rate adjustments to correct persistent external imbalances.

There was nothing naive or idealistic about the Geneva liberal commercial policy orientation. The view from Geneva eventually triumphed given the direction of trade policy reform post-1945; it commanded a consensus that, when national trade interventions have negative international consequences, international action is required. The profusion of trade policy research reports from Geneva in the 1930s and 1940s found many different ways of expressing this deceptively simple proposition. A study of the intellectual background to the GATT, as opposed to the much-discussed economic history setting, would seriously be incomplete without saluting the achievements of the Geneva research program. That program derived much of its fertility from contemporary developments in Scandinavian international economics and it ultimately proved pivotal in providing the intellectual rationale for the postwar freer trade machinery of the GATT.

6 Social Economics at the ILO: Scope, Content, and Significance

INTRODUCTION

The ILO constitution of 1919 enshrined the achievement of "social justice" as a core general objective of the organization. Following that broad objective, the International Labour Office proceeded to the specific task of investigating "every question appertaining to conditions of labor" (Thomas 1921a: 10–11). Studying "conditions of labor" requires a wide purview, encapsulating all the areas of research only later to be known as "social economics" (Clark 1936). Areas of study included working conditions and remuneration, population, health, housing, social services and pension schemes, unemployment insurance, and relief schemes and education. Later, one contribution to the Cambridge Economic Handbook Series succinctly outlined the social economist's *modus operandi*:

1. to apply economic theory to social problems;
2. to measure, where possible, the extent of social problems;
3. to study the social causes of economic behavior; and
4. to study the social consequences of economic behavior (Hagenbuch 1958: 2).

In all these respects, ILO researchers acted as social economists; the scope and method of their work was far from being narrowly confined by the conventional boundaries of contemporary economic theory. ILO social economists made generous allowances for "noneconomic," social, or institutional aspects of human behavior. Often these factors rendered irrelevant or inapplicable much received microeconomic economic theory.

From the outset, the ILO researchers were mindful that there were differing perceptions between workers or workers' organizations and employers on what constituted logically acceptable and complete principles of labor protection and labor market "justice" and on what would suffice to secure economic cooperation between these two social classes. The joint purpose of these two classes was to find "a regime of conciliation, an era of social peace" which would ensure a high, stable level of employment and output (Thomas 1921a: 12). These issues required analysis of the functions of government in labor markets at the national level as well as research on the role of government in the realm of macroeconomic stabilization policy. In considering these functions, the ILO and LON were driven to produce suggestions on how far rules and practices guiding government policy at the national level could be generalized to produce collaboration and joint standards at the international level.

Lacking clear, exact principles of "social justice" in labor markets, the ILO researchers adopted a pragmatic stance; they relied on the study of particular cases, that is, international practices, in order to give "justice" operational content. From a study of these cases presumably, some guiding principles could be articulated. In this chapter we focus on the microeconomic elements of ILO research output and associated, often implicit, policy implications that turned on improving the "conditions of labor."

In the 1920s new systems of social insurance, labor management and emerging trade union organizations were notable developments affecting labor markets. Renewed interest by economists in these developments, particularly the microeconomic aspects in the 1920s and 1930s, was usually separated for the purpose of analysis from macroeconomic forces affecting labor markets. Four principal interests may be distinguished:

1. unemployment compensation and income support;
2. the effects of various income support structures on labor market transitions, labor mobility, and labor market "rationalization";
3. the effects of unemployment compensation on incentives to participate in labor markets; and
4. the effects of union organization on labor market outcomes.

In the 1920s and early 1930s, income support and unemployment compensation schemes were widely referred to under the broad conceptual umbrella of "social insurance." By social insurance here we follow the contemporary definition which, mindful of the variegated nature of international practice, did not by any means imply state provision and financing of all risks facing workers:

> It means a right, which is legally enforceable, on the part of the workman to a certain sum in money, or goods and services in kind, as compensation against the loss resulting from certain specified emer-

gencies which lead to a diminished capacity to earn, or involve an increase of expenditure on his part. The term is actually applied today to the following twelve emergencies: industrial accident, industrial disease, non-industrial accident, ill-health, maternity, invalidity, blindness, old age, unemployment, burial, unprovided widowhood, and unprovided orphanhood (Cohen 1925: 475).

While the right to social insurance was legally enforceable in all the schemes observed by the ILO, there was nothing in the contemporary definition that excluded what the ILO economist Karl Pribram referred to in 1925 as the "individualist method[s] of solving a collective problem" (1925: 307). Individuals could freely choose to syndicate and provide insurance for risks faced in common; public or state authority was neither necessary nor sufficient. Indeed, under complete state responsibility for financing and provision, "social insurance" became a misnomer: "[S]ocial insurance becomes social relief and individual responsibility disappears" (Ibid., 308).

John Rogers Commons's (1921: 67) programmatic article in the first issue of the *International Labor Review* set the scene for social insurance investigation at the ILO. He noticed some "experiments" in industrial relations in which employers voluntarily encouraged profit sharing, health insurance, and unemployment insurance schemes. Some employers were "showing that it can be done, and the only question is: Is it sufficiently important to require all others to do it? . . . Capitalism can cure itself, for it is not the blind force that socialists suppose." Ostensibly, Commons was admiring experiments in voluntary insurance systems that had positive effects in encouraging labor force participation, labor force attachment, and regular rather than casual employment. For Commons, enlightened labor management relations were those in which employers attracted and held workers not through fear of unemployment but by bold experiments in social insurance.

The ILO researchers started their work in the 1920s without doctrinaire adherence to the state provision of income maintenance for the able-bodied unemployed in particular. State provision was not necessarily the route to "social justice" in labor markets. Similarly, the state's role in fixing wages at the national or industry level was not taken for granted. Notwithstanding their open-mindedness, ILO research presumed that it was desirable to create some semblance at least of uniformity in labor conditions in ILO member countries. ILO Deputy Director, H.B. Butler (1924) insisted that setting international standards or guidelines was the *raison d'être* of the organization; international, comparative research work conducted by ILO researchers was the principal means of assisting in creating workable, implementable standards.

INTERNATIONAL EXPERIENCE AND DEBATE ON SOCIAL INSURANCE UP TO THE 1930s: THE ILO PERSPECTIVE

The ILO's research on social insurance in the 1920s involved vast work programs across a variety of risk factors impacting on labor conditions. The official published output included several reports on compensation for industrial accidents; occupational health; comprehensive statistical work; and associated study related to the "risks" of sickness, maternity, old age, invalidity and premature death, and unemployment.[1] Taken together, these "risk" factors leave workers "in a state of perpetual uncertainty, which undermines his freedom of mind – the guarantee of good work – the organisation of production, and in the long run the peace of society" (ILO 1925e: 763). While these broad social and economic effects of not covering adequately these "risks" were recognized, it was not a straightforward matter to determine how such "risks" were to be minimized or allowed for. It was by no means a foregone conclusion in the 1920s that compulsory insurance should be required of all workers based on rules relating contributions to degree of coverage. Since the "risks" were very different depending on the problem, a unified compulsory insurance system was difficult to construct; international experience demonstrated that few such unified systems in fact existed. Thus, any search for unifying international standards seemed in vain.

The ILO began a dispassionate research program aimed first at determining "the extent of the evil in order to obtain a basis for establishing the probable future economic and social risks from [various] sources" (Nixon 1928a; Pribram 1926: 486–87). Internationally comparable data on the diversity of risk factors were in short supply and of low quality. The ILO-organized annual Conference of Labor Statisticians in the 1920s worked diligently to pass recommendations and resolutions exhorting nations to collect better statistics. The key analytical work assessing risk criteria, collecting and comparing available data, and surveying possibilities for provision and financing insurance was completed by the economist, Karl Pribram (1925, 1926), and statistician, John W. Nixon (1928a,b).[2]

Accounting for differential risks was problematic; the unification of social insurance under one monolithic scheme seemed nonsensical. Extensive ILO research (1925b,c) on a wide range of international practices and the myriad of institutional arrangements for the provision of

---

[1] Beginning with ILO 1922b and 1924e. The latter was later backed by strong analytical work reported in the *ILR* by P.H. Douglas (1925).

[2] Pribram and Nixon published their work independently in the *ILR*. They were also responsible for the ILO reports (1925b,c,e).

insurance across countries confirmed the diversity and particularities of the risks involved. The principal results were as follows:

1. the problem of measuring the extent of risk in connection with various labor market experiences may only be reduced to a common set of general principles;
2. large numbers must be subject to the risk in question in order to assess the risk "scientifically";
3. two different risks may generally be calculated: frequency and severity. The frequency component related to the probability of an event. Severity is a measure of the loss occasioned by the event (to the worker, workers' organization, employer, or state).

The policy prescriptions offered turned on insuring the worker (and dependants) against the "risk of incapacity for work." The form and amount of income compensation should vary according to the risk, contribution, and resources available for a specific purpose (for example, unemployment, invalidity, sickness). The common severity of industrial accidents normally meant that compensations for these were generally more substantial than other risks. Insurance against invalidism, old age, and premature death should provide annual pensions (in the latter case to dependants). ILO researchers approved of schemes which rewarded "the effort of thrift" accomplished by a worker (and sometimes employers) concerned. Thriftier workers deserved higher compensation. Incentive issues remained at the core of ILO deliberations. There was an identified imperative "to preserve in the individual a feeling of responsibility, and to encourage the habit of saving; otherwise social insurance would lose its moral value" (ILO 1925b: 125–26).

On the incentive question, international comparative study revealed only that there was no universally accepted criterion for dispensing responsibility be it solely to the individual, occupational group, union, employer, or society as a whole, especially in the cases of sickness, invalidity, and premature death. Allocating responsibility for industrial accidents was difficult given that statistics on the causes of accidents give different results across industries and countries. Nevertheless, occupational concentrations of accidents and illness underscored employer responsibilities to reduce risks and contribute to workers' insurance funds in order to alleviate the deleterious economic and social consequences of these factors. On the other hand, temporary unemployment carried with it significant employee responsibility to insure against unemployment and search avidly for employment. In all cases of income compensation, benefits must always be "less than actual wages lost in order to avoid abuses" provided that the insured person and dependants could live in "reasonable conditions of existence" (ILO 1925b: 126). This last proviso certainly lacked force: Standards of "reasonableness" at the international level could not be set without meaningful international comparisons of living standards. And the latter were nonexistent in the mid-1920s.

Overall, methods of raising and collecting insurance contributions, different rates of compensation, and the diversity of financing schemes across countries represented different social values for which there was no easy reconciliation, and no measuring rod of appropriateness. In fact, extant principles of responsibility did not seem to influence social insurance legislators so much as approaches founded on "workable compromises, which take into account [both] . . . the ability and willingness of insured persons and employers to contribute, and . . . the financial position of the State" in each country (Ibid., 128).

UNEMPLOYMENT INSURANCE: A CASE STUDY

The income maintenance-incentive nexus appeared as the centerpiece of research and policy advice emanating from the ILO throughout the 1920s and 1930s. There was no presumption in any ILO work in the 1920s that the state should assume most of the responsibility for the unemployed; governments were emphatically *not* to accept moral responsibility. For example, after a study tour of the United States in the mid-1920s, ILO economist, John R. Bellerby (1926: 8–9) concluded that two irreconcilable theses were identifiable in the various practices observed for responding to unemployment:

> the belief that the maintenance of individual responsibility will preserve virility in all branches of the nation's activity; and the view that the state, as the representative of the interests of the community as a whole has certain obligations when the principle of individual responsibility appears not to be effective.

Since trade unions were widely thought to act for large portions of "the community" the second thesis in the above passage did not have much appeal, at least in the United States. Therefore, Bellerby's report for the ILO equivocated on the matter: As far as unemployment insurance was concerned, the option of comprehensive state provision versus individual provision reduces to a "choice . . . which . . . depends essentially upon the conception held of the function of the State" (p. 8). Certainly, there were mostly negative lessons for creating international standards and practices from the U.S. study. The practical problems involved in coordinating unemployment insurance schemes in a federal system in order to produce a consistent, national scheme were significant. There was suspicion that the variety of income compensation schemes in operation in the United States hindered the mobility of labor between states and increased the duration of unemployment in some industries, but the evidence was anecdotal rather than substantial (pp. 10–12).

In 1925 an ILO study concluded that the

> cost of unemployment insurance should be borne partly by the insured persons, partly by the employers and partly by the state, on the hypothesis that unemployment is due to a minor degree to personal defects in the insured (laziness, physical unsuitability for work, etc.), and to a larger extent to defective organisation of production or credit, responsibility for which is shared by employers and the community as a whole (the policy of the state with regard to tariffs, taxation and banking) (ILO 1925b: 127).

Clearly there were microeconomic and macroeconomic aspects to this normative conclusion. Here we shall focus on the microeconomic issues, although we should remember from Chapter 3 that macroeconomic policy measures, especially monetary policy were regarded as more powerful instruments for dealing with unemployment. Indeed, in its first full study of unemployment, the ILO (1922a: 135) observed that the instrument of "unemployment insurance is merely a makeshift" and various methods of government-funded unemployment relief in different countries were "merely a palliative."

The value judgements underlying ILO thought in the 1920s on the concept of unemployment are of prime importance. The idea of "involuntary" unemployment constitutes the context of all ILO research on unemployment insurance. Evidence of systematic variations in unemployment considered as an aggregate permitted the view that unemployment was foremost a problem of the industrial system of production as a whole (much more than it was a private, personal problem for the individual) (ILO 1922a: 3–4). This conception was completely in accord with contemporary pre-Keynesian economic theory as represented, for instance, in Pigou's *Unemployment* (1914).[3] For Pigou, unemployment was involuntary when some aspect of the industrial system could be identified as a source of failure – frictional and cyclical unemployment may be caused by inadequate labor market practices, labor market failure, and institutional breakdowns. Unemployment was voluntary and not insurable when due to strikes, lockouts, and incapacity due to old age. The ILO report (1922a: 44) explicitly added to the voluntary (and not insurable) category any unemployment due to expectations of wages or work conditions higher than those previously enjoyed by a worker.

---

[3] Casson (1983: 28) distinguished pre-Keynesian theories of unemployment from Keynes's notion that involuntary unemployment was any unemployment "that could be alleviated by a mild inflation of produce prices."

Microeconomic coordination failures were key sources of unemployment in the pre-Keynesian perspective, and this view was promoted by ILO researchers. Public labor exchanges could improve coordination by disseminating information freely about available quantities and qualities of labor demanded and supplied. These exchanges acted as clearing houses, encouraging occupational and geographic mobility of labor (ILO 1931e: 410–17).[4] Exchanges brought "order and efficiency into the labour market." Improving coordination in labor markets was a key feature of all pre-Keynesian approaches to involuntary unemployment aimed at reducing the costs of insurance and responding to frictional and structural unemployment in particular.[5] Industrial "transference" solutions were widely observed in ILO studies in the 1920s; these information-based solutions provided by public labor exchanges were a necessary policy response to changing labor demand patterns. The underlying ideas are that workers are normally poorly informed about job opportunities and minimum job standards; sometimes employers are poorly informed about labor supply conditions. The amount of market information varies according to skill level and union membership status. Younger workers were noticed not to engage in systematic job search and were especially ill informed. Altogether, ILO research was optimistic about the public labor exchange institution as a policy response. Bellerby's (1926: 29) study of experience in the United States viewed exchanges as a "preventive" measure; they help "maximise labour mobility: and in the final analysis, increase total employment."

The state played an important part in the provision of unemployment insurance in some ILO member countries (the United Kingdom and Germany in particular). The role of government in these cases was vigorously defended by the ILO economists against the glib charges that, as with other forms of income maintenance, government-, or union-sponsored unemployment insurance schemes:

1. made wages inflexible downward;
2. made relative wages across occupations more inflexible;
3. contributed to labor immobility; and
4. caused permanent unemployment (Maurette 1931).

Pigou's (1927: 359) rough estimate that only five percent of observed involuntary unemployment in the United Kingdom was due to the combined effects of postwar collective bargaining over wages and the existing system of unemployment compensation, was cited with approval in the ILO response. Also adduced were data from the United States in the

---

[4] See also ILO (1933c).
[5] For an example from the mainstream economics literature at the time, see Cannan (1928).

1920s where there was no public unemployment insurance, no central-ized, collective wage bargaining institutions, high and rising wages, and comparatively lower rates of unemployment (Maurette 1931:672–73). It is argued that abolition of existing unemployment insurance schemes and the enforcement of greater money wage flexibility in the circum-stances prevailing in 1931 would not produce lower rates of unemploy-ment. There may be an implication of higher real wages:

> [A] fall in wages *would enable prices to fall still more rapidly*, and it has almost always been found that when prices are falling buyers delay their purchases as long as they can; the more rapid that fall in prices the more marked is this tendency to wait (Ibid., 683, emphasis added).

However, the pressure to require money wage reductions would be ongoing rather than a one-off event. There is "no proof," so this argu-ment proceeded, that the course of events described in the passage above – a downward money wage and price spiral – would lead to a reduction of unemployment. Now, what is notable at this point, is that Maurette's paper was published in December 1931 and it embodied an entirely new ILO position – an embryonic idea, coming out of the unemployment insurance debate, that ongoing money wage reductions in combination with (more than proportionate) output price reductions were not the desirable route to high levels of employment, and were not obviously deliverable of lower unemployment in practice. Doubtless, Pigou would have demurred and Keynes would have concurred. For Pigou (1933: 252), in general "unemployment as exists at any time is due wholly to the fact that changes in demand conditions are continually taking place and that *frictional resistances prevent the appropriate wage adjustments from being made instantaneously*" (emphasis added). Therefore, in the context of depressed demand, wages must adjust downward. In the context of mass, cyclical unemployment in 1931, the contrasting ILO position was made clear: There is "no substance behind the opinion that unemployment is largely caused by the maintenance of wage-rates at an uneconomically high level" (ILO 1931b: 277).[6] By implication, the main-tenance of unemployment compensation was also not largely responsi-ble for unemployment in 1931.

Several aspects of the pre-Keynesian theory of unemployment were in fact absent in ILO work. First, employers were not observed to have taken advantage of insurance schemes to extend the casualization of the labor force – as claimed by the English economist Henry Clay (1929). Second, there is no suggestion that because unemployment insurance gave workers benefits while they sought employment, it extended the

---

[6] Here we take "wage-rates" to mean *money* wage rates.

duration of job search or made workers more selective in the alternatives considered (a claim often attributed to Cannan 1930). Presumably these so-called pernicious aspects of unemployment insurance and related compensation schemes were not evident because existing benefits were low relative to minimum wages. Third, the idea contributed by Clay (1929) that unemployment insurance benefits gave trade unions more power to negotiate over wages and conditions and/or to shift the responsibility for the employment consequences of these negotiations on to governments was not compelling to ILO economists. Fourthly, instead of appreciating the negative consequences on the demand for labor following from any employers' costs associated with financing unemployment compensation (for example, through taxation), the ILO emphasized the effects of compensation schemes on labor force attachment. Greater labor force attachment benefited employers bidding for labor when business cycles entered an upswing. To some extent this position reinforces the claim that unemployment compensation could lead to occupational immobility and favor industries in which casual hiring and short-term work practices preponderated. Instead the ILO maintained a long-run growth perspective – one in which unemployment compensation via insurance or some other relief scheme stimulates labor force growth and makes it more attractive for individuals to enter the labor force in the first place.[7]

That the minimum supply price of labor (the "reservation wage") could be influenced by the magnitude of, and conditions applied to, unemployment compensation (and social insurance schemes generally) was implicitly understood in ILO work in the 1930s.[8] Researchers using modern techniques have since in part endorsed the ILO view at the time especially in finding that unemployment benefits (in the United Kingdom) had a strong positive effect on labor supply (Benjamin and Kochin 1979, 1982). However, Benjamin and Kochin interpret the strong positive association between unemployment compensation and unemployment (working through a strong reduction in labor demand given the high incidence of unemployment insurance costs falling on employers) in a manner that is alien to ILO deliberations in the 1930s. Benjamin's and Kochin's new found association is not recognized as significant in the admittedly impressionistic, international comparative studies of unemployment made by the ILO. Not long after the depres-

---

[7] Later in the twentieth century Friedman (1977: 458) in his Nobel Lecture recognized the positive effects on labor supply as one of the most important arguments in favor of generous unemployment insurance schemes.

[8] See Cohen (1929: 822). This understanding is given strong empirical support for the first time in the 1950s (Reynolds 1951: 109–10).

sion levels of unemployment experienced in the early 1930s, Woytinsky's (1935) study of the sources of that unemployment makes no mention whatsoever of any association between unemployment compensation, or the general level of money wages for that matter, on unemployment.[9] In that work, restrictions on immigration, the upsurge in various national experiments in unemployment relief, insurance, and compensation were regarded as reactions to an intractable problem that had *already* presented itself to policy makers.

WAGES AND WAGES POLICY: MICROECONOMIC ISSUES

Minimum Wages: ILO Preconceptions and Implications from Applied Research

In the field of labor protection and social justice in labor markets there was no more a commonly debated issue than wages and wages policy in the interwar period. ILO research was founded on the belief that labor must not be regarded as a commodity. Pribram (1928: 331) captures the prevailing ethos at the ILO: "human labour must not be treated as a commodity, an article of commerce whose price on the open market is determined solely by the forces of supply and demand." Again, however, this simple admonition had to be given an operational meaning and the pragmatic ILO economists rested their international comparative work on the idea that an adequate living wage should maintain a reasonable standard of life and that standard must be understood in context of time, occupation, and country (Ibid., 318). In addition, the setting of precise "reasonable minimum conditions" which would apply transnationally was regarded as difficult, if not impossible (ILO 1928: 9). It was keenly understood that international cooperation to create minimum standards might easily be accomplished between nations with comparable living standards, culture, and industrial structures. Otherwise, if some standard was applied to developing countries and relatively poorer countries and enforced, immediate economic losses resulting from a reduction in international competitiveness could follow. According to one economist acting as a consultant to the ILO:

> If international agreements establishing minimum conditions of labor are ratified by those countries in which conditions are now very much poorer than in the more effective industrial countries, the result will be to prevent the further expansion of industry in these countries unless and until they can meet this standard. The countries where conditions

[9] See also Woytinsky (1936: 172–82) which considers unemployment relief and supplementary allowances paid to the unemployed and their dependants in the early 1930s.

are poorest have as yet relatively few industries competing in the international market (Feis 1927: 504).

The Governing Body of the International Labour Organization was quite specific on the desirability of regulating and enforcing minimum wage standards across countries; where joint action was feasible, broad guidelines could be established. Partners to the ILO convention in 1928 undertook "to create or maintain machinery whereby minimum rates of wages can be fixed for workers employed in certain of the trades . . . *in which no arrangements exist for the effective regulation of wages by collective agreements* or otherwise and wages are exceptionally low" (McClure 1933: 307, emphasis added). For ILO economists trained and accustomed to thinking in terms of labor being remunerated in terms of its marginal product – that is wages equalling "the real value of the work done" (ILO 1928: 13) – the 1928 convention raised several questions: What were the main causes of wages falling below marginal product? What, if anything, ought to be recommended when industries could not remain viable without paying wages less than marginal product? What nonwage objectives could be achieved by minimum wage setting machinery?

The main causes of wages falling below marginal product were enumerated as (1.) cyclical economic depression in an industry; (2.) inefficient organization of production, and (3.) "inefficiency of the workers" (Ibid., 12). In respect of (1.), indefinite depression in a "deathbed" industry could not be ameliorated by minimum wage-fixing regulations; regulations, if applied would inevitably lead to unemployment. The ability of industries to pay some minimum wage needs to be considered on a case-by-case basis. Global regulation or standards setting would not necessarily benefit labor. Likewise, worker inefficiency as a result of inadequate capital or worker training could not be affected by minimum wages. In respect of (2.), any "improvement in the organisation of production which may result from the fixing of minimum rates is incidental . . . but nevertheless in many instances striking. If labor is cheap, there is less inducement to avoid waste of the working forces or to introduce labor-saving machinery. Where workers receive a high rate of remuneration, every effort is made to use their services to the best advantage" (Ibid., 12–13).

Where wages were not determined by collective agreements between unions and employers, evidence available from some ILO member countries indicated that minimum wage regulation promoted industrial peace, increased the level of output and sustained employment levels. In highly uncompetitive labor markets, where employers were exceptionally powerful in reducing wages, minimum wage legislation could help provide a measure of countervailing power in support of disorganized workers. Impressionistic ILO research as well as more formal LON's statistical work on particular country experiences from the late 1920s to the end of the 1930s on wages, reinforced earlier work on the effects of minimum wage fixing. That research was implicitly critical of the orthodox economic theory of wages resting on the principle of marginal productivity.[10]

Apart from questioning the completeness of competition in real case labor markets, the ILO was skeptical of the orthodox assumptions that employers and workers know the value of the marginal product of labor.[11] The propositions that labor is freely mobile and can transfer costlessly from job to job and that all freely mobile labor can find employment at prevailing wage rates were also treated with disdain.[12] On the subject of labor mobility, Feis (1927: 499) represented the ILO perspective: "within highly industrialised countries the mobility of labour and capital – their capacity to shift themselves from one industry to others under the pressure of competition – is slow, painful, and incomplete." The ILO rejection of orthodox wage theory emanated fundamentally from historically grounded, applied research on actual wage-fixing arrangements and practices across countries. There was no support for the belief in long-run tendencies in labor markets which would work within and through various market obstacles and imperfections, to establish outcomes consistent with marginal productivity theory. Paul Douglas (1934: 95) could well have included ILO economists in the following remarks:

> Many, who have seen the degree of variance between real life and the assumptions of the productivity school, have in their impatience declared that because of this defective basis, the conclusions which have been drawn from the productivity theory are not worthy of credence and hence should be disregarded. But such an attitude as this ignores the fact that the assumptions do represent real tendencies which in the aggregate are probably more powerful than those of a conflicting nature. There is a tendency for wage-rates which are lower than marginal productivity to be raised by the competition of the businessmen, and there is a tendency for wages in excess of the marginal product to be lowered by the competition of the laborers. The forces upon which

---

[10] The postulates of a marginal productivity theory of wages are discussed in two contemporary classics: Douglas (1934: 68–71) and Hicks (1932: 86–87).

[11] In more sophisticated work during the 1950s, Reynolds (1951: 45) found that if wages in comparable industrial occupations are used as a proxy, workers in fact only had a vague, inaccurate notion of their "worth" in other industrial plants. See also Lester (1948: 152).

[12] Mobility correlates used in formal economic research in the 1950s were also not supportive of the marginal productivity theory (Reynolds 1951: 27–28; 35–36).

the productivity school built their theories are, therefore, not fictitious, but are instead powerful.

Per contra, actual wage outcomes seemed to differ from what one might expect according to the narrow principles of the "productivity school." Preconceptions based on a market-determined, competitive wage structure were not regarded as very helpful for empirical studies of the kind conducted by the ILO. These studies, in terms of scope, compelled attention to unionism, collective bargaining, labor law, social insurance, and personnel management. And the ILO methodology had roots in history, law, and sociology more than economic theory.

Wage Determination and Wage Structures

Widespread evidence of collective bargaining institutions in many ILO member countries challenged the conclusions of the "productivity school," based as they were, on atomistic competition in labor markets. In short, imperfect competition in labor supply had to be considered as a vital influence on labor market outcomes. As already observed in the previous section, collective bargaining could protect workers from "exploitative" employers by assisting in the setting of uniform minimum wage (and nonwage) standards for different types of work. The conventional wisdom among researchers specializing in the study of labor market institutions in industrialized countries was that unions and/or government intervention had the potential to reduce industrial unrest and improve the living standards of certain groups of workers (for example, Burns 1926). In this respect, ILO research was entirely conventional. According to that research, collective bargaining over wages and working conditions, with or without direct government involvement, promised to raise labor's share in national income and change industry wage structures. We turn next to an investigation and exposition of the relevant empirical work.

The pages of the *ILR* and a plethora of ILO "Studies and Reports" throughout the interwar period are replete with research on various experiments conducted internationally on collective wages policy initiatives.[13] Collective wage setting usually involved organized labor and employers; some cases involved government compulsory arbitration and conciliation. The research documents a gradual transformation in wage determination arrangements from individual contracting toward systems of collective determination in the period from the early 1920s to circa 1950. ILO economist J.R. Bellerby, produced three papers that epito-

---

[13] See for example Condliffe (1924); ILO (1930, 1931f); McDaniel Sells (1924a,b,c); and Woytinsky (1931).

mized international comparative work in the period under review.[14] One important conclusion arising out of this work is that no single algorithm existed for setting wages, or for developing normative rules for desirable wage adjustments overtime (see also Martin 1927). Whether collectivist approaches to bargaining over wages and work conditions produced satisfactory results depended on a myriad of factors in each country. In fact, direct government involvement in establishing normative rules increased significantly from the mid-1930s.

ILO research on wage-setting practices established results which would be confirmed by formal labor economics as it evolved in the 1950s. First, unionization reduced personal differentials in wage rates by attaching remuneration to occupational categories, not to individuals. Union wage structures by industry had a strong impact on industrial differentials. The latter was especially marked in some countries where agricultural wages (often the nonunionized sector) fell relative to other unionized sectors (Belshaw 1933; Matthaei 1931; Woytinsky 1936: 214–20).

Secondly, and partly because of forces at work mentioned above, unions reduce wage differentials across plants in an industry (Richardson 1928: 196). Richardson's work for the ILO was prompted by Gustav Cassel's attack on the effects of unionization in a memorandum submitted to the WEC in 1927.[15] The memorandum claimed that monopolistic labor organizations maintained wage differentials between a "sheltered" export-oriented sector which was exposed to the vagaries of international competition. For Richardson (1928: 196), Cassel "appears to consider that organised labour is to be condemned." Richardson's first reposte is that "organized capital has equally concentrated upon endeavouring to make the most out of every given situation." Moreover, Cassel's argument is attributed to an overweening reliance on the Swedish context where

> owing to the exceptional strength of the trade unions, the influence of these organisations, within the limits of their effective action, has no doubt been greater than in certain other countries. It should be remembered, however, that the workers in various industries exposed to foreign competition are as strongly organised as those in the sheltered industries, but their strength has been largely unavailing on account of the economic difficulties with which these industries have been faced (pp. 196–97 n.2).

---

[14] See Bellerby (1927a,b,c).

[15] Cassel (1927) in a paper entitled "Recent Monopolistic Tendencies in Industry and Trade: Being an Analysis of the Nature and Causes of the Poverty of Nations." See especially pp. 26, 32–34.

On Richardson's reading of country experiences with unionization, collective bargaining reduced interindustry wage differentials in those industries dependent on home markets; whereas in those diversified industries dependent on foreign markets, collective bargaining had little impact on wage structures. Differences in underlying economic conditions prevailing in different countries and output market structures, more than trade union policy, were responsible for observed intersectoral wage differentials; such differentials would have existed without unionization. In short Cassel had not proven that institutional arrangements related to collective bargaining dominated all influences in product or output markets which affected wages. Finally while labor mobility was sluggish, the transference of workers from a poorly performing unsheltered sector toward a higher wage sheltered sector is "steadily proceeding" (Richardson 1928: 198). As before, the ILO position is reiterated: Appropriate industrial "transference" assistance through public policy initiatives such as free labor exchanges would be more effective than dismantling collective bargaining institutions. Collective bargaining was not in any way a demonstrable "cause" of relatively low wages in the unsheltered sectors.

Richardson's work extended to confirming copious evidence from industrialized countries. Unions considered in their entirety, were concerned with the employment of their members; that concern was sufficiently strong as to lead to observable trade-offs between wages and employment in certain wage negotiations (Richardson 1928: 197–99).[16] That evidence is in part derived from documented trends toward greater coordination in wage-setting systems, and the development of "just wage" principles in collective bargaining practices. Bargaining often involved trade union endorsed (or sympathizing) government agencies aiming to conjoin labor market outcomes with social policy initiatives (for example, family allowances). Wage structures may legitimately be altered by government tax and expenditure policies to change the distribution of incomes and engineer a more "fair" or "stable" share of total product accruing to the labor input. Legitimation for the practice is articulated in several ILO research papers (Bellerby and Isles 1930; ILO 1933e; Martin 1926c). The prescription here is that governments can alter

---

[16] It cannot, therefore, be maintained with any confidence that ILO economists provided a clear prediction that trade unions may be depicted as maximizing a wage bill for total membership. This prediction is first made for analytical purposes in Reder (1952). However, it is certainly correct to aver that ILO economists did *not* endorse Hicks's (1932: 184) view that "Trade Unionists bother so little about the connection between their wage policy and unemployment . . . [T]o the Trade Unionist wages and unemployment naturally appear to have little connection."

labor market outcomes to satisfy redistributional objectives though it was hardly a fashionable idea in the 1920s and only reflected prevailing public policy objectives from the mid-to-late 1930s.

The effects of unionization on wage changes does not obviously "distort," in any fundamental way, a hypothetical, perfectly competitive pattern of wage rates. And the perfectly competitive pattern was not observable. The allocative costs of union involvement in wage determination were inestimable. That is, given the absence of norms of wage relationships obtained under perfectly competitive labor markets with private, individualized wage bargains, it is difficult to quantify the extent of any distortion. The data sets with which ILO researchers had to work were admittedly primitive compared to those available to modern labor economists. The analytical techniques available in the interwar period were also unsophisticated by modern standards. Nevertheless, on the subjects of minimum wages, collective bargaining, unionization, and wage determination they perceived and made ground on some of the principal issues that were to interest applied labor economists of a later generation and they reported on international experience later corroborated by economists during the 1950s.

Real Income Wages Across Countries

ILO applied studies of wages policy in the United States and Canada during the 1920s conclude strongly in favor of patterns of industrial cooperation and associated increases in labor productivity (relative to other industrialized countries) exhibited in those countries (Butler 1927; Richardson 1929b). Here the cooperative spirit in industrial relations is correlated with a prevailing "doctrine of high wages" (Richardson 1929a). In this context trade unions were not considered obstacles to economic development as they were in some other countries. Richardson's study tour of the United States and Canada in 1928–29 confirmed that wage earners and employers were observed to be cooperating over wage setting in line with productivity changes; both employee and employer seemed keenly aware of the two-way relationship between wages and productivity. Higher real wages were an effect and a cause of higher productivity from the worker's point of view; and higher real wages encouraged employers to increase efficiency in the use of labor. Thus:

> An important aspect of the doctrine of high wages is the stimulus given to employers to improve their productive organisation and so reduce labour costs. In the United States a central element of the doctrine is that there is nothing incompatible between high wages and lower labour costs (Richardson 1929a: 803).

In short, real wages rise when output rises. The macroeconomic implication is that real wages tend to be procyclical rather than contracyclical.[17]

For employers in industries producing for a large domestic market, cooperation with workers in determining wages was rationalized because workers' income wages were a source of purchasing power for the employers' products. Richardson understood that the "doctrine of high wages" was popular among workers and employers producing mostly for a home market in market structures that were not especially competitive. Further, industries undergoing secular expansion (for example, motor vehicles), or in which important technological advances were being exploited, also promoted the high wages doctrine. In these industries, wages were sometimes paid on an output-incentive basis rather than a time basis. Hence the common observation in Richardson's work from U.S. data that wage rates tend to increase mostly in industries in which output, employment, and productivity are advancing the most and in concert. By way of contrast, in many countries with relatively open economies and older industries, wage movements were severely constrained by foreign competition. Here the method of raising wages "could only be applied to a much smaller extent; [an] increase in productivity would result in higher real wages mainly by lowering prices" (Richardson 1928: 200–01; Richardson 1929a: 806–07; 1929b: 815; Warming 1931: 31).

The disjunction of wage concepts of interest to the parties in wage negotiations in different parts of the world created a research problem.[18] Contemporary economic analysis did not make a sharp distinction between the marginal demand price of labor – the unit cost of labor to employers or the real product wage – and the marginal supply price of labor from the worker's point of view (or worker's earnings, the real income wage). By focusing on the equilibrium, market-clearing state in competitive labor markets, there was no need to make much of the distinction between real product wages and real income wages. Now the ILO economists were well aware that in practice, the indices used to deflate each of these "wages" behaved differently. In particular, the real *income* wage included the effects of changes in earnings as a consequence of fringe payments (possibly for value added), overtime rates,

---

[17] This result is noted more formally by Dunlop (1938). That it may have been quite country specific for the 1920s and 1930s is now well known (Freeman 1989: 321).

[18] Documents arising out of conferences held at the ILO in January 1929 and May 1930 indicate that the ILO Statistician J.W. Nixon was acutely aware of this problem. The conference papers and documents were edited by Clay and Jewkes (1930). See especially pp. 6–15 and 105–27.

taxes and, of course the prices of goods in the standard worker's basket of consumption goods. The "goods" of interest to employers – the whole range of producer input prices – were different from the goods of interest to workers making labor supply decisions. Therefore using identical units on the wages axis of a Marshallian labor market demand-and-supply diagram was indeed problematic. In recognition of this problem, ILO economists avoided that style of analysis which considered the pricing of labor in spot-market contexts, that is, in the manner that other inputs in the production process might be analyzed.

In the case of Canada and the United States, real product wages and real income wages were conflated in practice by seamless cooperative arrangements and progressive management practices at the individual plant level, sometimes extending to industries as a whole (Richardson 1929b). The "doctrine of high wages" to which much ILO work referred, amounted to some hybrid notion of "wages" particularly suited to discussions of rapidly growing industries where competitive pressures were weak. The plurality of wage concepts was brought into sharper focus in pioneering ILO research, commissioned by the Ford Motor company in the early 1930s. That (Ford) research project investigated the "cost of living" in Detroit and fourteen European cities. The objective was to ascertain the rate that ought to be paid by motor plants in each location in order to achieve approximate equality in real income wages (ILO 1931d).[19]

Important statistical work on methods of compiling index numbers of living costs and alternative methods for executing family budget enquiries were carried out in the 1920s and provided background for the Ford research (ILO 1924f, 1925d, 1926). In the early 1930s, several studies appeared in the *ILR* consequent upon appointment to the ILO research staff of the accomplished economist-statistician, and founder member of the Econometric Society, Hans Staehle.[20] Staehle (1932a) concentrated on methodological, conceptual, and technical difficulties faced by researchers intent on making international real income wage comparisons; he subsequently made several path-breaking enquiries into cost of living index numbers, published in leading journals. Technical difficulties aside, one summary result of the Ford research deserves consideration here. The results are calculated in a common currency on the basis of

---

[19] For the background to the research project including important correspondence on methodology, financing, and press commentary, see ILO Archives I 101/0/1.

[20] Staehle was made a Fellow of the Econometric Society in 1937; ILO Archives P2446. He came to the ILO with references from Schumpeter, Viner, and Douglas. For a brief intellectual biography see Milgate (1987). Carré (1961) is a most comprehensive obituary.

Table 6.1. Ford Research: Summary Results

City	Comparative Figures	City	Comparative Figures
Berlin	83–90	Antwerp	61–65
Frankfurt on the Main	85–93	Rotterdam	65–68
Copenhagen	83–91	Manchester	71–74
Stockholm	99–104	Cork	85
Helsinki-Helsingfors	83	Warsaw	67
Paris	80–87	Barcelona	58
Marseilles	75–81	Istanbul	65

Source: ILO (1931d: 29).

1931 Detroit expenditure = 100. Data in Table 6.1 estimate the purchasing power of the main European currencies in respect of the U.S. dollar, for workers of a given social and occupational group. Apart from Stockholm, it was inferred from these data that:

1. wage earners in the particular occupational and industrial category could achieve "parity" of earnings with workers in the Detroit plant by receiving wages less than US$1,000;
2. money wage comparisons between countries, even for a specific type of worker were not the appropriate basis for setting international wage standards; and
3. real wage comparisons faced complex technical and conceptual problems, not the least being the base city for setting a standard of normal consumption.

Norms of consumption based on "baskets of basic provisions" differed across countries; the quality of consumer goods was also variable (for example, rental costs for housing of "similar" quality were especially difficult to compare). While taxes on consumer goods were included in prices, income tax differences that determined after-tax income did not appear to have been taken into account.[21]

Public interpretation of these results lacked the caution desired by ILO researchers. In February 1932, the Director of the Twentieth Century Fund (a major U.S. funding agency which was later to contribute to ILO research) wrote to the director of the ILO, explaining the consequences of these pioneering ILO real income wage comparisons:

---

[21] Staehle (1932b) remained extremely uneasy about dismissing interpretative problems with these kinds of data. From 1932 he was concerned to find means of comparing well-being derived from given money incomes of social groups differing in milieu and tastes but he did not settle upon a satisfactory method of comparison until the late 1930s (see Staehle 1937).

The implication which the figures carry that the cost of living and wages are not automatically dependent one upon the other has made a deep impression here. As you know even the American Federation of Labor has recognized this principle and has opposed wage increases which also increase costs and prices. American employers find in the figures statistical proof of the possibility of paying comparatively high wages and at the same time reducing the prices of finished products through the application of scientific methods. The value of this proof is especially great at this time for it strengthens the hands of those employers who are trying to avoid the necessity of wage cuts by reducing other costs through further efficiencies in operating methods (ILO Archives, 19/6/1931, T101/01/1).

The success of the Ford research prompted the Rockefeller Foundation to fund work on international wage comparisons further for a wider range of occupational categories. The ILO's agenda was to point out the international policy implications of such comparisons, without however, drawing specific policy conclusions. First, the issue of "social dumping" came to the fore in the early 1930s and debate could be informed by making income wage comparisons. Tariff changes, for instance, "should take into account the standard of living and relative level of wages in the countries from which goods are imported."[22] Second, data could be used to set wages for migrant workers. Third, data on real income wage comparisons could act as an input in collective bargaining; where governments were involved in preparing principles of wage adjustment and minimum wage standards these data were potentially an important decision-making input. In any case, ILO research was to provide data, collected on a regular basis, "with the objective of arriving at recommendations for action which should be theoretically sound and practically feasible."[23]

While the purpose of real income wage comparisons was to arrive at "recommendations for action," the objective was thwarted by a research program which could not advance much beyond either debating fundamentals or producing a large number of unconnected family budget studies in different countries. Staehle's work on fundamentals, *inter alia*, on the concept of "the standard of living" and on index number

---

[22] This passage and the following discussion draws heavily on ILO Archives, N109/102. See also at that reference two memoranda: "International Enquiry into Wages and Cost of Living" 30/1/1934 and "Memorandum on the Work of the ILO on International Comparisons of Cost of Living" 2/2/1934.

[23] Results of the Rockefeller research project were published in numerous *ILR* articles. Family budget studies reported in the *ILR* between November 1933 and September 1937 constituted a significant research output and these are too numerous to list here. See the summary reports, ILO (1934, 1940b). Staehle's technical work on the project was reported in several scholarly journals.

problems involved in cost of living comparisons, proved disconcerting to his ILO superiors who were impatient to derive policy implications.[24] In particular, they wished strongly to relate the research to real income *wage policy*. As principal researcher, Staehle did not quickly arrive at definitive conclusions. Clearly, practical results were not merely required to satisfy the expectations of the funding agency; ongoing international wages policy debate, in which the ILO and League of Nations were actively involved, often turned on making money wage comparisons between nations. Such simple comparisons indicated that low wage "slavery" was the putative norm in many countries and international organizations had no means of responding to such conditions, or setting and enforcing some standards for minimum wages or living conditions. The only lesson from both the Ford and Rockefeller funded ILO studies, not unimportant in retrospect, was that any international convention on wages had to be concentrated on real income wages. Notwithstanding this preliminary insight, the appropriate standard could not easily be obtained from "scientific" comparisons of such wages; conceptual and technical problems associated with international comparisons were difficult to surmount. Further, pure conceptual and technical issues, as canvassed in Staehle's research, had not been resolved in the literature of economics and econometrics at the time (and have been controversial ever since).[25] Without Staehle's penchant to do the pure theoretical work first, while at the same time overseeing a massive international program involving family budget enquiries and not hastily drawing out policy implications, the ILO's high reputation for producing pioneering empirical work in the field would have been short lived. In the event, a decade after this research began, it was quietly shelved on Staehle's departure.

The abortive ILO cost of living research program in the 1930s was restricted to an assessment of real income wages at one remove. The link to wage comparisons was always implicit – always just a promise. The research was necessarily preliminary if some international policy implications were eventually to be drawn. If income tax policy, social policy

---

[24] Lewis Lorwin to Staehle: "Annual Report on Dr Staehle" 26/7/1938 and "Reply" by Staehle, ILO Archives 30/8/1938, P2446.

[25] According to Staehle: "[M]y work has often been found too technical for publication by the Office, to such an extent that, having gained this reputation, it is no longer even taken into account. I already have given my point of view as regards the impossibility of avoiding completely the use of scientific methods, sometimes a little technical, in the analysis of social problems which are always complex. And I again insist that the great human importance of any social policy makes it necessary to go to the limits of scientific knowledge in trying to foresee all its effects. This course I have also followed in my work on standards of living." ILO Archives, Ibid. 30/8/1938.

including family allowance and minimum wage legislation, and tariff policy were going to be relevant to setting conventions at the international level over wages, then a regular sampling of living costs across countries would be needed to inform debate. While holding the position that appraisals of wage levels and structures were essentially normative, ILO research sought an independent scientific basis for real wage comparisons. The latter amounted to a search for the Holy Grail.

Interrelations between Real Product Wages, Employment, and Unemployment

It was taken as an institutional datum, for the United States at least, that wage outcomes and wages policy were largely determined by the employed rather than the unemployed (Butler 1927). In countries where governments were involved in regulating labor market negotiations and setting wage standards that datum had to be modified. And governments were becoming increasingly active in labor market regulation from the early 1930s (ILO 1933e). In any institutional setting surveyed by the ILO up to the 1950s factors determining the prices of producers' inputs other than labor (capital, raw materials, property, intermediate goods), as well as product market pricing structures were preeminent determinants of wage structures and adjustments in those structures over time. Macroeconomic reasons for this position came to the fore in the early 1930s; mass unemployment did not seem to exert a strong influence on wages. Indeed unemployment and wage reductions were generally considered the results of changes in product prices in many countries.[26] Contemporary labor economics provided some support for this view. Dunlop (1944) for instance argued that when output prices were declining, those price declines, more than unemployment, put downward pressure on wages.

A vast body of literature from the ILO and LON supporting the influence of nonwage input costs and product prices on both wage setting and unemployment concentrated on microeconomic aspects of labor markets. In this literature the macrolevel causes, analyzed with reference to business-cycle analysis in the 1930s are set aside.[27] Many microeconomic factors are captured under the umbrella term *rationalization* and we shall attend fully to those factors in what follows. Before proceeding,

---

[26] An archetypal, small open economy case, was New Zealand, as reported by League of Nations economist J.B. Condliffe (1931). The tenor of his article is captured in the title: "The Effect of Falling Prices on Labor Conditions in New Zealand."

[27] The relationship between monetary developments including monetary policy and unemployment and international trade (including trade policy) and unemployment were also kept separate in ILO and League research. These matters are discussed in Chapters 3 and 5.

there is an important point to underscore at this juncture: Owing to their compartmentalization of a whole set of relationships in the economy between money and unemployment; trade and unemployment; business cycles and unemployment and rationalization and unemployment, the ILO and League economists throughout the interwar period did not possess a 1960s-style summary tool such as a Phillips curve vision of unemployment. The relationship between unemployment and wage changes was not a core consideration despite the influence of Irving Fisher's (1926) *ILR* article and its suggestion of a Phillips curve-type relation. As we note in Chapter 2, Fisher investigated a relationship between lagged price level changes and total employment. He collaborated with ILO researchers on the subject before publication.[28] He concluded that the relationship was causal, running unidirectionally from price changes to employment. The "causal relationship between inflation and employment or deflation and unemployment" (p. 792) had little *directly* to do with real product wage inflation. The price level variable leads employment changes crucially because of fixed contracts, custom, or inertia at the microlevel not only in labor markets but also in capital, property, and natural resource markets (p. 787). Fisher was exclusively concerned with the macroeconomic, business-cycle aspects of the causal relationship and macroeconomic policy responses to it, that is, "the inflation and deflation of money and credit" or monetary "stabilization" policy (p. 792).

For ILO researchers in the late 1920s and through the 1930s, the relationship between wage structures, employment, and unemployment was complex and uncertain; several causative factors were suspected to lurk behind wage changes and these deserved separate investigation. Collective bargaining institutions in different countries were just one factor. This perspective was due entirely to their firsthand, country-by-country assessments of the causes and consequences.

Real product wages, that is, the employment cost index of wages (of prime interest to employers), had some crucial connection to the demand for labor and hence to employment and unemployment. Real product wages were, in essence, the price of labor relative to the cost of other inputs demanded by employers. Processes of "rationalization" observable in many industries affected the real product wage. "Rationalization" summarized two broad trends: (1.) technological advancements leading to greater plant specialization and to capital intensive large-scale production systems aimed at achieving maximum economies of scale and (2.) advances in labor management and organizational practices in some

---

[28] In particular, he discussed the subject extensively with Albert Thomas and J.R. Bellerby from March 1924 onward. See ILO Archives I 106/74/1 to I 106/74/5.

industries. Both trends were a cause of, and driven by, product market pricing pressures, and changes in consumer demand. These trends inevitably and inexorably required employers to improve labor productivity and/or lay off workers.[29]

In nations experiencing high growth rates during the 1920s such as the United States, "rationalization" involved organizational developments prompted by a harmonious climate of labor relations. The unemployed had negligible influence on wage bargaining in this climate. Instead, workers' groups and individual employees embraced the employers' objectives variously to improve labor productivity; reduce labor turnover; preserve and develop workers' human capital in advancing industries. On organizational "rationalizations," a report for the League of Nations Economic and Financial Section referred glowingly to

> contributory unemployment insurance schemes [which] . . . put a premium on employers keeping their shops running as regularly as possible and on employees remaining loyal. Profit-sharing schemes, vacation with pay after certain terms of service, sickness, pension and death benefits are among the other material rewards to employees . . . Last, and probably not least, should be mentioned the constantly growing development of employees' stock ownership . . . And along with these factors has gone a development in personnel policies and industrial relationships which has made a profound change in the attitude of employees toward the job and employers toward employees (Houston 1926: 7).

The League of Nations' report to the World Economic Conference (LON 1927c: 192–93) resolved that "rationalization" should aim simultaneously at:

1. securing the maximum efficiency of labor with the minimum of effort;
2. facilitating by a reduction in the variety of patterns (where such variety offers no obvious advantage) the design, manufacture, use, and replacement of standardized parts;
3. avoiding waste of raw materials and power;
4. simplifying the distribution of goods; and
5. avoiding in distribution unnecessary transport, burdensome financial charges, and the inefficient interposition of middlemen.

When ILO research gave more precision to the meaning of rationalization and its link to employment and unemployment in the 1930s, it was uncategorically sanguine about its impact in the long term (ILO 1931c:

---

[29] The main ILO studies on this subject were: ILO (1931c, 1933d), Johnston (1929, 1930), Lederer (1938), and Woytinsky (1935).

8–9). The content of the term rationalization emphasized new human resource management techniques (dubbed "scientific management"), advancing material conditions in manufacturing by adopting modern "machinery," and expending resources on industrial research and development. The main operational variables were output per worker, hours of work, real product wages, levels of employment, industrial hygiene and accident prevention, and industrial relations practices more generally. Product market competition made rationalization an ongoing imperative. The short-term outcome may be greater unemployment, but this "is, however, only temporary" (Ibid., 371). Data could not be adduced clearly linking various forms of rationalization to higher total employment; the time horizons were especially problematic. The standard perfect competition model which depicted price taking in output markets and highly elastic demand responses provided the theoretical background for ILO deliberations. All forms of rationalization, including the adoption of technologically advanced, labor-saving machinery will result in a

> fall in prices . . . lead[ing] to increased sales and consequently to further production and the reabsorption of a section of those who are thrown out of employment. This is helped by the fact that the [rationalization process] . . . spreads gradually (Ibid., 370).

This passage embodies a confident, bold judgement in the midst of rapidly rising unemployment in the early 1930s. Various forms of scientific management will "lead to better adaptation of production to market needs" and this would reduce unemployment over the long term (p. 371). Furthermore, industrial transference policies promoted by labor exchanges and assisted migration schemes could assist in reducing the duration of unemployment consequent upon rationalization. As for wages before and after the process, the ILO observed that in countries where rationalization measures had been adopted with alacrity, "a certain rise in wages is often a necessary preliminary" to their introduction (p. 370). Apart from giving employers an incentive to adopt laborsaving technology more quickly, higher product wages made "labour more amenable to training" and more loyal once that training was complete, thus enabling employers to capture on-the-job training investments. In that happy outcome, real product wages rise together with productivity and profits.

The foregoing outlook on the benefits of rationalization becomes less rosy as the 1930s depression deepened. Research on the subject became more guarded, though not obviously influenced by the League of Nations research program in the 1930s on business cycles. During the 1930s, the issue of rationalization by adopting labor-saving machinery tended to overshadow forms of organizational rationalization based on scientific management and human resource management. This is not surprising given the appearance of mass unemployment. Short-term palliatives suggested to deal with inevitable adoption of new machinery included public works to relieve technological unemployment and the usual labor transference initiatives (Lederer 1938: 18–19). Employment subsidies and wage subsidies are surprisingly absent even though some contemporary economists favored them over trade policy – specifically over tariff responses.[30]

When various rationalization measures were ongoing at the same time as mass unemployment appeared in industrialized countries, a popular policy response effected by stringent legislation, was to place greater restriction on the employment of women (Fuss 1935: 465–69). Some progressive ILO studies in the 1930s condemned these misguided policies. Efforts to decrease the supply of woman workers had no beneficial long-run effects. According to Thibert (1933b: 620, 630) "abolishing women's employment as a remedy for ... unemployment" was reminiscent of "forms of social organisation belonging to a bygone age" and was anathema to the ILO principle of justice in labor markets.[31] Contrary to popular policy making in the late 1920s and early 1930s, ILO data demonstrated that well-trained women had been progressively entering new opportunities in nontraditional occupations that did not previously exist for either gender. Internal studies also confirmed that

> the occupations women are beginning to reject are either badly paid or entail much loss of freedom, and that the tendency is to seek better paid work, for which, too, better training is needed. The provisional and indeed haphazard employment of women, which under the lash of necessity drew masses of unskilled labor on to the market, is gradually giving way to a policy of more or less deliberate choice of occupations and direction of the labor market for women (Vallentin 1932: 498; see also Fuss 1935: 490–93).

Microeconomic forces requiring rationalization were, in this view, in fact beneficial to women's labor force participation and to the training of women.

Before the onset of mass unemployment in the 1930s, data from the United States indicated that in a rapidly expanding economy, higher labor productivity resulting from technological progress and total

---

[30] See Pigou (1927) and Casson (1983: 144–46).
[31] See also Thibert (1933a). Thibert's ILO work on the economic status of women (and children) extended over twenty years. Thibert was the chief author of ILO (1939b) and a prime mover in producing the ILO report for the League of Nations on "The Status of Women" (report submitted to the First Committee to the Assembly of the League of Nations, A. 60. 1935. V.). See ILO Archives WN9 and P1870, "Marguerite Thibert."

employment did not increase at the same rate. Employment grew more slowly. On the other hand, technological progress advanced labor productivity and was favorable to real product wages (Lederer 1938: 14, 17–19). These outcomes were greatly complicated, however, by the stage of the business cycle. Unravelling the wage and employment effects of technological forms of rationalization was made more difficult by the business cycle. Employment may indeed increase at the same rate as labor productivity in a business-cycle upswing:

> If labor-saving technological improvements are financed during the upswing, credit expansion will also enable the needs of the technically unchanged industries to be satisfied, so that not only will no secondary unemployment arise but the rising demand for capital will lead to extra employment. This will result in cumulative increases in production and employment (Ibid., 13–14; see also 235–48).

In the detail it is emphasized that when technological advancement is permitted freely to increase rapidly, wages tend to increase most in the affected industries (pp. 17–19). This positive emphasis is consistent with the ILO research orientation in the 1930s on the prime, long-term benefits for wages and employment of supply side factors. Product market developments (for example, new demands for modern consumer goods), product differentiation, and product market pricing were also seen as generally important *positive* influences on wages, employment, and unemployment. Certainly all these factors were more weighty influences than the negatively framed, oft-repeated bogeys in popular policy discussion, namely collective bargaining institutions, social insurance schemes, unionization, and the employment of women.

Increasingly during the 1930s and 1940s a wedge was driven between employers' labor cost or product wages and the income wages paid to workers. That wedge was exclusively the creation of governments wishing firstly to influence aftertax disposable income; secondly to play an increasing role in wage negotiations alongside unions and employers; thirdly to impose changes on nonwage working conditions in many industries; and fourthly to apply a new range of social security policies aimed at bolstering income wages. We turn next to some of these developments as assessed by ILO economists.

CHANGING THE LINKS BETWEEN SOCIAL AND ECONOMIC POLICY AND THE NEW SOCIAL SECURITY VISION

The first full-fledged study under the auspices of the ILO in the social realm – outside the direct analysis of remuneration in labor markets – was sponsored by the University of Chicago. Paul Douglas, later to become a renowned economist, presided over the study.[32] It sought to assess the arguments linking economic decisions of employers to demand labor at a particular real product wage, with the social objective to provide a "living wage" that included some form of family allowance (ILO 1924e: hereafter Douglas Report).

The research contrasted wage determination in a purely economic sense, understood in theory as an outcome of "the inter-relation between the demand and supply of labour" (p. 5) and the "productiveness of industry," with the worker's need to provide for a family of average size. Unmarried workers were advantaged in spot markets for labor in that their reservation wage did not usually include allowance for dependants. Since wage structures in the industrializing nations were determined by the wage policy stance of socially minded trade union members in negotiation with employers, the Douglas Report observed that many wage outcomes implicitly allowed for family allowances (for some average family size) (p. 10). Those unemployed (together with their families) and not receiving union-sponsored unemployment insurance where it existed, were excluded. If employers paid wages inclusive of some family allowance component – implicit or otherwise – this payment added to the cost of labor; such payments were observed either when union power was strong or government involvement required employer contributions, usually along with worker contributions in the 1920s, to family allowance funds. In addition, these payments were akin to social insurance premiums.

The object of family allowances in the 1920s, as reflected in the majority of schemes surveyed in the Douglas Report, was *not* to increase the size of the national income accruing to wage earners:

> The adequacy of the total wages paid in the community is not considered, nor is there any quantity as to the proportion of the total produce of industry which should go to labour. The problem is how to distribute the amount actually being paid in wages so as to secure the best social results (p. 12).

Conventional economic analysis of the family allowance question reinforced this judgement. Thus, Edgeworth (1922: 457) placed the responsibility for family allowances squarely in the hands of trade union organizations which should levy members and redistribute some earnings to workers with families. Moreover, the risk that the incentive to work would be eroded alarmed Edgeworth:

---

[32] ILO statisticians collected relevant data from ILO-member countries and Douglas completed the interpretative work. See Douglas (1972: 67).

[I]t does not require much knowledge of human nature to justify the apprehension that in relieving the average house-father from the necessity of providing necessaries for his family, you would remove a great part of his incentive to work (Ibid., 453).

For mainstream economists like Edgeworth, that unions or employers should choose to encourage workers to have large families is one thing; for the state to enforce or impose regulations making family allowance payments compulsory was anathema to him.[33] Certainly, in France family allowances were mandated explicitly in order to raise the birth rate although this was a rare case where the object of allowances was not directly related to the alleviation of poverty (ILO 1924e: 14).

The Douglas Report saw some significant long-term economic benefits arising from building family allowance considerations into wage negotiations. If the national income was better distributed *among* wage earners to take account of family size, then it would potentially reduce infant mortality, improve the health status of the population and enhance human capital, that is, "the qualities of future workers" (p. 14).[34] The idea of systematic income redistribution, effected through some broad system of social security to assist families, was not seriously considered by researchers in international organizations. In this, they merely reflected prevailing values and conventional economic analysis of the subject. In addition to incentive issues, that analysis insisted on raising labor productivity and on the imperative for employers to reduce production costs. So it is not surprising that the 1924 Douglas Report should declare the following self-denying ordinance: The "study is purely objective" and whether family allowances should be provided by employers, unions, individuals, state revenues, or some combination of these "involves consideration of the whole basis of public assistance and of the principles of taxation (e.g. equity, economy, etc.), which is outside the scope of this study" (p. 22). In retrospect, the Douglas Report is revealing for what it does *not* consider. It exhibited tentativeness in deriving policy implications on the family allowance question. It defined outside its scope crucial value judgements relating to income redistribution while at the same time giving ample space and support to the incentive argument for not paying generous allowances.

---

[33] Edgeworth's striking caveat was that his *"unbiased* economic conclusions," could be "overruled by moral considerations" (p. 431, emphasis added).

[34] Accordingly, pressure on married women to work would ease. To reduce this pressure was regarded as a *benefit* in the interests of raising the stock of human capital in the future (p. 14 n. 1). Taussig (1921: 152), a leading contemporary economist, concurred.

Individual "responsibility" and "incentive" arguments, so prevalent in ILO research and advisory papers in the 1920s, are all but expunged from similar work post-1935. The contrast is striking. Matters that the Douglas Report would not broach were taken for granted from the mid-1930s as a necessary part of any ILO survey of social insurance and family allowances. McClure's (1933: x) massive study of the work of the ILO and LON did not use the term *social security* at all, even though it proposed to offer "exposition of the economic work of the League of Nations." McClure defines economic work "in no narrow sense but rather seeks an understanding of all the endeavours directly to enhance the material prosperity of the world which have been undertaken by the international organization at Geneva." In keeping with ILO work up to the 1930s, McClure considers all the work in social economics as fragments without a unifying principle. Aspects of housing, health care, and social insurance are not directly linked to labor market outcomes.

Up to the late 1930s "social security was little more than a slogan" (Stein 1941: 249). Legislative initiatives in the United States, Chile, and New Zealand in the 1930s were especially influential in giving wider currency to the term.[35] Subsequently, ILO research endorsed and sustained national initiatives – it did not instigate them – and it proceeded to provide a full theoretical and philosophical rationale for them. Social security meant much more than social insurance. The latter was usually associated with a very limited scope of protection, and the dependence of entitlements on individual's contributions. The positive reaction at the ILO to "social security" initiatives is no better illustrated than in several of its key publications on the matter (ILO 1942, 1944; Stein 1941).

A constructive doctrine was developed at the ILO on the basis of preceding national practice in several countries. Most legislative initiatives on social security did not fully articulate a doctrine as such; they merely reacted to circumstances and changing social values by formulating practical schemes. The ILO thoroughly modernized its perspective on social insurance and gave meaning to the idea of "social security." First, a principle of universality – protection of all citizens irrespective of contributions – was established in ILO work. Thus the "policy of social security is based on a wide knowledge of social pathology and a study of the causes and effects of the common risks of life, to which low-income groups in particular are exposed" (Stein 1941: 249). These risks are not inherent in individuals; they are the consequence of "defective social organisation" (Ibid.). The risks are common to all

---

[35] We have not been able to locate the term *social security* in any ILO or League work before 1936. The term first appeared in legislation in the *United States Social Security Act* on 14/8/1935. See ILO (1936: viii).

individuals: unemployment, health, invalidism, and old age. Family allowances and public housing assistance could ameliorate some of the effects of these risks. If such risks are left to the free play of individual judgement and contribution, underprovision against them can have insidious, cumulative, negative effects on the level of economic output and on society as a whole (*viz.* "social disintegration," Ibid., 262).

The basis of comprehensive social security legislation was to arrest the problem of individual underprovision against a wide variety of risks – especially, though not exclusively, risks that reduced labor market participation and output growth. Monetary and in-kind benefits paid through comprehensive, universal social security schemes are therefore deemed most effective: They support a new principle of "solidarity" by giving "guarantee of minimum benefits, independent of contribution paid or even of the normal qualifying conditions" (Perrin 1969: 267). The purpose was to provide elementary protection for all, and no concern was held out for any erosion of labor supply incentives. The new social objectives were: (1.) to eliminate "poverty" defined by some national absolute standard in the first instance and (2.) to assure universal maintenance of some specified fraction of previous labor market income in the event of interruption or loss of earning power. These objectives were indistinguishable or converged for some social questions (for example, family allowances, old-age pensions, and invalid pensions).

The ILO preference by 1941 was clearly in favor of noncontributory benefit schemes financed out of public funds raised through progressive taxation regimes. Even so, methods of provision varied internationally, from compulsory social insurance schemes to full provision out of government taxation revenue. All observed schemes had an explicit egalitarian aspect. The ILO reports found less emphasis on the potential damage universalism and solidarity would do to individual responsibility and work incentive. From the late 1930s social security policies were "an institution for civic education" (Stein 1941: 274) and this conception had definite social engineering connotations. Moreover, the preventive function was vital in the case of health care assistance and housing; and information and vocational guidance provided with public unemployment compensation would reduce the duration of unemployment.

More narrowly economic research mentioned the place of social security policy in the operation of Keynesian-type aggregate demand management. Here the orientation was utterly pragmatic rather than doctrinal. Thus social security payments acted as automatic "economic stabilizers" – a form of compensatory government action as the case required. Unemployment benefits, for instance, "varied inversely with the level of employment" and helped counter a decline in aggregate demand in recessions (ILO 1950b: 77–78).[36] Social security expenditure complemented fiscal policy activism in countering fluctuations in aggregate demand. Reinforcing this pragmatic position on social security, Condliffe and Stevenson (1944: 210) reporting for the ILO, referred to the international, collaborative imperative of coordinating economic and social policy:

> [R]ising standards of living, full employment, social security and economic development *are now discussed more widely and in more practical terms* than ever before. There can be little doubt that national Governments will encounter a widespread and earnest demand for action designed to achieve these objectives. There is equally little doubt that independent and unco-ordinated action by national Governments is likely to hinder the international economic collaboration that is essential if employment and security are to be achieved together with high living standards (emphasis added).

After reacting to international developments, rather than in this instance leading them, the ILO researchers disseminated results from international experiences and legislative changes, and they did this approvingly. Social economics at the ILO from the 1940s contributed to the international transmission of Keynesian economic ideas insofar as social security was elaborated as a necessary adjunct of countercyclical macroeconomic policy. It may also have contributed to the perception that Keynesian macroeconomics carried with it a social engineering bias.

Research documents in the 1940s stress the desirability of "planning a complete social security program" in isolation from wages policy and labor market institutions (for example, ILO 1942: iii). Unemployment compensation, income maintenance, and industrial accident compensation were to be placed under the custodianship of social policy. Individual responsibility was downplayed and subordinated to a firmly held belief in the spirit of social responsibility somehow imbibed within and through the process of receiving social security benefits. A few years earlier the following admonition written in anticipation of a postwar revolution in economic and social policy would have seemed dangerously Utopian:

> Social security policy can only be planned as part of a larger programme which includes measures for promoting employment and maintaining

---

[36] That is, by "increasing and stabilising the level consumption of a large part of the population which in the past has had not only unstable, but also low, incomes, the economy is to that extent protected from the possibility of a large and sudden decline in aggregate demand" (ILO 1950b: 78).

it at a high level, for increasing the national dividend and sharing it more equitably, for improving nutrition and housing, multiplying facilities for medical care, and widening opportunities for general vocational education. Social security services are advantaged by economic adjustments that make for the expansion of employment and for the distribution of income in such a way as to produce the essentials of decent living. Such adjustments render it easier to finance social security services, for they not only keep benefit expenditure within bounds, but also tend to reduce it, since improved conditions of life and labor reduce the frequency and severity of social and industrial risks (ILO 1942: 97).

In this passage we find all key elements of the new policy vision emerging in the 1940s; it rested on social policy planning and deliberate employment promotion through macroeconomic management. Income redistribution was also becoming a more explicit economic and social policy goal. The new policy vision postdated by nearly thirty years John Maurice Clark's plea to formulate a general "social economics." Having purportedly "inherited an economics of irresponsibility," Clark foresaw movement "toward a sense of solidarity and social-mindedness" on an international scale (Clark 1916: 67). Confirming Clark's prescience ILO economists were to be found in the forefront promoting a new social economics of responsibility in the 1940s.

7 International Finance and Exchange Rate Policy

INTRODUCING NURKSE'S PIVOTAL WORK ON CURRENCIES AND INFLATION

Modern literature is replete with economic histories documenting international financial "crises," causes of crises, and lessons from policy responses with the 1920s and 1930s often given prominence. Studies concentrating on episodes of international monetary reform, the history of international monetary standards, and proposed new monetary orders also abound.[1] In all of this literature scant attention has been accorded to the doctrinal development of research work completed within and for international organizations.[2] Retrospectives available for the period from 1920 to 1950 are quite specific; they recount proposed arrangements for international economic cooperation and alternative monetary orders – that is, frameworks in which the international monetary system might operate – concentrating exclusively on the minutiae of negotiation over the Bretton Woods agreement in particular (for example, Eichengreen 1994; Gardner 1969; James 1996; Mikesell 1994).

The 1940s was widely conceived as a unique opportunity for reconstructing the international monetary order and gave rise to an array of intellectual constructs significantly different from the Keynes and White Plans – plans forming the basis for discussion at Bretton Woods in 1944 and for the final Bretton Woods agreement.[3] In this chapter we examine

---

[1] For example, Bordo and Schwartz (1999), Eichengreen and Portes (1987), Obstfeld (1995), and Tavlas (1997). On monetary orders past and present see Bordo and Eichengreen (1993), McKinnon (1996), and Schwartz (1987).

[2] Rare exceptions are Begg and Wyplosz (1993), Flanders (1989), and Guitián (1993).

[3] Some of those proposals are exposited in Halm (1945). J.H. Williams (1943: 150) lamented at the time that official preoccupation with the Keynes and White Plans meant "no other plan is likely to get an adequate hearing," and a recent celebrated historical overview gives just one unofficial proposal a footnote recognition (Bordo 1993: 33 n. 24).

the research of the LON and BIS on international finance and exchange rate policy in the 1940s, making Ragnar Nurkse's especially neglected work for the LON our primary focus. Nurkse studies various currency and inflation experiences as well as crisis periods in international monetary relations, and then offers a rule-based scheme to reduce the extent and frequency of exchange rate fluctuations.[4] Flanders (1989: 208, 209) observes that Nurkse's "classic" LON work, *International Currency Experience* (LON 1944; hereafter *ICE*) made him a "prototypical crisis writer."[5] That Nurkse systematically documents episodes of financial disturbance and currency upheaval and their putative causes, may account for some of his authority, but he also distills from these episodes a broadly applicable framework of rules and an approach to international policy coordination that was endorsed by other LON researchers.

Our discussion in this chapter initially considers relevant treatments of adjustment problems faced by countries in the interwar period undergoing crises in a context devoid of international monetary rules. The background and rationale for the LON position on the need for an exchange rate rule is then discussed. We then outline complementary stabilization rules for the principal dimensions of macroeconomic policy using Nurkse's second major work for the LON – *Course and Control of Inflation* (LON 1946; hereafter *CCI*) – as a guide. We conclude by assessing the LON doctrine on the international coordination of macroeconomic policy.

---

[4] A crisis, consistent with Nurkse's understanding, is a "disturbance of financial markets, associated typically with falling asset prices and insolvency among debtors and intermediaries, which ramifies through the financial system, disrupting the market's ability to allocate capital" (Eichengreen and Portes 1987: 10).

[5] By the 1950s, in Lundberg's (1961: 7) estimation, Nurkse had become "an economist of world fame." We also note Joan Robinson's (1945b: 407) review stating that Nurkse provided a "lucid and well-argued historical survey." Later Yeager (1966: 300) portrayed Nurkse as an economist who produced an "authoritative" study of interwar currency experience, and according to Haberler (1961: x), he produced a "classic in the field of international finance." See also Cooper (1999: 102), De Grauwe (1989: 13 n. 7), McKinnon (1996: 34), and Polak (1995: 738 n. 2). Nurkse's intellectual profile is briefly summarized by Lundberg (1961: 7–8) in his introduction to Nurkse's 1959 Wicksell Lectures: "[W]e were fortunate enough to have as our guest an economist of world fame – Professor Ragnar Nurkse from Columbia University, New York. Professor Nurkse had as early as . . . the middle of the 1930s published a book in Vienna on international capital movements. As research worker in the League of Nations' economic department he was active in this field for many years and one most important result of his work was a League of Nations' publication "International Currency Experience" published in the year 1944. I consider this study to be the best available one we have of the lessons of international monetary relations during the interwar period." Earlier in his career Nurkse studied for two years in Vienna from 1932 where the doctrines of the Austrian economists had some influence (as is clear in Nurkse 1935). He joined LON staff in June 1934 (Haberler 1961: vii).

ADJUSTMENT PROBLEMS IN THE CRISIS PHASE WITHOUT INTERNATIONAL RULES

While *ICE* is a detailed record of country experiences it contains a core set of ideas on currency management generated from a survey covering a period of international exchange and payments instability. Nurkse reviews an international (interwar) monetary system which was linked to gold but in which there were heterogeneous means of international payment (in addition to gold) in circulation with varying degrees of acceptability over time – a "mixed" system dubbed the "gold exchange standard" and officially sanctioned by the Financial Commission of the 1922 Genoa Conference.[6] As maintained by Nurkse (1933: 20–21) *en passant*, capital mobility can transmit and amplify business cycles and this point becomes a frequent refrain in *ICE*. To stave off these cycles, "synchronization" of the cycle and free capital mobility were understandably resisted at the national level. Specie flows were minimized. Given the widely presumed insufficient supply of gold in the 1920s to finance the exchange of tradeable goods, such an outcome was widely regarded as favorable. Actual practice resorted to "monetary 'autarky'" with the immediate purpose of retaining domestic price stability (avoiding an acceleration of inflation or deflation) (*ICE*: 14). International currencies and other liquid assets held as "buffer stocks" to meet payments imbalances obscured the link between official gold holdings and the domestic monetary base. Exchange rate stabilization in the 1920s took the form of participating countries fixing their exchange rates against one another, with at least one currency being anchored to gold (Eichengreen 1990: 247–48). Short-term foreign credits rather than specie movements were the hallmark of this arrangement. The immediate objective was not to balance international accounts; the purpose was to postpone, or avoid in some instances, the immediate domestic consequences of a short-run current account imbalance.

In Nurkse's estimation the gold *exchange* standard was employed to avoid the deleterious effects of deflation by ensuring that any gold flows decreasing the monetary base would be offset by exchange reserves. He recounts salutary experiences in some countries which attempted to use deflation as a means of restoring gold parities and such action reinforced widespread adoption of the exchange standard. In the 1920s, Denmark, Italy, and Norway attracted foreign capital inflows by allowing interest rates to rise. National concern to improve the current account was in fact subordinated to movements "through the capital account" – movements

---

[6] Pre-1914 antecedents to the gold exchange standard were substantial, for example, British Empire exchange arrangements (*ICE*: 28–30).

that to some extent turned out to be short term, speculative, and exaggerated by anticipations of exchange rate appreciation rather than economic fundamentals (*ICE*: 32).

ICE enters a judgement that countries should plan carefully to hold certain quantities of nonspecie reserves under the exchange standard because of the "common interest" to avoid "world-wide deflation" (p. 42). As a precaution against temporary payments difficulties, these reserves may obviate the necessity to make exchange rate adjustments "with all the disturbing effects on trade and production" that these putatively entail. Demand for liquid international reserves is likened to the holding of cash balances by individuals. *ICE* distinguishes between "(a) the need for such reserves . . . ; (b) the will or inclination to hold them . . . ; and (c) the ability to hold them" (pp. 91–92). Institutional factors such as country-specific political conditions will especially influence (b). Now Nurkse placed greatest weight on the degree of openness of an economy, measured by balance of payments variability over a long period, as a determinant of intercountry reserve distribution. Unequal reserve distributions could in fact represent an "equilibrium position" (p. 93). However, less-developed countries dependent on agriculturally based exports or countries affected by war, may hold suboptimal reserves (if any). The empirical rule derived in *ICE* for a "normal or equilibrium level of international liquidity" was a statistical demonstration of the variance in current account balances. The greater the variance, the higher the desired level of liquidity so long as (b) and (c) in the above quoted passage remained unchanged.[7]

A central bank's gold reserve requirement could not so easily be tied to an empirical rule: Legal stipulation by which the bank was required to keep a gold reserve minimum seemed mostly the result of convention. The primary objective was long term – to "maintain confidence in the currency" – that is, provide a backing for the domestic note issue and this depended "largely on psychological factors" (pp. 95–96). When gold, in addition to other reserves, is used for short-term purposes by some countries for effecting external transactions, matters become complicated. No simple international algorithm for setting a minimum gold reserve for central banks could be stated yet such a reserve was ultimately an indicator of the credibility of a nation's commitment to gold and thence the stability of its currency. Moreover, by the 1930s

> the link between central banks' international reserves on the one hand and domestic currency and credit on the other has become loose if not

---

[7] Modern commentators have rightly noticed that Nurkse anticipates discussion in the literature during the 1950s and 1960s on the optimal level of international reserves (Eichengreen 1990: 252–54; Flanders 1989: 210).

inoperative. The measures and tendencies which prevailed were such as to offset the domestic effects of shifts in international currency reserves; and this meant that legal reserve ratios had little if any influence on the money supply in industrial countries (*ICE*: 98).

In short, fractional gold backing for currencies lost its potency. Currencies therefore became more vulnerable to short-term capital flows.

In our view the intellectual advance in *ICE* relating to contemplation of optimal reserve requirements is of secondary doctrinal importance. Nurkse's core explanation of gold exchange standard *failure* is preeminent. Evidently the rules by which countries acted as if they were holding optimum reserves did not function for long; the liquidity crisis of the 1930s supervened and the antideflationary spirit of the gold exchange standard proved to be chimerical.[8] France, Germany, Italy, and Poland used the exchange standard as a transitory expedient. In France a principal motive for the central bank was to expand gross profits on its interest receipts from foreign bills and balances (p. 43). By contrast the sterling area exchange standard worked well, linked as it was to gold through the United Kingdom as "center country." The "psychological element" came into play again over the prestige of sterling which was rendered more credible by the British monetary authority's commitment to price stability and thence exchange rate stability (*ICE*: 46, 48, 61–64). The growth of sterling area financial activity in London "represented an influx of capital into the United Kingdom" which was well managed by the authorities and sterilized whenever the reserve balances of sterling area members were due to transactions unrelated to the United Kingdom. There was nothing automatic about the sterling exchange standard. British monetary leadership provided the reputation permitting credible use of discretionary policies to sterilize capital flows. Nurkse concluded that the growth in sterling area trade as a proportion of total world trade in the 1920s was due largely to the certainty created by exchange rate stability.

Why then did international efforts to stay linked to gold by experimenting with the various forms of exchange standard fail? The whole point of the first three chapters of *ICE* is to locate failure in disequilibrating capital flows.[9] The cause was fundamentally monetary and due to the diversity of institutional arrangements for international payments which permitted speedy capital mobility. The full crisis was of course

---

[8] Obstfeld and Rogoff (1996: 630) maintain that the exchange standard as it operated in the 1920s was a "powerful transmission mechanism for . . . deflationary impulse." Nurkse would have concurred with this summary judgement.

[9] This analysis was to form the accepted LON-UN view of the disequilibrating effects of short-term capital flows, and influence policy formation well into the 1950s (see LON 1945a: 106–08; UN 1949b: 65).

constituted by a significant fall in world trade. The institutional variation in international financial markets is illustrated by three cases, all of which broke the straightforward link between the volume of domestic credit and gold and/or foreign reserve holdings (*ICE*: 34–40):

1. *Germany*: Here the Reichsbank's holdings of reserves and domestic credit were not only a function of external transactions per se. The Reichsbank had to take account of endogenous variations in the preferences of German commercial banks which were such that liquid resources in various forms were held abroad according to interest rate differentials, expectations of exchange rate movements and the general "state of confidence."
2. *Italy*: Speculative short-term capital movements were exaggerated by exchange rate expectations. An exchange rate overshooting episode ensued.
3. *France*: An initial capital flight prior to 1926 was followed by deflation measures which were reinforced by capital inflows and exchange rate expectations. From 1928 the Banque de France officially accepted only specie and not foreign credits.

All three cases describe abnormal capital movements not clearly related to economic fundamentals.[10] These movements had more to do with the evolution of different international moneys – heterogeneous liquid assets – with varying degrees of acceptability over time (*ICE*: 66). For Nurkse, central banks were not to blame for these spontaneous institutional developments. Short-term interest rates connected with the demand for various forms of international money diverged from interest rates ruling for capital destined for facilitating trade and investment: One set of rates related to the preference for liquidity and the other for real, long-term investment.[11]

The "scramble for gold" and other preferred liquid assets not linked to the financing of international trade were due to sources of institutional weakness. Since the nucleus of the gold exchange standard system consisted of more than one center country, a disturbance in economic activity – even a misperceived macroeconomic performance problem in any one center – led to erratic variability in the center country's reserves and gold holdings with reverberations elsewhere. Insufficient cooperation between center countries, particularly when it was not anticipated that a new party wanted to become a full-fledged gold center (for example,

---

[10] Recent quantitative work provides qualified support for this conclusion. See Eichengreen (1990: 261–64).
[11] Here the similarities between *ICE* and the views expressed by Hayek (1937: 62 passim) are striking.

France) without international consultation and consensus, led to liquidity shocks and exchange instability. The gold exchange standard was a fragile, fair-weather system such that when "the comparative prospects of the various centre currencies became subject to discussion," sudden and disruptive capital movements were unleashed (*ICE*: 46).

Nurkse's model of exchange standard collapse, of financial crisis, is concertedly directed at malfunctioning international capital markets that are not governed by transnational rule-based frameworks. This is especially the case where norms of the international monetary system such as central bank provision of supplementary finance in cooperative efforts to stabilize exchange rates were adhered to weakly.[12] As *ICE* progresses, this core proposition is supported by two subsidiary themes. First, government-managed, exchange rate arrangements are required to facilitate, and spread the burden of, international payments adjustment. Second, international economic policy coordination, if it were possible at all, must operate under a rule-based regime.

In a detailed classification of international monetary relations in historical perspective, Ronald McKinnon (1996) identifies several "monetary orders" with attendant "rules of the game" for various subperiods, 1879–1992. However, notable for its absence is any characterization of an "order" prevailing for the period covered by *ICE*, 1919–40. Nurkse would have concurred subject to the qualification that there were short-lived episodes of "order" in the interwar period but these were not governed by any widely accepted rules of the game for central bank action in particular.

The idea that "rules" operated under the pre-1914 classical gold standard was in Nurkse's view to oversimplify a complex system in which the rules "were never laid down in precise terms" and were "never more than a crude set of signals or signposts" (*ICE*: 67). Rather, as Simmons (1994: 34) has since shown, there were implied norms guided by the notion that "external balance takes priority over the domestic economy." The object in principle was to secure quick, continuous adjustment to payments imbalances, with central banks merely facilitating by following the rules which applied equally to gold and foreign credits. Under a pure specie system *the* rule was straightforward, for example, when gold flowed out the central bank was supposed to contract its domestic assets by a factor

---

[12] Simmons (1994: 39–40) argues that provision of international liquidity under the gold-exchange standard norms faced two problems: "First, ad hoc exceptional financing was difficult to arrange because it was risky for the central banks or firms that made the bulk of the contribution. Furthermore, where the loan amount agreed upon was perceived as insufficient to salvage a currency under siege, market reactions would often render niggardly assistance packages counterproductive. In the absence of regularized channels and sources . . . surplus countries often delayed or shirked adherence to this norm."

dictated by its legal reserves ratio. With "a ratio of 33%, for instance, any net increase or decrease in the gold reserve was thus supposed to create a threefold expansion or contraction in the total credit base" (*ICE*: 66–67). Nurkse's focus was on central bank actions to offset changes in foreign assets and gold with opposite changes in the domestic money supply; he remains silent on sterilization under flexible exchange rates where domestic monetary policy is insulated from exchange rate market intervention.

Review of the historical record indicated that under the gold exchange standard regime there were crucial lags in central bank response to gold flows. First, there might be an inverse relation between a central bank's domestic assets and foreign assets from year to year; it may take "two or three years" for those assets to adjust in the same direction (*ICE*: 69). Thus a decline in foreign assets consequent upon an improved trade balance might not immediately be reflected in domestic credit conditions. Whether these delays were designed or undesigned depended on country-specific monetary policy reaction functions. For example, was there a deliberately built-in policy lag to make domestic adjustment more gradual? Second, the short-term commercial bank response to changes in the terms of central bank lending or to central bank open market operations might not be as expected, or might not be regular, thus sterilizing the impact of changes in foreign assets. Signals favoring domestic expansion, for instance, with a calculated, accommodating "degree of activity on the part of the central bank" may be thwarted by an interest-"inelastic demand" for credit or a newfound, more risk-averse approach in commercial bank lending portfolios (p. 71). In short, endogenous monetary responses dominate and sterilize capital flows in the short term ("two or three years" on Nurkse's reading).[13] Commercial banks can behave recalcitrantly and not be brought immediately under the control of crude rules of the gold standard or gold exchange standard which may have governed central banks.[14] A broader

---

[13] *ICE*: 69. It is very easy to misinterpret Nurkse's position. Thus, McKinnon (1996: 35): "[I]n noncrisis times, one would not expect sterilization to take place ... Nurkse's positive association between domestic and foreign assets of the central bank could hold. But this positive association is not itself a "rule" reflecting conscious policy." In fact Nurkse at no point sharply distinguishes between crisis and noncrisis periods. In *ICE* he discusses *lags* in central bank response or recalcitrant commercial bank reactions or both, whenever a divergence is observed between domestic and foreign assets of a central bank (and thence the domestic money stock) over periods of 2 to 3 years which are not necessarily "crisis" periods.

[14] *ICE* refers to three examples, the Netherlands, Switzerland, and the United States in the 1930s where "movements in international reserves were partly or wholly 'neutralized' in the sphere of commercial as distinct from central banking" (p. 71).

implication here is that on Nurkse's assessment of the evidence – that is, country-by-country surveys conducted over many years at the LON – economies did not exhibit the degree of price (and wage) flexibility required to make very quick adjustments to external payments imbalances.

A third factor making for sterilization was evident in cases where changes in fiscal policy were not coordinated with monetary policy. Here for example, *ICE* (pp. 76–77) recounts the French experience after 1926 in which changes in government debt retirement to the central bank automatically acted to sterilize the domestic impact of gold inflows. Monetary policy was rendered ineffective since the prevailing market "mood" was not favorable to taking up credit offered under an easy monetary policy. The sterilization of gold inflows in this case was not deliberate. Conversely, in the mid-1930s, a "whole range of fiscal, social and political contingencies" in France led to increased government borrowing from the central bank in the face of a monetary policy aimed to sterilize gold outflows.

Nurkse's fourth reason for "undesigned" sterilization turned on disequilibrating capital flows which weakened the control of central banks over monetary conditions. The heterogeneity of both international monies and monetary policy institutions compounded the problem. There was "a competitive rather than a complementary relationship between foreign and domestic credit, and the supply of money to any single market was highly elastic" (*ICE*: 72). The periods of time are hardly very short – being five years in the cases of Austria, Bulgaria, Czechoslovakia, and Germany where short-term capital movements made it difficult to discern a clear relationship between foreign and domestic assets. Capital flows aggravated a country's reserve position under fixed exchange rates rather than acting as passive financing instruments. Irrespective of central bank action, capital flowed toward countries in times of prosperity and conversely in times of recession; the problems of debtor countries were accentuated; adjustment by any supposed "rules" was thereby delayed.[15]

The systematic sterilization behavior of the Federal Reserve in the 1920s is adumbrated in *ICE*. The conjuncture of historical developments, including institutional arrangements, are represented as having created uncertainty in international financial markets. The increasing use of key currencies as financing instruments rested on confidence that such currencies would freely be convertible at a fixed rate into another asset and

---

[15] All this leads Nurkse formally to define "disequilibrating" capital flows: "a transfer which proceeds in such a direction that the discount or interest return on comparable assets is higher in the country of provenance than in the country of destination" (*ICE*: 72 n. 1).

ultimately if required into gold at any time. However, would the commitment of governments to honor the gold cover for national currencies be time-consistent given the costs of doing so?[16] A credibility problem lay at the core of the sterilization of U.S. balance of payments surpluses and the transmission of subsequent deflationary impulses elsewhere in the 1920s. More specifically, in the U.S. financial markets the gold influx up to 1925 was not regarded as long term, that is, not equivalent to specie flows if all nations' payments balances were settled on the basis of a genuine gold standard. Moreover, all monetary policies were no longer formally regulated by gold reserve ratios thereby raising doubts about commitment to convertibility. Lastly, Nurkse dismisses the proposition that credit expansion in the United States from 1925 was a lagged response to previous gold inflows. Credit expansion was primarily the result of endogenous factors, for example, "more economical use of the credit base through a shift from notes to commercial bank deposits" coupled with a growing preference for time over demand deposits (*ICE*: 74–75).

Throughout the 1930s sterilization of what contemporaries considered to be "disequilibrating" capital flows continued apace. *ICE* gives an account of associated bank failures, a loss of confidence in both central banks and currencies in the 1930s and the breakdown in financial intermediation – all of which led to a flight toward liquidity. There occurred "a hoarding of bank notes" in some currencies which rendered utterly ineffective monetary policies conducted according to any semblance of "rules" pertaining to a gold or gold exchange standard game (*ICE*: 81–82).

The distinction between deliberate and undesigned attempts to sterilize the impact of external shocks in the interwar years is considerably blurred. *ICE* documents a wide variety of sterilizing techniques some of which have little connection to intended central bank policy. The notion of a definite, existing set of "rules of the game" in the period under review is completely dispelled. Yet rules that bound committed monetary policy actions through significant periods of time were vital at least in lending credence to an exchange rate commitment, that is to improving the likelihood, but not guaranteeing, the success of sterilizing interventions. In any case, for Nurkse, foreign exchange intervention cannot be regarded as a separate instrument of policy; there is no substitute for monetary policy.

---

[16] Nurkse perceived that monetary policy must be subordinated to the fixed exchange rate – to the convertibility requirement – requiring substantial policy discipline in central, key currency countries (*ICE*: 121).

EXCHANGE MARKET DISTURBANCES AND THE RATIONALE FOR AN EXCHANGE RATE RULE

Much of the LON research in the 1940s considered frequent, large exchange rate fluctuations damaging to international trade. According to Nurkse, leaving currencies "free to fluctuate from day-to-day under the influence of market supply and demand" was likely to "result in chaos" (*ICE*: 137). Similarly, Gottfried Haberler (1945: 309), who contributed actively to discussion on draft reports by the LON Delegation on Economic Depressions in the 1940s, held the view that fully flexible exchange rates would lead to "extremely undesirable results" including "capital flight and violent fluctuations." More precisely, exchange rate over- and under-shooting of equilibrium levels, as determined by economic fundamentals and purchasing power parities, were considered pernicious results of flexible rates. The movements of exchange rates in practice were much larger than movements justified by changes in relative national price levels.[17] The prime cause of exchange rate volatility were disturbing, abnormal "self aggravating," short-term capital movements driven by "market psychology" in some cases inducing a "cumulative process of capital flight" (*ICE*: 114, 118, 126; also Haberler 1946: 70, 444–51). Of note was the quite common case of a "dramatic suddenness" of a fall in a flexible rate after a long period of slow downward momentum. Loss of confidence made for discrete disturbances in line with the lumpiness of market information flows (*CCI*: 47).

The costs of exchange rate instability were price instability and social unrest, both of which damaged output and trade (*ICE*: 118–22). There was no obvious automaticity in economic adjustment under flexible rates. A flexible exchange rate system in theory might insulate the domestic economy from international monetary flows – "the most important carrier of the boom and depression bacillus." In practice, the overwhelming weight of evidence indicated that cyclical movements in output were not independent "if capital moves freely" (Haberler 1946: 446, 449). Further, the noise created by exchange rate fluctuations might confuse signals consistent with the need to ensure efficient allocation of capital in the long run. The "fundamental test of real capital needs" is beyond the purview of foreign exchange rate markets concerned to act as conduits for internationally mobile capital. Notwithstanding these

---

[17] Nurkse would not therefore have accepted unqualifiedly Friedman's (1953: 158) argument: "Instability of exchange rates is a symptom of instability in the underlying economic structure." Friedman (pp. 175–77) expressly built a case against Nurkse's position in *ICE*.

strong judgements against completely flexible exchange rates, is to accept Cooper's (1999: 102) interpretation of the LON position as represented by Nurkse (and also Haberler in the 1940s) as one which perceived two extremes: Exchange chaos and capital misallocation due to flexible exchange rates as *the* alternative to some fixed but adjustable exchange rate associated with efficient international capital allocation would be to trivialize their contribution.[18] Indeed, it is accepted that speculation under flexible rates, given the right conditions, could be equilibrating (*CCI*: 46, 48; *ICE*: 116, 192–93; LON 1945a: 106–07). Nevertheless flexible rates encouraged disequilibrating speculation more often than not in the interwar years.[19] There is skepticism that monetary policy could quickly thwart speculative activity. Under a free float

> an outflow of capital has no tendency to reduce the domestic money supply, and there need therefore be no *early* check on the outflow through . . . a rise in interest. Besides, the credit system is usually elastic enough to meet a pressing demand for additional exportable funds either out of previously inactive reserves or out of additional bank credits (*ICE*: 121, emphasis added).

Furthermore, Nurkse's research for the LON (*CCI*: 47) identified the public's unwillingness to renew or buy treasury bonds in some cases so that a money supply expansion could be the *effect* of a currency depreciation and capital flight.

Under various fixed but adjustable exchange rate arrangements short-term speculative capital flows "seeking safety rather than employment" could also be disruptive (*ICE*: 103; UN 1949b: 66–67). Capital flight "may well have serious effects on employment and incomes" unless the country resorted to depreciation or exchange controls. Furthermore, these capital movements did not "represent basic investment decisions" and therefore did not have employment-generating effects in the recipient country (LON 1945a: 108).[20] With unrestricted capital mobility the

---

[18] Cooper (Ibid.) describes "Nurkse's antipathy to flexible exchange rates" (quoting *ICE*: 210), but neglects to mention Nurkse's comments that fixed rates may also be "equally harmful" (*ICE*: 211).

[19] Some empirical generalizations to this effect in *ICE* have been justifiably disputed. See Yeager (1966: 284–85) and Bordo (1993: 30–31). However, this does not entail that Nurkse's views on the negative effects of exchange rate speculation under flexible rates are universally invalid or irrelevant. See Aliber (1987: 211–12).

[20] In other research at the LON, Folke Hilgerdt (1935: 180) had described such short-term capital flows "vagabond capital" – "large amounts of short term capital" that gravitated to the major financial centers causing "most unfavourable" economic effects on the depleted country *viz.* reduction in reserves, currency depreciation, and cessation of domestic investment.

option for a single country in isolation of fixing the exchange rate is not feasible because of the self-destructive speculation that may be engendered by such a policy. Any suspicion in the market that the rate is misaligned may not initiate a crisis but could aggravate the situation; it would become self-feeding unless a realignment was made credible. Lack of credibility may be the result of market expectations that official reserves were inadequate to support a realigned rate, further inciting "abnormal" capital movements which will be "overpowering" irrespective of ruling interest rate differentials (*ICE*: 114, 116–17, 121). Prolonged interest rate rises or marked volatility in interest rates, depending on the case, could stem capital flows but the domestic costs may be unbearable. In modern parlance this is the familiar case of sudden and costly speculative attacks on a currency.[21]

Nurkse confronts the issue of the time-consistency of a government's commitment to a particular exchange rate rule: It might be infracted for local reasons, or it might not be optimal at all future periods which is so well illustrated by the demise of the gold standard in the interwar years. Before offering solutions *ICE* considers the "epidemic" of exchange fluctuations in the 1930s which began in agricultural-commodity-dependent countries in response in some cases to burgeoning current account deficits; in others where the current accounts were balanced or even in surplus the exchange rate was devalued in response to large-scale unemployment.[22] Here the rudiments of the Mundell-Fleming, Keynesian approach to exchange rates and the balance of payments is anticipated:

> [B]alance-of-payments equilibrium alone is not a sufficient criterion; at different levels of income and employment, *equilibrium in the balance of payments can be secured at different rates of exchange*. It may be better therefore to define the true equilibrium as one that maintains the balance in equilibrium without the need for mass unemployment at home (*ICE*: 126, emphasis added).

The Delegation on Economic Depressions (LON 1945a: 243) concurred, defining the "appropriate" exchange rate as that "which will secure long-run equilibrium in the balance of payments without imparting deflationary influences" on the domestic economy – specifically, balance of payments equilibrium at "a high level of employment without inflation." The "without inflation" proviso is not something unique to the (mostly Princeton-based) Delegation reports: Inflation also played on Nurkse's

---

[21] These matters have been broached many times since the publication of *ICE*. See for example, Dornbusch, Goldfajn, and Valdes (1995: 255–57) on episodes of currency collapses and their causes since 1978 brought on by speculative attacks.

[22] For a similar line of argument see also later UN research (1949b: 60–61).

mind. For it was all very well to desire an exchange rate that was consistent with balance of payments equilibrium *and* full employment – achieving these objectives was another difficult matter for an economic policy that also wished to stabilize the price level: "If we want stability at a level of 'full employment,' this may be very hard to achieve. The past has shown that inflationary or speculative processes are liable to develop long before that level is attained."[23] Just as in the Delegation reports on business-cycle management, Nurkse's work at the LON was acutely attuned to the dangers of inflation. As we shall see presently, only a macroeconomic policy mix based on clear rules of procedure and reaction, could reconcile conflicts between policy objectives.

That policy makers must consciously choose an equilibrium exchange rate in the sense elaborated above assumed that it may easily be identified. In a review of *ICE*, Joan Robinson (1945b: 406) applauds the space devoted to discussing the deleterious economic effects of the "wrong" rates of exchange while warning against overconfidence at the LON in finding the "right" rates. The purchasing power parity approach to real exchange rate adjustment is rejected by LON researchers ostensibly on Keynesian grounds because it "tends to neglect the important conditions affecting the volume of demand . . . leaving out of account wide shifts in aggregate income and expenditure" (*ICE*: 126). In the context of the period 1930–36, Nurkse was sympathetic to the many currency devaluations that took place, even though they were not carried out according to some international rule.

The position taken lately in Obstfeld and Rogoff (1996: 630) that Nurkse "viewed devaluation as a 'beggar-thy-neighbour' policy that raises . . . income mainly at trading partners' expense" is questionable. To be sure, Nurkse mentions contemporary debate on the dangers of "competitive aspects of currency devaluation." Then he proceeds to champion exchange rate adjustment in the 1930s when,

> as *was more frequently the case*, devaluation was followed by a domestic expansion of investment and national income, that expansion was a net expansion from the world point of view, tending to stimulate foreign trade all around (*ICE*: 129–30, emphasis added).

The duration of the economic crisis in the early 1930s was shortened by an activist exchange rate policy combined with, and accommodated by, monetary expansions which were "completely uncoordinated in time as well as degree" (*ICE*: 130).[24] What Nurkse adds to modern empirical

---

[23] R. Nurkse to W.A. Brown 23 September 1943, LON Archives C1738.

[24] It is therefore inaccurate to refer to "Nurkse's account of the *evils* of competitive currency depreciation in the context of the Great Depression" (Obstfeld 1995: 183, emphasis added).

work reported in Obtsfeld and Rogoff (1996: 628) is the stimulus given by internationally uncoordinated exchange rate adjustments to the "striking" systematic positive correlation between cumulative inflation and output growth. This correlation can explain how some countries recovered faster than others from the Depression.[25] In recognizing the favorable effects of devaluation on trade balances Nurkse was an elasticity optimist after the fact. He also ascribed economic recovery through devaluation to the interaction between foreign trade multipliers and the accelerator. Capital movements in these circumstances became autonomous, leading to long-term investment in tradeable goods industries. The disposition of the international stock of capital was equilibrating. The previously maligning influence of capital flows seemed to dissipate by the mid-1930s. Capital markets became fair-weather partners in economic recovery.

Disorganized international monetary relations led to economic recovery in the 1930s only fortuitously. The speed of adjustment could have been more rapid with "international coordination of anti-depression policies." The method of coordination was secondary: Anticipated disorganization creates financial market disruptions which in turn have real effects. What principally mattered was "coordination among the leading industrial countries." If these countries succeed in keeping their national income at high levels *and* manage to control the rate and variability of inflation, the problem would be resolvable (*ICE*: 111). In addition Nurkse recommended international organization to create buffer stocks of instruments for international payments so that countries could weather *temporary* balance of payments shocks without resorting to exchange rate adjustments. But he was realistic in not placing too much faith in buffer stocks. In situations where the incentives to hold reserves were low and international capital could take flight, buffer stocks – and other stabilization funds or clearing unions – would be inadequate (*ICE*: 218–19). He distanced the LON line of thought on this matter from the White (stabilization fund) and Keynes (clearing union) proposals perceiving these as insufficient in maintaining exchange stability in an international system with "unequal distribution of wealth among the nations" and as inadequate given the historical evidence pointing to regular, conscious decisions by governments to sacrifice exchange rate stability for domestic import requirements (Ibid.).[26] The interwar experience, on

---

[25] Obstfeld and Rogoff (1996: 630) formally model, but without acknowledging it, Nurkse's conclusion: "We will look at a model that suggests . . . countries that devalued their currencies (in order to inflate) may have actually helped their neighbours by expanding global aggregate demand."

[26] Nurkse represented the Economic, Financial, and Transit Department of the LON at the Bretton Woods Conference in July 1944. There is no record of his contribution to Conference discussion. His ambivalence to the Keynes Plan evident in *ICE* stands in marked

Nurkse's interpretation, illustrated that to proceed with inconsistencies between domestic policies and vague exchange rate commitments could precipitate conditions where the stability of the international monetary system would be threatened.

THE POSTWAR INTERNATIONAL MONETARY SYSTEM: STABILIZATION RULES FOR THREE MAIN DIMENSIONS OF ECONOMIC POLICY

Jacques Polak's (1995: 737) recent review of IMF research on exchange rates maintains that from the mid-1940s there was a "broad common understanding" of the structure of the postwar international finance system and that structure was to be based on "the international applica-tion of the main tenets of Keynesian economics in a spirit of coopera-tion among sovereign countries." This reading is acceptable if one concentrates on exchange rate research and policy at the IMF *in vacuo*. However, LON work providing the background for much of later IMF research (Pauly 1996; Polak 1995: 737–38) also included the Nurkse–Haberler view turning on the inextricable and crucial interde-pendencies between domestic and international policy settings within a rule-based system.[27] This system was constructed in contradistinction to, and was sometimes explicitly critical of, Keynesian economics.[28]

While not wishing to provide a Utopian plan, Nurkse insists that means should be sought to achieve a "maximum degree of international stability consistent with freedom to pursue autonomous policies to mod-erate the violence of economic fluctuations" (*ICE*: 191). The focus is on preparing a stabilization mechanism to avoid "violent" crisis episodes. Failing that, the degree of policy autonomy would inevitably be reduced. With growing international demand for high levels of employment, stable incomes, and social security in major industrialized countries post-

---

contrast to other LON researchers. Rasminsky (1988: 152–53) recalls the feeling of "relief" that Keynes had put forth a proposal on postwar currency arrangements, and how Keynes was "obviously excited and completely seized by the Clearing Union idea," imbuing others "with his enthusiasm and with the feeling they were participating in something important."

[27] That Nurkse's work for the LON was consistent with Haberler's is in no doubt. Haberler cited Nurkse's strong influence (see Haberler 1944: 179; 1947). Samuelson (1948: 407) refers to a "Nurkse and Haberler" position on international monetary rela-tions in the 1940s. Willett (1982: 166) states that Haberler followed "Nurkse's influen-tial analysis" in *ICE*.

[28] Certainly, Polak (1995: 738) acknowledges that "the broad consensus on international financial policy still left many questions of application unsolved." Nurkse would go further in questioning the fundamental assumptions behind the ability of international organizations to establish long-term binding agreements, although he would have agreed on the necessity for some form of cooperation to maintain exchange rate stability.

1945, it was a mistake to attempt to achieve these goals using aggressive bilateralism, extension of commercial policy, and exchange control. Exchange control in particular is described as generally "harmful and obnoxious," often used to protect misaligned currencies and delay inevitable adjustment (*ICE*: 222, 224). To minimize resort to these devices the LON offers a set of general rules for three dimensions of economic policy: exchange rate management, monetary and fiscal policy, and international lending policy. In this rule-based scheme there is clear awareness of what has been more recently termed the *open economy trilemma*: Fixed exchange rates and monetary autonomy to achieve high employment levels would only be sustainable if some rules were set to stabilize capital flows (Rodrik 2000: 180).

Exchange Rate Policy

Exchange rates should be fixed but adjustable in an orderly manner. Exchange rate policy is best assigned to the balance of payments. An exchange rate should be set initially using a center country currency as numeraire – a currency which may not necessarily be tied to gold. The establishment of postwar "equilibrium rates of exchange" was difficult and would involve consultation between policy makers representing major economies.[29] There needed to be a willingness to accept adjustments in order to avoid "incentives to such unilateral action" as import restrictions, export subsidies, or other trade restrictions (*ICE*: 141; see also BIS 1944: 31). Short-term cyclical movements in the current account would use central bank reserves, supplemented as the case demanded by short-term finance and credits from trading partners, the center country, or an international institution.[30] Any short-term external deflationary or inflationary shock that threatens internal balance is not to be reinforced by policy; sterilizing interventions are the rule in these instances.

A "crisis," that is, an exceptional "severe and protracted slump" (Nurkse 1945a: 32) requires exchange rate realignment in order to spread

---

[29] The BIS gave guidance. True equilibrium rates were those "consistent with the purchasing power of the different currencies" (1944: 42) – the calculation of parities using wholesale price indices was "the simplest method of approaching the problem" and formed "a useful starting-point" (1946: 80–81). As we argued above, Nurkse rejected the purchasing power parity approach to setting exchange rates. Joan Robinson (1945b: 405–06) appeared critical of the insufficient thought given to providing operational guidance on choosing the "right" rate. In general, Nurkse argued that an adjustable, fixed-rate system would be the best practical method of successively approximating the "right" rate.

[30] See *ICE*: 92–94; 221–29 and *CCI*: 57–58. The following discussion also draws heavily on Nurkse (1945a,b) – work that was completed when Nurkse was engaged by the Princeton Mission of the LON.

the burden of necessary relative price adjustment on domestic income and employment. This position rests on the viability of effecting relative price changes through exchange rate realignment under conditions of "rigidity of wages and prices." If exchange rates are not adjusted, it could be "difficult or impossible to secure adjustment of domestic money incomes needed to close a persistent gap in the balance of payments" (*ICE*: 225).[31] It is preferable to restore confidence *and* long-term capital flows by currency realignment provided that the real exchange rate does not suffer further pressure by allowing the underlying inflation rate to accelerate. Deficit countries could, on the other hand, achieve slower adjustment by cutting money incomes with all the attendant initial output losses and unemployment. Much needed capital inflows would then, he predicted, be sluggish to respond.

The well-known ambiguities associated with the constitution of the IMF which provided for discrete changes in exchange rates of member countries, is dealt with succinctly in Nurkse's writings for the LON during 1944 and 1945.[32] The IMF rule stipulated a "fundamental disequilibrium" in the rate of exchange as grounds for realignment. In *ICE* (1944: 226) there is already use of the phrase "a fundamental and persistent disequilibrium." Nurkse (1945a,b) was quick to offer operational guidance. Seasonal and cyclical current account fluctuations of "less than a year" were emphatically not grounds for rate changes, whereas a cumulative deterioration over "two or three years" was an indication of disequilibrium. A sudden, exceptional net change in a country's international currency reserve brought on by short-term capital flows would have to be assessed against real trade activity, and the threat of exogenous shocks such as political and social upheaval or war. In these cases exchange rate devaluation could be warranted (1945a: 7–11). Further, there were three additional indicators of some importance. First, long-term capital investment may slow or halt. Second, and this point remains implicit in Nurkse's treatment, the introduction of new trade restrictions – for instance active use of export subsidies and import duties – indicates an inappropriate exchange rate. There was some debate among the LON research economists on the dearth of commercial policy advice in early drafts of *ICE*.[33] In fact, as we point out in Chapter 5, *ICE* represents a

---

[31] At the same time Haberler was also convinced of the need for some exchange rate flexibility in a fixed exchange rate system (Willett 1982: 166).

[32] Nurkse was well placed to comment on the Bretton Woods scheme given his attendance (see footnote 26) at the Bretton Woods Conference (LON 1945b: 41). Other former LON researchers at Bretton Woods included Jacques Polak (Dutch Delegation) and Louis Rasminsky (Canadian Delegation) (Pauly 1996: 33).

[33] For instance, Folke Hilgerdt expressed concern over "the sharp dichotomy between monetary and commercial policy when analyzing the concept of equilibrium levels of currency" in *ICE*. Hilgerdt to Nurkse 8 March 1944, LON Archives C1738.

long line of LON publications dating at least from the mid-1930s favoring a more active exchange rate policy, and hence use of the price mechanism, over refinements in commercial policy. Third, "it is hardly proper to call the exchange rate a true equilibrium rate" if it is maintained for several years by depressing aggregate money income; sticky wages and prices may, under these conditions, produce large-scale unemployment without a corresponding current account deficit. Therefore at "different levels of national income and employment in a given country, equilibrium in the balance of payments can be secured at different rates of exchange" (1945a: 11). Nurkse settles on defining a "fundamental disequilibrium" as that exchange rate which can only be maintained over the business cycle – a two- to three-year period – in conjunction with mass unemployment, major changes in capital flows, and price-level instability.[34] Instability here means *accelerating* deflation or even inflation occasioned by social and political unrest and fiscal mismanagement (Nurkse 1945b: 292). Usually the indicators Nurkse refers to are observed in combination. In the final analysis exchange rate realignment contains elements of science and art, but it must be decisive to dampen the impact of anticipatory, speculative capital flows.

Nurkse's contingent "rule" on exchange rates, as with all his policy rules, crucially turned on having a "publicly recognized and recognizable criterion" (1945a: 13). In fact it reduces to a set of imprecisely weighted operational indicators which, even if afforded quantitative expression still have to be included in a stable, transparent policy reaction function of some kind.

Nurkse was well aware that his contingent exchange rate rule was not by its own right credible. Credibility had to be earned. Firstly, it was assisted by using exchange realignments only as a defensive measure and not as an aggressive device to gain competitiveness and expand an extant trade surplus. Second, by securing international support, either formally or semiformally, using trading partners or newly developed international

---

[34] Bordo (1993: 84) reflects the modern view that the Bretton Woods rule on exchange rate adjustment collapsed because it was "defective," since the "fundamental disequilibrium contingency was never spelled out." Early on, Nurkse attempted to address this problem. Williamson and Miller (1987: 10–11) provide an operational definition of "fundamental disequilibrium" substantially identical to that of Nurkse. The BIS was more sympathetic to the difficulties of defining "fundamental disequilibrium," arguing that one reason why no attempt was made was "probably that many different situations may arise" *viz.* structural disequilibrium (such as those identified by Nurkse), fiscal imbalances, and sharp declines in export prices in commodity-dependent economies. One operational definition was offered: Disequilibrium (undefined) could not be eliminated by any other means than exchange rate adjustment. But the BIS also warned that "fashions" in economic and monetary thought may lead to countries opting for exchange rate adjustment rather than "'disagreeable' measures on the home market" (BIS 1945: 109 n. 1).

institutions, realigned exchange rates can be rendered more credible. Sterilized intervention to support a new rate may need international support to be effective, and exchange rate adjustment would be made only by multilateral agreement. Third, publicly transparent monetary and fiscal policy rules must be consistent with the exchange rate setting over time. Specifically, as we point out below, these rules must make it costly to pursue a policy that accelerates the inflation rate.

Fiscal and Monetary Policy Rules

The foregoing exchange rate rule is underwritten by Nurkse's plea for international cooperation on exchange rates which required "major powers" to determine exchange rates "by mutual agreement" (*ICE*: 230). To speak "as if all countries were more or less economically equal" is a "dangerous simplification" (Nurkse 1945a: 21). As we argued in Chapter 5, *Pax Americana* ramified throughout international trade and monetary relations in the mid-1940s. Here was an opportunity to establish international economic policy coordination on a hegemonic basis with one or two key currencies at the center (*ICE*: 217–18). Stable, disciplined monetary and fiscal policies were a prerequisite for center countries; antiinflation policy was critical in this schema, unlike its subsidiary role in the list of objectives of the Bretton Woods system's founders, or later in the UN Committee's (1950a) proposals for international policy coordination to achieve full employment.[35] As we argued in Chapter 2, Haberler was cautious over applying countercyclical public expenditure policies to smooth out income at *all* levels of gross domestic product – more analysis of the complexities of economic management at or near full employment was required than was available in Keynes's *General Theory*. Like Nurkse, Haberler (1945: 309) favored an antiinflation emphasis in early postwar years, arguing that "the creation of employment" should "play only a subordinate role" in the hierarchy of national policy objectives."[36]

---

[35] Bordo (1993: 30 n. 15) claims that "Nurkse's interpretation of the lessons of interwar experience should be viewed as largely reflecting the views of Keynes, White and others." Perhaps so as far as *ICE* is concerned. But more than the architects of Bretton Woods, Nurkse and Haberler wrote extensively on antiinflation discipline. Giovannini (1993) rightly maintains that monetary discipline was not among the objectives of the Bretton Woods system.

[36] Similar sentiments were held by the BIS which by the mid-1940s had accepted that expansionary fiscal policy was an important part of policy response to depression, although "there is certainly much to learn as to the proper methods of adding to the money volume and of timing such additions" (1944: 312). No less important were supply-side policies "required to get business going" – cost adjustment, resource reallocation, and provision of credit (Ibid., 313).

The LON concern with postwar inflation and a macroeconomic policy-making environment favoring full employment over other economic goals motivated the 1946 study on the *Course and Control of Inflation* (LON 1946). Again Nurkse led the research team and wrote Part I of the Report. *CCI* contributes the conviction that inflation "is a monetary phenomenon" and it must be controlled. Antiinflation credibility has to be achieved if the exchange rate rule is to endure. Nurkse (1946: 347) lamented the lack of explicit rules on both monetary and fiscal policy in the IMF constitution.[37] The incentive to rapidly inflate or deflate must be avoided to negate destabilizing capital flows. The pernicious costs of inflation are fully discussed in *CCI* (65–68, 76–79). The fiscal policy rule should target long-term fiscal balance given that the "main threat of inflation arises from a current excess of government expenditure over government revenue." In *CCI* we also have the proposition that "government deficits were the primary cause of inflation" (p. 68). Government deficit reduction was always slow given the seemingly "irreducible" items in government expenditure (*CCI*: 76, 68). Notwithstanding fiscal rigidities, in the exceptional case of a crisis occasioning downward exchange rate adjustment, "inflation is to be avoided" by canceling "some or all the compensatory increase of expenditure" that might have been triggered by automatic fiscal stabilizers or discretionary fiscal actions (Nurkse 1947a: 56). Otherwise, taxation arrangements should be supportive of investment – both domestic investment and foreign capital imports (*CCI*: 47–48).

What is Nurkse's monetary policy rule? He wants an "appropriate . . . financial policy inaugurated" as a necessary "preliminary" to exchange rate stabilization at any newly desired level. And this requires a disciplined policy aimed ultimately at price stability (*CCI*: 131). He presumptively exhorts the "major powers" to use both fiscal and "banking policy" in tandem to "combat violent fluctuations in incomes and as a by-product to secure more stable outlets for raw-materials producing countries." He recites the familiar Keynesian article of faith: "price stability does not ensure stability of income and employment, and cannot in fact be achieved through stable income and employment" (*ICE*: 230, 231). Nurkse allows that all participating countries will pursue "good and steady employment without inflation" (1945a: 20). He qualifies this position by insisting that the policy mix must at least not accelerate the inflation rate. There is in fact more than one rule for monetary policy in all this, although it may be considered a "single" sequential rule. The source

---

[37] As we have shown in Chapter 3, Nurkse's colleagues at the ILO had earlier offered such rules, specifically monetary rules, and had recommended central bank independence.

of the disturbance to an economy matters and in some circumstances a decision to sacrifice internal balance in the short term may be a legitimate response of monetary authorities. Monetary policy (supported by fiscal policy) must in the long run maintain output and employment while avoiding a "general and rapid rise of prices." It must, in other words, be focused on the rate and variability of inflation (*CCI*: 75). Monetary policy is essential to accommodating the growth of output up to a level of employment consistent with a nonaccelerating rate of inflation and an exchange rate commitment. In the short term (for example, during a crisis, but not exclusively so) monetary policy may be used in tandem with international reserve utilization to defend an exchange rate when sterilized intervention using reserves will not suffice (*ICE*: 100, 104).[38] The return to high incomes and employment may in this case take time after a protracted crisis.

A rigid monetary policy rule cannot be specified across countries; that would also threaten policy autonomy in the adjustment to a crisis, and any possibility of international coordination. Coercion in the sense of a binding rule would be self-defeating. It was necessary to have an exchange rate commitment coupled with stable, time-consistent monetary policy attuned to a commonly held ultimate goal of "full" employment. Exceptional exogenous disturbances may well require a future exchange rate realignment, but the reputation of monetary policy makers in holding the line on inflation as the proximate objective, would not thereby evaporate so long as the one-off exchange rate adjustment was appropriate. Altogether, Nurkse (*ICE*: 131), Haberler (1946), and the BIS (1944: 42; 1945: 114) stressed that there was a causal linkage between macroeconomic instability and exchange rate volatility. Credible fiscal and monetary policy rules would contribute more to global monetary stability than would official regulation of exchange rates in isolation.[39]

---

[38] Cf. Obstfeld (1995: 185) which, in reflecting on "lessons learned or relearned" since the publication of *ICE* enters the following judgement: "[T]here was no compelling evidence that sterilized foreign exchange intervention, even when carried out by several countries acting in concert, is a reliable tool of expectations management *independent of monetary and fiscal policies*" (emphasis added). This lesson is made lucid in *ICE* even if the language of "expectations management" is absent.

[39] See also contemporary BIS pronouncements: "The truth is that exchange rate values are affected by all kinds of domestic conditions and policies in various countries, such as the relation between costs and prices, between savings and investment, between debts and the national income, etc." (1944: 42). In order to gain stability of exchanges, IFIs needed to "gain influence" on domestic policies, especially public finances and tariffs (1945: 114).

International Lending Policy

The central message in LON research in the 1940s is that controls on private capital flows should in general be liberalized.[40] Specifically, exchange controls restrict and misallocate international investment. Therefore, in line with the spirit of contemporary Bretton Woods discussion (and subsequent IMF articles on this matter), LON research established the principle that restrictions imposed on payments and transfers for current account transactions, as well as interest on dividends on foreign direct investment, should be removed. Intermittent movements of capital for other purposes, and destabilizing speculative capital flows were best avoided in the long run by consistent domestic macroeconomic policies rather than rigid controls on capital account convertibility.[41]

The slow down in net private capital flows and the relatively underdeveloped nature of capital markets in immediate postwar years understandably shifted the international policy focus to intergovernmental lending issues. Now short-term capital and intergovernment stabilization loans, or funds from IFIs, provide liquidity to defend exchange rates in the face of current account fluctuations. Once confidence in the future of a currency has returned, long-term private funds and foreign portfolio investments follow (*CCI*: 58).[42] These arguments contrast with later UN (1949b; 1950a) policies on international investment loans which stated that "general developmental" project investment could generate exchange rate stability. The UN (1949b: 67) argued that it was trivial and unhelpful to set a "simple rule" that loans should only be for "productive purposes" and that IFIs leave development finance largely to the private sector. General development loans would allow governments to invest in "unproductive" social overhead capital and make available "domestic capital otherwise not available for productive investment."

---

[40] There was nothing new in this message as far as policy recommendations in international organizations are concerned. Originally, Cassel (1927: 12) reported for the LON that "the free movement of capital between nations is of great importance for the favourable development of the world's economy." Again, the LON *Report on Exchange Control* (1938b) carried over this general belief into the 1930s.

[41] For the most lucid account of Bretton Woods discussion on this matter see Bernstein (1946).

[42] Implicitly Nurkse (LON 1946) recognizes problems associated with international lending under fixed rates. As Bordo and Schwartz (1999: 707) have shown, unless adherence to an exchange rate is "durable and credible" international loans must take into account exchange rate risk. However, Nurkse does not address the moral hazard features of international lending that lead to investment "boom-bust episodes" (Ibid., 706).

Intergovernmental loans would therefore create confidence in the local economy and avoid conditions associated with capital flight and exchange rate crises. Like Viner (1950), Nurkse was more cognizant of government failure and placed emphasis on the need for sound domestic economic fundamentals.[43] He provides a warning which should have been heeded since Bretton Woods: While exchange rate stability was essential, direct international loans and credit facilities "were neither sufficient by themselves to bring about effective stability" (*CCI*: 131). Monetary and fiscal policy consistency was indispensable.

Ideally capital movements for direct investment should move in countercyclical fashion with creditor countries lending more when they were buying less from debtor countries. Capital reconstruction loans following a crisis or war were also relevant here. That conditions be attached to such capital flows was axiomatic. Sometimes IFIs should provide funds by pooling risks and equalizing risk premia through the procedure of joint international guarantees (Nurkse 1945b: 293); by comparison with the Bretton Woods role for IFIs such as the IMF, these funds would go beyond provision of resources for short-term current account problems. Loan agreements must specify more consistent monetary and fiscal policies. Loan capital may be restricted where appropriate to the support of, or direct production of, tradeable goods. The rule for creditor countries in terms of their domestic policies was to maintain incomes at a high enough level to induce imports from debtor countries (*CCI*: 82).

Foreign control over some aspects of borrowing country policies was "inevitable and, if wisely exercised, desirable." Austerity programs were a necessary evil, the more so when stabilization loans were not provided before a crisis had produced "desperate necessity" in which case monetary disorder and price instability had already been destructive. The potency of such concerted, internationally organized lending, not to mention long-term private capital flows, in the crisis recovery or economic reconstruction period is reduced unless carefully targeted and conditional on specific structural and policy changes (*CCI*: 56–59). In all of this, Nurkse's proposals assumed a preference for public over private international investment – a stance also later adopted by the UN (1950a) report on full employment (see Chapter 8). The fact that a newly created

---

[43] The performance and function of IFIs is still vigorously debated. According to Krueger (1998) there is no agreement on the appropriate methodology for dealing with questions such as the effectiveness of IMF conditionality and surveillance, the contribution of the World Bank to economic development, and so forth. Guitián (1995: 819) argues that any such assessment will "be normative and reflects a particular interpretation of events in the international economy." There are substantive grounds for believing that IFIs fail in their actions along the same lines that national governments fail to correct perceived market failures (Frey 1997; Krueger 1998: 1999–2004; Vaubel 1994).

International Financial Institution (IFI) such as the International Bank for Reconstruction and Development (IBRD) had little experience in direct loans and did not have historical data on default rates of developing country sovereign debt from which to draw guidance did not deter recommendations favoring public investment through the IFI. Similarly, there was little guidance on how lending institutions should deal with cases of noncompliance with repayments schedules or outright default, and methods by which risk between lender countries could be diversified so that the costs of default are borne by all member nations rather than solely by the IBRD.

TOWARD INTERNATIONAL COORDINATION
OF MACROECONOMIC POLICIES

The LON's coherent "doctrine of international coordination of national policies" has a distinctly modern flavor partly because it eschews capital controls and avoids the option of relying on trade policy interventions. Immediately upon leaving the international civil service research role at the LON, Nurkse continued work on the theme of international policy coordination. He distinguishes naively ambitious postwar plans to abolish the business cycle using Keynesian policies; badly designed attempts at international policy coordination aimed to "synchronise . . . business fluctuations" thereby forcing countries to endure high variability in price levels (including deflation); and finally policies which would realize higher levels of employment and output with lower rates and variability of inflation (Nurkse 1947a: 58–62). He favored the last approach and there is complete continuity here with the ideas generated at the LON in immediately preceding years.

Policy coordination would aim to achieve "international monetary equilibrium." It would rest on the broad rules for the main dimensions of economic policy outlined above. In pleading for autonomy for each country to use broad monetary and fiscal rules Nurkse was allowing each country to choose the best domestically acceptable compromise given short-run variability in local awareness of the relationship between the conduct of fiscal and monetary policy and employment. The length of the transition path to the long run remains opaque in Nurkse's work, presumably varying initially between countries undergoing adjustment.

The LON macropolicy rules were intended to produce internationally aligned price levels, freer multinational trade, and some correspondence among national stabilization policies. They depend on a hegemon (in the sense of a powerful leader or leaders). Monetary stabilization in the leading center was important: That way an exchange rate anchored to the center currency could import credibility but some monetary independence would be sacrificed.[44] If the center country strayed, the stability of income, output, and prices elsewhere would be jeopardized.

Nurkse harbored scepticism about the prospects for a global regulatory agency or international governance structure, preferring instead spontaneously developed, mutually self-interested responses to organizing cross-border monetary arrangements. That the IMF had been created did not mean that it need be anything more than a flexible agency for coordination and consultation among countries with similar macroeconomic objectives and for coordinating crisis advice and recovery measures. In the predicted turbulent reconstruction period post-1945 Nurkse provided a distinctive LON approach to institutional emergence in this respect: "[E]ven without an international agreement, the spontaneous adoption and pursuit by different countries of the same basic objective – economic stability and full employment – is not an impossible hypothesis in these circumstances" (*ICE*: 231). When the Bretton Woods system had been established he averred that

> this idea of "combined international action," pleasing though it may be to the imagination, can be carried too far . . . Any scheme aiming, however discreetly, at some super-national regimentation of domestic fiscal and monetary policies would be certain to encounter political and psychological obstacles in the world as we find it. Besides, it would be unnecessarily ambitious (1947a: 60).

Nurkse attributed only loose policy rules to the pre-1914 gold standard. Just as that standard emerged "freely and spontaneously" among participating nations with common objectives, any new successful system of loose rules must be the undesigned product of spontaneous intercountry collaboration (1947b: 74). The potential conflict between national and international stability "could only be resolved if the various countries spontaneously adopted the same objective – a stable level of good employment – . . . or if they expressly arranged to coordinate and synchronize their policies for the maintenance of economic activity" (*ICE*: 110). Nations should unilaterally earn a reputation for adhering to a common set of rules. Different collaborative forms are conceivable so that multipolar global monetary arrangements could evolve.[45]

---

[44] This is the "imported credibility" argument made popular in modern international monetary economics. See for example, Giovannini (1993: 113).

[45] Nurkse did not extend this argument for multipolar arrangements beyond presuming that there would be some incentive compatibility justifying their existence. By contrast, as Rogoff (1999: 32) has maintained, today "[t]he idea that a certain degree of international governmental competition can be healthy for promoting investment and productivity is well-known in the literature on international macroeconomic policy coordination."

Centrally planned international cooperation utilizing a treaty, that is formal binding rules, could not be regarded as universally optimal. Indeed, as the BIS (1947: 166) argued, it was almost impossible to find "uniform solutions" given "diversity" of economic systems; IFIs should have "respect for, and noninterference in, the internal affairs of the individual countries." Optimal design of the international monetary system must therefore be an ongoing collaborative process. International financial crises were unique, requiring episodic cooperation in different forms and in different geopolitical regions or groupings. Crossborder spillover effects were also often spatially and temporally concentrated. The existence of a hegemon and "spontaneous recognition of a common policy objective" were usually required to provide that rationale for some modicum of explicit multilateral coordination (*ICE*: 232).[46] Nurkse was in fact proposing a liberal method toward achieving effective international monetary arrangements which relied on organic development, rather than on conscious design by a supranational agency, on a rigorous blueprint or treaty. Now *ICE* was in fact offering a more mature statement of a view that had formed in the Economic and Financial Section of the LON in the late 1930s: "It rests with each Government to take the necessary measures . . . Internal action by each of the countries concerned [with policy coordination] . . . is an essential prerequisite to the restoration of a sound [global] economic system" (LON 1938b: 5). This method was more recently delineated by Anna Schwartz (1987: 391): "[S]table international arrangements can only develop as *individual* countries adopt appropriate monetary and fiscal policies to stabilize their own economies" (emphasis added). Yet the liberal method, leaving open the possibility for organic development in the evolution of the international monetary system, ran against the ideational stream prevalent in the 1940s. The British, Canadian, and U.S. plans submitted to the debate at Bretton Woods were all represented as essentially formal and treaty based.[47]

The scope for a weak form of policy coordination is delimited by the need to preserve some policy autonomy at the national level. The self-interest of national policy makers wishing to retain some semblance of power over national policy objectives is *not* underestimated. Nurkse favored minimal cooperation insofar as macroeconomic policy decisions should normally be decentralized to nation-states. It is recognized that

---

[46] Many of Nurkse's insights on policy coordination compare well with modern treatments, especially Bryant (1995), Frenkel and Goldstein (1996b), and Frenkel, Goldstein, and Masson (1996).

[47] At least this is the manner in which these plans are outlined by the ILO (see Jack 1943). There is no reason to take issue with this representation.

there might be political and economic "difficulties" in maintaining correspondence between internal and external policy settings – differential rates of capital formation, government powers and administrative machinery, labor mobility, business "psychology," and so forth (*ICE*: 111).[48] Countries must be prepared to adhere to the "common policy objective" behind any monetary system that evolved by internalizing (rather than externalizing) these difficulties, that is undertaking policy choices to maintain trade liberalization and stable fiscal-monetary policy settings. By contrast, externalization would threaten the system's stability by "exporting" difficulties to neighbors and creating incentives for defection from the trade and currency system (Rodrik 2000: 182; Simmons 1994: 278–83).

The LON scheme rested on the existence of a nascent consensus about international economic policy objectives. There would be mutual recognition of the potential for disruptive crossborder consequences from monetary mismanagement and regular intercountry consultation and information exchange. Significant trade interdependencies may give rise to spontaneous development of more formal arrangements especially if one or other trading partner endures a major disturbance in which case the crossborder spillovers would be significant. The incentive to coordinate on an ongoing basis may in fact depend on the degree of an economy's openness. Indeed, the BIS (1944: 44) reviewed several earlier monetary groupings where "countries freely join such a group" given a hegemon and expected transaction cost minimizing benefits in international trade and payments. Nurkse's doctrine of spontaneity allows implicitly for the possibility of monetary unions, and as we noted in Chapter 5, in 1944–45 some preliminary work was completed at the LON on complementary customs unions.

The depth of coordination will vary but at least the method is clear: Macroeconomic policy would follow some broad rules, policy instruments being assigned specific macroeconomic objectives in common across coordinating countries. Rules, including the fixed, adjustable exchange rate rule, were means of enhancing the reputation and predictability of policy actions among freely coordinating countries (*ICE*: 222; Nurkse 1945a: 19–21). The assignment weightings will vary depending on circumstantial tradeoffs. For example, monetary and fiscal policy

---

[48] Simmons (1994: 276) demands that any theory that purports "to explain why states select strategies of internal over external adjustment must develop an explanation of the political pressures and incentives to externalise." The LON approach in *ICE* was to explore the heterogeneity in economic institutions and arrangements that, from time to time in the interwar years, severely constrained policy makers' ability to select a strategy founded on high principle.

Table 7.1. The LON Rule-Based Scheme for Macroeconomic Policy in an Open Economy

Policy Instruments	Assignment	Rule
Exchange Rate Policy	External balance	Contingent rule: fixed, adjustable rate
Fiscal Policy	Internal balance, but external balance in the crisis	Sequential rule: balanced budget in long run; short-run expansion of income and employment subject to a low rate and variability of inflation
Monetary Policy	Internal balance, but external balance in the crisis	Sequential rule: price stabilization in the long run; subordinate to fiscal policy in the short run
Commercial Policy	External balance	Liberalize: surplus countries to lower barriers
International Lending Policy	External balance	1. Liberalize capital controls: free capital account convertibility in the long run and no restrictions on current account transactions in the short run 2. Cooperate with trading partners to enhance liquidity for credible sterilization 3. Provide intergovernmental, conditional loans and special facilities in crisis

would have to be strongly supportive of the exchange rate rule in a full-scale economic reconstruction postwar or postfinancial crisis. Finally, if IFIs were to be successful in coordinating an international monetary system then confidence in their operations must be engendered and some "principles of national behaviour" established and maintained (BIS 1945: 114; 1946: 66; *ICE*: 111).

These general assignment prescriptions for macroeconomic policies and broad rules are represented schematically in Table 7.1. The analytical standard of modern approaches to international policy coordination emphasizing credibility and time consistency in policies adopted by coordinating nations, far outstrips the simple scheme in Table 7.1 (for example, Keohane 1984; Simmons 1994: 284–86). The LON scheme was analytically inchoate though striking in several respects because it: (1.)

contained a well-made distinction between normal conditions and crises (including reconstruction periods); (2.) delivered a rudimentary lesson in the theory of policy credibility and commitment to rules of different types; (3.) understood inherent complexities involved when both operational criteria for achieving policy objectives and the effects of applying different macroeconomic policy instruments are dispersed over a range of time horizons; and (4.) presumed, contrary to developments in the theory of macroeconomic policy in the last quarter of the twentieth century, that anticyclical government policies could be effective if applied systematically according to simple rules.

CONCLUSION

The LON's broad rule-based approach is not sufficient by the standards of modern research to secure long-lasting effective international economic policy coordination.[49] Nonetheless, in the context of the 1940s the LON research section made pioneering contributions on international finance. They attempted to address the assignment problem. Policy coordination does not necessarily require significant modification of existing national policies. There must be a common framework of objectives available *ab initio*. This presumption is acceptable in retrospect given the increasing degree of international economic integration in prospect in the mid-1940s.

The LON doctrine advanced specifically for the 1940s depended critically on three factors: (1.) multilateral, spontaneous adherence to common policy objectives, especially high employment; (2.) the stabilizing role of the hegemon's (or center countries') inflation discipline; and (3.) a common attitude to maintaining a low rate and variability of inflation. It is not expressly mentioned that these three factors may make for wide variation in attainable unemployment rates among participating countries which policy makers would need to accept. The implications of adopting all three have been discussed in many guises since the 1940s, for example, in the European Monetary Union debate.

The antiinflation and imported credibility messages embodied in monetary and fiscal rules; the insistence that rules be founded on "publicly recognizable" criteria; the avowed macroeconomic policy constraint represented by the need to ensure price level stability; and the negative attitude to trade restrictions and exchange controls all accord with orthodox, late-twentieth-century ideas. Nurkse and Haberler set aside early solicitude in such matters as the disruptive effects of short-term capital flows, preferring instead to articulate a rule-based scheme which, taken

---

[49] Crockett's (1996) survey of post-1945 episodes of policy coordination indicates that loose rules-based schemes have eventually broken down.

as a whole, would render these flows less pathological or more stabilizing. All this was tantamount to making their perspective different from that which dominated proposals submitted for consideration at Bretton Woods. Moreover, Nurkse and the BIS renounced a rigidly planned, global treaty for the solution of specific crisis difficulties and for governing international monetary relations in general.

At the core of *ICE* is an explanation of gold exchange standard failure. Immanent in that explanation is recognition that arrangements for the transfer of savings from suppliers to demanders in the international economy were inherently fragile so long as there were many national fiat monies and multiple reserve assets of variable quality. Coexistence of the fixed exchange rate rule and a liberal attitude to capital mobility was always seen as difficult to reconcile with the former being taken as a prerequisite for the expansion of world trade and high employment. Capital flows were indirectly manageable in a system of transparent, commonly adopted policy rules, supplemented by concerted intergovernmental action in crises. There is no presumption that blueprints for international monetary reform of the Bretton Woods-type would be optimal, only that greater power must be ceded to a hegemon in multilateral schemes that might be organized in postwar years. The latter is more often viable in crisis and recovery episodes when the common objective is to reduce transition costs and effect major global economic reconstruction.

The LON contribution in the 1940s represents one of the most outstanding mid-twentieth-century attempts to explain how responses to international financial reform and to more mundane monetary relations among countries, can be made more credible by commitment to rules. Policy coordination through broad rules could occur spontaneously and was very likely to be historically contingent, episodic, and transient. This was the LON message: It was modest, less detailed, and more general by comparison with the Bretton Woods Agreement, though also more enduring.

8   The Full Employment Movement from the 1940s

INTRODUCTION

Much research work in international organizations during the 1940s focused on policies associated with full employment. The experience of worldwide depression in the 1930s and the rise of Keynesian macroeconomics played a significant part in research on the problem of transition from wartime in both developing economies and developed economies. The late 1930s and early 1940s were described as a "great transformation ... in economic thought" at the ILO where "the economy was no longer regarded as being fundamentally self-directing" and "the possibility of an equilibrium at a low level of employment for an indefinite period of time had been recognised" (ILO 1950a: 25). Research effort on the immediate policy problems associated with postwar transition drew upon earlier LON work on economic developments post-First World War. Major issues involved economic reconstruction, relaxation of price controls, and the containment of inflation, restoration of international trade, demobilization of labor, and the avoidance of mass unemployment. Employment policy continued to feature prominently in ILO and UN work throughout the decade due to recognition of the link between unemployment and social and political problems. The international community in the new postwar world order appeared to establish a consensus predicated on the belief that countries could exploit "the possibilities for concerted government action to attain global social objectives" (Lee 1994: 474).

While the economic problems facing countries postwar were familiar to researchers, the international policy institutions that were born after the Second World War placed a new set of responsibilities on international organizations. The reincarnation of the League of Nations in the United Nations led to many key research secretariats being reformed in constituent bodies such as the International Monetary Fund, the World

Bank, and various United Nations committees. For the ILO the Declaration of Philadelphia (1944) was an "attempt to adapt itself to the new world order and, specifically, to carve out a role for staff within the new system of international organizations that was being established" (Lee 1994: 467–68). The declaration included objectives of full employment and rising living standards, extension of social security, nutritional and housing goals, equality of opportunity in education, child welfare, and maternity protection. To this was added Article V of the Atlantic Charter which empowered the UN to provide "the fullest collaboration" in economic policy formation "with the object of securing for all, improved living standards, economic advancement and social security" (Staley 1945: 1).

The commentaries of Franklin (1969: 299) and Lee (1994: 472–73) separate the ILO, LON, and UN research during the 1940s into two distinct phases: attention during the war years to policies necessary to avoid recurrence of mass unemployment, and longer-term policies that could be used by developed and developing economies once postwar transition was complete. We accept this division of subject matter although for expositional purposes it will prove more appropriate to examine the second phase of research in two sections: development policies and the full employment movement in the late 1940s. Firstly, we describe the early 1940s research on employment policy in wartime and the transition to peace. This section extends our discussion in Chapter 2 on the Reports of the LON Delegation on Economic Depressions and highlights continuity in research themes at the LON despite the war. Second, we address the rise of development economics at the LON and ILO in the mid-1940s as both organizations sought to understand the dynamics of economic development for "backward" areas by contrast with developed countries. A rich-country-poor-country model was used to form the intellectual basis for development policies later formulated by the United Nations. Finally, we examine the rise of the full employment movement of the late 1940s and early 1950s, specifically the United Nations (1950a) Report.

EMPLOYMENT POLICY IN WARTIME AND THE TRANSITION TO PEACE

Economic policies formulated to deal with transition and postwar economic conditions were the topic of much debate in the mid-1940s. James Meade (1948: v–vi) summarized the prevailing view among academic economists that

> a large measure of state foresight and intervention is required to guide the economy from war to peace, to prevent inflationary and

deflationary pressures, to ensure a tolerably equitable distribution of income and property, and to prevent or to control the anti-social rigging of the market by private interests, but ... these objectives can be achieved in an efficient and free society only if an extensive use is made of the mechanisms of competition, free enterprise and the free market determination of prices and output.[1]

"To plan or not to plan" was a simple phrase hiding a more complex set of policy conundra concerning the state's role in achieving major objectives of full employment, economic stability, equity, and freedom. The Delegation on Economic Depressions (LON 1943, 1945a) provides analysis of the particular policy issues involved in wartime and transition economies, the attainment of economic stability, and the prevention of monopolistic tendencies noted by Meade. The reports deserve revisiting in this context as they form the basis of contemporary debate on transition economics within international organizations and of later UN policy prescriptions on the full employment objective.

The problems of transition were the focus of the first Delegation report in 1943, although several other publications had addressed transition issues (for example, LON 1942a). While wartime provided the state with opportunity to experiment in commandeering and directing resources usually impossible in a liberal economic system in peacetime, the LON was more interested in investigating how a country moved from a control system to peacetime economic organization. The maintenance of high employment and the avoidance of postwar inflation were more pressing issues than wartime resource allocation. Certainly, the characteristics of the wartime economy allowed the attainment of a *type* of full employment given that the ultimate objective of any belligerent country was to direct all available resources to the production of goods and services for war. War imposed a structural change in production leading to depreciation and depletion of durable and nondurable consumer goods in favor of capital goods used in war goods production (LON 1943: 31–41). Now such a system of governmental control and direction of resources could not prevail in peacetime. The transition problem at its basic level involved the replacement of a control-based system (that was underpinned by a simple set of war demands and restraints on consumption) with a price-based resource allocation system.[2] In wartime the state

---

[1] As Meade (1948: v) noted, the extent of government planning necessary in the postwar economy was a central theme of some contemporary economic classics: R. Harrod's *Are these Hardship's Necessary?*, F. Hayek's *Road to Serfdom*, L. Robbins's *The Economic Problem in Peace and War*, J. Jewkes's *Ordeal by Planning*, and of lectures by H. Henderson and D.H. Robertson.

[2] Similar sentiments were expressed by the BIS in several Annual Reports after 1945. For example, "[t]he greatest mistake of all, however, would be to imagine that peacetime reorganisation could be achieved by perpetuating the often improvised methods of the

substitutes its own preference schedule for the aggregate preference schedule of the various income groups of the population . . . It is simple in [wartime] conditions and with so large a proportion of each country's manhood under arms to assure full employment. It is incomparably more difficult to assure it when production has to be geared to meet not almost unlimited repeat orders by the state, but the infinitely miscellaneous demands of the individual (1943: 34–35).[3]

The transition problems for most war-affected economies derived from either the production and resource allocation system used in the war effort, or destruction due to the war. The transition period involved reemploying demobilized labor and satisfying a range of postwar demands: consumer goods, raw materials for consumer and capital goods, and social infrastructure. However, focusing solely on redeployment ignored the change in capital structure that had taken place where older industries may have redundant processes or machinery, agriculture had deteriorated, and human capital had been depleted (1943: 45). Capital depreciation meant that countries may need to write off completely plant that could not be adapted, accepting that scrap value is "an unavoidable part of the total war outlay" rather than utilizing less efficient capital equipment (Ibid., 49). Similarly, as labor skills had depreciated over wartime, new demands for skills would not immediately be met. The state's role here is to assist in labor placement and guidance for job search, retraining, transfer of workers to areas of labor shortages, and vocational rehabilitation of injured workers and soldiers (Ibid., 66).

Macropolicy coordination in the transition economy involved the planning of public works expenditures concentrating on those projects that are indispensable in postwar reconstruction; the "time schedule . . . should . . . be guided by the overruling necessity to maintain full employment not simply in the first year or two after the war but, in so far as that is possible, permanently" (Ibid., 63). The financing issues involved were important, especially given that short-term increases in budget deficits stimulated aggregate demand and posed a threat to the maintenance of

war economy." And the use of physical controls over raw materials, prices, wages, movement of labor, and investment "seem always to involve a strong admixture of inflation" (BIS 1948: 163).

[3] The LON researchers (mostly Princeton based in the early 1940s) were in good company in arguing that postwar employment problems could not be solved using the planning techniques developed and refined during the war. In a series of lectures at Cambridge Lionel Robbins (1947: 76), one of Britain's leading wartime economists, summarized a prevailing academic view that an obvious temptation "to imagine a transfer of ownership and control to the state . . . [such that] the disharmonies of competitive or monopolistic production were automatically eliminated". Robbins warned that such a temptation must be resisted; his experiences had hardened him against "collectivism" as a viable policy regime (Ibid.).

price stability. Overall, the success of public sector expenditure programs in the transition to peace depends upon governments having the administrative structure that allows "postponable government projects [to] be employed to fill gaps rather than to compete with an active market demand" (Ibid., 65).

As the immediate transition problems were alleviated, LON researchers urged governments to withdraw from active involvement in capital reconstruction and labor markets, and focus on the macroeconomic policy instruments available to maintain a "high and stable level of employment" (1945a: 205). The Delegation's reports provided a theoretical rationale for contracyclical economic policies drawing upon the previous LON work by Haberler and Tinbergen. As we have seen in Chapter 2, the Delegation focused on the domestic and international macroeconomic policy issues involved in attaining high levels of employment. Employment policy required finely designed fiscal and monetary policies to maintain confidence and support private investment. Public expenditure and revenue decisions could be altered in times of economy-wide unemployment in order to maintain aggregate demand. These contracyclical expenditure plans necessitated, in the first instance, a movement in philosophy toward accepting budgetary balance over the business cycle, rather than annually (Ibid., 167). Policy options then depended upon country-specific circumstances. In advanced economies the use of tax policy would often be more effective in boosting national income than the timing of public works expenditure to coincide with deficient private sector demand. In economies facing cyclical stagnation a characteristic Keynesian response was advocated where governments could "counter fluctuations in private spending by budgeting for deficits." In less-developed countries fiscal policies may not be as effective in reviving business as "fluctuations in private investment do not play so important a role in determining economic activity" – such countries may need to resort to an active credit policy more in sympathy with pre-Keynesian monetary policies advocated by the ILO in the 1920s (Ibid., 166, 184, 156).

All three contracyclical fiscal policies – tax relief, public works timing, and deficit-financed expenditures – were analyzed in some detail with clear recognition of the differential impact each of these instruments had on aggregate demand and aggregate supply. Potential problems included changes to the composition and size of national indebtedness, and the crowding out of private sector investment through higher interest rates and increased competition from the state for scarce resources (pp. 167–88). The Delegation drew upon formal academic work – Hansen (1941) – in warning that the (internally funded) deficit financing of public works may have different effects depending upon the size of debt and the taxation system designed to finance interest payments.[4] In circumstances where debt was held by wealthier individuals and the tax system was regressive "the financing of the debt leads to a continued redistribution of income from the poor to the rich." The multiplier effects of such a redistribution depended upon country-specific factors:

> In a highly dynamic economy where savings are a limiting factor on development, this redistribution of income may facilitate the accumulation of real capital without depressing the level of employment, though at the cost of depressing real wages. In a mature or stagnant economy, if savings tend to exceed investment outlets, it will lead to chronic underspending and unemployment (LON 1945a: 181).

The impact of the debt also depended upon assumptions about the "demographic pattern of society" and the likelihood of aggregate supply changes that determined per capita debt burden – the economy's taxable capacity.

In terms of the crowding out effects of compensatory public expenditures the Delegation delineated three possibilities: an unintended impact on expectations such that business confidence would fall due to "unfounded mistrust of the policy of government spending"; a reduction in investible funds in countries where the "financial mechanism is seriously disorganized" such that increases in government expenditure may cause capital flight; and price and cost increases in sectors where public expenditure may "keep [wages and other costs] rigid at an uneconomically high level" and so hinder private consumption. Despite all these qualifications the Delegation concluded that in cases of "the *threat* of serious unemployment" compensatory fiscal policies were required and "should be undertaken with promptitude and courage" (Ibid., 182–85, 188; emphasis added). The Delegation always seemed to forsee favorable outcomes from the operation of compensatory policy. Accordingly, D.H. Robertson (1945: 402), in reviewing the 1945 LON report, was moved to write that the Delegation failed "to set out more explicitly the reasons for supposing that the successful *stabilization* of demand would result, not in a mere redistribution of the total volume of unemployment over time, but in its *reduction*" (emphasis in original). That the Delegation did not make a distinction between stabilizing and expanding aggregate demand is testimony to the intellectual domination of Keynesianism by the mid-1940s.

Finally, the LON experts recognized the need for minimal government involvement in labor markets and the avoidance of monopolistic tendencies, although like Meade they argued that a return to a liberal

---

[4] See Hansen (1941: 152–68).

economic system would provide the best means of achieving high levels of employment (LON 1945a: 21–22). The state's prime role was macroeconomic: To ensure "the fullest possible employment of resources" through the mitigation of economic depressions – it did not involve assuming responsibility for the economic implications of all labor reallocation at the microlevel. The concept of the "right to work," as we have discussed in Chapter 6, specifically excluded those unemployed by choice or by sectoral changes in labor demand. The right to work did not imply "that the state should assume responsibility toward each individual severally to secure him employment when he is temporarily disengaged" (LON 1943: 17). Indeed, a postwar employment policy entailed distributing, "as far as possible, the risk to the individual resulting from interruption or reduction of earning power" (Ibid., 14; 1945a: 22). This allocation of risks to the individual was part of a wider belief at the LON that high levels of employment were only possible over the long term if all sections of society were involved. Governments needed support from business and trade unions. If either group exercised their monopoly power the achievement of employment goals would be jeopardized. Thus, the LON researchers believed that

> governments will be best able to secure the full backing of both entrepreneurs and workers if they give their representatives as full a share as possible in both the elaboration and execution of anti-depression policies. What is necessary is that all three parties should face up to the difficulties together and feel a joint responsibility (1943: 17–18).

In short, the LON saw the maintenance of high employment as "a community effort from which all will benefit and to which all must make their appropriate contribution" (1945a: 210–11). The role of national governments was to provide compensatory fiscal policy (tax relief, public works, or deficit-financed expenditures) at times when the private sector components of national income led to economy-wide unemployment (Ibid., 166–67, 188).

The Delegation on Economic Depressions provided the dominant view emanating from the League on transition and postwar employment policy. On most points the ILO concurred, with E.J. Riches and L.B. Jack (1943: 5) reminding readers that the economic objectives proposed by the Delegation should be reminiscent of "discussions of economic and social policy in the International Labour Conference during the past decade." By contrast, the BIS performed a lone vigil guarding principles of fiscal rectitude and monetary stability. Economic transition to peace during 1946 and 1947 demanded policies bringing about balanced budgets, reduction in deficits outstanding, monetary reform, and establishment of "realistic rates between various currencies" (BIS 1948: 162). The use of public expenditures in a compensatory fiscal policy scheme should be avoided, and policy makers should return to "measures of financial control" – measures such as open market operations and discount rate adjustment that "in conjunction with the price mechanism, have repeatedly proved their usefulness in adjusting the balance of payments and in giving stability to the national currency" (Ibid., 165, 164). The BIS stressed some essential open economy points commonly overlooked at the time. Transition economics must not, in the BIS view, ignore the enduring link between a nation's domestic financial policies on the one hand and the state of its balance of payments on the other. In particular, interest rate variations appropriately managed by central banks could be used more frequently to deal with the open economy problems.

Apart from the BIS there was one ILO research program on the postwar employment prospects in developed economies that stands in contrast to the LON work – M. Kalecki's pioneering work on forecasting employment trends for the United States and the United Kingdom. In 1942, LON researchers had examined post-World War One economic transitions in the United States and the United Kingdom in order to predict short-run cyclical effects of transition from war to peace (LON 1942a), and their 1945 report devotes space to analyzing the economic structure of the major economies in order to predict expenditure commitments required postwar to achieve high employment levels. Kalecki introduced a major change in theoretical perspective taken at the ILO by introducing analytical techniques to forecast budgetary commitments for the United States and the United Kingdom – if these countries were to achieve full employment.[5] Whereas the LON reports generalize from data collected for the 1920s and 1930s about the potential financial commitments, Kalecki is estimating parameters in each economic system and extrapolating results up to 1950 to obtain an understanding of future macroeconomic challenges facing the two countries.

Kalecki's (1945b) article in the *ILR* drew upon his previous work on economic planning undertaken at the Oxford Institute of Statistics. It examined the technical difficulties of achieving full employment in a capitalist economy and presented a new style of analysis utilizing national income accounting and statistical forecasting.[6] Certainly the LON Delegation (1945a: 110–200) had couched its discussion of postwar economic

---

[5] Kaldor (1944) had already undertaken similar analysis of the full employment problem for the United Kingdom – an analysis that "created quite a stir, and became a prototype of far more sophisticated econometric models to serve the purpose both of economic management and forecasting" (Kaldor 1989: 24). There is no evidence to suggest that Kaldor and Kalecki had communicated on the topic.

[6] Kalecki was to later be appointed Director of the Economic and Stability section at the UN in New York (Sawyer 1985: 7). His contribution to UN reports on inflation and employment policy is discussed in more detail later in this chapter.

policy in broad national income accounting terms but it was technically deficient compared with Kalecki's effort. Kalecki advanced further by estimating future components of national income using various national income accounting approaches. Before one could discuss full employment policies definitively, national balance sheets (with base year, current, and projected figures) needed to be constructed in order to provide a comparative framework. These balance sheets incorporate personal consumption, net private investment in fixed and working capital, net exports, and public expenditure levels for a base year as close to the beginning of war as available (United States 1940; United Kingdom 1938). Assumptions were then made about likely tax levels, savings ratios, public expenditure, and investment based upon labor force and productivity growth in the two economies, and national income forecasts made for 1950 (United States) and 1951 (United Kingdom) (1945b: 459–61). Kalecki presents the problem of full employment as one where, net of private sector consumption, "with a balanced budget, a given level of employment can be maintained only if savings at that level are in fact "offset" by investments plus export surplus" (Ibid., 452). If the savings gap was positive (in the sense that a country had excess savings and reduced aggregate demand), a budget deficit could be run in order to bring about full employment equilibrium.

Kalecki's statistical analysis of the United States and the United Kingdom national income accounts indicated that postwar employment problems would be greater in the former country. The main structural differences between the economies lay in a higher U.S. savings rate and the need for government to manage its budget deficit wisely. The forecasted budget deficit *at full employment* in the United States was 8.6 percent of aggregate income (net of tax), as compared with 2.6 percent in the United Kingdom. The higher savings rate was "at least partly" due to the distributions of personal income, with the United States possessing a greater proportion of wealthier citizens who had lower propensities to consume (pp. 457, 459). Alternative reasons for the differences in savings rates such as differences in the distribution of income between workers and capitalists, or differences in tax law treatment of death duties were indicated, within the national income framework, to have little explanatory value (p. 458). The policy alternatives available to the United States and the United Kingdom related to improving various components of aggregate demand in order to close the savings gap at full employment equilibrium. For the United States "the problem of employment after the transition will require [an] . . . unorthodox policy in public finance." Public deficits *could be avoided* if working time was reduced, a taxation system redistributed income from higher to lower income groups leading to higher average consumption, or if a "vigorous policy of foreign lending" led to positive net exports (p. 463). Kalecki had elsewhere made a strong case for the use of progressive taxation and income redistribution (the "income tax system" over the "budget deficit system"; 1945a: 54) in employment policy.

In the Oxford Institute analysis of full employment policy options, Kalecki's "Three Ways to Full Employment" compares and contrasts the policies of deficit spending, the stimulation of private investment, and income redistribution. There he argued "that the second method i.e. stimulating private investment, is not satisfactory, but that both the first method and the third method provide adequate means to maintain full employment" (1945a: 39). Kalecki favored the income redistribution method which "not only secures full employment, but at the same time renders the distribution of income (after taxation) more egalitarian" (Ibid., 55). However, he argued that progressive taxation would encounter greater political resistance and left open the possibility that a budget deficit policy may still be required to achieve and maintain full employment. In all of this there was no discussion of the administrative problems associated with controlling the rate of investment, a point made by Joan Robinson in her review of the Oxford Institute paper.[7] Furthermore, as Robinson (1945a: 101) argues, there was little analysis of the case "where the rate of investment required . . . exceeds the full-employment rate" – a case likely to take place in wartime transition where the government is "to adjudicate between urgent claims for the available resources of the nation."

In representing the ILO, Kalecki presented similar arguments on the preference for contracyclical fiscal policy. The use of budget deficits to close the savings gap and maintain aggregate demand at full employment was preferable to leaving employment policy to the vagaries of private sector investment. And what mattered for countries such as the United States was not the level of national debt but the "burden of the debt" as represented in the relative growth rates of debt to national income. Government expenditure on goods and services (as in the classic ILO public works argument) *and* transfers were justified in that both types of expenditure impacted disproportionately on lower income classes thereby raising aggregate and average consumption levels in the economy (1945a: 49–50; 1945b: 464). Overall, Kalecki's sojourn at the ILO altered the focus of analysis on employment in the wartime transition economy by linking macropolicy concerns with income distribution and relative consumption and living standards between social classes.

---

[7] Robinson's (1945a: 102) review compliments Kalecki on the clarity of argument and presentation of alternatives, but chides him for believing that public authorities could easily garner knowledge of the private investment plans of firms.

THE RISE OF DEVELOPMENT ECONOMICS IN INTERNATIONAL ORGANIZATIONS: THE RICH-COUNTRY-POOR-COUNTRY DEBATE

The Declaration of Philadelphia pledged the ILO to work with other international organizations in achieving world economic growth, high levels of employment, economic stability, and high levels of world trade. Of particular importance was the recognition that world economic growth would involve the development of "backward" countries, posing a range of new policy questions associated with the impact of international economic interdependence on those countries as well as on developed nations. The rise of research on development economics in international organizations came in response to popular fears that economic development and industrialization would harm the trade of developed countries, as well as "a concern for policy rooted . . . in a mixture of moral commitment and what might be called historical excitement at the drama of intensified efforts at modernization that began to unfold in Asia, the Middle East, Latin America and Africa" (Rostow 1990: 373–74; see also Hilgerdt 1945: 7; Staley 1945: 12–15). Forming the foundation of this research was the LON trade and industrialization study by Hilgerdt (1945), and the ILO development studies by Staley (1945) and ILO (1946).[8]

The rich-country-poor-country model which we might reconstruct from research in international organizations in the 1940s describes the development paths of two countries at different stages of growth with the poor country having lower real income per worker, lower capital stock, and older technology. Trade between these countries increases world welfare and leads to technological progress in the poor country, especially in cases where there is a backlog of technology in the rich country that the poor country can draw upon. Hilgerdt and Staley focused on similar aspects of the rich-country-poor-country case: That a rise in trade and the provision of development capital to poor countries would raise world living standards, and provide new markets for rich countries so long as they maintained "adaptive" or flexible economic structures. These path-breaking studies have been acclaimed by Myrdal and Rostow – preeminent academic researchers in the field during the following two decades.[9] We shall examine Hilgerdt's and Staley's contri-

---

[8] Franklin (1969: 310) believed that ILO (1950b) provided the "first substantial ILO discussion of employment problems in developing countries." This position is not quite correct for there were several important reports produced on the subject from 1945.

[9] Myrdal (1957: 147) has described Hilgerdt's work as one of the "outstanding contributions to our ideas about the 'network of international trade' and related matters . . . [which] . . . are now classic texts" while Rostow (1990: 320) argued that Hilgerdt "evi-

butions with reference to three major themes: the benefits to rich countries from international investment in poor countries; the benefits to rich and poor countries as longer-term development takes place; and the role of international organizations in the formulation of development policy.

The benefits to rich countries from encouraging poor country development rested on trade-creation effects from higher world income, the reduced threat to security by improving living standards and income distribution, reduced pressure on "immigration barriers," and future social infrastructure expenditures as migration flows were curtailed (ILO 1946: 3; Staley 1945: 11). Much anxiety arose from a fear that the development of poor countries, through the provision of greater access to the markets of developed countries in particular, would threaten income and employment in developed countries. This issue was initially addressed in LON trade studies on the world trade network and industrialization. Hilgerdt (1945: 8) sets out to establish the conditions under which "an industrial expansion in backward countries would be favourable also to the older industrial countries." International investment flows that helped poor countries industrialize led to stimulation of poor country demand boosting agricultural production and incomes. Agricultural expansion conferred spillover benefits for domestic commerce and trade, creating new demands for goods and services. By analyzing historical-statistical data on trade and economic structures, Hilgerdt found that "*among countries of similar size*, a high manufacturing production per capita was usually associated by a high per capita import of manufactured goods" (p. 118; emphasis in original). Thus, the growth of poor countries through industrialization tended to be trade creating and did "not encroach upon the market for imported commodities" in those countries (p. 116).

The stimulus of poor country aggregate demand through international investment and the resultant rise in manufacturing imports presented two opportunities for rich countries. First, in the immediate postwar period the timing and direction of capital goods orders by poor countries would help stabilize rich country employment and income. International investment therefore was an important part of a rich country's

dently anticipated a good deal in the postwar prescriptive literature on development." Rostow also found Staley's work "a remarkably fresh and germane tract for the 1980s and beyond" (Ibid., 374). Staley's research was funded by the Rockefeller Foundation program "The Economics of Transition and Adaption" at the Fletcher School of Law and Diplomacy (United States) and enjoyed research support from the U.S. Bureau of Foreign and Domestic Commerce (Staley 1945: i–ii). Both organizations had expressed interest in postwar security. Furthermore, a presumed increase in political and economic security consequent upon international investment fitted well with the ILO's Declaration of Philadelphia, and motivated Staley to prepare the study "specially for, in collaboration with, the International Labour Office" (p. ii).

full employment policy, leading to a decrease in the savings gap characteristic of rich countries: "A great international programme of development, fitting the capital needs of some areas to the abundant savings of other areas, might provide just the extra stimulus needed to put the post-war era into the upward phase of a new 'long wave' in economic activity" (Staley 1945: 47). Second, rich country exporters faced changing demand patterns for manufactures favoring more consumer goods and different types of capital goods (Hilgerdt 1945: 23–25). The fear that poor countries might use infant industry tariffs excluding rich country exporters was ill-founded; such trade barriers would have only "a limited and temporary restrictive effect on imports" (Ibid., 117).

The longer-term implications of development investment were less straightforward as the outcomes from rich-country-poor-country interaction potentially involved multiple equilibria. The preconditions for growth depended upon population density and the extent of technological absorptive capacity, which determined the receptiveness to technology from rich countries. Sparsely populated countries were more likely to have conditions facilitating industrialization as they had limited home markets leading to the early development of foreign trade, development of internal transportation, and capital (Hilgerdt 1945: 38–40). Their technological uptake was relatively quick allowing them to utilize efficiently the backlog of technology available from rich countries. Densely populated poor countries did not have the preconditions for what Rostow (1960) was later to call "takeoff" – they were characterized by low labor productivity, poverty, old-fashioned and inert social organization, and deficient savings.[10] Industrialization could take place only if policies were introduced to check "excessive population growth," foster domestic savings (as "experience shows that only limited amounts of [foreign] capital are likely to be available for building up a manufacturing industry"), and improve social overhead capital and social well-being (p. 121). Under these conditions the role of public investment too must be different. Public works serving national development functions were valuable for their "product" as much as their much less visible, though often potent, "process" effects (ILO 1946: 23–24).[11] Better housing, increased well-being, and declines in mortality constituted some of the product effects that created the preconditions for growth. In summary, in the

---

[10] That Hilgerdt anticipated many of the features of Rostow's stages theory of growth was later acknowledged by Rostow (1960: 17–35).

[11] "Process effects" were the stimulus to employment and income deriving from public works due to (1.) direct employment/income, (2.) multiplier effects, (3.) induced private consumption, (4.) related demands for goods used in public works, and (5.) confidence effects of public works on private sector investment (ILO 1946: 23–24).

sparsely populated countries we would observe industrialization and increased international trade, while in densely populated countries "the greatest opportunities for raising productivity and income . . . will lie in modernization of their agriculture, their forestry, their fisheries, etc., and not, at least at first, in the increase in manufacturing" (Staley 1945: 5).

The increase in poor country incomes changes the composition of international demand for goods and services. Rich countries now need to be industrially adaptable in order to profit from the growth of poor countries, rather than respond to competition with a "policy of restriction" (Ibid., 188–89). Hilgerdt's study suggested that as long as multilateral trade endured, rich countries would face increases in third market competition as poor countries exploited comparative advantages associated with low wage labor in manufacturing. Third market *demand* would also rise implying that the overall trade effects were uncertain:

> Price competition from younger industrial countries may involve losses in the market for particular commodities; but normally such losses tend to be offset by gains resulting from the new demand that is released, in various ways, by competition (p. 115).

Rather than adopting policies which would deny poor country exports access, industry-specific industrial policies (for example, subsidies assisting factor transference) in rich countries were required to minimize the adjustment costs associated with the transition to a new set of trade conditions. Staley (1945: 197–217) presents a comprehensive set of "adaptation" policies to smooth out adjustments through stimulating industrial mobility and distributing the burden of changing economic conditions by having the state provide assistance to contracting industries.[12] Stimulating industrial adjustments involved the maintenance of an active competition policy, use of research and development tax shields to encourage development and marketing of new products and processes, and less direct means such as public health and education (which could alter the nature of domestic demand) (pp. 201–02). State assistance to contracting industries required resource reallocation policies such as vocational retraining, social security aid for retraining and relocation, and tax breaks to help firms write off obsolete capital equipment (pp. 204–05). It was these kinds of policies which were becoming more popular in the mid-to-late-1940s also in the context of a desire to raise and maintain high levels of employment. Finally, any infant industry support should be oriented toward short-term adjustment. Subsidies were the best policy instrument in that they remain transparent whereas tariffs and quotas

---

[12] Staley draws upon the work of William Beveridge, Allan Fisher, Joseph Schumpeter, and Colin Clark in developing these "adaptation" policies.

involved a *"concealed* subsidy in the form of higher prices collected directly from the consumer" which entrenched industry interests (p. 215; emphasis in original).

The role of economists in international organizations during the mid-1940s was to point out the compelling rationale for increasing interaction between capital abundant and capital scarce countries. Problems associated with information asymmetries, home country bias of private sector capital flows, and short-term speculative capital flows were minimized with the researchers preferring to view international capital as being patiently invested in the form of foreign direct investment or equity in local industry. Such capital would only receive repayment in principal after "a considerable increase in productivity has taken place" and, barring changes in political risk, is "likely to be left intact for an indefinitely long period" (Ibid., 49, 65). A range of international development authorities, not unlike the International Bank for Reconstruction and Development and the World Bank, would form a multilateral governance structure to provide "guidance, supervision and encouragement" to private sector and intergovernmental developmental enterprises. Key roles of the proposed authorities included:

1. launching a world survey of resources and coordinate data collection by national governments;
2. raising capital by selling securities to national governments and the public, to provide capital for developmental projects, and serve as an intermediary in development finance and technical assistance;
3. establishing a framework to guarantee "a minimum rate of return on approved developmental projects undertaken by private enterprise, in order to spread risks and encourage venture capital";
4. setting contract standards for international investment, and linking attainment of labor standards to financing; and
5. acting as a mediator to minimize political conflicts and regulate relations between lenders and borrowers (Staley 1945: 103–04).

Like many of his contemporaries, Staley is sanguine about the prospects for international economic organizations; he ignores potential difficulties ensuring rule enforcement in the provision of development finance between nations. There is no recognition that moral hazard might arise if international organizations committed to economic development are involved in underwriting investment projects, or that the establishment of guaranteed rates of return would distort international capital flows by replacing the market mechanism. Multilateral development organizations would solve market failure issues associated with financing poor countries, but there is no account taken of the dangers of governmental failure and bureaucratic inertia in these organizations. Indeed, Staley envisaged no disadvantages in progressing from their initial establishment to worldwide coordination of development policies, and to world federalism: to "some sort of responsible and effective world government" (p. 103).

Despite elements of idealism, development economics at the LON and ILO in the 1940s established some profound policy prescriptions shown later to be theoretically consistent and eminently applicable in some countries. The rich-country-poor-country analysis of Hilgerdt and Staley indicated that economic growth in developing countries may lead to some closing of the growth rate disparities between nations, and presumably improvements in world welfare. They understood the static two-country, two-good, two-factor trade model outcome that trade flows would be altered so that the rich nations move to specialize in the capital-intensive industrial good and poor nations specialize in less-capital intensive production. In Chapter 5, we demonstrated a persistent line of thought in international organizations from the mid-1930s favoring freer trade, turning on the argument that freer trade will be conducive to more efficiency in the utilization of the world's scarce resources. Now in the mid-1940s additional weight to the freer trade case is added: Freer trade is likely to have beneficial effects on the expansion of incomes and employment in poor countries. In addition, the LON and ILO researchers developed an appreciation of the dynamic, long-term benefits of greater international trade and associated investment flows which hastened technological uptake, investments in research and development, thereby improving growth rates in all countries.

DIMENSIONS OF THE FULL EMPLOYMENT OBLIGATION

Devising Full Employment Policies for a New World Order

The research roles of the ILO and UN agencies after the Second World War became intertwined as full employment was seen as an important, if not primary, economic goal. This is most clearly illustrated by the publication of the ILO's *Action Against Unemployment* (1950b) and the UN's *National and International Measures for Full Employment* (1950a). Both reports were expressly designed to complement each other in style and focus. Up to this point, however, postwar research activity on employment policy in the various organizations had been more piecemeal and overlapping, as we demonstrate below.

Formal statements on full employment policy were approved at ILO conferences in 1944 and 1945 giving direction to the research secretariat to undertake a comprehensive study of employment policy.[13] Debate ensued on whether the report should be written primarily by an academic of a planned economy persuasion such as Joan Robinson, or by a group of writers. Robinson was favored because she was "well versed in the Keynesian school of economics, with ability to write in a popular style and with a certain bias in favour of a planned economy which would be in contrast to Condliffe's bias in favour of free enterprise."[14] However, there was also strong argument for the ILO sponsoring a report that would "carry the subject further than the familiar generalizations of the Keynesian theory which, valuable as they are, leave almost untouched the great problems of structural change (and particularly the international aspects of those problems)."[15] Only joint work from authors representing a range of intellectual traditions could do justice to the issues associated with devising full employment policies in a postwar world constituted by free enterprise, mixed and planned economies.[16] It was envisaged that the multiauthored ILO report would

> discuss certain specifically international aspects of the problem (such as the regulation of international capital movements to the level and regularity of employment in industrial countries) and certain aspects which are common to many or all countries (such as problems of labour mobility and labour market organization raised by technological change or by changes in the composition or geographical distribution

---

[13] These statements were prompted by the earlier recognition by ILO officials that the Keynes mission to Bretton Woods (representing the United Kingdom) and the United States discussion on postwar organization had given little attention to the role of the ILO. It was feared that the ILO would be marginalized. For example, "It appears that there has been a certain hostility to the ILO in these discussions and it seems to me that there is a grave danger that the ILO may be left out in the cold so far as the essential problem of full employment is concerned" (D. Christie Tait to Waelbroeck (ILO Director) 23 November 1943 p. 1, ILO Archives EC 24).

[14] Tait to Waelbroeck, 23 November 1943, p. 2, ILO Archives EC 24.

[15] E.J. Riches "Proposed Study on Full Employment" internal report 31 January 1944, p. 1; ILO Archives EC 24.

[16] As Riches argued, "A symposium of this kind would, of course, be more difficult to arrange and it might take longer to complete than a study by a single author. It would, however, carry more weight, be international in character and more likely to take account of the different circumstances and problems of different countries; and it would represent more of a contribution on the part of the Office to a problem which transcends the vision and resources of any single individual." Potential collaborators included Robinson, Geoffrey Crowther, or A.C. Pigou (from the United Kingdom), Oskar Lange, J.H. Pierson, or P.A. Samuelson (United States), G. Myrdal or B. Ohlin (Sweden: "[T]here are elements both in the Swedish situation and experience and in Swedish economic thought which should be of considerable interest for other countries"), and E.R. Walker (Australasia: "representing countries which are in a less advanced stage of industrialization and depend largely on exports of primary products"); Riches, "Proposed Study on Full Employment," pp. 1–2; ILO Archives EC 24.

of population or by changes in the domestic or international location of industry).[17]

This discussion of research options was based upon a perception that the closed economy Keynesian policies for full employment were insufficient as a basis for international policy consideration. In the event, the proposed comprehensive study on full employment was to be delayed until the late 1940s and the ILO researchers spent the next five years investigating particular aspects of postwar planning and employment policy (for example, ILO 1946, 1948).

Research on employment policy at the UN was motivated by Article 55 of the UN Charter which stated that "the UN shall promote . . . higher standards of living, *full employment* and conditions of economic and social progress and development" (UN 1950a: 5; emphasis in original). In 1946, the UN established the Economic and Employment Commission (UNEEC) to advise on "the prevention of wide fluctuations in economic activity and the promotion of full employment by the coordination of national full-employment policies and by international action" (Asher et al. 1957: 235). The UNEEC appointed the Sub-Commission on Employment and Economic Stability to undertake employment-related studies until its abolition in 1949.[18] The Sub-Commission was charged with examining international economic policy issues associated with economic stability and development *viz.* national and international measures to influence credit conditions, real incomes of primary producers, and timing of development projects and capital expenditures to aid developing and developed countries. The economic secretariat to the Sub-Commission was directed by Kalecki, who provided "the guiding and controlling spirit not only as regards the theoretical framework . . . but also in the practical analysis carried out" (Dell 1977: 32).

The UNEEC paid particular attention during 1948 and 1949 to the danger of postwar inflation during the implementation of full employment policies. Analysis and comment was presented on the replies by national policy makers to UNEEC questionnaires on employment policies (UN 1949a) and surveys were undertaken of "inflationary tendencies" in member countries using macroeconomic data on components of gross domestic product, inventories, wholesale and retail prices, and monetary reserves (UN 1947: 7–22).[19] Kalecki's influence on the UN

---

[17] Ibid.

[18] The Sub-Commission included prominent economists R. Frisch and R.F. Harrod. Other members were L. Melville (Chairman), P. Chernyshev, E. Goldenweiser, and G. Leduc (Dell 1977: 34 n. 4).

[19] The surveys were organized by groups of countries facing alternative inflation-unemployment scenarios. For example, in the 1949 survey (1.) "non-controlled" or partially economies without rationing or price control systems (France, Italy, Poland, India,

reports was to highlight the distributional implications of alternative full employment policies, an orientation we have already noticed in his work for the ILO in 1945. This influence is illustrated best with the UN (1949d: 5–14) discussion of the dynamics of inflation (demand and supply-side) at full employment.

Kalecki (UN 1949d) delineates three types of inflation at full employment: inflation caused by increases in nonconsumption private sector demand; inflation caused by increases in government expenditures; and inflation caused by a supply-side shock such as a change in productivity. Demand-side inflation due to increases in exports or investment (non-consumption private sector demand) leads to negative wealth effects for households (reducing real wages and consumption) and a redistribution of income from labor to profits. The distributional effects were slightly different if inflation was observed largely in food prices. In that case, lower income groups would suffer a greater decline in real wages than higher income groups (due to higher propensities to consume out of current income), and it was from these groups that income shifted to producers. Depending on the structure of the economy, inflation in food prices would also cause a redistribution from workers to small farmers accentuating the decline in real wages. The second type of inflation was caused by increases in government expenditure at full employment. Here the distributional effect of inflation would depend upon how the expenditure was financed. Direct taxes levied on higher income groups would reduce consumption and savings, implying that to "prevent inflation the taxes should exceed expenditures sufficiently to offset this effect." By contrast, if taxes fall more heavily on lower income groups real labor income would fall initiating demands for higher money wages and, potentially, a wage-price spiral. Finally, supply-side inflation caused by crop failure or declines in productivity implied a different macroeconomic relationship between inflation and employment outcomes. In these circumstances, "inflation is not necessarily incompatible with unemployment" and if left unchecked could develop into an "inflationary spiral . . . in spite of the existence of unemployment" (1949d: 7–8, 9–10, 11).

The implications for policy makers from the UNEEC reports on inflation under conditions of high (or full) employment were that policy responses should be tailored to specific institutional and historical

Latin America); (2.) controlled economies (United Kingdom, Scandinavian countries and the Netherlands, Czechoslovakia, and Australia); (3.) countries in the process of removing controls (United States, Canada, Belgium); (4.) national planned economies such as the Union of Soviet Socialist Republics; and (5.) hyperinflation economies such as China in 1947 and 1948 (UN 1949d).

circumstances in order to reduce, or eliminate, the welfare costs of inflation. There was no presumption that broad compensatory aggregate demand policies would always be effective in controlling inflation. The experience of UN member countries was that a range of demand and supply-side policies were available from which policy makers could choose. This position is illustrated clearly in the UNEEC argument that direct controls could be effective in containing inflation at full employment *in certain circumstances.*[20] A rationing and coupon system could prevent the redistribution of income from labor to profits in cases where government had control over the total supply of the rationed good (UN 1949d: 11–12). When there were alternative sources of supply a control system would create a black market for the good concerned, complicating the economic effects of controls. Even then a continuation of the controls would provide social welfare benefits "despite the fact that the prices of the unrationed supplies reflect the prevailing inflationary pressures." Controls would maintain the real income of lower income groups (for whom "rationed supplies constitute a high proportion of . . . consumption") while market processes allocated the scare rationed good for higher income groups. A similar distributional outcome could be achieved by designing a compensation system which would raise all prices to the "free price" and provide transfer payments for lower income groups funded from taxes (or reduced subsidies) on producers and merchants (Ibid., 12 n. 1). The underlying point of the UN analysis of inflation was that the type of inflation at full employment dictated the appropriate policy response. The set of policy responses should be left as large as possible, and include the option of controls, given the primacy of full employment.

Increased unemployment in industrialized countries in 1949 prompted the UN and ILO governing bodies to invite updated research on full employment (ILO 1950a: 26).[21] The UN Committee of Experts

---

[20] Kalecki's (UN 1949d: 11–12) discussion of price controls is one of only a few examples where policy options are discussed in UNEEC reports. We accept Dell's (1977: 35–36) argument that Kalecki fostered a culture in the Employment and Economic Stability section that eschewed political controversy and adopted a position of "technical experts on the analysis of economic trends and issues but not as participants in the debate about such issues."

[21] The Economic and Social Council of the UN was dissatisfied with the quality of research undertaken at the Sub-Commission, and invited a small group of experts to prepare a report to aid the Council in its deliberations – a move seen later by Asher et al. (1957: 240) as an attempt "to obtain reports of a higher order of economic analysis, relatively unmarred by the intrusion of political considerations" that previously characterized the Sub-Commission's pronouncements. The 1950 UN Committee to report on full employment comprised prominent economists of the day: John Maurice Clark, Nicholas Kaldor, Arthur Smithies, Pierre Uri, and E. Ronald Walker. The Committee was supported by

and the ILO research team communicated over initial structure and coverage of their respective reports, and proposed a complementary program of work.[22] E.R. Walker (Chair of the UN report) and Riches (ILO) agreed that the ILO focus attention on frictional and seasonal unemployment, and the problems of capital scarce (developing) countries. The UN report would "deal primarily with the problem of maintaining effective demand and the problem of handling international disturbances" and make "specific references in our report to the work which the ILO is doing and the way in which it is able to advise governments on many aspects of government unemployment policies."[23] We now examine the content and intellectual pedigree of the 1950 reports adopting the conceptual framework undertaken in the original work: frictional unemployment, the developing country case, and demand deficient unemployment. We then assess contemporary reaction to the reports.

Frictional Unemployment

The ILO report's stated aims were to review and analyze unemployment experience since the Second World War, and to suggest action that might be undertaken to "prevent, relieve and reduce unemployment" (1950b: 2). A considerable amount of unemployment in any developed economy came from the normal workings of an economy through frictional and seasonal factors. In order to ensure that labor markets worked as efficiently as possible, ILO researchers investigated features of the labor market that might prevent its smooth working, and suggested policies that could be undertaken to reduce frictions and rigidities (p. 83).

   In order to reduce frictional unemployment to "a minimum consistent with national principles and traditions of action," governments should review and consider implementing policies that (1.) reduced

---

Kalecki and his staff at the UN. In July the ILO Conference adopted a resolution to initiate "the preparation without delay of a comprehensive report on the problem of unemployment" and directed the research secretariat to "cooperate with the United Nations and the specialized agencies directly" in analyzing policy alternatives (ILO 1950a: 45).

[22] See E.R. Walker to A.A. Evans (ILO) 28 November 1949; ILO Archives EC 24.

[23] Ibid. ILO Economic Advisor Edwin Riches had no doubt that the researchers succeeded in their aims. In a letter to Leon Keyserling on the U.S. Council of Economic Advisers, he stated the reports "usefully complement one another. The UN report goes into greater detail on such matters as full employment targets, automatic compensatory devices and measures to stabilise the flow of international trade. The ILO Report has more to say about employment market organisation and other measures to deal with frictional unemployment, and breaks some new ground in its analysis of special problems of the less developed regions and the policies which might be followed in dealing with them" (Riches to Keyserling 29 May 1950; ILO Archives EC 21–1).

information asymmetries in the labor market; (2.) provided vocational guidance and job retraining; and (3.) facilitated structural readjustment by decreasing costs associated with labor mobility. As for information provision, governments enjoyed economies of scale in information collection and were able to supplement ad hoc private sector agency information on the demand and supply of labor. Employment services could collect and analyze quantitative and qualitative data on vacancies, number on unemployment benefits, school leavers, and labor trends and turnover to enable workers and employers to job search more efficiently (pp. 84–88). It was also important that broad indicators of macroeconomic trends were made available quickly in order to discern employment trends. Overall, "[t]he development and organisation of adequate economic information services, private as well as public, national and well as international . . . constitute[d] . . . one of the first necessary steps in the formulation of a concrete program of action against unemployment" (p. 207). Vocational guidance and job retraining were important in reducing the duration of unemployment and avoiding the negative psychological aspects of unemployment (pp. 89–91). Experience during the 1930s depression and the transition from war to peacetime production indicated that adequate funding was required in order for counseling to benefit labor market participants.

Greater attention was given to the third policy on facilitating labor mobility. ILO researchers argued that in all countries regardless of their stage of development "a substantial proportion of post-war unemployment can be traced to the lack of sufficient occupational or geographical mobility in the labour force" (p. 91). Increasing labor mobility was a complex problem that needed to "be considered against the background of broader economic and social policy" (Ibid.). Labor was immobile due to a range of personal, financial, and structural factors: resistance to change; mismatching of skills and unwillingness to retrain; switching costs influenced by lack of information on new job opportunities; lack of suitable housing; and labor market conditions such as working conditions, wage differentials, restrictions in certain occupations (pp. 92–106). Thus, in the first instance reducing immobility involved employment policies reducing the costs of labor transference through subsidized private sector vocational training, training allowances, continuation of social security while on training schemes, employment information services, and special grants for relocation. Little action could be taken to alter the structure of the labor market determining wage differentials or working conditions unless governments worked in close cooperation with employers' and workers' representatives. Not considered were potential distortionary effects on incentives to supply labor following government policies reducing wage differentials.

Apart from lowering mobility costs the ILO concluded establishing new industries in depressed areas would not be advantageous. In planned economies such an approach might involve the nationalization of industries, or state direction of industrialization. Often these investments involved no profit – they perpetuated inefficient production. In free enterprise economies the policy choices rested on the reasons for economic depression. In situations where unemployment was due to a poorly diversified industrial base, entrepreneurship could be encouraged by establishing supportive institutional arrangements for investment. Local development policies might include tax shields and tax holidays, provision of new social infrastructure, concessional land and planning benefits, and seed-finance for venture capitalists (pp. 118–25). When unemployment was due to reduction in employment opportunities in resource extraction industries experience indicated that the most efficient policy response was to relocate communities.

State support for frictional unemployment could be united with social security policy. Unemployment insurance alleviated the negative effects of unemployment and replaced "at least part of the wage loss which the worker suffers," and it prevented "drastic reduction" in workers' standard of living (p. 58). The ILO reviewed the organization, scope of protection, qualifying and waiting periods, rate of benefit, and duration of payments of major state and private sector unemployment schemes (pp. 39–59). It concluded that support for unemployment was an important part of any full employment policy, but that any scheme should be linked to a precise definition of "genuineness of unemployment" leading to payment of benefits which minimized disincentives to search for work. If such schemes are to provide relief for frictional workers, "it is desirable that the organisation of unemployment insurance in each country be closely linked with that of the employment service" (p. 58). The primary focus of any scheme must be to restore workers to employment.

The Developing Country Case

Research by international organizations on frictional unemployment focused primarily on microeconomic aspects of employment policy relevant to industrial and developed economies. Employment problems in developing economies were associated with capital scarcity and chronic underemployment rather than frictional or cyclical unemployment. Economic policies to achieve high levels of employment required countries "to alter their economic structure, to revolutionize their techniques of production and, above all, to achieve a sufficiently rapid increase in capital accumulation to counteract the depressing effects of a rapidly growing population" (ILO 1950b: 128). Thus, unlike policies proposed to deal with deficient aggregate demand, research on the developing economy case involved assessing a myriad of microeconomic and regional development policies rather than the national macroeconomic fiscal-monetary policy mix. The ILO drew upon earlier research by Hilgerdt and Staley for the ILO, Kalecki's work for the UNEEC (and other UN reports) on the nature of economic development and the benefits of trade between rich and poor countries.[24] Two problems in particular were seasonal unemployment in agriculturally dependent developing countries, and underemployment in less-developed economies.

The social and economic effects of seasonal unemployment were greater in developing countries because agriculture tended to be labor intensive based on small production units operating at subsistence level. Here, large-scale rural development policies were relevant: modernizing cottage and craft industries and encouraging mechanization. Governments should ensure that the conditions for development were in place by providing technical assistance, cheap rural credit, and legislative support for the formation of cooperatives (ILO 1950b: 137). Where rural industrial development was not practical the encouragement of mixed farming entailing new crops (or livestock) with different growing cycles and markets would diversify farmers' income streams and alleviate seasonal unemployment problems (Ibid., 139–40). In addition, contracyclical policies might be appropriate in certain circumstances – public works timed to offset seasonal variations in agricultural employment, and government assistance for seasonal migration to help farmers supplement income. Any rural-urban labor movement, however, needed careful monitoring and controlling to avoid labor exploitation by setting legal minimum working standards.

Chronic underemployment represented a challenge to less-developed countries in that its elimination involved changes to institutions and social traditions (Ibid., 134). Furthermore, a regional approach was needed in order to allow for the uneven nature of economic development. The ILO favored government-sponsored regional plans arguing that state assistance was required to establish preconditions of economic growth and applauded India for taking a "middle course" where government and private sector initiatives had led to rural development and economic growth in that country. Land resettlement and encouragement of industrial development in surplus labor regions needed to be coordinated in

[24] For example, reports on financing economic development through domestic and foreign sources (UN 1949c), the UNEEC (UN 1947, 1949a, 1949d) reports on the problems of inflation and economic stability (which included analysis of the developing country case), and ILO regional conference deliberations on Asian economic development (ILO 1947, 1949).

situations where the region might be experiencing population growth, and where technological development may cause adjustment problems (Ibid., 168–72). Domestic financing for development would be supplemented by international development loans as in many countries capital scarcity posed a poverty trap, and a dearth of domestic savings restricted economic policy options. International aid should also be made available in terms of technical assistance and project-specific financing either directly through the IBRD or private sector loans with the Bank's endorsement (Ibid., 197). In summary, ILO researchers warned against the slavish application of Keynesian macroeconomic policies to developing countries where the transformation of certain institutions was a prerequisite for economic growth. Their expertise in country-specific analysis and data collection placed the ILO in a pivotal position to illustrate and disseminate a form of "best practice" economic development. By the late 1940s the employment problems of *developed* countries were being relegated to secondary importance at least in ILO research.

Demand-Deficient Unemployment

The UN Report focused on unemployment due to the "insufficiency and instability of effective demand" (1950a: 11). Like the previous LON (1943, 1945a) and UNEEC (1947, 1949a, 1949d) reports the UN Committee presented its analysis in a national income framework with Keynesian macroeconomic foundations.[25] The aggregate relationship between demand and supply determined full employment equilibrium, and "the condition necessary for balance is that the sum of factors having a plus effect on expenditure – private investment, government expenditure and exports – shall equal the sum of the minus factors – savings decisions, taxes and imports." Private sector investment, government expenditure, and exports were exogenous variables while savings, taxes, and imports were positively related to national income. There was no reason "to assume that the full employment level will be reached automatically or that, if reached, it will be maintained at that level" (UN 1950a: 21). Cyclical variations in national income and employment were

---

[25] One major criticism from several countries was that the Committee did not examine unemployment caused by institutional rigidities such as wage rate setting (ILO 1950c: 387). Indeed, in the UN (1950a: 100–04) Report J.M. Clark had, in a separate "concurring statement," stated that greater attention in the Report needed to be given to the wage-price structure and how it might limit the ability of countries to maintain full employment policies (see also Wallich 1950: 878). Instead the Committee focused almost exclusively on effective demand failure as the cause of *all* unemployment of a nonfrictional nature (ILO 1950c: 387–88; Viner 1950: 386–87). That effective demand did not require definition is testimony to the dominance of the Keynesian framework in the UN Report.

caused largely by instability in private sector investment giving *raison d'être* for governments to operate contracyclical policies to stabilize demand. The Committee's reading of theoretical research in the 1930s and 1940s was that investment instability was due to overinvestment cycles where expansion of capital stock "resulted in a more rapid increase in the stock of capital equipment than in investment opportunities" (Ibid., 23). Other disturbing factors were structural changes such as inventions and innovations, war, the fiscal policy stance of public authorities, and different capital good durabilities leading to sharp spikes in capital expenditures at different times.

While the Committee used a closed-economy, Keynesian framework they were cognizant of international spillovers from, and to, domestic business cycles, especially in a multilateral trading system with currency convertibility and fixed exchange rates that was the foundation of the Bretton Woods system. Primary emphasis was given to the hegemonic role played by the United States in setting full employment policy given that trade and monetary interdependencies synchronized national growth rates (Ibid., 29–33). Smaller countries would be constrained in attaining full employment if the major economies did not pursue consistent macropolicies designed to reduce income fluctuations at home. Only in the small open economy case could primacy be given to external factors as causes of decreases in aggregate demand. The contemporary preference for bilateral trading systems that led to trading blocs should not be seen "in itself [as] a major source of economic instability" or "an obstacle to the successful pursuit of domestic full employment policies by any country" (Ibid., 32). However, over time it was expected that international policy discussion needed to encourage movement toward a multilateral (rather than bilateral) trading system as a precondition for a smoothly functioning international economic system and the attainment of internal stability and full employment.

The UN Report was neatly divided into analysis of domestic and international policy prescriptions. In both settings, the first requirement for governments was to set "a full employment target that will provide a guide-post for their policy."[26] The target was determined by what would

---

[26] The proposal for an employment target was adopted in the UN Economic and Social Council Resolution 290 (XI): Each member government should "publish as soon and as precisely as is practicable the standard by which it defines the meaning of full employment as a continuing objective of policy, such standard being expressed, wherever possible, in terms either of employment percentages or of absolute numbers of unemployed or in ranges of such percentages or numbers; and thereafter publish such revised standards as may become necessary from time to time" (quoted in Dell 1977: 34–35). Kalecki was in agreement with the proposal.

now be termed a "natural" rate of unemployment empirically estimated to be between 2 and 4 percent of the total labor force, and governments were to treat growth of unemployment beyond this level as "evidence of an inadequacy of effective demand" (Ibid., 74). It was clear that the natural rate was institutionally and historically contingent, and was "expected to vary to a limited degree from season to season and from year to year, depending on the nature and extent of economic change and on other circumstances" (Ibid., 14). In all this it is taken for granted that unemployment rates were the appropriate indicator in terms of accuracy and timeliness to inform policy settings for maintaining high levels of employment. Measurement complexities were of secondary importance.

Policy options to stabilize effective demand depend upon whether governments wish to target (and compensate for) private sector investment instability directly or use more general compensatory aggregate demand policies. Countercyclical monetary policy (via changes in interest rates) could stimulate investment although it was recognized such a policy may be ineffective in liquidity trap situations. Supply-side policies such as tax incentives and subsidies were less effective in that they involved cumbersome administrative machinery and unreliable forecasting techniques. Public sector investment was considered more effective; it altered effective demand at both under- and above-full-employment income levels. Public authorities would target the long-term trend of private sector investment and be ready to compensate fluctuations with a reserve of readily implementable projects. Also of importance were policies dealing with the problem of "adapting the structure of the economy to a higher ratio of consumption demand to investment demand which may be necessary in order to secure adequate total demand" (Ibid., 36).

Unless private sector investment could be monitored accurately, stabilizing aggregate demand more generally with a compensatory fiscal policy would be the appropriate policy response to declining effective demand and associated unemployment. Flexible tax policy targeting consumption was preferred to public expenditure in that it could be implemented automatically and complemented the operation of automatic stabilizers which also tended to affect purchasing power directly. Sales tax, income tax, and social security contributions influenced consumer demand "with a sufficient degree of reliability to warrant application." The compensatory scheme used a range of "signals" to bring automatically into action differential tax changes, and involved rules which were "announced beforehand . . . [and] . . . automatically come into operation in clearly defined eventualities." The Committee also recognized that compensatory aggregate demand policy may be applied in graduated steps rather than in on-off settings: "The automatic compensatory mea-sures may be operated in a more flexible manner by setting more than one signal; so that certain expansionary action is taken at the first signal, further action if unemployment continues to grow until a second signal is reached, and so on" (Ibid., 41 n.). Employment indicators from "sen-sitive industries in which employment fluctuations are normally concen-trated" would be used in measuring changes in the business cycle (Ibid., 38, 40; see also 81–83). Confidently it was assumed that elasticities of demand and supply were easily estimated, and that the multiplier effects of changes in consumption were greater than those associated with exogenous changes in public expenditure.

The UN's use of targets and preference for rules over discretion in macroeconomic policy making was based upon the possibility of policy lags such as slow recognition of an unemployment problem and slowness of decision making. Policy inconsistency and credibility would be lost when policies were left *entirely* to the discretion of executive govern-ment: "[T]here is a strong presumption that the uncertainties of the future will generally weigh the scales in favour of inaction rather than action, and the adoption of positive counter-measures will be delayed until a downward movement in production and employment is well under way" (Ibid., 39). While the inflexibility of rules was acknowledged, the costs associated with discretion outweighed inflexibility at least in respect of responding to demand deficient unemployment. In other cir-cumstances "the executive organs of the government should have the power to waive the obligations . . . with respect to automatic compen-satory measures" but in doing so "they should announce the precise reasons for their action" (Ibid., 83–84).

Other macroeconomic policy settings should be consistent with the automatic compensatory scheme. "Flexible fiscal policy" that balanced budgets over the cycle was to be substituted for a traditional balanced budgetary policy. Indeed, government debt per se was deemed to have few negative externalities, the Committee noting that "past fears con-cerning the harmful economic effects of a large public debt were very much exaggerated" (Ibid., 42). Budget deficits were sustainable so long as debt servicing payments remained manageable proportions of gross domestic product. More importantly, inflationary effects of aggregate demand policies were assumed to be easily dealt with as side effects of a countercyclical policy approach. Simply, wage-price inflation could be avoided by preventing "an excess of effective demand." Other types of inflation due to supply bottlenecks or monopolistic tendencies in partic-ular industries did not "present serious difficulties to an effective full-employment policy." It was understood that using macropolicy to deal with inflation from these sources would only result in quantity adjustment rather than any change in relative prices. Therefore, "selective measures of a direct or indirect nature" were preferred and should be left for individual governments to determine, and should probably take the form of "qualitative or quantitative credit control . . . , direct controls over inventories and selective controls over prices" (Ibid., 85). Contrary to the lack of faith in discretion at the macrolevel, it was assumed by the Committee that governments could act, as the case demanded, to correct market imperfections at the microlevel – and act, for that matter, without producing significant policy failures or additional imperfections.

The international measures to maintain full employment proffered by the Committee have been assessed by several commentators as transcending "the 'closed economy' framework of the original Keynesian system" thereby making "international aspects of full employment an integral part of the problem" (Wallich 1950: 881–82). Its recommendations on international aspects were seen as "largely pioneering work" and "conceptually more novel" than the domestic policy recommendations (Ibid.; also Asher et al. 1957: 245). The Committee founded this point of its work on the argument that an international economic system required incentive-compatible rules minimizing the opportunities for countries to renege on their responsibilities. Three major requirements were identified: balance of international trade and finance flows; stabilization of international investment; and stabilization of international trade.

The balancing of international trade involved countries acting cooperatively to avoid balance of payments deficits or surpluses which may require adjustment of domestic policies (UN 1950a: 88–90). Cooperation would be achieved through ongoing multilateral bargaining and negotiation. In the process, policies would be harmonized and targets set to give a "quantitative expression of the rate and direction of economic adjustment" desired. While the outcomes of these negotiations were not to be binding, reputations effects were expected to operate when countries were faced with "inconsistencies in . . . policies and aspirations." Indeed, targets and conditions could not be imposed unilaterally – "[o]nly the governments themselves, by acting together in agreement with one another, can take the steps necessary to eliminate conflicts between their national economic policies" (Ibid., 52, 54). Problems associated with disciplining recalcitrant members or dealing with countries that opted out were not addressed.

Historical experience had shown that "foreign investment, if left to private initiative, tends to be extraordinarily unstable" and direct intergovernment involvement was needed to supplement private capital flows. Long-term lending through the IBRD should be encouraged so long as the IBRD is modified by (1.) increasing resources so that it relies less on borrowing on international capital markets, and (2.) expanding the range of projects the Bank can lend on so that larger development projects are encouraged. The Bank would "make the market" for long-term development loans by borrowing from member states, selecting projects and allocating funds, and charging interest rates on loans "no higher than required to cover the cost of the loans, the bank's operating expenses and a *fixed allowance* for the risks of default" (Ibid., 56, 57; emphasis added). There is no recognition here of the possibility of institutional failure in project selection, or that recipient governments would misallocate funds when the Bank changed from a project-based approach to "general developmental lending." The moral hazard effects that might arise from the assumption of a uniform risk distribution were ignored.

Finally, a major threat to the maintenance of full employment policies were fluctuations in effective demand originating from the external sector. The Committee focused specifically on situations where a country experienced a decline in exports, and subsequently reduced import demand. In order to prevent trade disruption from a decline in import demand from country A and a transmission of recession – a "cumulative contraction in world trade" – to trading partners, country A should deposit currency at the IMF which is then made available to exporters. Exporting countries could then draw the "scarce" currency "in an amount not exceeding the fall in the value of their [net] exports" in order to stabilize export income at a level determined by a reference year. The system was to have clearly defined conditions under which countries could draw currency, and was designed to be "self-liquidating" to ensure that the financial resources of the IMF were not unduly affected. The international currency reserve system could be supplemented by trade interventions by national governments such as import stockpiling in a primary product stabilization scheme. The restrictive nature of these schemes (in terms of the types of commodities it included) meant that "within a permanent and systematic international scheme" the depositing and replenishing of monetary reserves of trading partners "would be the most important single contribution that could be made in the international sphere towards protecting the world economy against the spread of recurring deflationary influences" (Ibid., 95–96).

CONTEMPORARY EVALUATION OF THE ILO AND UN FULL EMPLOYMENT REPORTS

The ILO report was well received by commentators who felt that it "made modest but useful contributions to the diagnosis and treatment of all three types of unemployment," was less dominated by Keynesian analysis and had "pioneered in the adoption of concrete measures" which contribute to the maintenance of full employment (Asher et al. 1957: 248–49, 234). The UN Report received wider condemnation for (1.) its general framework; (2.) its penchant for policy rules; (3.) the use of controls over market forces; and (4.) primacy given to full employment over other economic goals such as inflation. We examine each of these points *seriatim*.

General Framework

The UN Committee of Experts presented a Keynesian analysis "in the simplest and most mechanical sense of that adjective." The analysis of full employment was reduced to "a small set of algebraic equations" that involved policy makers having "confidence in forecasts and targets and in formulae, and in its unqualified pursuit of a single social goal" (Viner 1950: 386).[27] We could debate the costs and benefits of simplicity as a rhetorical device in policy discussion – a straightforward rationale for presenting a "mechanical" Keynesian analysis might have been that it was easy for policy makers at the national level to grasp.[28] Certainly, the general Keynesian analytical bias was quite obvious to reviewers. Apparently, from the confident way Keynesian ideas and concepts are paraded in their reports, the ILO and UN researchers presumed that they were orthodox, uncontroversial, readily measurable, and even incontrovertible.[29] Wallich (1950: 879) argued that "[t]hose who treat the aggregate of investment, saving, and consumption as the focal points of their analysis beyond which it is unprofitable to go, naturally incline toward quantitative remedies operating directly upon effective demand." Macroeconomic policy, particularly fiscal policy, was the preferred policy instrument. Wallich found the Keynesian conceptual framework useful as a "shorthand method" believing that the causes of fluctuations in components of aggregate demand were "sufficiently clear-cut to be isolated conceptually and controlled by policy" (Ibid., 878). Ostensibly, other more specific employment policies would address the price-cost struc-

---

[27] Similar sentiments were held by the Danish representative on the UNEEC who argued that "the influence of Keynes had led the [UN] experts to overemphasise the need for expansion and confine themselves too exclusively to the negative question of how to avoid unemployment" (quoted in Asher et al. 1957: 248).

[28] In the United States for example, the "economic theory underlying the compensatory [fiscal] policy had a directness which made it believable to non-economists" (Stein 1969: 461).

[29] Johnson (1971: 6) estimates that "beginning perhaps sometime in the mid-1950s . . . Keynesianism [became] . . . an established orthodoxy." Going by the reception given to the UN Report and that Report's slavish acceptance of Keynesian concepts and policy instruments we would be inclined to change that estimate to the late 1940s and 1950 at the latest (see also Jones 1972).

ture, competitive conditions, and special situations of regions with high unemployment – policies that were institutionally contingent, and not "sufficiently clear-cut to fit into a positive program of action."

Automacity versus Discretion

The recommendations of the Committee for explicit targets and automatic compensatory fiscal policy were supported in principle. Both Viner (1950: 394–95) and several government representatives on the UNEEC acknowledged that governments could obtain a credibility bonus by adopting explicit targets and a rule-based policy regime (ILO 1950c: 389–90). However, doubt was expressed over the spurious precision and the mechanical nature of the compensatory policies attached to the indicators recommended for use in changing policy settings. Two points made by contemporary critics were pertinent. First, the use of targets and indicator variables suggested movement to a rule-based domestic policy regime ranking full employment at the top of the list of policy goals and denied, for the most part, opportunities for policy makers to use their discretion. While the Committee (UN 1950a: 39) had argued that discretion often led to policy inaction, Viner (1950: 395) and Wallich (1950: 881) suggested that government failure may arise if policy makers were forced to make hasty commitments under conditions of uncertainty. The rule-based system also assumed there were no circumstances under which discretion in policy settings would be superior to "automatic measures." Even Viner, in a more promarket oriented review, conceded that "*ad hoc* legislative or administrative action, tailored to the special circumstances, the perceived lags and trends, of the moment" would be useful. The guarded use of leading indicators in employment policy making is preferred; their judicious (rather than automatic) use would "relieve us of any excuse for the pretension that we know how to design a completely effective employment thermostat" (1950: 395; see also ILO 1950c: 396–97).

Second, the measurement issues involved in target setting and designing indicators was severely criticized. The Committee (UN 1950a: 74) suggested that the unemployment rate should serve as the appropriate signal to alter policy settings. Yet the use of unemployment rates posed problems in that such a "residual phenomenon is much more variable and much harder to define and identify for specific purposes than is employment" (Viner 1950: 394). Unemployment definitions varied by region and institutional settings. Furthermore, the pool of unemployed varied in size by the opportunity cost of job search (and thus might underestimate hidden unemployment), and no account was taken of changes in the composition (duration, skill levels) of the unemployed;

depending on their actual configuration both factors could potentially reduce the potency of aggregative compensatory policy to reduce unemployment (ILO 1950c: 390–91; Viner 1950: 394–95; Wallich 1950: 881).[30]

In addition to the criticisms above, the Committee also failed to provide systematic analysis of the large body of contemporary research on the design of compensatory tax policy. The topic had been hotly debated in the United States after the publication of the U.S. "think-tank" Committee for Economic Development report *Taxes and the Budget* (1947). Furthermore, as we noted earlier, Hansen's (1941) analysis of compensatory fiscal policy had informed LON researchers in 1945. Hansen examined the use of cyclically adjusted taxes in bringing about changes in aggregate demand, and analyzed the differential incentive and elasticity effect on sales, savings, income, and corporate taxes on consumption, savings, and business behavior. In terms of smoothing national income fluctuations Hansen (1941: 297) concluded that "the boom would develop in a more stable manner under a cyclical adjustment of payroll or sales taxes than under a cyclical adjustment of highly progressive corporate and individual income taxes." He was also careful to establish conditions under which such a policy would be effective – "for a dynamic, expanding economy enjoying vigorous booms a fluctuating consumption tax may be the appropriate tax policy" – but for milder cyclical fluctuations "offsetting fluctuations in governmental expenditures" are more appropriate (Ibid., 300). It was enough, though, to assume that automatic tax policies affected expenditure in similar fashion, or that tax policy can be used in all types of economies. Hansen's message was incorporated into earlier LON work but is conspicuously absent from the UN Report.[31]

The UN Committee's failure to acknowledge relevant policy research from other international organizations is best illustrated by the lack of interest in BIS proposals. The BIS had cogently and consistently argued throughout the 1940s that not all underemployment equilibria could satisfactorily be corrected with compensatory fiscal policy. In situations of capital depletion and low domestic savings, increases in investment

---

[30] The system of currency reserves and convertibility that would operate during recession was also prone to definitional and measurement difficulties, rogue behavior by member countries and timing problems that were assumed away (Viner 1950: 407; Wallich 1950: 882).

[31] By the end of the decade Hansen (1949: 183) was of the opinion that economists had "not learned how to make government an effective, flexible, and responsive instrument in a fluctuating and highly complex society." Viner (1950: 394, 393) also warned that "the technical problems of designing flexible taxes are formidable and have scarcely been explored as yet" although he was in favor of the "flexibility of taxes as an alternative to flexibility of expenditure programs as a budgetary compensatory device."

would lead to a deficit in the balance of payments which might outweigh any gain to employment. Thus, "the employment theories of Mr. J. Maynard Keynes" were not applicable when unemployment was caused by factors other than deficient demand; open economy considerations also tended to confound Keynesian economists who really believed they could boost aggregate demand without paying attention to costs, inflation effects, and balance-of-external-payments effects of their favored policies (BIS 1950: 78–79). In open economy cases "there is every reason to encourage a recovery in individual saving . . . and . . . avoid all steps which might arouse doubts as to the continued stability of the currency." Further, "there can . . . be no doubt that an increase in savings would, [in such countries] be a source of greater employment, and not the reverse" (Ibid., 79). There was some force in these BIS observations. The UN recommendations on responses to unemployment caused by deficient demand had concentrated on the short-run unemployment-demand nexus. In attempting to redress the balance, the BIS reports at this time insisted that instead of relegating open economy issues to the background as if they were secondary considerations, the balance of international payments was in fact a significant constraint on the operation of domestically focused compensatory policies. To ignore the foreign exchange constraint (in open economies with fixed exchange rate policies) would be to imperil the level of employment in the medium term. This was definitely a minority concern in 1950, though as we explained in Chapter 7, the message would not have been lost on LON economists – Ragnar Nurkse in particular.

Controls versus Market Forces

The Committee's attitude to inflation and international trade imbalances favored using price and quantity restriction rather than leaving the price mechanism to allocate resources. As for inflation, the Committee (UN 1950a: 85) argued that it was difficult to set price level targets at the macroeconomic level, and that inflation was best dealt with through price controls. Viner (1950: 388–92) warned against treating inflation in such a manner; controls only disguised inflation and changes in relative prices, leading to "absenteeism, the unpenalized inefficiencies, the padded personnel in plants, the upgrading for pricing and downgrading for quality and service, the queues, the bottlenecks, the misdirection of resources, the armies of controllers and regulators and inspectors."[32]

Similar warnings were directed to the artificial maintenance and control of balances in trade relationships for each country. Government-

---

[32] This point had also been made by Kalecki in earlier UN reports (for example, 1949d: 11–12).

or multilateral-sponsored balance of payments agreements would in-volve restricting capital flows and enforcement of rigidly fixed exchange rates (Viner 1950: 398). The establishment of targets was particularly worrisome for market oriented economies and ignored the complexities of intergovernment negotiation, the difficulties of monitoring and enforcement, and the likelihood of incompatibilities between domestic and international policy targets (Ibid., 401). Viner was ready to accept a multilateral fixed exchange rate regime so long as allowances were made for discretionary changes (*à la* Bretton Woods): A system that would relax controls when fundamental disequilibrium in the balance of pay-ments could be identified and then dictate changes in exchange rates. However, the Committee went well beyond the level of control neces-sary in international trade and finance to achieve full employment (Viner 1950: 400). By contrast, throughout the 1940s the BIS advocated a return to fully flexible exchange rates based upon purchasing power parities (see BIS 1948: 102–03).

Relationship between Full Employment and other UN Objectives

The ranking of full employment as the primary economic goal came under severe criticism by commentaries and governments, that "consid-ered the handling of this question the weakest part of the Report" (ILO 1950c: 399). The assumption that multiple economic goals could be reduced to a clearly defined hierarchy unnecessarily misled policy makers in situations where goals conflict. Indeed, policy tradeoffs usually make it "necessary . . . to balance degrees of the one [goal] against degrees of the other" (Viner 1950: 396). Similarly Wallich (1950: 881) cau-tioned that the question of "how to reconcile economic stability, eco-nomic freedom, and maximum employment is an extremely serious one" and that it was not for the Committee to pronounce on a ranking of goals.

The focus on employment policy and the downgrading of inflation problems, in particular, was characteristic of Keynesianism in the 1940s. As Harry Johnson (1971: 6) was to later write, "[t]he corollary of the Keynesian view of the primacy of the unemployment problem has been a pronounced tendency to play down the adverse economic consequences of inflation." As we have seen above, Viner (1950: 388–92) devoted much of his review of the Report to the dangers of accepting the Committee's view that inflation was less important than employment, and that using selective price controls was sufficient. Similarly, Wallich (1950: 880) argued that the emphasis on employment led the Committee to provide "a much stronger set of defenses on the unemployment front than on the inflation front." The BIS presented the strongest contemporary case among international organizations against the primacy of full employment and against downplaying the dangers of inflation when attempting to achieve that goal. BIS research suggested that "the essential task is to secure a relatively stable price level" and only then would a situation "be created in which fluctuating prices for individual commodities (that is, relatively moderate divergencies from the stable average) would have a definite economic role to fill as a guide to producers and traders" (BIS 1950: 114). This view is reminiscent of a policy line developed by the LON and ILO in the 1920s; it maintained that a genuine, sustainable level of employment would be subsequent to creating a stable price level.

The recommendation that governments move to balancing the budget over the course of the business cycle, and to relegating the goal of fiscal balance to a lower place in the hierarchy of policy goals was largely endorsed by commentators (Viner 1950: 393–94). Again the BIS (1949: 69) offered a dissenting view among international organizations:

> [T]he creation of new money may be justified as a means of keeping up demand in relation to the available resources; but that is very far from having been the case in the sellers' markets of the last few years, with a shortage of goods in most lines and *no lack of employment* (emphasis added).

For the BIS, monetary policy was the most effective policy instrument in producing "a proper limitation of effective demand" in these circumstances, and specifically avoiding deficit monetization. Notable here is the focus on limiting rather than expanding demand. As for fiscal policy, the crucial rule must be to keep government budgets "in order" so as to avoid an "inflationary gap" appearing in the domestic economy. Conversely, countercyclical fiscal policy could be justified under conditions of above full employment by "budgeting for a surplus," but the disincentive effects of higher taxation should be acknowledged: "[H]eavy taxation makes for rigidity in economic life and in that way represents an obstacle to economic enterprise and progress as well as to individual liberty" (BIS 1949: 61–62, 69; see also BIS 1950: 50, 64–65). Overall, the BIS countenanced small spending governments and restraint in using fiscal instruments, especially as part of a discretionary policy-making regime: "[T]he problem is not merely one of equilibrium in the public finances; it is also a question of the level of government expenditure on all counts" (1949: 62). In this last respect – on the importance of creating an enduring rule-based domestic fiscal policy regime – the UN and BIS were on common ground. The precise content of the rules for operating fiscal policy nonetheless differed markedly between these organizations.

CONCLUDING REFLECTIONS ON THE FULL EMPLOYMENT LITERATURE

The full employment movement in international organizations in the late 1940s promoted government policies preventing declining demand on the domestic market by active fiscal policy accommodated by monetary policy and if necessary supported by microeconomic control measures to remove supply bottlenecks and monopolistic tendencies. The movement generally accepted compensatory finance as the basic principle of fiscal policy; it gave quite a minimal, cameo role for monetary policy and it relegated stability of exchange rates and external stability, making them secondary to internal stability understood as maintaining high levels of employment. As protagonists of full employment policy the ILO and UN Committee did not regard the external stability issue as problematic as long as it was possible to coordinate national full employment policies (along Keynesian lines) on an international scale. Perhaps they were justified in doing so given the prevailing consensus around the Bretton Woods system? In their minds at least, many of the open economy issues relating to international capital movements, currency management, and external stability were settled.

We can now see that the research undertaken as part of the full employment movement of the 1940s illustrates a reversal of fortunes for particular doctrinal orthodoxies. The orthodox 1920s policy focus on cost-price alignment faded into the background by the 1940s; the BIS was almost on its own in making this matter central to its deliberations. Orthodoxy in the 1920s dictated a limited governmental fiscal policy role and strict monetary policy rules. Keynesianism definitely became the *new* orthodoxy in international organizations and with it came the new focus on employment expansion and maintenance using general macroeconomic policy instruments according to some transparent rules. The ILO and the UN Committee provide an early version of open economy Keynesianism that was to be the hallmark of academic work in the 1950s. They raised the status of the full employment obligation within international economic policy making. Countries were advised to set clear domestic policy targets, specifically high levels of employment, in the knowledge that international spillover effects were important. A rule-based system of fixed-adjustable exchange rates *à la* Bretton Woods would give external stability and international loans would advance world welfare by aiding less-developed country growth and fostering trade relationships.

With respect to closed economy policies some of the key UN Committee fiscal policy insights deserve to be recounted here: (1.) the real possibility that the character and structure of taxation could affect the level and rate of private investment; (2.) the possibility in some circumstances of affecting the level of consumption by redistributive tax policies; (3.) the real possibility of balancing internal government budgets over the business cycle at the same time as using expansionary fiscal policies to raise output and employment; (4.) tax and expenditure changes could be calculated so as to generate a desired level of output; and (5.) errors of timing in tax and expenditure policies could be minimized by following well-designed fiscal policy rules.

ILO research during the 1940s and the last pieces of economic work from the LON focus on growth, trade, labor, and employment issues in developing economies. There is an awareness of complexities in specifying the determinants of economic growth in less developed economies given the dynamics of rich-country-poor-country economic relations. For less developed countries it was critical that the developed industrial nations adopted measures to expand their economies and open their domestic markets to maximize employment on a global basis. The growth of international trade was championed by international organizations in tandem with promotion of full employment policies.

The UN Committee, by contrast, assumes the mantle of providing policy advice to governments in more developed economies. In its 1950 report the UN Committee takes for granted that compensatory fiscal policy has determinate effects on national aggregates. There is more emphasis placed on developing data sets and indicators which would signal need for fiscal response (passively supported by monetary policy and actively supported by microeconomic policies to prevent sector-specific inflation), and less emphasis on the need to develop statistical monitoring techniques to demonstrate the effects of policy actions. It was a highly presumptive line maintaining that the effects of fiscal activism will be strong on the desired objectives (and conversely weak on generating inflation). By contrast, earlier LON work had argued that whether or not the effects of fiscal activism were strong would depend on national circumstances and certain measures of national economic aggregates, and the ILO carried this view through to developing economy cases.

Recent historiography on the experience of Keynesianism in the United States and the United Kingdom in the 1940s and early 1950s reinforces the modern view that Keynesian economics and policy advice is associated with active *discretionary* management of the *domestic* economy (Barber 1996: 161 ff.; Jones 1972; Stein 1969; Winch 1969). Our analysis has presented a previously undocumented variant on this view. By 1950 a predominately *rule-based* Keynesianism was articulated by UN researchers. Why do we find this variant in international organizations? In the first place, full employment research in international organizations in the late 1940s was conducted in environments somewhat detached from the day-to-day policy-making pressures experienced by member governments. Second, international organizations drew together economists from a wide range of countries who brought with them knowledge of policies applied in an equally wide range of circumstances. That rules were considered necessary within a Keynesian policy framework was a sign of healthy skepticism over the ability of politicians and national policy makers successfully to apply the new, Keynesian economics. That scepticism would have been aided by caution given recognition of policy lags associated with compensatory aggregate demand measures – lags that researchers in international organizations were made aware through familiarity, by 1950, with diverse experiences implementing Keynesian policies.

9　Conclusion

Epilogue: Investigating Economics and Policy Analysis in International Organizations

In Chapter 1 we portrayed economists engaged by international organizations as practitioners of "international political economy," subsequently defined in the Schumpeterian sense as including the articulation of a set of economic policy recommendations or policy orientations advocated on the basis of certain underlying normative precepts. We set the objective for this book to produce an account of the economic thought of economists associated in one way or another (as employees, consultants, advisers) with international organizations up to 1950. Usually, the ideas of these economists were developed in response to policy questions – questions connected directly with government action – established by resolutions and recommendations of the governing bodies and conferences of respective international organizations.

A more specific expositional objective was to accept from the outset the value laden content of research work on policy questions in international organizations and then analyze as a separate matter, the "unifying principles," as Schumpeter (1954: 38) called them, underpinning policy proposals. Moreover, we were interested in considering the uniqueness and distinctiveness of analysis undertaken within the locus of an international organization, and the extent to which associated economic doctrines supported or invalidated particular lines of approach adopted by policy makers. When reviewing explicit or implicit advocacy contained in a piece of analysis or research work surveyed in the foregoing chapters it must be borne in mind that historical accounts or reconstructions analyze the character and content of economics as applied to policy issues at one remove from the motives of those who produced the analysis. The direction and special nuances in the analysis may well have been motivated by what Schumpeter (1954: 337n) referred to as the "most stubborn class interest" – yet the analytic content may be apprehended in its own right as representing insights (error-ridden, idealistic, pathbreaking, original, trivial, or otherwise) gained from working and interacting within the ambit of international organizations.

Given our intellectual history theme, it is vital, as argued in Chapter 1, not to misunderstand the difference between a history of ideas for the most part constructed with an appreciation of the ideational context (for example, in the context of a reconstructed contemporary profile of ideas and opinions on economic policy questions), and the flow of events that may have given impetus to the appearance of those ideas. We therefore distinguish between the origination or source of interest in a particular economic policy question, that is the politico-economic history context, and the analysis associated directly or loosely with this question. It is upon the latter – the analysis – that this book has concentrated. Who might have been implementing a specifically formulated economic policy or supporting the adoption of a policy in some country was of minor interest; more important for our account is the internal consistency or defensibility of what was contributed by economists in international organizations to policy discussion. These contributions have undergone scrutiny in the light of contemporary analysis, later developments in economic analysis, and given subsequent vicissitudes, fads, and fashions in economic thought. One undercurrent in the foregoing chapters is that while contemporary events, policies, and circumstances in different nations made the analysis more or less relevant, immediate policy relevance as a criterion of validity or defensibility for a piece of analysis was not accorded as much importance as it might have been in a standard history of actual economic policy. We might therefore anticipate complaints from economic and political historians interested in the effects of international organizations on policy making at the national level; our perfunctory treatment of the history of national economic policies is however justified by the intellectual history theme. To be sure, much of the work we survey is in fact closely tied to events (sometimes with a time lag); for example the ILO economists' research on unemployment and public works in the early 1930s had immediate relevance. Some work was not immediately relevant to policy: Haberler, Tinbergen, and Polak worked at the LON on aspects of business-cycle analysis, Hilgerdt on a "network" of world trade and payments relationships, and these contributions did not hinge on providing solutions to pressing policy issues. Nevertheless, we could detect in the work on cycles and trade networks the indirect effects of a long period of anxiety among national policy makers from the early 1920s on the vexed questions of international business-cycle transmission and the impact of artificial obstacles to international trade respectively.

All the work of economists in international organizations was policy relevant to questions posed at some stage in the 1919–50 period by those charged with formulating responses to concrete problems. However, policy-making processes at the national government level or within and through international organizations was not a pertinent consideration in our intellectual history. What really mattered in our account was not what governments achieved, or implemented in response to work completed or resolutions passed by international organizations. What the economists offered in terms of ideas, scenarios, and policy orientations remained a critical focus throughout. Of course this focus did not gainsay the likelihood of an iterative feedback process operating between economic ideas propounded in international organizations and the development of events and policies at the national level. The effects of feedback were usually diffuse, so much so as to render statements on precise links in the process highly speculative. We doubtless observe a feedback process at work in the way ILO economists studied the design of monetary policy in the United States during the 1920s and then developed their own recommendations partly founded on those observations. Nonetheless certain doctrinal presuppositions on how monetary policy should be conducted were sourced from their own distinctive synthesis of existing monetary literature. The ideas of ILO researchers on public investment were transformed by the searing experience of worldwide economic crisis in the early 1930s – here the impact of events on ideas was immediate and feedback from the impact of different types of public works policies in various countries also assisted ILO thinking on the subject. By contrast, the effect of the economic crisis on the doctrines held by LON economists was far less immediate and they took some time to jettison older international monetary ideas. As well, economic analysis at the BIS held grimly to the notion that monetary policy had primacy throughout the period, as seen in the similarity of remarks on public works and unemployment policy options in the 1930s and the 1940s – here we observe very little impact of events and policies on ideas. Much of the work surveyed on trade policy and social economics was informed by the variety of national practices in these fields. Further, some of that work had relevance for work on international economic policy issues at a much later date and beyond the period under review. We might mention as one illustration the far-reaching insights of Bellerby's work at the ILO on the importance of central bank independence in the conduct of a rule-based monetary policy and on the valuable role of statistical indicators in formulating a macrostabilization policy in the 1920s.

CHARACTERIZING POLICY ANALYSIS PRODUCED FOR INTERNATIONAL ORGANIZATIONS

A noticeable theme in much of the work of international organizations on economic policy questions was an overriding cautiousness in advisory style as evidenced by many guarded policy pronouncements. The only major exception to this theme occurred in the late 1940s, notably in the UN report on full employment which exuded strong faith in the concepts and policy implications of the new Keynesian economics.

The danger of overconfidence concerning the prime function of national governments in advancing international cooperation and economic integration is signalled strongly in research prior to the mid-1940s. For example it was not merely adventitious that research on the management of business cycles (Chapter 2), on exchange rate policy (Chapter 7), and on producing sustainable full employment outcomes (Chapter 8) warned of the dangers of inflation – wage, price, and profit inflation – arising from an inappropriate macroeconomic policy mix. The *international* dimension in all the work reported here introduced uncertainty as to the effectiveness of policies designed and conducted with exclusive reference to the nation-state; it emphasized conflicts of policy objectives and international spillover effects of some policy stances which were not recognized when governments took up the challenge to implement policy measures derived from the foundational contributions of leading economists (for example, Fisher-Hawtrey-Keynes-type price level stabilization policies in the 1920s; Keynesian countercyclical policies in the 1940s). Nurkse's work on the failure of the gold standard and gold exchange standard currency regimes also communicated the lesson that nations operating on their own and without recourse to international rules on currency policy could introduce disturbances leading to international financial crises.

Also evident in the research reported in this book are tentative, carefully hedged suggestions that traditional, widely accepted policy responses may have weaknesses. For instance Ohlin and Haberler in the early 1930s proposed that monetary policy reforms on their own could be insufficient to dampen all variants of business cycles. ILO economists in the early 1930s set aside the price level stabilization objective for monetary policy which their colleagues had favored only a few years earlier, and proposed that there may be other objectives for monetary policy depending on the circumstances. Furthermore, when much of the preceding work on business cycles at the LON had concluded that business cycles exhibited a "natural rhythm" coinciding with a modest policy *in*effectiveness theme, Tinbergen completed work at the LON which hinted that government stimulation of investment expenditure could indeed be effective over the long term. It was only after a significant time lag – recall the work of the LON Delegation on Economic Depressions in the 1940s – that the confidence introduced by Keynes (1936) in the effectiveness of a broad macroeconomic policy is carried over to the work of international organizations. In our exposition and commentary on business-cycle management we argued that Tinbergen, Haberler, and the LON Delegation were not slavish followers of any orthodoxy, including by the 1940s, Keynes's *General Theory*. International coordination of macroeconomic policy along Keynesian lines was envisaged as feasible, though realizing effective coordination, as opposed simply to desiring it, is recognized as exceedingly problematic.

Another major element indicating the guarded, cautious character of policy analysis surveyed here is the low expectation that the logical consistency, and completeness of economic doctrines considered in isolation were sufficient to make those doctrines applicable and clinch the argument as to how a particular policy should be formulated. In short, economic analysis was not always consistent with conventional political wisdom. Far from proceeding as promoters of nostrums for the edification of national governments and their officials, economists in international organizations developed independent lines of analysis on policy questions; they were not deluded by a belief that, at least in the short run, day-to-day political issues must be subordinated to rationality embodied in an economic proposition.[1] Jacques Polak, whose career began at the LON and proceeded to high office at the IMF, reported that economists in international organizations "must understand . . . the depth of domestic political constraints on joint policymaking at the international level" (Pauly 1996: 37). Polak was not alone in this recognition – all his LON associates would have endorsed this view. The sentiments expressed by LON officials in a publicity statement attached to LON reports on trade policy in the mid-1940s are also representative:

> [T]hese studies emphasise that, though indeed wise economic measures are one of the bases of durable peace, they provide in themselves no solutions to the post-war political problem. And on the solutions of that problem the success or failure of all efforts to create a better economic world ultimately depends.[2]

Throughout the 1940s Ragnar Nurkse remained wary of the complications and difficulties involved in formulating blueprints for international monetary relations. Workable rules for international action were difficult to design, implement, and enforce. In general, economists working in international organizations up to the creation of Bretton Woods institutions in the mid-1940s, were dubious about the efficacy of blueprints. The onus was placed on individual countries to make

---

[1] They would not therefore have been surprised, for example, by the findings of "[s]tudents of postwar European economic integration [which] generally acknowledge the primacy of political over economic forces driving the sequence of events" (Coats 2000: 248).

[2] Official Statement attached to the printer's copy of Viner (1943), LON Archives R4408, p. 3.

economic policy adjustments which were aligned spontaneously with others; the development of aligned policy rules would be guided and informed, rather than planned from above, by researchers in international organizations. There is no evidence that economists' work for international organizations carried messianic status; the economists did not think of themselves as shaping the world economic order, the goals or the expectations of officials and politicians in member governments. In fact they would roundly have condemned this self-perception as the outcome of hubris. It is better to describe their position as akin to Levites serving the high priests of politics in their holy work for national governments.

That the work reported here may be considered in retrospect as having created laudable, distinctive orientations in economic policy analysis is another matter which transcends what the authors would probably have thought of their own work at the time. While there were occasions in the 1940s when the work surveyed expressly records a "transformation" or "major change" in economic thought there is nothing emphatic in all this to suggest that the work was understood as remarkably new, distinctive, or revolutionary. We may now refer to extensive, derivative use of Keynesian conceptual categories in LON reports during the 1940s, in UN work at the end of the 1940s, and even in BIS reports near the end of the period under review, all of which may now be deemed to have contributed to a Keynesian "revolution" broadly conceived. However that characterization would be inaccurate if it represented unfailing confidence in Keynesian concepts and policy implications. For example, the LON Delegation on Economic Depressions in the 1940s, the work on development by Hilgerdt and Staley, and Nurkse's two important books – the first on international currency and finance and the second on inflation – did not accept Keynesian ideas uncritically. They were cautious about the potentialities of compensatory fiscal policies and aggregate demand management. We are therefore restricted to generalizing as follows: As compared with economists working outside the ambit of international organizations, those within were not won over rapidly to the new economics. To maintain that they assisted in the international diffusion of Keynesian ideas seems defensible though not easily verifiable.[3] Certainly for economics as a body of analysis in international

---

[3] Publications of the LON Delegation on Economic Depressions and BIS in the 1940s were widely available to economists and policy makers in national governments. This point has been overlooked in otherwise thorough research on the making of the Keynesian Revolution in the interstices between academic economics and economic policy analysis undertaken by economists in government (Clarke 1988). Pauly (1996: 29) makes the plausible claim that the "studies of the Delegation were widely acknowledged as having a significant impact on policymaking, both during and after the war"; no substantiation is offered.

organizations we should agree with Blaug (1991: 184) that it would be "a mistake to insist . . . that the Keynesian Revolution was a *theoretical* revolution and not a normative revolution in the policy prescriptions of economists" (emphasis in original). We identified doctrinal discontinuities in the treatment of business cycles, macroeconomic management, and social economics associated with Keynesian ideas. We also documented reluctance among economists in international organizations – the UN in the late 1940s to 1950 excepted – easily to accept the favorable ideational consensus which had formed around Keynesian policy analysis and its implications.

Perhaps overshadowing all other considerations in characterizing the economic policy analysis surveyed here, when they turned to definite policy recommendations the ideas of economists in international organizations were exceedingly modest in their expectation of the role of government up to the mid-1940s. Post-1944, and especially in the fields of public investment, social economics, development economics, and fiscal policy, policy recommendations were more forthright in articulating a governmental role. Notwithstanding developments post-1944, the policy-related ideas discussed in foregoing chapters carried obvious connotations of advocacy; yet it was advocacy informed by the laws of Solon – that policy making at the national and international level should not be conducted as if people could be moved about (and have their lives and well-being altered) like pieces on a chessboard.[4] While they developed independent lines of thought and doctrinally eclectic positions on many policy questions, economists in international organizations were not detached from their subject matter as we might expect of academic purists. It is possible the vast array of international practice on so many policy questions (for example public works policy in the 1930s or wage setting policy in the 1920s and 1930s) induced humility and a perspective emphasizing the point that what is optimal under one set of institutions and country-circumstances is seldom optimal for others. Correspondingly there was widespread doubt at the LON about the sustainability of binding international treaties which contracted nations to particular policy stances. The BIS and Nurkse at the LON proposed a form of voluntary international monetary cooperation that may lead to more formal policy coordination. Voluntary cooperation within a loose framework of international consultation supported by robust economic policy analysis and broad international agreements, was the preferred

---

[4] Here reference to the laws of Solon and to the chessboard analogy are not original; they come courtesy of remarks made by Adam Smith in the *Wealth of Nations* and *Theory of Moral Sentiments* respectively, on the appropriate manner for conducting political economy. See Winch (1983: 502–11).

course post-1944. In this view global blueprints are difficult to enforce. The experience of the ILO on policy harmonization 1919–45 was salutary; securing international cooperation and ensuring enforcement over the most basic labor standards proved difficult. That the same could be achieved for economic policy, including trade policy and exchange rate management would be to entertain naively ambitious objectives and, in any case, could not be a one-time event. Cooperation must perennially be renewed and often the degree of renewal is linked to significant events in the world economy. It is scarcely surprising that LON and BIS economists and to a lesser extent ILO economists did not openly hail arguments in support of the Bretton Woods agreement as unassailable, or regard the institutions created thereby as vital or essential. On reconstructing the work of economists in international organizations up to and including 1944, there is no clear message demanding the creation of formal, binding international policy regime environments, and requiring that the economists concerned wished to act as architects for such a regime. None of this was considered a good substitute either for the practical solution of unique national economic difficulties or for minimizing adjustment problems following major shocks such as economic depression or war.

ON THE DISTINCTIVENESS OF ECONOMIC THOUGHT IN INTERNATIONAL ORGANIZATIONS

Despite the air of humility pervading many of the contributions to economic policy analysis surveyed in the foregoing chapters, it became clear as our exposition proceeded that those contributions were differentiated in important respects from similar work outside the loci of international organizations. Below we provide a selective list of distinctive doctrines recognizing that readers may choose to mention others. Our choice is based on distinctive contributions which hitherto have been neglected in standard histories of economic thought and policy for the period 1919–50:

1. pathbreaking research at the ILO on the conduct of monetary policy in the 1920s (Chapter 3);
2. proto-Keynesian developments in the analysis of public investment policy in the early 1930s (with an added international dimension), along with the application of underconsumptionist ideas in this connection (Chapter 4);
3. elaborate, ongoing defense of freer trade policy from 1927 at the LON, later using an original and informal model of the world economy based on trade and payments data (Chapter 5);

4. interdisciplinary work by the ILO economists (using institutional knowledge and legal, sociological, and historical insights) on social economics and labor market policies in the 1930s and 1940s (Chapter 6);
5. the first cogent historical analysis of gold standard failure, open economy macroeconomics and international currency analysis at the LON in the 1940s with policy conclusions that may be distinguished both from formal reports produced for Bretton Woods and from the policy regime constructed at Bretton Woods (Chapter 7); and
6. contributions to development economics at the LON and ILO in the mid-1940s which, *inter alia*, linked unique economic problems in developing countries to international forces including trade and capital movements (Chapter 8).

Naturally this list is seriously incomplete if we wish to consider the overall evolution of (Schumpeterian) international political economy. Recognition should also be given to the originality and prescience involved in contributing what may now be regarded as a mere allusion to a new or better policy orientation or resolution of a policy problem. Sometimes the economists concerned moved beyond mere hints of recognition to present some partial analyses of note. Again we mention selectively:

7. Ohlin's and Haberler's suggestion that monetary policy reform may not be enough to overcome deep economic crises;
8. alternative lines of macroeconomic thought to Keynes's in the 1930s – Tinbergen's econometric work on business cycles, Haberler's and Polak's recognition of open economy complications in the propagation and transmission of business cycles;
9. the Delegation on Economic Depressions, the LON, and the BIS in the 1940s only cautiously entertained Keynesian policy implications, pointing to dangers if policy makers ignored the consequences of inflation;
10. the ILO's insistence throughout the period under review that governments, and governments cooperating with each other internationally, had a significant macroeconomic stabilization role and that aggregate employment should be a prime policy goal;
11. the ILO's rejection of price stabilization as the sole objective of monetary policy in the 1930s;
12. the transformation of policy language in ILO reports in the 1940s on public "works," social "expenditure," and public "investment" indicating a deeper change in economic thought

equating a wider variety of government expenditure in the 1930s and 1940s with genuine investment;

13. a clear statement of the idea, supported by evidence, that trade policy tools are not an effective defense against the international transmission of business cycles;

14. the use of real wage data at the ILO to support the proposition that trade dependence need not imply domestic impoverishment;

15. pre-Keynesian ideas on the problem of coordination in labor markets and associated microeconomic policy responses retaining a place in ILO policy analysis after Keynesian macroeconomics came into vogue;

16. on the subjects of minimum wage policy, collective bargaining, and the role of unions in wage determination, generalizations from ILO research were later given support in more formal labor economics from the 1950s;

17. on open economy issues, given fixed exchange rates, the strong links between monetary and fiscal policy, domestic inflation, and the state of a nation's balance of payments consistently stressed by the BIS and Nurkse's analytical work at the LON in the 1940s;[5]

18. the importance accorded to rule-based policy regimes in the work of the LON on international macroeconomic policy coordination in the 1940s;

19. the rule-based fiscal policy ideas presented by the UN in 1950 probably aimed at controlling the excesses expected to arise from zealous application of demand management policies; and finally,

20. an innovative variant on Keynesianism at the ILO in the mid-1940s demonstrating the link between the level of employment, macropolicies designed to raise the level of employment and macropolicies involving income redistribution.

There were also frequent instances where international political economy depended critically on the dictates of current fashion in the discipline of economics and in the practice of economic policy in several countries. On those occasions the work of economists in international organizations became a reflection of the prevailing orthodoxy; rather than leading or innovating, that work followed orthodox economics closely. Here we might mention:

---

[5] This subject was not widely discussed during the fervid uptake of Keynesian closed-economy macroeconomics during the 1940s. Strict formalization of Keynesian-type policy choices, and the consequences of these policy choices in an open-economy situation had to wait until the work of Mundell and Fleming in the early 1960s.

1. early work at the LON and ILO on a monetary approach to business cycles and on business-cycle measurement;
2. economic analysis produced by the LON Economic and Financial Committee as background to the deliberations and reports of the Gustav Cassel-led LON Gold Delegation which favored monetary responses based on a gold standard mechanism right up to the 1933 WEC;[6]
3. pre-Keynesian thought on public investment at the ILO in the 1920s;
4. the progold standard prescriptions of the BIS in the early 1930s;
5. research on unemployment, unemployment insurance, and unemployment policy at the ILO in the early 1920s, including the Douglas Report which was consistent with standard individual incentive and individual responsibility themes in contemporary, orthodox economics;
6. the efflorescence of ideas and policies in the 1940s turning on Keynes's aggregate economic constructs which was paralleled in the space devoted to these constructs in research reports of the ILO, LON, BIS, and UN from 1940 to 1950; and
7. the ILO's reflection of contemporary attitudes and policies in linking closely wages policy and social security from the late 1930s and the ILO's penchant to *report* on policy developments in social economics rather than lead by creating new policy initiatives.

It is tempting to employ conventional rhetorical techniques in histories of economic thought such as identifying crucial "precursors," or important "anticipations" of future developments in economics and policy. We have identified some intellectual linkages in the foregoing chapters concentrating (though not exclusively) on contemporary linkages. To read ideas exposited and reconstructed here as "important" simply because they supposedly, as if by design, "anticipated" a future development involves not only elements of anachronistic reconstruction; it also imposes on the subject matter a mythology of logical necessity and coherence through time and well outside of the immediate context in which some economic idea or policy prescription appeared. However, there were some ideas of distinction which may be drawn to the

---

[6] Our mention of the LON Gold Delegation's work and associated research cannot be taken as supporting Pauly (1996: 41) which reproves the LON up to 1933 for its treatment of "monetary and financial" matters precisely because it did not "question reigning orthodoxies." Pauly overlooks Ohlin's and Haberler's work for the LON containing reservations about prevailing orthodoxies. He also neglects the fact that the ILO was an integral part of the LON in an institutional sense and the economic analysis provided by ILO economists openly challenged orthodox gold standard ideas from an early date.

attention of modern economists given the state of economics and international political economy in the late twentieth century. Two motivations for this practice seem reasonable: to imply that progress in the analysis of economic policy is not always easy to discern and to demonstrate the continual ebb and flow of intellectual fashion. So without further hesitation we cite: The ILO's work on objectives and indicators for monetary policy in the 1920s, for that work demonstrates that there was nothing very new in monetary policy developments in the 1990s which set price level stabilization as the prime policy objective; while the language is different from modern textbooks, LON economists emphasized the importance of credibility and consistency in economic policies both within and between nations over time; at different points in the history of research at the LON, the role of expectations is considered crucial (though again the term was not often used) and more so when assessing the applicability and effectiveness of activist monetary, fiscal, and exchange rate policies; ILO social economics dealt with incentive issues and the complex links between social policies and labor market policies which have continuing relevance; the same point may be made for artificial separation of efficiency and equity questions in trade policy debate; and the relationship between trade, trade policy, and domestic economic development (including employment) were dealt with competently by LON and ILO economists given the tools of analysis and data sets available and their general conclusions seem hardly to differ from many modern economists who use more sophisticated techniques and more comprehensive data sets. Finally, LON work on international economic policy coordination in the 1940s clearly grasped and accepted the idea that many different forms of coordination were possible; that the scope and extent of economic cooperation could differ; and economic crises and hegemons could be important in creating international policy regimes, preferably rule-based procedures and policy coordination would need to be credible and enforceable. In short, basic guideposts used in the modern literature on the subject have not changed substantially since the 1940s at least.

REFLECTING ON PRINCIPAL INTELLECTUAL (AND OTHER) INFLUENCES

The cosmopolitan set of intellectual influences acting on research in international organizations has been noticed at various junctures. Certainly the national culture from which economists emerged to work in the locus of an international organization seemed to matter. From the mid-1920s ILO and LON research openly cited its indebtedness to individual academic contributions; it is unusual to find recognition of sources for research methods and analytical frameworks in "schools" of economic thought. When we should most expect it, the work of the Delegation on Economic Depressions, and UN on full employment do not give priority to "Keynesian" economics as such. Always referred to are key influential contributions (for example, A.H. Hansen's) yet the reports reason with a style and conceptual tools which may now clearly be recognized as Keynesian.

For some fields of policy analysis there is a strong Scandinavian influence – aspects of ILO research on monetary policy in the 1920s had intellectual antecedents in Swedish economics though it was equally influenced by the work of Keynes, Hawtrey, and Fisher. The result was an interesting amalgam, perhaps a hybrid intellectual construct, incorporating a range of contributions. The Swedish economist Per Jacobsson dominated economic research at the BIS from its inception and his special brand of practical, liberal international political economy promoted belief in the self-adjusting forces of the market price system and was certainly critical of the idea that Keynesian policy prescriptions could be applied with impunity and without reference to specific country circumstances. Condliffe's and Hilgerdt's "network of world trade" model and associated commentary derived from Scandinavian influences (Ohlin featuring directly and prominently here). A general Scandinavian outlook on the international economy was pivotal in giving impetus to trade policy analysis in Geneva from 1927, culminating in the freer trade orientation of international trade agreements toward the end of the period under review. American economics and statistical work in the 1920s had significant bearing on business-cycle research at the ILO and LON in the 1920s. Haberler's Austrian training came to the fore in his early work on cycles at the LON and it is likely that this training was responsible for his skeptical attitude to Keynesian policy developments which he thought were potentially blinded to the danger of creating inflationary tendencies. Here, Haberler's consistent inclination to think in terms of structures rather than aggregates had Austrian overtones. Martin's underconsumptionist reasoning at the ILO had American roots in the work of Foster and Catchings. Tinbergen's and Staehle's special brands of quantitative work owe much to early training in quite different European intellectual contexts. Work at the ILO on social economics seemed to be the outcome of American and European institutional and historical economics. We may speculate that Ragnar Nurkse's early study in Vienna had given rise to his doctrine of voluntary cooperation and spontaneous international monetary order which he propounded in 1944; he seemed naturally inclined against formal international *plans* for restructuring the international monetary system; otherwise he developed a genuinely independent set of ideas on international finance and open economy macroeconomics and succeeded in distinguishing his work from the Keynesian and Bretton Woods orthodoxy in the 1940s.

It is not altogether satisfying merely to recount intellectual influences. As suggested in Chapter 1, the consequences of such influences matter in terms of the style and content of the analysis and policy prescriptions derived thereby. What our study highlights is the hybrid nature of many contributions in that they were not a clear-cut result of work within the bounds of a particular tradition or school of thought. Economic thought in international organizations up to 1950 was not concerned with a universally held set of ideas, methods, and techniques for a single economics or international political economy.[7] A good proportion of the work surveyed was not unduly abstract, mathematical, or quantitative compared with contemporary work in pure economic theory. As a corollary, much of the research produced in international organizations was institutional because the very nature of policy analysis demanded that account be taken of international-comparative cases, experiences, data, and country-specific policy arrangements.

The diversity of approaches to economic policy questions over the thirty-year period is remarkable as between organizations at the same time (compare for example the ILO and LON on the gold standard and the role of monetary policy in the early 1930s) and within organizations at different times (compare for example the ILO on public works on the 1920s and 1930s). The governing bodies of international organizations would normally deny having an "official line" on any policy question. Whether the work of economists in those organizations could be represented as the "official line" is entirely otiose as far as this study is concerned. Through all the noise – international conferences and resolutions of international organizations – there were some clear signals that the intellectual atmosphere in Geneva had some impact on what economists thought on policy questions. We identified and traced developments in a "policy of Geneva" on international trade; in the 1920s the ILO economists developed a differentiated position to the pre-Keynesian line on aspects of social economics such as unemployment; an international dimension was added to the study of business cycles at the LON; the full employment reports in the 1940s differentiated a common ILO-UN line from those of national governments on the same subject; Ragnar Nurkse's independent work in 1944 on international monetary policy and policy coordination appeared to have been nurtured in the Geneva

---

[7] The results of a very recent study in a related field – on the development of economics in Western Europe after 1945 – are consistent with ours: Economics as applied to public policy issues cannot be considered a "universal science, at least in its totality" (Coats 2000: 253).

environment over a long period of research starting in 1934; the Condliffe-Hilgerdt trade policy analysis and the Hilgerdt-Staley reports on development economics and policy contained truly internationalist elements that might only have been produced in the intellectually open, cosmopolitan Geneva environment where no rabid doctrinal or national interest could easily prevail. Mixed doctrinal origins evident in particular contributions – where they could be traced – must on no account be regarded as a symptom of confusion, for policy-oriented work often considered what was feasible in a practical, implementable sense rather than what could be justified from a purely theoretical standpoint. As well, the primacy of national considerations tended to be set aside in work completed in international organizations. For instance pre-Keynesian approaches to the causes of unemployment and to the function of public works in the 1920s was mostly articulated by British writers and contemporary ILO reports on the subject modified these approaches to suit a wider range of observed cases; Keynes's position on trade policy in the 1930s focused on British interests and therefore ran against research in Geneva which embodied a strong internationalist message; and the British and American plans submitted at Bretton Woods contained significant points of difference from Ragnar Nurkse's LON report on international monetary questions in the mid-1940s. Other examples of individual contributions to work in international organizations could not be considered to have an especially regional (Anglo-American or European) bias: Viner produced outstanding reports for the LON on trade policy; Kalecki contributed fleetingly to full employment policy discussion at the ILO; and Douglas's work for the ILO in the 1920s had a lasting influence on thinking about social security policy.

In attempting to apprehend influences on the vast array of research in international organizations to 1950 it is vital to recall the wide range of country-specific cases and policy reactions that had to be accounted for in that research. Consequently, economists' reports for international organizations produced a distinctive style of policy analysis and a blend of doctrines. While governing bodies of organizations usually set the broad topic for investigation, researchers were free to develop the scope, method, and research agendas of their investigations in discussion with peers and policy makers inside and outside the locus of their governing organization.[8]

---

[8] The LON-ILO committee of economists established to discuss Tinbergen's work is perhaps one of the most notable examples of internal peer influence (see Chapter 2); on the wide range of outside audiences desiring to hear addresses from, and discuss issues with, LON economists see: "Invitations to Members of the Economic and Financial Section to Lecture 1934–1939," LON Archives R4606.

NORMATIVE AGENDAS FOR INTERNATIONAL POLITICAL
ECONOMY 1919–1950

The notion that a world economy relying mostly on market forces to
allocate resources would lead automatically to high rates of economic
growth, widespread peace, and prosperity is not universally accepted in
the literature surveyed in this book. Moreover, it was not widely proposed by economists in international organizations that international
peace and economic cooperation could be effected simply by limiting the
economic role of government – both national government and international "government" through international organizations. As we foreshadowed in Chapter 1, economists in international organizations for
most of the period up to 1950 may not easily and convincingly be labeled
as "liberal fundamentalists" (cf. Murphy 1994: 159, and also Pauly 1996:
25–26). The "liberal" label is inappropriate if it means that the economists concerned held a normative position directly sourced from
nineteenth-century classical liberal economics. They did not argue
unqualifiedly for an unregulated global economy that promotes international prosperity. Indeed, on some issues contriving a common interest
across nations in economic growth through the use of market forces was
considered impractical; learning from (and perhaps widely adopting)
interventionist policies used in some countries (for example in the fields
of labor and social economics) might be more effective in achieving
global peace and prosperity.[9] Economists in international organizations
generally did not presume that governments must gradually relinquish
control over a wide spectrum of domestic policies in order to effect
higher growth rates.

There is also no convincing evidence in favor of using the term *fundamentalist* if this means that economists in international organizations
were doctrinaire advocates of a liberal international political economy.
From the 1920s, macroeconomic questions were addressed with a view
to providing policy rules for macroeconomic stabilization, specifically
monetary policy rules. Increasingly from the 1930s LON and ILO econ-

---

[9] Kirshner (1995: x) maintains that "the founders of the Bretton Woods-GATT system"
sought to recreate an ideational context based on "faith in classical liberal economic
theory" supported by the putatively positive "experience of the relatively open world
economy of the nineteenth century." If by "classical liberal" is meant that the economists
concerned entertained the benefits in principle of market processes allocating resources
internationally, then the majority of work surveyed in this book would attract that label.
However we find no *strong* evidence supporting any proposition in favor of replicating
nineteenth-century circumstances, institutions, or policies save perhaps for some *very
early* pre-Keynesian work on aspects of social economics and LON reports favoring
restoration of the pre-1914 gold standard.

omists attempted to promote a range of fiscal, monetary, and exchange rate policies all of which may legitimately be described as implying varying degrees of government intervention. Our summary judgement is that most of the international political economy surveyed in previous chapters was reformist insofar as it was motivated by a desire continually to alter the role of government in the economy (both national and international) rather than replace governments with the markets or recklessly deregulate in every case where governments were observed to be intervening to change market outcomes. Now of course the reformist strategy meant that international political economy (by definition) in its various dimensions did not resist commentary upon criteria of legitimacy for particular policy responses – legitimacy was always relative to historical conditions and institutions. It is scarcely surprising that international governmental interventions are also promoted on a range of issues throughout the period under review though the most obvious policy recommendations at this level related to trade policy, international currency matters, labor standards, and international investment policy.

Except perhaps for the LON Gold Delegation and its dogmatic position on reestablishing the gold standard in the early 1930s, even the obvious liberal position consistently taken by LON economists on trade policy from 1927 cannot be described as "fundamentalist." Clearly, the LON economists implacably opposed quantitative trade controls; they preferred using tariffs and exchange rate changes. Yet few economists at the LON, ILO, and BIS favored untrammeled capital account convertibility. On trade policy, subtle shifts in the LON argument on the functions of tariffs are discernible from 1927–50; there is grudging acceptance of discriminatory bilateral trade policy arrangements as at least encouraging *some* trade. The oft-argued case for *freer* multilateral trade coextensive with binding international trade agreements to produce that outcome is based on extensive empirical work and full understanding of existing trading arrangements and country-specific policy interventions. Certainly the Geneva trade policy line identified in Chapter 5 does not imply laissez faire or the unconditional abandonment of protectionist policies; equally it is not compatible with an overarching system of state control over tradeable goods and services.

Typically, as we should expect of economists analyzing economic problems, work on trade policy concentrates on resource allocative efficiency. Distributional issues between countries and to a lesser extent, the freer trade-employment conundrum were not so deeply or frequently discussed at least up until the mid-1940s. In the 1940s the rich-country-poor-country problem was more fully analyzed, starting with the work of Hilgerdt and Staley and it features again in the UN full employment literature. Here, as earlier in the work of the LON and ILO, a key policy prescription turns on the need for larger, more prosperous industrial countries to open their markets and give greater access to the products of poorer countries (and especially to labor-intensive products). Relative underdevelopment and relative poverty is not separated from absolute levels of living. In respect of trade policy literature discussed in Chapter 5 and the Hilgerdt-Staley work on development economics in Chapter 8, the beneficial effects of more trade on the level of world income is underscored. Freer trade arrangements would tend to raise absolute income levels in poorer countries. It is not expressly desired or presumed that freer trade rather than more restricted trade would be conducive to greater efficiency in the disposition of the world's resources *and* to a more equal distribution of world income.

According to ILO research, when trade flows impinge on human values, including labor standards and employment conditions, trade flows need not thereby be unduly restricted; instead, national governments should cooperate with each other and create internationally enforceable conditions including minimum wage codes and basic standards to protect the employment conditions of certain types of workers. As well, factor subsidies, social transfer payments, and various forms of industry assistance were widely recommended in the work surveyed – these would assist with labor and capital mobility and provide vocational training. Freer trade enthusiasts they were, though not without insisting on a supportive structure of government interventions.

INTERNATIONAL ECONOMIC INTEGRATION AS A DOMINANT THEME TO 1950

In Chapter 1 we established a time span for our study beginning with creation of the LON in 1919 and ending with reports on full employment issued by the ILO and UN in 1950. Needless to say the period from 1950 to the end of the twentieth century invites a similar analysis. As the twentieth century came to a close increasingly international organizations were grappling, as usual, with policy questions relating to the nature and consequence of global economic integration.

Our analysis demonstrates that discussion of the process of internationalization or international economic integration is not new. The work of economists surveyed here often considered the benefits, costs, and methods involved when nations loosely cooperate over, or formally coordinate, their policy actions. The term *globalization* (to use a modern idiom) and its implicit content would have been broadly familiar to those economists whose work we have exposed here, although they may not have anticipated the extent to which rapid technological progress would break down traditional economic barriers between nations (such as geographical distance) and reduce transactions costs associated with international trade and exchange. Various approaches to international political economy outlined in this book do not consider precisely how much international economic integration might take place or how far economic integration could proceed at a very general level. On an issue-by-issue basis there was some indirect consideration of these matters: Goal harmonization was deeply considered over macroeconomic policies designed to achieve full employment in the 1950s; international agreements on exchange rate policy, trade policy, and the treatment of labor were all indicative of a concern to integrate policies among individual national economies. In treating these issues there was always tension between the place of national jurisdictional sovereignty and "integration" where the latter meant harmonization facilitated by international organizations and international agreements embodying rules enforced through international organizations. Attempts to promulgate universal standards for action on trade, monetary and fiscal policy, social economics, international money, and so forth were also symptomatic of a desire to promote integration. Indeed there was keen realization that the balance between sovereignty and integration was fragile and easily changed by events. Where policy harmonization was in evidence it appeared episodic and was understood as such in most of the work discussed here. For example, Bretton Woods arrangements for a fixed adjustable exchange rate regime combined with national monetary autonomy were not accompanied by clear operational rules for the conduct of domestic fiscal and monetary policy. The absence of clear rules left the way open for the Bretton Woods regime to be undermined by policies which led to an upsurge in inflation – and this danger is well recognized in skeptical BIS reports and in the work of economists associated with the LON.

As we look over the thirty-year period surveyed here, it is difficult not to be struck by the extent to which so much confidence is expressed in international economic integration actively involving international organizations *and* national governments. In fact, a lodestar for much of the work considered in this book is that economic integration connotes harmonization of government policies and policy objectives – it was not necessarily a function of the degree of free reign given to market processes.[10] The central organizing principle of open global markets as the sole, most potent economic integrating mechanism, while present on

---

[10] This theme was also a feature of Hobson (1915) mentioned at the very beginning of this book. cf. Rodrik (2000: 178), which declares the "natural benchmark for thinking about international economic integration is to consider a world in which *markets* for goods, services and factors of production *are perfectly integrated*" (emphasis added).

some issues such as international trade and payments, was not universally accepted by economists whose work is exposited in the foregoing
chapters. They had another message: While more open markets operating across national boundaries increase international pressures to reduce
production costs and improve economic competitiveness and efficiency,
they have deleterious spillover effects elsewhere. The latter must be
ameliorated by social policies; policies designed to maintain high levels
of employment; industry assistance policies and special lending and
trade policy arrangements to raise the rate of economic growth in poor
countries.

In the 1920s economic nationalism attracted disapproval *sotto voce*,
though more virulent strains were inveighed against in the work of international organizations where they were held to account for a long period
of contraction in world trade in the 1930s. There were also many examples where ideological trends are documented without taking a definite
position, for example:

> The present situation [circa 1936] is characterized by a vigorous reac-
> tion against individualism and economic liberalism, the abuse and
> excesses of which are widely held to bear a large part of the responsi-
> bility for the development of the depression.[11]

Overall, the work we have surveyed is less inclined expressly to condemn
trends toward "economic liberalism" especially on trade policy and open
economy macroeconomics. Economists in international organizations
were aware that points of reference in respect of international integration can change, so that the balance between market processes and the
role of governments in the internationalization process could also shift.
There was no possibility that the issue of integration would recede in
research conducted by international organizations – it underwrote discussion on most of the topics considered in this book. While not using
the same terminology as economists in the late twentieth century, economists in international organizations in the 1919–50 period presumed
that economic integration would be ongoing and never complete; interactions and interdependencies among nations are driven by natural economic imperatives and these would not disappear.

Ideally, it was thought that voluntary cooperation aligned closely to
economic policies would give a semblance of order and stability to the
process of internationalization. International organizations would act as
enabling institutions or as advisory agencies on international economic
interactions and their consequences. Our main criticism of research com-

---

[11] Economic Committee "Trend of Commercial Policy since March 1935. Note by Secretariat," August 1936, LON Archives R4407.

pleted by economists in international organizations during the 1940s, and this point came to the fore more especially when addressing exchange rate policy, international lending policy, and the full employment question, was that it appeared to demonstrate egregious faith in government institutions (national and international). In short, while market failure in many instances forms the rationale for policy proposals, government failure seems to receive short shrift. Again, the reference point is important: Successful government planning during wartime was doubtless a focal point. Nevertheless we also detect many rule-based arrangements proposed in the period under review designed to increase policy transparency: monetary policy rules, compensatory fiscal policy rules, exchange rate rules, guidelines for international lending policy, and the desire for formal, enforceable, multilateral trade policy agreements. These proposals if implemented would have a countervailing influence on *ad hoc* changes dictated by short-term, political expediencies but they do not remove the danger of bureaucrats extending their influence and capturing a growing share of resources in both national governments and international organizations.

The diversity of approach and strong empirical grounding in economic work carried out by international organizations up to 1950 is matched by a many-sided outlook on the nature of international organizations that might evolve to assist in managing economic integration. Organizations and the international regime or order in which they operated would have to be formed in a voluntary, cooperative process. Forcing nations to join a policy harmonization arrangement managed through an international organization would be counterproductive. In the view of the economists whose work we have been concerned with here, and Nurkse's work for the LON is a splendid example, nations would be better off choosing their own policy stances and then perceiving advantages in coordinating policies with others. Pluralistic, geopolitical, or regional economic arrangements appear especially suited to this line of thinking; it forms part of an international political economy reflecting familiarity with diverse national and regional experiences on a range of economic problems and it reflects awareness of historical relativities. Lastly, it was a perspective promoting international economic integration as desirable so long as it could be supported by persuasive research conducted by international organizations.

References

Åkerman, J. 1932. *Economic Progress and Economic Crises*. English translation. London: Macmillan.

Alcock, A. 1971. *History of the International Labour Organisation*. London: Macmillan.

Aldcroft, D.H. 1993. Depression and Recovery: The Eastern European Experience. In W.R. Garside ed. *Capitalism in Crisis: International Responses to the Great Depression*. New York: St. Martin's Press, 166–96.

Aliber, R.Z. 1987. Exchange Rates. In J. Eatwell et al. eds. *The New Palgrave A Dictionary of Economics*. London: Macmillan, 210–13.

Ansiaux, M. 1931. Disturbances in International Trade and Their Effects on Unemployment. In *Unemployment Problems in 1931*. Geneva: ILO Studies and Reports Series C No. 16.

1932. Underconsumption as a Factor in the Economic Cycle. *International Labour Review* 26: 8–25.

Asher, R.E., Kotschnig, W.M., Adams Brown, W., and Associates. 1957. *The United Nations and Economic and Social Co-operation*. Washington DC: The Brookings Institution.

Auboin, R. 1955. *The Bank for International Settlements, 1930–1955*. Princeton University Essays in International Finance No. 22. Princeton, NJ.

Bailey, S.D. 1964. *The Secretariat of the United Nations*. London: Pall Mall Press.

Balogh, T. 1944. The League of Nations on Post-War Trade Problems. *Economic Journal* 54: 256–61.

Bank for International Settlements. 1931. *First Annual Report 1930/31*. Basle: BIS.

1932. *Second Annual Report 1931/32*. Basle: BIS.

1935. *Fifth Annual Report 1934/35*. Basle: BIS.

1937. *Seventh Annual Report 1936/7*. Basle: BIS.

1942. *Twelfth Annual Report 1941/42*. Basle: BIS.

1944. *Fourteenth Annual Report 1943/44*. Basle: BIS.

1945. *Fifteenth Annual Report 1944/45*. Basle: BIS.

1946. *Sixteenth Annual Report 1945/46*. Basle: BIS.

1947. *Seventeenth Annual Report 1946/47*. Basle: BIS.

1948. *Eighteenth Annual Report 1947/48*. Basle: BIS.

1949. *Nineteenth Annual Report 1948/49*. Basle: BIS.

1950. *Twentieth Annual Report 1949/50*. Basle: BIS.

Barber, W.J. 1985. *From New Era to New Deal: Herbert Hoover, the Economists, and American Economic Policy, 1921–1933*. Cambridge: Cambridge University Press.

1996. *Designs Within Disorder: Franklin D. Roosevelt, the Economists and the Shaping of American Economic Policy, 1933–1945*. Cambridge: Cambridge University Press.

Barkai, H. 1993. Productivity Patterns, Exchange Rates, and the Gold Standard Restoration Debate of the 1920s. *History of Political Economy* 25: 1–37.

Baumol, W.J. 1991. On Formal Dynamics: From Lundberg to Chaos Analysis. In L. Jonung ed. *The Stockholm School of Economics Revisited*. Cambridge: Cambridge University Press, 185–98.

Begg, D. and Wyplosz, C. 1993. The European Monetary System: Recent Intellectual History. In *The Monetary Future of Europe*. London: CEPR, 11–27.

Bellerby, J.R. 1923a. *Control of Credit as a Remedy for Unemployment*. London: P.S. King.

1923b. The Controlling Factor in Trade Cycles. *Economic Journal* 33: 305–31.

1924. The Monetary Policy of the Future. *Economic Journal* 34: 177–87.

1925. *Monetary Stability*. London: Macmillan.

1926. *Stabilisation of Employment in the United States*. Geneva: ILO Studies and Report Series C No. 11.

1927a. The Evolution of a Wage-Adjustment System: I. *International Labour Review* 16: 1–25.

1927b. The Evolution of a Wage-Adjustment System: II. *International Labour Review* 16: 196–215.

1927c. The Evolution of a Wage-Adjustment System: III. *International Labour Review* 16: 328–60.

Bellerby, J.R. and Isles, K.S. 1930. Wages Policy and the Gold Standard in Great Britain. *International Labour Review* 22: 137–54.

Belshaw, H. 1933. Agricultural Labour in New Zealand. *International Labour Review* 28: 26–45.

Benjamin, D.K. and Kochin, L.A. 1979. Searching for an Explanation of Unemployment in Interwar Britain. *Journal of Political Economy* 87: 441–78.

1982. Unemployment and Unemployment Benefits in Twentieth Century Britain: A Reply to our Critics. *Journal of Political Economy* 90: 410–36.

Bernstein, E.M. 1946. Monetary Stabilization: The United Nations Program. In S.E. Harris ed. *Economic Reconstruction*. New York: McGraw Hill, 336–52.

Beveridge, W.H. 1944. *Full Employment in a Free Society*. London: George Allen and Unwin.

Beyen, J.W. 1949. *Money in a Maelstrom*. New York: Macmillan.

Bhagwati, J. 1994. Free Trade: Old and New Challenges. *Economic Journal* 104: 231–46.

Black, S.W. 1987. International Monetary Institutions. In J. Eatwell, M. Milgate, and P. Newman eds. *The New Palgrave: A Dictionary of Economics*. London: Macmillan, 917–20.

Blaug, M. 1991. Second Thoughts on the Keynesian Revolution. *History of Political Economy* 23: 171–92.

Blinder, A. 1987. The Rules-versus-Discretion Debate in the Light of Recent Experience. *Weltwirtschafliches Archiv* 123: 399–414.

Booth, A. 1993. The British Reaction to the Economic Crisis. In W.R. Garside ed. *Capitalism in Crisis: International Responses to the Great Depression*. New York: St. Martin's Press, 30–55.

Bordo, M.D. 1993. The Bretton Woods International Monetary System: A Historical Overview In M.D. Bordo and B. Eichengreen eds. *A Retrospective on the Bretton Woods System: Lessons for International Monetary Reform*. Chicago: University of Chicago Press, 3–107.

Bordo, M.D. and Eichengreen, B. eds. 1993. *A Retrospective on the Bretton Woods System: Lessons for International Monetary Reform*. Chicago: University of Chicago Press.

Bordo, M.D. and Schwartz, A.J. 1999. Under What Circumstances, Past and Present, Have International Rescues of Countries in Financial Distress Been Successful? *Journal of International Money and Finance* 18: 683–708.

Bridel, P. 1987. Public Works. In J. Eatwell, M. Milgate, and P. Newman eds. *The New Palgrave: A Dictionary of Economics*. London: Macmillan, 1072–73.

Brown, W.A. 1957. International Trade and Payments. In R.E. Asher, W.M. Kotschnig, and W.A. Brown and Associates eds. *The United Nations and Economic and Social Co-operation*. Washington, DC: Brookings Institution, 96–159.

Bryant, R.C. 1995. *International Coordination of National Stabilization Policies*. Washington DC: Brookings Institution.

Burns, E.M. 1926. *Wages and the State*. London: P.S. King.

Butler, H.B. 1924. Mr. H.B. Butler's Speech. In *Unemployment and Its National and International Aspects*. Geneva: ILO Studies and Reports Series C No. 9, 213–23.

1927. *Industrial Relations in the United States*. Geneva: ILO Studies and Reports Series A No. 27.

1931a. The Social Effects of Economic Depression in North America. *International Labour Review* 23: 301–23.

1931b. *Unemployment Problems in the United States*. Geneva: ILO Studies and Reports Series C No. 17.

Cairncross, A.K. 1944. League of Nations Studies of Transition Problems. *Economic Journal* 54: 252–56.

Cammarosano, J.R. 1987. *The Contributions of John Maynard Keynes to Foreign Trade Theory and Policy 1909–1946*. New York: Garland Publishing Inc.

Cannan, E. 1928. Review of Report of the Industrial Transference Board. *Economic Journal* 38: 673–77.

1930. The Problem of Unemployment: A Review of the Post-War Unemployment Problem, by Henry Clay. *Economic Journal* 40: 45–55.

Carré, P. 1961. Brief Note on the Life and Work of Hans Staehle. *Econometrica* 29: 801–10.

Cassel, G. 1927. *Recent Monopolistic Tendencies in Industry and Trade: Being an Analysis of the Nature and Causes of the Poverty of Nations*. Geneva: League of Nations C.E.C.P. No. 98.

——— 1932. World Economic Reconstruction: A Criticism of the Economic Resolution Adopted by the International Labour Conference. *International Labour Review* 26: 643–48.

Casson, M. 1983. *Economics of Unemployment: An Historical Perspective*. Oxford: Martin Robertson.

Clark, J.M. 1916. The Changing Basis of Economic Responsibility. Reprinted in *Social Economics: Essays on Economic Theory and Social Problems*. New York: Rinehart.

——— 1936. *Preface to Social Economics: Essays on Economic Theory and Social Problems*. New York: Rinehart.

Clarke, P. 1988. *The Keynesian Revolution in the Making*. Oxford: Clarendon Press.

Clarke, S.V.O. 1967. *Central Bank Cooperation: 1924–1931*. New York: Federal Reserve Bank of New York.

Clay, H. 1929. *The Post-War Unemployment Problem*. London: Macmillan.

——— 1939. The League of Nations Monetary Review. *Economic Journal* 49: 575–77.

Clay, H. and Jewkes, J. eds. 1930. *International Wage Comparisons*. Manchester University Press, Social Science Research Council of New York.

Coats, A.W. ed. 1981. *Economists in Government: An International Comparative Study*. Durham: Duke University Press.

——— 1986. *Economists in International Agencies: An Exploratory Study*. New York: Praeger.

——— 1997. *The Post-1945 Internationalization of Economics*. Durham, NC: Duke University Press.

Coats, A.W. 2000. Concluding Reflections. In A.W. Coats ed. *The Development of Economics in Western Europe since 1945*. London: Routledge, 245–56.

Cohen, J.L. 1925. The Administrative Machinery of Social Insurance. *International Labour Review* 11: 474–508.

——— 1929. The Incidence of the Costs of Social Insurance. *International Labour Review* 20: 816–39.

Committee for Economic Development. 1947. *Taxes and the Budget: A Program for Prosperity in a Free Economy*. New York: Committee for Economic Development.

Commons, J.R. 1921. Industrial Government. *International Labour Review* 1: 61–68.

Condliffe, J.B. 1924. Experiments in State Control in New Zealand. *International Labour Review* 9: 334–60.

——— 1931. The Effect of Fall Prices on Labour Conditions in New Zealand. *International Labour Review* 23: 476–506.

——— 1933a. Some Problems of International Equilibrium. *Svenska Handelsbanken: Index* 8: 226–37.

——— 1933b. Vanishing World Trade. *Foreign Affairs* 11: 645–56.

1935a. Exchange Rates and Prices. *Svenska Handelsbanken: Index* 10: 1–17.

1935b. *War and Depression*. New York: World Peace Foundation World Affairs Pamphlets No. 10.

1938. Summary of Discussion. *International Affairs* 17: 803–04.

1941. *The Reconstruction of World Trade: A Survey of International Economic Relations*. London: Allen and Unwin.

1951. *The Commerce of Nations*. London: Allen and Unwin.

Condliffe, J.B. and Stevenson, A. 1944. *The Common Interest in International Economic Organisation*. Montreal: ILO Studies and Reports Series B No. 39.

Cooper, R.N. 1999. Exchange Rate Choices. In J. Sneddon Little and G.P. Olivei eds. *Rethinking the International Monetary System*. Federal Reserve Bank of Boston Conference Series No. 43: 99–123.

Craver, E. 1986. Patronage and the Direction of Research in Economics: The Rockfeller Foundation in Europe, 1924–1938. *Minerva* 24: 205–22.

Crockett, C.R. 1996. International Institutions, Surveillance and Policy Coordination. In J.A. Frenkel and M. Goldstein eds. *Functioning of the International Monetary System* Vol. I. Washington DC: International Monetary Fund.

De Grauwe, P. 1989. *International Money: Post-War Trends and Theories*. Oxford: Clarendon Press.

De Marchi, N. 1991. League of Nations Economists and the Ideal of Peaceful Change in the Decade of the 'Thirties. In C.D.W. Goodwin ed. *Economics and National Security: A History of Their Interaction*. Durham: Duke University Press, 143–78.

Dell, S. 1977. Kalecki at the United Nations 1946–54. *Oxford Bulletin of Economics and Statistics* 39: 31–46.

1986. Economics in the United Nations. In A.W. Coats ed. *Economists in International Agencies: An Exploratory Study*. New York: Praeger, 36–52.

Diebold, W. 1952. *The End of the ITO*. Princeton, NJ: Princeton University, Department of Economics and Social Institutions, International Finance Section, October.

1996. From ITO to GATT – And Back? In O. Kirshner ed. *The Bretton Woods-GATT System. Retrospect and Prospect After Fifty Years*. New York: M.E. Sharpe, 152–73.

Dimand, R.W. 1993. The Dance of the Dollar: Irving Fisher's Monetary Theory of Economic Fluctuations. *History of Economics Review* 20: 161–72.

1995. Macroeconomics With and Without Keynes. *History of Economics Review* 24: 23–42.

Dimsdale, N.H. 1988. Keynes on Interwar Economic Policy. In W. Eltis and P. Sinclair eds. *Keynes and Economic Policy: The Relevance of the General Theory After Fifty Years*. London: Macmillan, 317–35.

Dornbusch, R., Goldfajn, I., and Valdes, R. 1995. Currency Crises and Collapses. *Brookings Papers on Economic Activity* 2: 219–93.

Douglas, P.H. 1925. Some Precedents For the Family Wage System. *International Labour Review* 12: 353–65.

1934. *The Theory of Wages*. New York: Macmillan.

1972. *In the Fullness of Time: The Memoirs of Paul H. Douglas*. New York: Harcourt Brace Inc.

Dowd, K. 1995. Deflating the Productivity Norm. *Journal of Macroeconomics* 17: 717–32.

Dulles, E.L. 1932. *The Bank for International Settlements*. New York: Macmillan.

Dunlop, J. 1938. The Movement of Real and Money Wage Rates. *Economic Journal* 48: 413–34.

1939. Cyclical Variations in Wage Structure. *Review of Economics and Statistics* 21: 30–39.

1944. *Wage Determination Under Trade Unions*. New York: A.M. Kelley.

Edgeworth, F.Y. 1922. Equal Pay to Men and Women For Equal Work. *Economic Journal* 32: 431–57.

Eichengreen, B. 1984. Keynes and Protection. *Journal of Economic History* 44: 363–73.

1985. International Policy Coordination in Historical Perspective: A View From the Interwar Years. In W. Buiter and R. Marston eds. *International Economic Policy Coordination*. Cambridge: Cambridge University Press, 139–78.

1990. *Elusive Stability: Essays in the History of International Finance 1919–1939*. Cambridge: Cambridge University Press.

1994. *International Monetary Arrangements for the 21st Century*. Washington DC: Brookings Institute.

Eichengreen, B. and Portes, R. 1987. The Anatomy of Financial Crises. In R. Portes and A. Swoboda eds. *Threats to International Financial Stability*. Cambridge: Cambridge University Press, 10–58.

Evans, A.A. 1995. *My Life as an International Civil Servant in the International Labour Office*. Geneva: International Labour Organization.

Fair, R.C. and Howrey, E.P. 1996. Evaluating Alternative Monetary Policy Rules. *Journal of Monetary Economics* 38: 173–93.

Feis, H. 1927. International Labour Legislation in the Light of Economic Theory. *International Labour Review* 15: 491–518.

1940. *The Changing Pattern of International Economic Affairs*. New York: Harper Brothers.

Fisher, I. 1923. Business Cycle Largely a "Dance of the Dollar." *Journal of the American Statistical Association* 18: 1024–28.

1926. A Statistical Relation Between Unemployment and Price Changes. *International Labour Review* 13: 785–92.

1928. *The Money Illusion*. New York: Adelphi Co.

1933. The Relation of Employment to the Price Level. In C.F. Roos ed. *Stabilization of Employment*. Bloomington, IN: Principia Press Inc., 152–59.

1935. *Stabilised Money: A History of the Movement*. London: Allen and Unwin.

Flanders, M.J. 1989. *International Monetary Economics 1870–1960: Between Classical and New Classical*. Cambridge: Cambridge University Press.

Fleming, G.A. 2000. Foreign Investment, Reparations and the Proposal for an International Bank: Notes on the Lectures of J.M. Keynes in Geneva, July 1929. *Cambridge Journal of Economics* 24: 139–51.

Foster, W.F. and Catchings, W. 1925. *Profits*. Boston: Houghton Mifflin.

1928. *The Road To Plenty*. London: Pitman and Sons.

Franklin, N.N. 1969. Employment and Unemployment: Views and Policies, 1919–1969. *International Labour Review* 99: 293–314.

Freeman, R.B. 1989. *Labor Markets in Action: Essays in Empirical Economics*. New York: Harvester Wheatsheat.

Frenkel, J. and Goldstein, M. eds. 1996a. *Functioning of the International Monetary System* Vol. I. Washington DC: International Monetary Fund.

1996b. Introduction. In J.A. Frenkel and M. Goldstein eds. *Functioning of the International Monetary System* Vol. I. Washington DC: International Monetary Fund, 1–14.

Frenkel, J., Goldstein, M., and Masson, P. 1996. International Coordination of Economic Policies. In J.A. Frenkel and M. Goldstein eds. *Functioning of the International Monetary System* Vol. I. Washington DC: International Monetary Fund, 17–59.

Frey, B.S. 1997. The Public Choice of International Organisations. In D.C. Mueller ed. *Perspectives on Public Choice: A Handbook*. Cambridge: Cambridge University Press, 106–23.

Friedman, M. 1953. *Essays in Positive Economics*. Chicago: University of Chicago Press.

1977. Nobel Lecture: Inflation and Unemployment. *Journal of Political Economy* 85: 451–72.

Friedman, M. and Schwartz, A.J. 1963. *A Monetary History of the United States 1867–1960*. Princeton, NJ: Princeton University Press.

Frisch, R. 1933. Propagation Problems and Impulse Problems in Dynamic Economics. Reprinted in R.A. Gordon and L.R. Klein eds. *Readings in Business Cycles*. London: Unwin, 155–85.

Fuss, H. 1926. Unemployment in 1925. *International Labour Review* 14: 203–31.

1927. Money and Unemployment. *International Labour Review* 16: 601–17.

1935. Unemployment and Employment Among Women. *International Labour Review* 31: 463–97.

Fuss, H. and Tait, D.C. 1933. Unemployment Benefits and Measures for Occupying the Unemployed in Great Britain. *International Labour Review* 27: 595–619.

Gardner, R.N. 1969. *Sterling-Dollar Diplomacy*, 2nd edition. New York: Macmillan.

Garraty, J.A. 1978. *Unemployment in History: Economic Thought in Public Policy*. New York: Harper Row.

Garvy, G. 1978. Carl Snyder, Pioneer Economic Statistician and Monetarist. *History of Political Economy* 10: 454–90.

GATT. 1952. *General Agreement on Tariffs and Trade: Basic Instruments and Selected Documents* Vol. I. Geneva.

Gavin, M. and Rodrik, D. 1995. The World Bank in Historical Perspective. *American Economic Review* 85: 327–34.

Gayer, A.D. 1935. *Public Works in Prosperity and Depression*. New York: National Bureau of Economic Research.

Ghosh, A.R. and Masson, P.R. 1994. *Economic Cooperation in an Uncertain World*. Oxford: Basil Blackwell.

Giovannini, A. 1993. Bretton Woods and its Precursors: Rules versus Discretion in the History of International Monetary Regimes. In M.D. Bordo and B. Eichengreen eds. 1993. *A Retrospective on the Bretton Woods System: Lessons for International Monetary Reform.* Chicago: University of Chicago Press, 109–52.

Goodrich, L.M. 1947. From League of Nations to United Nations. *International Organization* 1: 3–21.

Graham, F.D. 1923. Some Aspects of Protection Further Considered. *Quarterly Journal of Economics* 37: 199–227.

Groom, A.J.R. 1988. The Advent of International Organization. In P. Taylor and A.J.R. Groom eds. *International Institutions at Work.* London: Pinter Publishers, 3–20.

Groom, A.J.R. and Taylor, P. eds. 1990. *Frameworks for International Cooperation.* London: Pinter Publishers.

Guitián, M. 1993. The European Monetary System: Recent Intellectual History – A Commentary. In *The Monetary Future of Europe.* London: C.E.P.R.

    1995. Conditionality: Past, Present, and Future. *IMF Staff Papers* 42: 792–835.

Haberler, G. 1932. Money and the Business Cycle. In Q. Wright ed. *Gold and Monetary Stabilization: Lectures of the Harris Foundation.* Chicago: University of Chicago Press, 43–74.

    1936. *The Theory of International Trade with its Applications to Commercial Policy.* London: William Hodge and Co.

    1937. *Prosperity and Depression: A Theoretical Analysis of Cyclical Movements,* 1st edition. Geneva: League of Nations.

    1938. Some Comments on Mr. Kahn's Review of *Prosperity and Depression. Economic Journal* 48: 322–33.

    1943a. *Prosperity and Depression: A Theoretical Analysis of Cyclical Movements,* 3rd edition. New York: United Nations.

    1943b. *Quantitative Trade Controls: Their Causes and Nature.* Princeton: Princeton University Press, League of Nations Economic and Financial Publications II.A.S.

    1944. Currency Depreciation and the International Monetary Fund. *Review of Economic Statistics* 26: 178–81.

    1945. The Choice of Exchange Rates After the War. *American Economic Review* 35: 308–18.

    1946. *Prosperity and Depression: A Theoretical Analysis of Cyclical Movements,* 3rd edition revised. New York: United Nations.

Haberler, G. 1947. Comments on National Central Banking and the International Economy in International Monetary Policies. Washington DC: Board of Governors Federal Reserve System Postwar Economic Studies No. 7.

    1961. Introduction. In R. Nurkse *Equilibrium and Growth in the World Economy.* Cambridge, MA: Harvard University Press.

Hagenbuch, W. 1958. *Social Economics.* Cambridge: Cambridge University Press.

Hall, R.E. 1984. Monetary Strategy with an Elastic Price Standard. In *Price Stability and Public Policy.* Kansas City: Federal Reserve Bank of Kansas City, 137–59.

Halm, G.N. 1945. *International Monetary Cooperation*. Chapel Hill: University of North Carolina Press.

Hancock, K.J. 1960. Unemployment and the Economists in the 1920s. *Economica* 27: 305–21.

1962. The Reduction of Unemployment as a Problem of Public Policy, 1920–1929. Reprinted in S. Pollard ed. *The Gold Standard and Employment Policies Between the Wars*. London: Methuen 1970, 99–121.

Hansen, A. 1941. *Fiscal Policy and Business Cycles*. New York: W.W. Norton.

1949. *Monetary Theory and Fiscal Policy*. New York: McGraw Hill.

Harberger, A.C. 1984. Reflections on the Present and Future Role of the World Bank. Report for the World Bank, mimeo.

Harrod, R.F. 1937. Review of World Economic Survey 1936–37. *Economic Journal* 47: 706–07.

Hawtrey, R.G. 1919. *Currency and Credit*. London: Longmans Green.

1922. The Genoa Resolutions on Currency. *Economic Journal* 32: 290–304.

1923. *Monetary Reconstruction*. London: Longmans Green.

1925. Public Expenditure and the Demand for Labour. *Economica* 5: 38–48.

1930. Money and Index Numbers. *Journal of the Royal Statistical Society* (New Series) 93: 64–85.

Hayek, F.A. 1925. The Monetary Policy of the United States After Recovery From the 1920s crisis. In R. McCloughry ed. *Money, Capital and Fluctuations: Early Essays*. London: Routledge, 2–32.

1932. The Fate of the Gold Standard. In R. McCloughry ed. *Money, Capital and Fluctuations: Early Essays*. London: Routledge, 118–35.

1933. *Monetary Theory and the Trade Cycle*. London: Macmillan.

1937. *Monetary Nationalism and International Stability*. London: Macmillan.

Heilperin, M.A. 1946. *The Trade of Nations*. London: Longmans Green.

Henriksson, R.G.H. 1996. The Early Contribution of Erik Lundberg: A Commentary to his Licentiate Thesis "On the Concept of Economic Equilibrium" (1930). *Structural Change and Economic Dynamics* 7: 347–60.

Hicks, J.R. 1932. *Theory of Wages*. London: Macmillan.

Higgins, B. 1944. The United States Public Work Reserve: An Experiment in the Co-ordination of Public Investment Planning. *International Labour Review* 50: 581–602.

Hilgerdt, F. 1933. Foreign Trade and the Short Business Cycle. In *Economic Essays in Honour of Gustav Cassel*. London: Allen and Unwin, 273–91.

1935. The Approach to Bilateralism – A Change in the Structure of World Trade. *Svenska Handelsbanken: Index* 10: 175–96.

1942. *The Network of World Trade*. Geneva: League of Nations Economic Intelligence Service.

1943. The Case for Multilateral Trade. *American Economic Review* 33: 393–407.

1945. *Industrialization and Foreign Trade*. Geneva: Economic, Financial and Transit Department League of Nations.

Hill, M. 1946. *The Economic and Financial Organisation of the League of Nations A Survey of Twenty-Five Years Experience*. Washington DC: Carnegie Endowment for International Peace.

Hobson, J.A. 1915. *Towards International Government*. London: Unwin.

Horsefield, K. 1969. *The International Monetary Fund 1945–1965: Twenty Years of International Monetary Cooperation* Vol. 1–3. Washington DC: International Monetary Fund.

Houston, D. 1926. *Memorandum on Rationalisation in the United States*. Geneva: League of Nations C.E.C.P. 20 Economic and Financial Section.

International Institute of Intellectual Cooperation. 1934. *A Record of a Second Study Conference on the State in Economic Life*. Paris.

International Labour Organization. 1922a. *Unemployment Enquiry: Remedies For Unemployment*. Geneva.

　1922b. Unemployment Insurance: An International Survey. *International Labour Review* 6: 365–75.

　1923. Employment and Unemployment. *International Labour Review* 7: 298–320.

　1924a. *Unemployment 1920–23*. Geneva: ILO Studies and Reports Series C No. 8.

　1924b. *Economic Barometers*. Geneva: Studies and Reports Series N No. 5.

　1924c. Bank Credit and Unemployment. *International Labour Review* 9: 78–94.

　1924d. *Unemployment in its National and International Aspects*. Geneva: ILO Studies and Reports Series C No. 9.

　1924e. *Family Allowances: The Remuneration of Labour According to Need*. Geneva: ILO Studies and Reports Series D No. 13.

　1924f. Comparison of the Levels of Real Wages in Certain Capital Cities. *International Labour Review* 9: 620–54.

　1925a. *Unemployment Insurance: A Study of Comparative Legislation*. Geneva: ILO Studies and Reports Series C No. 10.

　1925b. *General Problem of Social Insurance*. Geneva: ILO Studies and Reports Series M No. 1.

　1925c. *The International Labor Organization and Social Insurance*. Geneva: ILO Studies and Reports Series M No. 12.

　1925d. *Methods of Compiling Cost of Living Index Numbers*. Geneva: ILO Studies and Reports Series N No. 6.

　1925e. The International Labour Organisation and Social Insurance. *International Labour Review* 11: 763–83.

　1925f. Unemployment in 1924 and the Beginning of 1925. *International Labour Review* 12: 186–224.

　1926. *Methods of Conducting Family Budget Enquiries*. Geneva: ILO Studies and Reports Series N No. 9.

　1927. *Report of the Director*. Geneva: ILO Conference, Fourth Session.

　1928. *Minimum Wage-Fixing Machinery*. Geneva: ILO Studies and Reports Series D No. 17.

　1929. *Unemployment: Some International Aspects 1920–1928*. Geneva: Studies and Reports Series C No. 13.

　1930. *Wages and Regulation of Condition of Labour in the USSR*. Geneva: ILO Studies and Reports Series D No. 19.

1931a. *Unemployment and Public Works*. Geneva: ILO Studies and Reports Series C No. 15.

1931b. *Unemployment Problems in 1931*. Geneva: ILO Studies and Reports Series C No. 16.

1931c. *The Social Aspects of Rationalisation*. Geneva: ILO Studies and Reports Series B No. 18.

1931d. *A Contribution to the Study of International Comparisons of Costs of Living*. Geneva: ILO Studies and Reports Series N No. 17.

1931e. The Use of the Employment Exchange Service in Great Britain as a Labour Clearing House. *International Labour Review* 24: 410–17.

1931f. *Principles and Methods of Wage Determination in the Coal-Mining Industry: An International Survey*. Geneva: ILO Studies and Reports Series D No. 20.

1931g. *Unemployment and Monetary Fluctuations. Unemployment Committee Report*. Geneva: International Labour Organization Doc. U.C.7. 26–27 January.

1932. Resolution Adopted by the Sixteenth Session of the International Labour Conference Concerning Action to be Taken to Remedy the Crisis. *International Labour Review* 26: 220–21.

1933a. The Problem of the Unemployment of Young Persons. *International Labour Review* 27: 499–523.

1933b. *Report of the Director*. Geneva: ILO Conference Seventeenth Session.

1933c. *Employment Exchanges: An International Study of Placing Activities*. Geneva: ILO Studies and Reports Series C No. 18.

1933d. Technological Changes, Productivity of Labour, and Labour Displacement in the United States. *International Labour Review* 27: 519–23.

1933e. Economic Depression and Wage Policy. *International Labour Review* 27: 392–97.

1934. *International Comparisons of Cost of Living*. Geneva: ILO Studies and Reports Series N No. 20.

1935. *Public Works Policy*. Geneva: ILO Studies and Reports Series C No. 19.

1936. *The International Labour Organization and Social Insurance*. Geneva: ILO Studies and Reports Series M No. 12.

1938. Public Works as a Factor in Economic Stabilisation. *International Labour Review* 38: 727–57.

1939a. *Report of the Director*. Geneva: ILO.

1939b. *The Law and Women's Work: A Contribution to the Study of the Status of Women*. Geneva: ILO Studies and Reports Series I No. 4.

1940a. *Employment, Wages and International Trade*. Geneva: ILO Studies and Reports Series B No. 32.

1940b. *Methods of Family Living Studies: Income-Expenditure-Consumption*. Geneva: ILO Studies and Reports Series N No. 23.

1942. *Approaches to Social Security: An International Survey*. Geneva: ILO Studies and Reports Series M No. 18–19.

1945. Full Employment in the Transition Period. *International Labour Review* 52: 589–608.

1946. *Public Investment and Full Employment.* Montreal: Studies and Reports New Series No. 3.

1947. *The Economic Background of Social Policy including Problems of Industrialisation.* New Delhi: ILO Preparatory Report IV Asiatic Regional Conference.

1948. *Housing and Employment.* Geneva: Studies and Reports New Series No. 8.

1949. *Report of the Director-General.* Geneva: ILO Asian Regional Conference.

1950a. *Fourth Report of the International Labour Organisation to the United Nations.* Geneva: International Labour Office.

1950b. *Action Against Unemployment.* Geneva: International Labour Office Studies and Reports New Series No. 20.

1950c. Reports and Enquiries: National and International Measures for Full Employment. *International Labour Review* 614: 385–409.

Irwin, D.A. 1996. *Against the Tide: An Intellectual History of Free Trade.* Princeton, NJ: Princeton University Press.

Jack, L.B. 1943. Proposals for International Exchange Stabilisation: Analysis of the British, Canadian, French and United States Plans. *International Labour Review* 48: 157–73.

Jacobsson, E.E. 1979. *A Life For Sound Money: Per Jacobsson, His Biography.* Oxford: Oxford University Press.

Jacobsson, P. 1928. The Theoretical Solution as Seen From the Conference. In *The Economic Consequences of the League.* London: Europe Publishing Co, 43–53.

1958. *Some Monetary Problems, International and National.* In E. Jucker-Fleetwood ed. Oxford: Oxford University Press.

James, H. 1996. *International Monetary Cooperation since Bretton Woods.* Oxford: Oxford University Press.

Johnson, H.G. 1971. The Keynesian Revolution and the Monetarist Counter-Revolution. *American Economic Review* 61: 1–12.

Johnston, G.A. 1929. Rationalisation and Industrial Relations. *International Labour Review* 20: 619–40.

1930. The Technique of Discussion in Management-Worker Relationships in the United States. *International Labour Review* 21: 623–45.

1932. Social Economic Planning. *International Labour Review* 25: 58–78.

Jones, B.L. 1972. The Role of Keynesians in Wartime Policy and Postwar Planning 1940–1946. *American Economic Review, Papers and Proceedings* 62: 125–33.

Jonung, L. 1979. Knut Wicksell's Norm of Price Stabilization and Swedish Monetary Policy in the 1930s. *Journal of Monetary Economics* 5: 459–96.

1991. Introduction and Summary. In L. Jonung ed. *The Stockholm School of Economics Revisited.* Cambridge: Cambridge University Press, 1–37.

Kahler, M. 1995. *International Institutions and the Political Economy of Integration.* Washington DC: Brookings Institution.

Kahn, R.F. 1931. The Relation of Home Investment to Unemployment. *Economic Journal* 41: 173–98.

1937. The League of Nations Inquiry into the Trade Cycle. *Economic Journal* 47: 670–79.

1938. A Rejoinder. *Economic Journal* 48: 333–36.

Kaldor, N. 1944. The Quantitative Aspect of the Full Employment Problem in Britain Appendix C. In W.H. Beveridge ed. *Full Employment in a Free Society*. London: Allen and Unwin, 344–401.

1989. Recollections of an Economist. Reprinted in F. Targetti and A.P. Thirlwall eds. *Further Essays on Economic Theory and Policy* by Nicolas Kaldor. New York: Holmes and Meier, 13–37.

Kalecki, M. 1945a. Three Ways to Full Employment. In T. Balogh, F.A. Burchardt, M. Kalecki, K. Mandelbaum, E.F. Schumacher, and G.D.N. Worswick eds. *The Economics of Full Employment*. Oxford: Basil Blackwell, 39–58.

1945b. The Maintenance of Full Employment after the Transition Period: A Comparison of the Problem in the United States and the United Kingdom. *International Labour Review* 52: 449–64.

Keohane, R.O. 1984. *After Hegemony: Cooperation and Discord in the World Political Economy*. Princeton, NJ: Princeton University Press.

Keynes, J.M. 1923. *A Tract on Monetary Reform*. In *The Collected Writings of John Maynard Keynes: Activities 1931–39*. Vol. IV. London: Macmillan.

1924a. A Comment on Professor Cannan's Article. In D. Moggridge ed. *The Collected Writings of John Maynard Keynes: Economic Articles and Correspondence*. Vol. XI. London: Macmillan 1983, 415–19.

1924b. Mr. J.M. Keynes's Speech. In D. Moggridge ed. *The Collected Writings of John Maynard Keynes: Activities 1922–1929*. Vol. XIX. London: Macmillan 1981, 182–93.

1924c. Discussion on Monetary Reform. In D. Moggridge ed. *The Collected Writings of John Maynard Keynes: Activities 1922–1929*. Vol. XIX. London: Macmillan 1981, 206–14.

1930. *A Treatise on Money* 2 vols. London: Macmillan 1930. In D. Moggridge ed. *The Collected Writings of John Maynard Keynes*. Vols. V and VI. London: Macmillan 1971.

1933. National Self-Sufficiency. In D. Moggridge ed. *The Collected Writings of John Maynard Keynes: Activities 1931–39*. Vol. XXI. London: Macmillan 1982, 233–46.

1936. *General Theory of Employment Interest and Money*. London: Macmillan.

1939a. The League of Nations. Professor Tinbergen's Method. *Economic Journal* 49: 558–68.

1939b. The Process of Capital Formation, Review of League of Nations 1938a. *Economic Journal* 49: 569–75.

1940. Comment. *Economic Journal* 50: 154–56.

1945. The Anglo-American Financial Agreements. (Speech Delivered to the House of Lords, December 18, 1945.) Reprinted in S.E. Harris ed. *The New Economics*. New York: A.A. Knopf 1947, 380–95.

1979. *The Collected Writings of John Maynard Keynes: Activities 1940–43*. Vol. XXIII, D. Moggridge ed., London: Macmillan.

1981. *The Collected Writings of John Maynard Keynes, Activities 1929–31.* Vol. XX. D. Moggridge ed., London: Macmillan.

Keynes, M. and Henderson, H.D. 1929. *Can Lloyd George Do It? An Examination of the Liberal Pledge.* London: The Nation and Athenaeum.

Kindleberger, C.P. 1986. International Public Goods Without International Government. *American Economic Review* 76: 1–13.

1989. Commercial Policy Between the Wars. In P. Mathias and S. Pollard eds. *The Cambridge Economic History of Europe, Vol. VIII: The Industrial Economies.* Cambridge: Cambridge University Press, 161–96, 1153–55.

King, J.E. 1990. P.W. Martin and the Flaw in the Price System. La Trobe University, Melbourne, November: 36pp.

Kirshner, O. 1995. Introduction. In O. Kirshner ed. *The Bretton Woods-GATT System. Retrospect and Prospect After Fifty Years.* New York: M.E. Sharpe, ix–xiii.

Krueger, A.O. 1998. Whither the IMF and the World Bank? *Journal of Economic Literature* 36: 1983–2020.

Laidler, D. 1991. The Austrians and the Stockholm School: Two Failures in the Development of Modern Macroeconomics? In L. Jonung ed. *The Stockholm School of Economics Revisited.* Cambridge: Cambridge University Press, 295–327.

1999. *Fabricating the Keynesian Revolution: Studies in the Inter-War Literature on Money, the Cycle and Unemployment.* Cambridge: Cambridge University Press.

League of Nations. 1920. *Report of the International Financial Conference 1920, Brussels.* 2 Vols. Brussels: T. Dewarichet.

1922. *Papers Relating to International Economic Conference Genoa 1922.* London: H.M. Stationery Office.

1927a. *Report and Proceedings of the World Economic Conference.* Geneva: League of Nations Document C.E.I.46, 2 Vols.

1927b. *Report of the Economic Work of the League of Nations.* Geneva: League of Nations Economic and Financial Section.

1927c. Final Report of the [World Economic] Conference, Geneva 1927. Reprinted in P. Jacobsson ed. *The Economic Consequences of the League.* London: Europe Publishing Co., 160–207.

1928. *Report of the Economic Consultative Committee on its First Session.* Geneva: League of Nations Documents, Economic and Financial.

1929. *Report of the Economic Consultative Committee on its Second Session.* Geneva: League of Nations Document, Economic and Financial.

1930a. *Interim Report of the Gold Delegation of the Financial Committee.* Geneva: League of Nations.

1930b. *Principles and Methods of Financial Reconstruction Work Undertaken Under the Auspices of the League of Nations.* Geneva: Economic and Financial Section Secretariat 1930. II. 6.

1931. *Interim Report of the Gold Delegation of the Financial Committee.* Geneva: League of Nations.

1932a. *Report of the Gold Delegation of the Financial Committee.* Geneva: League of Nations Archives Doc. II.A.12.

1932b. *World Economic Survey, 1931–2*. Geneva: League of Nations.

1933a. *World Economic Survey, 1932–3*. Geneva: League of Nations.

1933b. *Balance of Payments 1933*. Geneva: League of Nations.

1936a. *World Economic Survey, 1934–5*. Geneva: League of Nations.

1936b. *Equality of Treatment in the Present State of International Commercial Relations*. Geneva: League of Nations Document II.B.

1937a. *World Economic Survey, 1935–6*. Geneva: League of Nations.

1937b. *Report of the Committee: The Study of the Problem of Raw Materials* Geneva: League of Nations Document A.27.II.B.

1938a. *Statistics Relating to Capital Formation. A Note on Methods by the Committee of Statistical Experts*. Geneva: League of Nations Studies and Reports on Statistical Methods No. 4.

1938b. *Report on Exchange Control*. Geneva: League of Nations Economic and Financial Section Document II.A.10.

1939a. *Fiscal Committee, Report to the Council on the Work of the Ninth Session of the Committee*. Geneva: League of Nations.

1939b. *The Development of International Cooperation in Economic and Social Affairs, Report of a Special Committee*. Geneva: League of Nations.

1939c. *World Economic Survey, 1937–8*. Geneva: League of Nations.

1941. *Europe's Trade: A Study of the Trade of European Countries With Each Other and With the Rest of the World*. Geneva: League of Nations Economic Intelligence Service.

1942a. *Economic Fluctuations in the United States and the United Kingdom 1918–1922*. Geneva: League of Nations.

1942b. *Commercial Policy in the Interwar Period: International Proposals and National Policies*. Geneva: League of Nations.

1943. *The Transition from War to Peace*. Geneva: League of Nations.

1944. *International Currency Experience: Lessons of the Inter-War Period*. Geneva: Economic, Financial and Transit Department.

1945a. *Economic Stability in the Post-War World: The Conditions of Prosperity after the Transition from War to Peace*. Geneva: League of Nations.

1945b. *Report on the Work of the League*. Geneva: League of Nations.

1945c. *Commercial Policy in the Post-War World*. Geneva: League of Nations.

1946. *The Course and Control of Inflation*. New Jersey: Economic, Financial and Transit Department.

Lederer, E. 1938. *Technical Progress and Unemployment*. Geneva: ILO Studies and Reports Series C No. 22.

1939. Industrial Fluctuations and Wage Policy: Some Unsettled Points. *International Labour Review* 39: 1–33.

Lee, B.A. 1989. The Miscarriage of Necessity and Invention: Proto-Keynesianism and Democratic States in the 1930s. In P.A. Hall ed. *The Political Power of Economic Ideas: Keynesianism across Nations*. Princeton, NJ: Princeton University Press, 129–70.

Lee, E. 1994. The Declaration of Philadelphia: Retrospect and Prospect. *International Labour Review* 133: 467–84.

Lerner, A.P. 1936. Mr. Keynes' "General Theory of Employment, Interest and Money." *International Labour Review* 34: 435–54.

Lester, R. 1948. *Company Wage Policies: A Survey of Patterns and Experiences.* Princeton: Princeton University Industrial Relations Section.

Lorwin, L. 1936. The ILO and World Economic Policy. *International Labour Review* 33: 457–67.

Loveday, A. 1938a. Problems of Economic Insecurity. In *The World's Economic Future*, Sir James Halley Stewart Lectures for 1937. London: Allen and Unwin, 17–42.

    1938b. The Economic and Financial Activities of the League. *International Affairs* 17: 788–809.

Luard, E. ed. 1966. *The Evolution of International Organizations.* London: Thames and Hudson.

Lundberg, E. 1930. On the Concept of Economic Equilibrium. Reprinted in *Structural Change and Economic Dynamics* 7 1996: 361–90.

    1937. *Studies in the Theory of Economic Expansion.* London: P.S. King.

    1961. Introduction. In R. Nurkse ed. *Patterns of Trade and Development.* Oxford: Basil Blackwell.

MacBean, A.I. and Snowden, P.N. 1981. *International Institutions in Trade and Finance.* Boston: Allen and Unwin.

Macmillan Committee. 1931. *Committee on Finance and Industry: Report.* London: H.M. Stationery Office, Cmd. 3897.

Manoilesco, M. 1931. *The Theory of Protection and International Trade.* London, P.S. King.

Martin, P.W. 1926a. *The Limited Market.* London: Allen and Unwin.

    1926b. Overproduction and Underconsumption: A Remedy. *International Labour Review* 14: 37–54.

    1926c. The Conciliation and Arbitration of Industrial Disputes I. *International Labour Review* 14: 640–59.

    1927. The Conciliation and Arbitration of Industrial Disputes III. *International Labour Review* 15: 78–97.

    1931a. Finance and Industry: The International Significance of the Macmillan Report. *International Labour Review* 24: 359–75.

    1931b. Finance and Industry: The Macmillan Report as a Basis for International Action. *International Labour Review* 24: 685–98.

    1932. World Economic Reconstruction: An Analysis of the Economic Resolution Adopted by the International Labour Conference. *International Labour Review* 26: 199–220.

    1933. Public Works and the World Crisis: The Frontal Attack on Industrial Depression and Unemployment. In Geneva Institute of International Relations, *Problems of Peace*. London: Allen and Unwin Eighth Series, 226–45.

    1936. The Present Status of Economic Planning I. *International Labour Review* 33: 619–45.

    1937. The Present Status of Economic Planning II. *International Labour Review* 35: 177–97.

Martin, P.W. and Riches, E.J. 1933. The Social Consequences of a Return to Gold: An Analysis of Certain Current Proposals for an International Monetary Standard. *International Labour Review* 27: 25–50.

Mason, E.S. and Asher, R.E. 1973. *The World Bank Since Bretton Woods*. Washington DC: The Brookings Institution.

Matthaei, L.E. 1931. Some Effects of the Agricultural Depression on Agricultural Labour. *International Labour Review* 23: 453–75.

Maurette, F. 1931. Is Unemployment Insurance a Cause of Permanent Unemployment? *International Labour Review* 24: 663–84.

McCallum, B.T. 1987. The Case for Rules in the Conduct of Monetary Policy: A Concrete Example. *Weltwirtschafliches Archiv* 123: 415–29.

McClure, W. 1933. *World Prosperity as Sought Through the Economic Work of the League of Nations*. New York: Macmillan.

McDaniel Sells, D. 1924a. The Development of State Wage Regulation in Australia and New Zealand. *International Labour Review* 10: 607–29.

1924b. The Development of State Wage Regulation in Australia and New Zealand. *International Labour Review* 10: 779–99.

1924c. The Development of State Wage Regulation in Australia and New Zealand. *International Labour Review* 10: 962–1004.

McKinnon, R. 1996. *The Rules of the Game: International Money and Exchange Rates*. Cambridge, MA: MIT Press.

McLean, R.I. 1980. *Civil Servants and Public Policy: A Comparative Study of International Secretariats*. Ontario: Wilfred Laurier University Press.

Meade, J.E. 1932. Public Works in Their International Aspect. Reprinted in *The Collected Papers of James Meade Volume 1: Employment and Inflation*. London: Allen and Unwin, 6–25.

1933. International Economic Cooperation. *Journal of the Proceedings of the Agricultural Economics Society* 2: 275–82.

1948. *Planning and the Price Mechanism*. London: George Allen and Unwin.

Meltzer, A.H. 1988. *Keynes's Monetary Theory: A Different Interpretation*. Cambridge: Cambridge University Press.

Menzies, A.A. 1983. Technical Assistance and the League of Nations. In *The League of Nations in Retrospect*. New York: Walter de Gruyter.

Meron, T. 1977. *The United Nations Secretariat*. Lexington, MA: Lexington Books.

Metzler, L.A. 1949. The Theory of International Trade. In H.S. Ellis ed. *A Survey of Contemporary Economics*. Philadelphia: Blakiston Co.

Meyer, R.H. 1970. *Bankers' Diplomacy: Monetary Stabilization in the Twenties*. New York: Columbia University Press.

Mikesell, R.F. 1994. The Bretton Woods Debates: *A Memoir*. Princeton University Essays in International Finance No. 192.

Milgate, M. 1987. Staehle, Hans 1903–1961. In J. Eatwell et al. eds. *The New Palgrave A Dictionary of Economics*. London: Macmillan, IV 470.

Mitchell, W.C. 1913. *Business Cycles*. Berkeley, CA: University of California Press.

1923. *Business Cycles and Unemployment*. New York: McGraw Hill.

Mitnitzky, M. 1934. The Effects of a Public Works Policy on Business Activity. *International Labour Review* 30: 435–56.

1935. Wage Policy To-day and Tomorrow. *International Labour Review* 32: 344–73.

Morgan, M.S. 1990. *The History of Econometric Ideas*. Cambridge: Cambridge University Press.

Morgenstern, O. 1943. On the International Spread of Business Cycles. *Journal of Political Economy* 51: 287–309.

Mouré, K. 1992. The Limits of Central Bank Co-operation, 1916–36. *Contemporary European History* 1: 259–79.

Murphy, C.N. 1994. *International Organizations and Industrial Change: Global Governance Since 1850*. New York: Oxford University Press.

Myrdal, G. 1957. *Economic Theory and Under-Developed Regions*. London: Gerald Duckworth.

Nixon, J.W. 1928a. The Measurement of Risk in Connection with Labour Statistics. *International Labour Review* 17: 633–50.

1928b. Some Problems of Statistics of Accidents as Illustrated by the British Statistics. *International Labour Review* 17: 731–59.

Northedge, F.S. 1986. *The League of Nations: Its Life and Times 1920–1946*. Leicester: Leicester University Press.

Nurkse, R. 1933. Causes and Effects of Capital Movements. Reprinted in R. Nurkse 1961. *Equilibrium and Growth in the World Economy*. Cambridge, MA: Harvard University Press, 1–21.

1935. *Internationale Kapitalbewegungen*. Wien: Verlag von Julius Springer.

1944. The Gold Exchange Standard. Reprinted in B. Eichengreen ed. *The Gold Standard in Theory and History*. New York: Methuen, 1985, 201–25.

1945a. Conditions of International Monetary Equilibrium. Essays in International Finance, No. 4 Princeton University. Reprinted in A.E.A. *Readings in the Theory of International Trade*. London: Allen and Unwin, 1950, 3–34.

1945b. International Money and Credit – Discussion. *American Economic Review* 35: 291–94.

1946. Review of G.N. Halm, International Monetary Cooperation. Reprinted in R. Nurkse 1961. *Equilibrium and Growth in the World Economy*. Cambridge: Harvard University Press, 346–47.

1947a. Domestic and International Equilibrium. Reprinted in R. Nurkse 1961. *Equilibrium and Growth in the World Economy*. Cambridge, MA: Harvard University Press, 41–71.

1947b. International Monetary Policy and the Search for Stability. Reprinted in R. Nurkse 1961. *Equilibrium and Growth in the World Economy*. Cambridge, MA: Harvard University Press, 72–86.

Obstfeld, M. 1995. International Currency Experience: New Lessons and Lessons Relearned. *Brookings Papers on Economic Activity* 1: 119–95.

Obstfeld, M. and Rogoff, K. 1996. *Foundations of International Macroeconomics*. Cambridge, MA: MIT Press.

Officer, L.H. 1982. Prosperity and Depression – And Beyond. *Quarterly Journal of Economics* 97: 149–59.

Ohlin, B. 1928. The Plea for Freer Trade. In *The Economic Consequences of the League*. London: Europe Publishing Co, 123–28.

1931a. *The Course and Phases of the World Depression: Report Presented to the Assembly of the League of Nations*. Geneva: Secretariat of the League of Nations.

1931b. Protection and Non-Competing Groups. *Welwirtschafliches Archiv* 33: 30–45.

1933a. *Interregional and International Trade.* Cambridge, MA: Harvard University Press.

1933b. On the Formulation of Monetary Theory. English translation reprinted in *History of Political Economy* (1978) 10: 53–69, 221–40.

1935. Economic Recovery and Labour Market Problems in Sweden: II. *International Labour Review* 31: 670–99.

1936. *International Economic Reconstruction.* Paris: International Chamber of Commerce.

1937. Employment Stabilization and Price Stabilization. In A.D. Gayer ed. *The Lessons of Monetary Experience.* New York: Farrar and Rinehart, 318–28.

1938. Review of Haberler 1936. *Economic Journal* 48: 498–507.

Oudegeest, J. 1929. The Functions of the International Labour Organisation. *International Labour Review* 20: 1–14.

Patinkin, D. 1976. Keynes and Econometrics: On the Interaction Between the Macroeconomic Revolutions of the Interwar Period. *Econometrica* 44: 1091–1123.

Pauly, L.W. 1996. *The League of Nations and the Foreshadowing of the International Monetary Fund.* New Jersey: Princeton University Essays in International Finance No. 201.

Peden, G.C. 1984. The "Treasury View" on Public Works and Employment in the Interwar Period. *Economic History Review* 37: 167–81.

Perrin, G. 1969. Reflections on Fifty Years of Social Security. *International Labour Review* 99: 249–92.

Persons, W.M. 1916. Construction of a Business Barometer Based Upon Annual Data. *American Economic Review* 6: 739–69.

1919. An Index of General Business Conditions. *Review of Economic Statistics* 1: 111–205.

Pigou, A.C. 1914. *Unemployment.* London: Williams & Norgite.

1927. Wage Policy and Unemployment. *Economic Journal* 37: 355–68.

1933. *Theory of Unemployment.* London: Macmillan.

Polak, J.J. 1937–39. International Propagation of Business Cycles. *Review of Economic Studies* 5–6: 79–99.

1995. Fifty Years of Exchange Rate Research and Policy at the International Monetary Fund. *IMF Staff Papers* 42: 734–61.

1997. The Contribution of the International Monetary Fund. In A.W. Coats ed. *The Post-1945 Internationalization of Economics.* Durham, NC: Duke University Press, 211–24.

Pribram, K. 1925. The Unification of Social Insurance. *International Labour Review* 12: 303–17.

1926. The Scope of Labor Statistics. *International Labour Review* 13: 476–88.

1928. The Regulation of Minimum Wages as an International Problem. *International Labour Review* 17: 317–31.

Rappard, W.E. 1925. *International Relations as Viewed From Geneva.* New Haven, CT: Yale University Press.

1930. *Uniting Europe: The Trend of International Cooperation Since the War.* New Haven, CT: Yale University Press.

1938. *Post War Efforts for Freer Trade.* Geneva: Geneva Research Centre.

Rasminsky, L. 1988. Planning the Postwar International System. In O.F. Hamouda and J.N. Smithin eds. *Keynes and Public Policy after Fifty Years Volume 1: Economics and Policy.* Aldershot: Edward Elgar, 151–56.

Reder, M. 1952. The Theory of Union Wage Policy. *Review of Economics and Statistics* 34: 34–45.

Reisman, S. 1996. The Birth of a World Trading System: ITO and GATT. In O. Kirshner ed. *The Bretton Woods-GATT System. Retrospect and Prospect After Fifty Years.* New York: M.E. Sharpe, 82–88.

Reynolds, L. 1951. *The Structure of Labor Markets.* New York: Harper.

Richardson, J.H. 1928. Some Aspects of Recent Wage Movements and Tendencies in Various Countries. *International Labour Review* 17: 179–203.

1929a. The Doctrine of High Wages. *International Labour Review* 20: 797–815.

1929b. Recent Developments in Industrial Cooperation in the United States and Canada. *International Labour Review* 20: 67–83.

Riches, E.J. and Jack, L.B. 1943. The Transition from War to Peace Economy: Analysis of an International Report. *International Labour Review* 48: 1–22.

Robbins, L. 1947. *The Economic Problem in Peace and War.* London: Macmillan.

Robertson, D.H. 1945. Review of League of Nations. Economic Stability in the Post-War World. *Economic Journal* 55: 401–04.

1983. J.M. Keynes and Cambridge in the 1920s. *South African Journal of Economics* 51: 407–18.

Robinson, J. 1945a. The Economics of Full Employment. *Economic Journal* Reprinted in *Collected Economic Papers* Vol. 1. Cambridge MA: MIT Press 1951, 99–104.

1945b. Review of International Currency Experience. *Economic Journal* 55: 405–07.

Rodrik, D. 2000. How Far Will International Economic Integration Go? *Journal of Economic Perspectives* 14: 177–86.

Rogoff, K. 1999. International Institutions for Reducing Global Financial Instability. *Journal of Economic Perspectives* 13: 21–42.

Rostow, W.W. 1960. *The Stages of Economic Growth.* Cambridge: Cambridge University Press.

1990. *Theorists of Economic Growth from David Hume to the Present.* Oxford and New York: Oxford University Press.

Salter, A. 1928. The League's Contribution. In P. Jacobsson ed. *The Economic Consequences of the League.* London: Europa, 1–11.

1932. *Recovery: The Second Effort.* London: Allen and Unwin.

1934. Presidential Address. In International Institution of Intellectual Cooperation *A Record of a Second Study Conference on the State in Economic Life.* Paris: 13–18.

Samuelson, P.A. 1938. Welfare Economics and International Trade. *American Economic Review* 28: 261–66.

1939a. A Synthesis of the Principle of the Accelerator and the Multiplier. *Journal of Political Economy* 47: 786–97.

1939b. The Gains from International Trade. *Canadian Journal of Economics and Political Science* 5: 195–205.

1948. Disparity in Postwar Exchange Rates. In S.E. Harris ed. *Foreign Economic Policy for the United States*. Cambridge, MA: Harvard University Press, 397–412.

Santaella, J.A. 1993. Stabilization Programs and External Enforcement: Experience From the 1920s. *IMF Staff Papers* 40: 584–621.

Sawyer, M.C. 1985. *The Economics of Michal Kalecki*. London: Macmillan.

Schloss, H.H. 1958. *The Bank for International Settlements: An Experiment in Central Bank Cooperation*. Amsterdam: North Holland.

Schneider, M. 1987. Underconsumptionism. In J. Eatwell, M. Milgate, and P. Newman eds. *The New Palgrave Dictionary of Economics*. London: Macmillan, IV 741–45.

Schumpeter, J.A. 1954. *History of Economic Analysis*. New York: Oxford University Press.

Schwartz, A. 1987. Lessons of the Gold Standard Era and the Bretton Woods System for the Prospects of an International Monetary System Constitution. In M. Bordo ed. *Money in Historical Perspective*. Chicago: University of Chicago Press, 391–406.

Scitovsky, T. 1942. A Reconsideration of the Theory of Tariffs. *Review of Economic Studies* 9: 89–110.

Selgin, G. 1995a. The "Productivity Norm" Versus Zero Inflation in the History of Economic Thought. *History of Political Economy* 27: 705–35.

1995b. The Case for a "Productivity Norm": Comment on Dowd. *Journal of Macroeconomics* 17: 733–40.

Silverman, D.P. 1982. *Reconstructing Europe After the Great War*. Cambridge, MA: Harvard University Press.

Simmons, B.A. 1993. Why Innovate? Founding the Bank for International Settlements. *World Politics* 45: 361–405.

1994. *Who Adjusts? Domestic Sources of Foreign Economic Policy During the Interwar Years*. Princeton, NJ: Princeton University Press.

Snow, E.C. 1923. Trade Forecasting and Prices. *Journal of the Royal Statistical Society* 86: 332–76.

Snyder, C. 1923a. The Stabilisation of Gold: A Plan. *American Economic Review* 13: 276–85.

1923b. A New Index of the Volume of Trade. *Journal of the American Statistical Association* 18: 949–63.

1924. New Measures in the Equation of Exchange. *American Economic Review* 14: 699–713.

Staehle, H. 1932a. An International Enquiry into Living Costs. *International Labour Review* 26: 313–63.

1932b. Ein Verfahren zur Ermittlung gleichwertiger Einkommen in verschiedenen Ländern. *Archiv für Sozialwissenschaft* 67: 436–46.

1937. A General Method For the Comparison of the Price of Living. *Review of Economic Studies* 4: 205–14.

Staley, E. 1945. *World Economic Development: Effects on Advanced Industrial Countries.* Montreal: International Labour Organization Studies and Reports Series B No. 36.

Stein, H. 1969. *The Fiscal Revolution in America.* Chicago: University of Chicago Press.

Stein, O. 1941. Building Social Security. *International Labour Review* 64: 249–74.

Stolper, W. and Samuelson, P.A. 1941. Protection and Real Wages. *Review of Economic Studies* 9: 58–73.

Taussig, F. 1921. *Principles of Economics* Vol. II, 3rd edition. New York: Macmillan.

Tavlas, G.S. ed. 1997. *The Collapse of Exchange Rate Regimes: Causes, Consequences and Policy Responses.* Boston: Kluwer Academic Publishers.

Taylor, J.B. 1981. Stabilization, Accommodation, and Monetary Rules. *American Economic Review* May: 145–49.

Taylor, P. 1990. A Conceptual Typology of International Organization. In A.J.R. Groom and P. Taylor eds. *Frameworks for International Cooperation.* London: Pinter Publishers, 12–26.

Thibert, M. 1933a. The Economic Depression and the Employment of Women I. *International Labour Review* 27: 443–70.

1933b. The Economic Depression and the Employment of Women II. *International Labour Review* 27: 620–30.

Thomas, A. 1921a. The International Labor Organisation: Its Origins, Development and Future. *International Labour Review* 1: 5–22.

1921b. The First Year of the International Labour Organisation. *International Labour Review* 1: 23–40.

Tinbergen, J. 1938. *The Statistical Testing of Business Cycle Theories: Volume 1, A Method and Its Application to Investment Activity.* Geneva: League of Nations.

1939. *The Statistical Testing of Business Cycle Theories: Volume 2, Business Cycles in the United States of America, 1919–1932.* Geneva: League of Nations.

1940. On a Method of Statistical Business-Cycle Research: A Reply. *Economic Journal* 50: 141–54.

United Nations. 1947. *Survey of Current Inflationary and Deflationary Tendencies.* New York: Department of Economic Affairs.

1949a. *Maintenance of Full Employment.* New York: Department of Economic Affairs.

1949b. *International Capital Movements during the Inter-War Period.* New York: Department of Economic Affairs.

1949c. *Methods of Financing Economic Development in Under-Developed Countries.* New York: Department of Economic Affairs.

1949d. *Inflationary and Deflationary Tendencies, 1946–1948.* New York: Department of Economic Affairs.

1950a. *National and International Measures for Full Employment.* New York: Department of Economic Affairs.

1950b. *Implementation of Full Employment Policies.* New York: Department of Economic Affairs.

United States Committee on International Economic Policy. 1944. *World Trade and Employment*. New York: Report from the Advisory Committee on Economics, Carnegie Endowment for International Peace.

Vallentin, A. 1932. The Employment of Women Since the War. *International Labour Review* 35: 480–98.

Vaubel, R. 1994. The Political Economy of the IMF: A Public Choice Analysis. In D. Bandow and J. Vasquez eds. *Perpetuating Poverty: The World Bank, the IMF and the Developing World*. Washington DC: CATO Institute, 37–55.

Vaubel, R. and Willetts, T. eds. 1991. *The Political Economy of International Organizations*. Boulder, CO: Westview Press.

Viner, J. 1926. *A Memorandum on Dumping*. Geneva: League of Nations, Reprinted New York: A.M. Kelley, 1966.

1943. *Trade Relations Between Free Market and Controlled Economies*. Geneva: League of Nations.

1950. Full Employment at Whatever Cost. *Quarterly Journal of Economics* 50: 385–407.

Walker, E.R. 1938. Wages Policy and Business Cycles. *International Labour Review* 38: 728–93.

Wallich, H.C. 1946. The Path From Bretton Woods. In S.E. Harris ed. *Economic Reconstruction*. New York: McGraw Hill, 366–77.

1950. United Nations Report on Full Employment. *American Economic Review* 40: 876–83.

Walters, F.P. 1952. *A History of the League of Nations*. London: Oxford University Press.

Warming, J. 1931. A Theory of Prices and Wages. *International Labour Review* 24: 24–54.

1932. International Difficulties Arising Out of the Financing of Public Works During Depression. *Economic Journal* 42: 211–24.

Weir, M. and Skocpol, T. 1985. State Structures and the Possibilities for "Keynesian" Responses to the Great Depression in Sweden, Britain and the United States. In P.B. Evans, D. Rueschemeyer, and T. Skocpol eds. *Bringing the State Back In*. Cambridge: Cambridge University Press, 107–63.

Willett, T.D. 1982. Gottfried Haberler on Inflation, Unemployment and International Monetary Economics: An Appreciation. *Quarterly Journal of Economics* 97: 161–69.

Willetts, P. 1990. Transactions, Networks and Systems. In A.J.R. Groom and P. Taylor eds. *Frameworks for International Cooperation*. London: Pinter Publishers, 255–84.

Williams, J.H. 1934. The World's Monetary Dilemma – Internal *Versus* External Stability. Reprinted in J.H. Williams *Post-war Monetary Plans and Other Essays*. Oxford: Basil Blackwell 1949, 300–05.

1943. Currency Stabilization: The Keynes and White Plans. Reprinted in J.H. Williams *Post-war Monetary Plans and Other Essays*. Oxford: Basil Blackwell 1949, 141–54.

1947. International Trade With Planned Economies: The ITO Charter. Reprinted in J.H. Williams *Post-war Monetary Plans and Other Essays*. Oxford: Basil Blackwell 1949, 85–102.

Williamson, J. and Miller, M. 1987. *Targets and Indicators: A Blueprint for the International Coordination of Economic Policy*. Washington DC: Institute for International Economics.

Winch, D. 1969. *Economics and Policy: A Historical Study*. London: Hodder and Stoughton.

1983. Science and the Legislator: Adam Smith and After. *Economic Journal* 93: 501–20.

World Economic Conference. 1933. *The Program for the World Economic Conference: The Experts' Agenda and Other Documents*. Boston: World Peace Foundation.

Woytinsky, V. 1931. New Statistics of Collective Agreements in Germany. *International Labour Review* 23: 506–32.

1932. International Measures to Create Employment: A Remedy for the Depression. *International Labour Review* 25: 1–22.

1935. *Three Sources of Unemployment*. Geneva: ILO Studies and Reports Series C No. 20.

1936. *The Social Consequences of the Economic Depression*. Geneva: ILO Studies and Reports Series C No. 21.

Yeager, L.B. 1966. *International Monetary Relations: Theory, History and Policy*. New York: Harper and Row.

Zarnowitz, V. 1992. *Business Cycles. Theory, History, Indicators and Forecasting*. Chicago: University of Chicago Press.

Zeiler, T.W. 1999. *Free Trade, Free World. The Advent of GATT*. Chapel Hill: University of North Carolina Press.

Index

Åkerman, Johan, 26

balance of payments
  anticipated Keynesian approach to, 179–80
  effect of monetary policy on (Cassel), 89
  exchange rate policy assigned to, 183–6
Balogh, Thomas, 124n26, 129n32
Bank for International Settlements (BIS)
  advice during postwar transition, 204–5
  on central bank international cooperation,
    73–5
  as central international institution, 74
  on compensatory fiscal policy, 230–1
  on exchange rate stability, 188n39
  monetary issues (1930s), 71–5
  on transition economics, 205
  view of Keynesian policy implications, 245
Bellerby, J.R., 20
  case study of Federal Reserve by, 66–9
  contribution to ILO monetary policy
    research, 61–9
  report on employment in United States
    (1926), 85–6
  on responsibility of the state, 138
  on U.S. labor exchanges, 140
  on wage setting, 146–7
  work at ILO, 22, 27
Benjamin, D.K., 142
Beveridge, W.H., 84
Bhagwati, Jagdish, 105
Blaug, Mark, 90, 243
Blinder, Alan, 70
Bordo, M.D., 185n34, 189n42
Bowley, Arthur L., 26, 82, 84
Bretton Woods
  Keynes and White Plans related to, 167
  LON support for proposed institutions of,
    54
  role for IFIs, 190
  See also International Monetary Fund
    (IMF); United Nations; World Bank

Bridel, P., 84
Brussels Financial Conference (1920), 9, 58
budget, balanced, 86, 89
budget deficits
  BIS on loan-financed investment spending,
    99–100
  deficit financing (Bellerby; Martin), 86,
    88
  to finance public works (Keynes), 90–1
  government management of (Kalecki),
    206–7
business cycles
  criteria for data in index of, 27, 64–6, 68–9
  Haberler's research on, 35–8, 41, 46, 49–50,
    55
  ILO-LON research on (1920s, 1930s,
    1940s), 9–20, 26–57, 64
  ILO-LON theory and research program
    (1920s), 21–6
  indicator variables in, 27, 64–6, 68–9
  international cooperation to counteract
    (1920s), 58
  Keynesian influence on LON analysis and
    policy of, 42–54
  Keynes's review of Tinbergen's work,
    39–41
  LON and BIS belief in rhythm of, 54
  LON Gold Delegation conception of,
    29–30
  Mitchell's work on, 25–6
  1920s monetary theory of, 20–2
  Polak's research on, 41–2
  sources of research about (1920s, 1930s),
    17–18
  Swedish research on, 30–1
  Tinbergen's research on, 38–41, 46, 55–6
business cycles, international
  in context of protectionism (LON),
    110–11
  idea of immunization from, 111–12
  ILO-LON research (1930s), 30–42, 56–7